Generative AI for Cyber Risk Management

Yassine Maleh
https://orcid.org/0000-0003-4704-5364
Sultan Moulay Slimane University, Morocco

Lahby Mohamed
https://orcid.org/0000-0002-8272-0487
Hassan II University, Casablanca, Morocco

Ahmed A. Abd El-Latif
Prince Sultan University, Saudi Arabia

IGI Global
Scientific Publishing
Publishing Tomorrow's Research Today

Vice President of Editorial Melissa Wagner
Director of Acquisitions Mikaela Felty
Director of Book Development Jocelynn Hessler
Production Manager Mike Brehm
Cover Design Jose Rosado

Published in the United States of America by
IGI Global Scientific Publishing
701 East Chocolate Avenue
Hershey, PA, 17033, USA
Tel: 717-533-8845 | Fax: 717-533-7115
Website: https://www.igi-global.com E-mail: cust@igi-global.com

Library of Congress Cataloging-in-Publication Data

LCCN: 2025038320 (CIP Data Pending)
ISBN13: 9798369383971
Isbn13Softcover: 9798369383988
EISBN13: 9798369383995

British Cataloguing in Publication Data
A Cataloguing in Publication record for this book is available from the British Library.

Table of Contents

Detailed Table of Contents

S. Priya, Vel Tech Rangarajan Dr. Sagunthala R&D Institute of Science and Technology, India
S. Thirumal, Vels Institute of Science, Technology, and Advanced Studies, India
S. P. Santhoshkumar, Vel Tech Rangarajan Dr. Sagunthala R&D Institute of Science and Technology, India
S. Ramamoorthi, Vel Tech Rangarajan Dr. Sagunthala R&D Institute of Science and Technology, India
M. Mohamed Sithik, Vel Tech Rangarajan Dr. Sagunthala R&D Institute of Science and Technology, India

The importance of cyber risk management cannot be overstated in the digital era because the companies rely on technologies such as cloud computing, AI, IoT, and 5G which increases the attack surface and puts up against advanced threats. Fundamentals of Cyber Risk Management chapter discusses the main principles of identifying, evaluating, and eliminating cyber risks and enhancing the resilience. It describes the risk lifecycle, including identification, assessment, treatment and monitoring and presents standards, including NIST CSF, ISO/IEC 27005, COBIT and FAIR. The challenges that are identified in the chapter are the measurement of risks, human factors, resource constraints of SMEs, and vulnerability of supply chains. It emphasizes the need to prevent, detect, respond and recover, and be in compliance with GDPR and CCPA. Lastly, it focuses on leadership, culture, and accountability in instilling cybersecurity into enterprise governance to develop adaptive, secure organizations.

Cyber threat intelligence (CTI) is of great importance in the proactive nature of the cyber defense process, allowing organizations to make actionable plans for evolving threats. Historically, acquiring cyber threat intelligence has been beset by the lack of comprehensiveness, immediacy, and the ability to synthesize disparate data from undefined sources of threat intelligence. Generative AI affords an opportunity to rise above these deficiencies from the perspective of the depth, speed, and readability of threat intelligence. This chapter assesses how generative AI may be of assistance in driving forward the study of cyber threat intelligence from the millennial perspective, but from an initial perspective – how generative models do indeed have the capability of producing threat hints and warnings, modelling essential threat/attack scenarios and augmenting sources of data for training detection systems.

We present a systems-theoretic framework coupling Generative AI with multi-agent systems to make cyber-risk management a continuous, anticipatory control loop. The architecture: (i) risk-evaluation agents fusing telemetry with a knowledge graph; (ii) generative threat agents (GANs/diffusion/LLMs) synthesizing counterfactual attacks; and (iii) control agents trained with CTDE to allocate defenses under safety

driven cyber defense capabilities. The chapter concludes by identifying emerging research directions and outlining future trends that will shape AI-augmented incident response ecosystems.

The rapid growth of cybersecurity risks has led organizations to build stricter frameworks, with Zero Trust Architecture (ZTA) emerging as a significant paradigm. Based on "never trust, always verify," zero trust involves ongoing user and device identification verification, even inside the network perimeter. ZTA has a solid foundation, but cyberattacks are becoming more sophisticated, requiring more flexible solutions. AI improves ZTA by enabling real-time threat detection, behavioral analytics, and automated security event responses. A complete review of AI-powered tools and methodologies such natural language processing, anomaly detection, and predictive analytics is presented in this chapter to improve ZTA. It discusses AI implementation challenges, how AI interacts with ZTA components to improve security, and future research objectives.

The integration of generative AI into software engineering is transforming how developers write and secure code. Tools like GitHub Copilot and ChatGPT enhance productivity but also introduce risks to code quality, security, and accountability. This study explores how generative AI intersects with secure software engineering by examining its role within the Secure Software Development Life Cycle (SSDLC). It investigates how AI-generated code can propagate vulnerabilities and how prompt engineering may mitigate these risks. Emphasis is placed on the importance of explainability, code auditing, and human oversight in AI-augmented development environments. Through case studies in DevSecOps (Prates & Pereira, 2025), the paper illustrates both the promise and the pitfalls of AI-assisted coding. Findings underscore the need to evolve traditional practices to ensure safe, transparent, and ethical AI integration, offering actionable strategies for aligning intelligent automation with secure development standards.

Generative Artificial Intelligence is transforming continuous monitoring and regulatory compliance across sectors. Since there is heightened cybersecurity, financial reporting, and legal requirement compliance complexity, organizations require intelligent, scalable, and flexible solutions. GenAI brings robust capabilities such as report automation, anomaly detection, detailed risk reporting, and regulatory scenario simulation with low-level minimal intervention. The book presents a comprehensive end-to-end explanation of GenAI architectures, frameworks, ethics, and real-time applications in monitoring dynamic systems and compliance in the real world. Every chapter is based on flagship sectors such as finance, healthcare, manufacturing, and cybersecurity, and includes in-depth case studies, implementation plans, and upcoming trends. The book is geared towards policymakers, researchers, and practitioners alike, bridging theory and practice. It provides a comprehensive guide to applying GenAI in the development of smart, transparent, and ethical compliance solutions

Preface

Cybersecurity has experienced a huge transformation since the last decade. Cybersecurity was once an industry based on perimeter-based defensive measures, signature detection, and regular audits of compliance now consists of an agile on-going intelligence-driven practice with ever-changing adversaries faster than most organizations can defend against. The scale of this challenge is well understood: since 2023 attack activity related to ransomware has increased each year since 2020, supply chain attacks have put whole networks at risk from cascading failure, and the number of connected devices means much greater attack surfaces than what was built for with traditional security models.

Generative AI creates an opportunity to fill this gap by automating the process of threat classification, generating synthetic training data for security models, augmenting the analyst's workflow in a Security Operations Center (SOC), and providing a mechanism for ongoing compliance monitoring; thus transforming cyber risk management from a manual/periodic process to a continuously evolving and data-driven discipline. However, this opportunity comes with risk, as generative models have the potential to hallucinate (create non-existent data), be adversarially manipulated with adversarial input(s), encode the biases within the underlying training data and/or create a false sense of trust in an organization when used without appropriate levels of oversight.

Each side of the equation is addressed in this book; a thorough technical grounding in how generative AI is used in cyber risk management, as well as the limitations, unresolved research questions, and governance challenges associated with this technology, will also be addressed.

The convergence of generative AI and cybersecurity is not a future scenario. It is happening now, and it is happening unevenly. Large technology companies and well-resourced financial institutions have already integrated generative AI into their security operations, using it for automated triage, threat hunting, and code review. Meanwhile, small and medium enterprises, public sector organizations, and institutions in developing countries are still grappling with basic cybersecurity hygiene, let alone the adoption of AI-driven tools.

The cybersecurity workforce gap compounds the challenge. The global shortage of qualified cybersecurity professionals, estimated at over 3.5 million unfilled positions, means that organizations cannot simply hire their way to better security. Generative AI is increasingly seen as a force multiplier, a way to extend the reach of existing teams by automating routine tasks, accelerating analysis, and reducing the cognitive load on analysts who are already overwhelmed by alert volumes that far exceed human processing capacity.

At the same time, adversaries are using the same technology. Generative AI has lowered the barrier to entry for sophisticated attack techniques. Phishing campaigns powered by large language models are more convincing and harder to detect. Automated vulnerability discovery tools can scan codebases at scale. Deepfakes and synthetic media can be used for social engineering. The arms race between attackers and defenders has entered a new phase, and organizations that do not understand how generative AI is being used on both sides of the equation will find themselves at a structural disadvantage.

This book was conceived in this context. It is not a speculative exercise about what might happen in the future. It is an attempt to document, analyze, and critically evaluate what is already happening, and to provide researchers, practitioners, and decision-makers with the knowledge they need to navigate this rapidly evolving landscape.

TARGET AUDIENCE

This book targets a broad, yet informed audience, including cybersecurity researchers, academics, security practitioners, SOC analysts, CISOs, risk managers, software engineers, DevSecOps professionals, graduate students, and doctoral researchers.

BOOK ORGANIZATION

Chapter 1: Fundamentals for Cyber Risk Management. This opening chapter establishes the conceptual and methodological foundations upon which the rest of the book is built. It provides a structured overview of cyber risk management principles, covering risk identification, assessment, treatment, and monitoring within the context of established frameworks such as ISO 27001, ISO 27005, NIST CSF, and COBIT. The chapter also introduces the key concepts of generative AI that are relevant to cybersecurity applications, including large language models, generative adversarial networks, and diffusion models. By grounding the reader in both domains before they are combined, this chapter ensures that subsequent discussions of AI-driven risk management are accessible to readers from either a cybersecurity or an AI background.

Chapter 2: Improving Cyber Threat Intelligence Through Generative AI — From Data to Actionable Intelligence. Threat intelligence has traditionally relied on manual analysis of indicators of compromise, threat feeds, and intelligence reports. This chapter examines how generative AI transforms the threat intelligence pipeline by automating the extraction, correlation, and synthesis of threat data from diverse sources. It covers techniques for natural language processing of threat reports, automated generation of threat profiles, and the use of large language models to bridge the gap between raw data and actionable intelligence. The chapter also addresses the risks of hallucination and fabrication in AI-generated intelligence, and proposes validation strategies to ensure that automated outputs meet the reliability standards required for operational decision-making.

Chapter 3: Multi-Agent Generative AI Systems for Cyber Risk Evaluation and Control. This chapter explores the application of multi-agent architectures to cyber risk evaluation, where specialized AI agents collaborate to perform distinct functions such as risk identification, analysis, evaluation, and treatment. The chapter discusses the design principles behind agent decomposition, inter-agent communication protocols, and the integration of explainable AI techniques to ensure that agent-driven decisions remain interpretable and auditable. It also examines the challenges of validating multi-agent systems, including the difficulty of testing emergent behaviors and the security risks associated with shared message buses and inter-agent trust.

Chapter 4: Synthetic Risk Environments for Next-Generation Cybersecurity. One of the persistent challenges in cybersecurity research and training is the scarcity of realistic, labeled datasets that capture the full spectrum of attack scenarios. This chapter addresses that gap by examining how generative AI can create synthetic risk environments: realistic but artificial datasets, network traffic patterns, and attack scenarios that can be used for model training, red team exercises, and security testing. The chapter covers generative adversarial networks for synthetic data generation, the use of large language models for scenario construction, and the critical question of how to validate that synthetic environments are representative of real-world conditions without introducing systematic biases.

Chapter 5: Autonomous Defenders — Generative AI for Smarter Incident Response: AI-Augmented Security Operations in Modern SOCs. Security operations centers are the front line of organizational defense, and they are under pressure. Alert volumes routinely exceed the capacity of human analysts, leading to missed detections, delayed responses, and analyst burnout. This chapter examines how generative AI is being deployed to augment SOC operations, covering automated alert triage, natural language summarization of security events, AI-assisted investigation workflows, and the generation of response playbooks. The chapter draws on operational experience to discuss the practical challenges of integration, including the risk of automation bias, the need for human oversight at critical decision points, and the organizational changes required to make AI augmentation effective rather than disruptive.

Chapter 6: The Role of AI in Zero Trust Architectures. Zero Trust has moved from a conceptual framework to an operational requirement for many organizations, driven by the dissolution of traditional network perimeters and the adoption of cloud-native architectures. This chapter examines how generative AI can enhance Zero Trust implementations across several dimensions: continuous identity verification, adaptive access control, real-time risk scoring of user and device behavior, and automated policy generation. The chapter also addresses the tension between the deterministic verification requirements of Zero Trust and the probabilistic nature of AI-driven decisions, and discusses strategies for maintaining security guarantees when AI components operate within trust boundaries.

Chapter 7: Secure Code Generation and Software Engineering with Generative AI. The adoption of AI-assisted coding tools has accelerated rapidly, with generative models now capable of producing functional code, writing tests, generating documentation, and suggesting refactors. This chapter examines the security implications of this shift. While AI-generated code can improve developer productivity, it can also introduce vulnerabilities through hallucinated APIs, insecure default configurations, outdated dependency recommendations, and patterns that compile correctly but fail security review. The chapter covers secure prompting strategies, validation pipelines for generated code, the integration of security checks into AI-assisted development workflows, and the broader implications for software supply chain security.

Chapter 8: Generative AI for Continuous Monitoring and Compliance. Compliance with cybersecurity standards and regulations is a continuous obligation, but the mechanisms for verifying compliance have traditionally been periodic: annual audits, quarterly assessments, point-in-time certifications. This chapter explores how generative AI can transform compliance monitoring into a continuous, automated process. It covers the use of large language models for policy interpretation and gap analysis, automated evidence collection and mapping to control frameworks, real-time compliance dashboards, and the generation of regulatory reports. The chapter also examines the risks of automated compliance, including the danger of treating model outputs as authoritative without human validation, and the regulatory acceptance challenges that automated reporting still faces in many jurisdictions.

Chapter 9: Directly Relevant to Finance and E-Commerce—Fraud Detection, Credit Scoring, and Transaction Analysis. Financial services and e-commerce operate in an environment where cyber risk has immediate, quantifiable financial consequences. This chapter examines how generative AI is being applied to the specific risk management challenges of these sectors, including real-time fraud detection, adversarial robustness of credit scoring models, anomaly detection in transaction flows, and the generation of synthetic financial data for model training. The chapter also addresses the regulatory dimension, covering the requirements of financial regulators for model explainability, fairness, and auditability, and discussing how generative AI tools can be deployed in a manner consistent with these obligations.

Chapter 10: Case Studies and Real-World Applications of Generative AI. The final chapter brings the theoretical and technical discussions of the preceding chapters into contact with operational reality. It presents a collection of case studies drawn from diverse industries and geographies, documenting how organizations have deployed generative AI for cyber risk management in practice. Each case study covers the problem context, the solution architecture, the outcomes achieved, and the lessons learned, including failures and unexpected challenges. By grounding the book in real-world evidence, this chapter provides readers with concrete reference points for their own deployment decisions and highlights the gap between what is theoretically possible and what is practically achievable in today's operational environments.

CONTRIBUTION TO THE FIELD

This book makes several contributions to the cybersecurity and AI communities. First, it provides one of the first comprehensive treatments of generative AI specifically focused on cyber risk management, as opposed to cybersecurity operations more broadly. This distinction matters because risk management involves governance, compliance, and strategic decision-making functions that require different AI capabilities and different validation standards than operational detection and response.

Second, the book bridges the gap between technical AI research and cybersecurity practice. Too often, AI research in cybersecurity is evaluated on benchmark datasets and synthetic scenarios without adequate consideration of operational constraints, organizational realities, and regulatory requirements. Conversely, cybersecurity practitioners often adopt AI tools without a deep understanding of their limitations, failure modes, and governance implications. This book speaks to both communities and attempts to create a shared vocabulary for productive collaboration.

Third, the book addresses the international dimension of cyber risk management. The contributors represent multiple institutions across several countries, and the discussions engage with regulatory frameworks from different jurisdictions, including the European Union, the United States, and Morocco. This international perspective is essential because cyber risk does not respect national boundaries, and governance approaches that work in one regulatory environment may not transfer directly to another.

Fourth, and perhaps most importantly, this book maintains a commitment to intellectual honesty about the current state of the technology. Generative AI is powerful, but it is not infallible. It can augment human judgment, but it cannot replace it. It can accelerate processes, but it can also introduce new categories of risk that did not exist before. Every chapter in this book was reviewed with these tensions in mind, and the contributors were encouraged to discuss the limitations of their work as thoroughly as they discussed its contributions.

The field of cyber risk management is at an inflection point. The organizations that will manage risk most effectively in the coming years will be those that understand both the capabilities and the limitations of generative AI, and that deploy it within governance frameworks robust enough to catch its failures. This book is intended to equip its readers with the knowledge they need to be among those organizations.

Yassine Maleh
Sultan Moulay Slimane University, Morocco

Mohamed Lahby
Hassan II University, Casablanca, Morocco

Ahmed Abd El-Latif
Prince Sultan University, Saudi Arabia

Chapter 1
Fundamentals for Cyber Risk Management

S. Priya
http://orcid.org/0009-0003-3305-745X
Vel Tech Rangarajan Dr. Sagunthala R&D Institute of Science and Technology, India

S. Thirumal
http://orcid.org/0000-0002-8497-8764
Vels Institute of Science, Technology, and Advanced Studies, India

S. P. Santhoshkumar
http://orcid.org/0000-0001-8531-759X
Vel Tech Rangarajan Dr. Sagunthala R&D Institute of Science and Technology, India

S. Ramamoorthi
http://orcid.org/0000-0001-5152-278X
Vel Tech Rangarajan Dr. Sagunthala R&D Institute of Science and Technology, India

M. Mohamed Sithik
http://orcid.org/0009-0005-3989-7198
Vel Tech Rangarajan Dr. Sagunthala R&D Institute of Science and Technology, India

ABSTRACT

The importance of cyber risk management cannot be overstated in the digital era because the companies rely on technologies such as cloud computing, AI, IoT, and 5G which increases the attack surface and puts up against advanced threats. Fundamentals of Cyber Risk Management chapter discusses the main principles of

DOI: 10.4018/979-8-3693-8397-1.ch001

identifying, evaluating, and eliminating cyber risks and enhancing the resilience. It describes the risk lifecycle, including identification, assessment, treatment and monitoring and presents standards, including NIST CSF, ISO/IEC 27005, COBIT and FAIR. The challenges that are identified in the chapter are the measurement of risks, human factors, resource constraints of SMEs, and vulnerability of supply chains. It emphasizes the need to prevent, detect, respond and recover, and be in compliance with GDPR and CCPA. Lastly, it focuses on leadership, culture, and accountability in instilling cybersecurity into enterprise governance to develop adaptive, secure organizations.

1. INTRODUCTION

In the digital age, companies in all industries are becoming increasingly reliant on technology, interdependent systems, and process-driven, which are based on data. Whereas these innovations are highly beneficial in terms of efficiency and innovation, it is also creating a wide range of cyber threats to organizations. Cyber risk is a term used to describe the possibility of loss, disruption or damage due to cyber threats, including data breach, ransomware, phishing, insider abuse or critical infrastructure attack. Cyber risks are dynamic, borderless, and ever-changing unlike traditional risks, and they are due to the rapid change in technology, globalization and the increasing sophistication of the adversaries, since they are dynamic.

Cyber risk management can be defined as a methodical way of detecting, evaluating, reducing and tracking risks caused by cyber threats. Besides being a technical problem, it is also a strategic requirement that affects business continuity, compliance with regulations, consumer trust and national security.

1.1. Problem Statement

Contemporary cybersecurity risks are always transnational, often being both initiated and affected by multiple countries at the same time. The vulnerabilities to cyberattacks are regulatory gaps, haphazard legal frameworks, and the absence of coordinated international policies. Though each country is taking cybersecurity-related steps, effective prevention, detection, and response of cross-border cyber threats has not been achieved due to lack of effective global coordination of actions against such threats. Thus, the urgent necessity to develop coordinated international cooperation systems and alignment of policy frameworks to respond to changing global cyber threats is a pressing issue.

1.2. Motivation

The swift digitalization of the economy, vital infrastructure, financial systems and communication systems has most certainly risen the global interconnectivity. Ransomwares, intrusions sponsored by the state, data breaches, and cyber espionage are the main types of cyber attacks that are collectively sensitive to countries due to this interconnected ecosystem.

The factors that prompted this chapter are:

- The growing intensity and advancement of internationally-related cyberattacks.
- Absence of international regulatory and legal standards.
- The necessity of combined threat intelligence dissemination.
- The relevance of joint incident response mechanisms.
- The increasing reliance on international information infrastructure.

The enhancement of international collaboration can make them stronger, enhance collective defense, and minimize threats to cybersecurity across the globe.

1.3. Research Gap

Despite the fact that international cooperation in cybersecurity is identified as a necessity, there are still a few gaps:

a) Absence of Consistent International Frameworks – The current policies on cybersecurity differ considerably in different countries, which results in implementation and jurisdictional issues.
b) Poor Real-Time Threat Intelligence Sharing- Existing systems of disseminating cyber threat intelligence are ineffective and slow.
c) Policy inconsistency and regulatory misalignment– The variation in the national legislation, data protection rules and definition of cybercrimes makes it difficult to take coordinated action.
d) Trust and Sovereignty Problems, The political conflicts and issues of national sovereignty do not allow complete cooperation on a large scale.
e) Lack of Coherent Incident Response Procedures - There is no internationally recognized quick-response model in case of massive cross-border cyber incidents.

Accordingly, the international system of cybersecurity governance, which is comprehensive, collaborative, and policy-congruent to overcome legal, technical, and operational gaps needs to be implemented.

2. TYPES OF CYBER RISK MANAGEMENT

2.1. Risk avoidance

Risk Avoidance in cyber risk management is a concept that involves the practice of ensuring that there are no activities, processes, or technologies that have possible security risks instead of trying to control or lessen them. The strategy is normally used in cases where the possible effect of cyber risk is too high or cost of mitigation is too high relative to the cost of taking a risk altogether. To illustrate, an organization might not wish to employ a given cloud service because it does not have sound security measures or stop using the old applications that are no longer one with new updates. Risk avoidance takes full advantage of the protection against a certain threat, and at the same time, it can suppress business opportunities or innovation in case it is conducted too strictly; thus, the balance between security and the aims of an organization should be considered.

2.2. Risk Mitigation

Cyber risk management risk mitigation aims at minimizing the possibility or the effects of future cyber attacks through proactive security controls and implementation of security measures. This is a risk reduction strategy in which the risk source is removed by reducing the vulnerabilities and reinforcing the defense in place to assure the continuity of the business. The most common methods are the use of firewalls, intrusion detection system, multi-factor authentication, data encryption, frequent patch management, as well as, employee cybersecurity training. An example is when sensitive customer information is encrypted; the consequences of a possible data breach will be minimized, despite the possibility of unauthorized access by attackers. When the risks are mitigated effectively, organizations always strike a balance between security and the operations of the organization, where the cyber threats are mitigated effectively without affecting the productivity.

2.3. Risk Transfer

Risk Transfer Cyber risk management through the use of risk transfer is using a third party to take the risk of financial/operational impact of cyber threats instead of the organization bearing the whole responsibility. The mechanisms that are normally used in accomplishing this strategy include: buying cyber insurance, outsourcing IT services, and even the managed security providers who share the risk. In case of an example, a firm can purchase a cyber insurance policy to cover expenses associated with data breaches, ransomware or regulatory penalties. Risk transfer does not eliminate the risk but ensures that in case of cyber attacks, the risk is financially and resource safeguarded, and the businesses will be more able to counter the impact without bearing the whole responsibility alone.

2.4. Risk Acceptance

Risk Acceptance in cyber risk management can be described as a deliberate choice made by an organization to accept and accept some cyber risks and not take any immediate steps to avoid, reduce or transfer them. This method is normally pursued in the situations where the expense of applying security measures is greater than the potential risk impact, or the risk is considered as having a low probability or low impact. In the example, an organization could tolerate the risk of the small phishing attacks that are not likely to lead to serious damages. Risk acceptance enables the organizations to allocate resources to greater threats but it cannot be left without constant monitoring that overtime the risks that are accepted now do not become serious vulnerability.

2.5. Risk Monitoring and Review

The continuous process of monitoring, assessing and revising the risk environment within an organization in cyber risk management is known as Risk Monitoring and Review which requires periodic monitoring of the identified threats and maintenance of their control as well as verification of the effectiveness of security measures. As the cyber attacks are dynamic and new vulnerabilities are introduced every day, continuous monitoring is beneficial to keep track of the changes to the risk level and makes the necessary changes in mitigation practices. This includes routine security audits, vulnerability testing, penetration testing, and compliance checking along with the incident report analysis to improve risk response. Systematic review of risks by organizations will help them to identify vulnerabilities, enhance resilience, and stay within the objectives of the business and regulatory demands, which will provide active protection against constantly evolving cyber threats.

2.6. Regulatory and Compliance-Based Risk Management

The Risk Management of cybersecurity on Regulatory and Compliance-Based is aimed at the management of the risks on the basis of making sure that the practices used by the organization are in compliance with the existing laws, industrial norms, and regulatory frameworks aimed at the system and data protection. The practice can assist an organization to prevent legal fines, financial losses, and reputational losses due to compliance with requirements such as the General Data Protection

Regulation (GDPR), Health Insurance Portability and Accountability Act (HIPAA, Payment Card Industry Data Security Standard (PCI DSS) and frameworks like NIST CSF or ISO/IEC 27005 . As an example, applying robust data privacy settings would not only guarantee that fast compliance with GDPR but also chances of breach would be minimized. In addition to the legal requirements, compliance-based risk management creates trust in the stakeholders, customers, by showing responsibility, transparency, and willingness to ensure the security of sensitive information.

Figure 1. Cyber risk management strategies infographic.

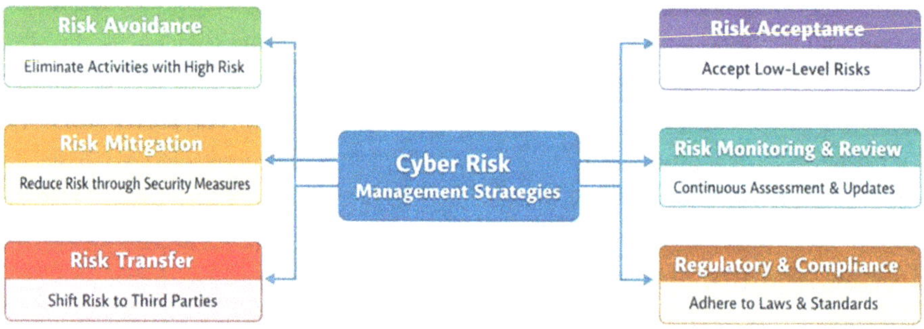

3. LITERATURE SURVEY

The new literature that the concept of cyber risk management (CRM) is no longer considered to be a best-practice recommendation but is a regulatory expectation in the majority of industries. According to experts, CRM transforms the model of cybersecurity in which it is viewed as stable, technology-oriented and in which business-risk orientation is viewed as dynamic in which a security posture can not be viewed as fixed and put aside. It has been identified in research that not many organizations implement CRM adequately, partly due to the impossibility to quantify cyber risks but due to overestimation with references to purely quantitative metrics. In its turn, the scholars advance the necessity to alter the risk assessment approach to qualitative and hybrid in order to facilitate strategic decision-making. Furthermore, according to the literature, an effective, ongoing cyber asset management and threat-informed defense measures are critical enablers that support the business entities in ensuring that they are operating in complex IT environment, reducing the probability of occurrence of incidents and reduction of financial and operational costs of cyber incidents, respectively (Donegan, 2024).

The new study was introduced by (Sobhy Abdelkader et al., 2024) who proposed that the active evolution of electric vehicles, smart electronic devices, and digital technologies has put a huge strain on the energy need that places a heavy load on the traditional power systems in both reliability and resilience. The theorists propose the concept of smart grid digitalization as the answer to the effective monitoring and controlling of the power networks remotely. However, the literature also points out that the smart grids are susceptible to cybersecurity risks, which were demonstrated by massive attacks, such as the one on the Ukrainian power grid. The existing research is to conceptualise cyber-threats, empower the defence systems and deployment of emerging superior security innovations to protect the critical grid resources. Overall, the past works come to the conclusion that the high quality of cybersecurity systems is needed to be able to ensure continuous power supply, system stability, and long-term stability of existing power infrastructures.

Available literature indicates that the rate of the Internet of Things (IoT) expansion has aggravated the need to manage cyber risks well since it has been integrated into the essence of the daily and organizational operations. Literature review of the literature on IoT security frameworks shows that the majority of the models concentrate on technical risks, but the risks and issues related to people have not been addressed thoroughly and in a comprehensive manner. The comparison of various studies proves that the standardized risk management procedures have gaps, interdomain security assurance and user awareness. The studies in this direction are therefore recommended by researchers which ought to be human centered on vulnerability, adaptive risk paradigm and domain based security mechanisms in order to improve overall cyber resiliency to IoT (Emily Kate Parsons et al., 2023).

According to the recent studies, integrated cyber risk management frameworks are proposed, which involves risk assessment; besides capital management to address the complex financial and operational effects of cyber risks. In literature, it is highlighted that frequency-severity models of insurance were to be coupled with cybersecurity impact and cascade models in order to increase the accuracy of risk estimation. Studies also focus on the importance of cost benefit and sensitivity analysis analysis to the organization that is limited in budget in the sense that they are able to make balanced decisions on security investment, insurance and reserve assignment. Generally, the literature available has a conclusion that dual-pillar and data-driven solutions are more strategic, flexible, and economically learned cyber risk management in various organizational environments (Chong et al., 2024).

According to the recent literature, the application of Artificial Intelligence (AI) and Machine Learning (ML) can be a highly valuable addition to the cyber risk management process because it allows analyzing a large amount of data within a limited time frame, foreseeing the threats, and automatizing the security processes. It is also emphasized in the research that more than ever before modern techniques such as deep learning, edge computing, federated learning, and explainable AI have become more significant towards improving the risk detection and decision-making process. However, in any case, researchers cannot but find certain unresolved problems related to the quality of the information, the clarity and understandability of the model, confidentiality, and the morality of using the information. In general, the above literature therefore concludes that despite the fact that AI-based solutions can be revolutionary to the cybersecurity systems, the future research ought to find the balance between the technological advancement and the equity, responsibility, and regulatory compliance as the means of ensuring sustainable cyber resilience (Ishrag Hamid et al., 2025).

According the current studies, (Yiu Ting Yan Azura et al., 2025) have discovered that the rapid adoption of an online banking platform has increased the challenges of insecurity, privacy and resiliency in operations. Previous literature notes that the traditional security models fail to address domain-specific threats, regulatory policies as well as sensitivity of information in a digital banking environment. The newest literature therefore advocates inherent threat- and risk-oriented models of management with a systematic risk assessment, vulnerability audit, and preset mitigation strategies. To make the implementation practical, researchers emphasize that it is important to detect the threats which can be identified at the context level, measure the risk, and follow the alignment. Overall, the contemporary work concludes that there is a need of vast dynamic structures that can enhance consumer confidence, protect financial information, and enhance the physical online banking platform security status.

The recent literature shows that (Bashee, 2024) the threat of the blistering development of the Internet of Things and the environments has been increasing, and the necessity to introduce the systematic practice of managing cyber risks is quite obvious. The reviews of the available literature indicate that the researchers in the field primarily focus on the identification of the main IoT security risks, the development of mitigation best practices, and integration of the cyber risk management within the IoT ecosystem that could ensure the confidentiality, integrity, and safety. The review of the existing literature indicates that the majority of developed frameworks are applied in the form of ISO and NIST, models such as OCTAVE are in use, and other models like PDCA Cycle, Cyber Kill Chain, COBIT 5, and Cyber Value at Risk (CVaR) are also used. The variety of these methods testifies that there is a growing consensus that the use of dynamic, context-based, and industry-specific risk management models are significant in order to have the emerging IoT infrastructures properly secured.

According to the current literature, (Sasha Romanosky et al., 2024) note that the rising rate and economic price of data breaches have caused cyber risk to become a board issue in organizations. Whether cyber risk represents a radically new form of risk or whether the Enterprise Risk Management (ERM) systems can adapt to it is open to research. The results of the research are typically that regardless of the high profile of cyber events, the quantifiable losses that are measured in financial terms are related to those that are caused by other operational risks. Thus, cyber risk, according to the scholars, has to be rationally integrated into the existing ERM frameworks, which are to be monitored and managed with strategic control rather than being a per se risk domain.

According to literature, recent times have depicted increased exposure of organizations to cyber attacks such as ransomware and data breaches due to the growing use of digital technologies which have made organizations incur significant losses in their economies and derail their operations. Studies identify that dealing with cyber risks is a multi level approach which incorporates both a preventive approach, rapid response in the event of an attack and continuous security upgrades. Cases of the ransomware attack of Norsk Hydro ASA demonstrates that proper incident response planning and post-attack resilience strategies can help the incident to reduce the financial and reputational losses of the incident in the long-run. Overall, the scholarly sources conclude that companies that invest in the implementation of the comprehensive cyber risk management system can both increase the degree of security posture and ensure a higher level of economic resilience and competitive advantage in the digital environment (Andrae, 2024).

The risk of information security in relation to the public cloud is increasing exponentially due to mass adoption of the virtual machine and the open-source software dependencies, (Benjamin M et al., 2024). It has been pointed out that maladjustments at the user level and the installation of packages can significantly increase the vulnerability space, and the process of vulnerability evaluation and ranking can become difficult when done manually by security personnel. Traditional signatures-based and rule-based vulnerability management measures are no longer satisfactory, at large scale on the clouds. Thus, the application of machine learning and deep learning algorithms, particularly the unsupervised clustering and anomaly detectors, to process the multi-dimensional security data automatically have been explored by scholars. (M. M. Rahman et al., 2024) Identifying the cyber risk management is an invaluable study field because businesses are finding it hard to implement optimal models available at the highest layers. The traditional methods tend to use qualitative measures which are not comparable and cannot be applied in the organization. As a response to this challenge, Rahman et al. proposed AssessITS, which is an idea in which the procedural rules are combined with an empirical assessment measures of the IT and cybersecurity risk evaluation.

(G. F. Burch et al., 2024) Bridged this gap by the study proposing a model of relating the incident classification and prioritization mechanisms to the capability maturity models. The approach is based on the established practice of maturity assessment, such as the Capability Maturity Model Integration (CMMI) and the levels of the Cybersecurity Framework of NIST, but to the details of IR functions.

4. UNDERSTANDING CYBER RISK

4.1. Cyber Risk

Cyber risk is a risk that arises due to malicious intent or loss, damage or interruption to the data, electronic assets, systems or operations of an organization due to cyber threats such as unauthorized access, data breach, malware attack, ransomware, phishing, or insider abuse. It is the likelihood and the consequences of the adverse events caused by vulnerabilities in the technology, processes, or human behavior and may be misused by malicious actors.

4.2. Sources of Cyber Risk

Cyber Risk Sources refer to the sources or reasons that expose vulnerabilities and sources of threats to the digital assets of an organization. These sources may be internal or external and many times are caused by the weaknesses that may be technological, human and process. Key sources include:

a) Human Factors: Errors, carelessness, or ill intent of employees, contractors or insiders e.g. clicking on phishing emails, weak passwords or deliberate sabotage.
b) Technological Vulnerabilities: Software, hardware, or network infrastructure flaws or bugs, such as unexpired systems, old applications, configured devices, and insecure APIs.
c) External Threat Actors: Hackers, cybercriminals, hacktivists, or nation-state offenders that use vulnerabilities to steal information, cause denial of service, or ransomware.
d) Third-Party Risks: There are weak links among vendors, partners or outsourced service providers who can inject security gaps into the systems of an organization.

5. TYPES OF CYBER THREATS AND VULNERABILITIES

5.1. Malware (Malicious Software)

Malware (Malicious Software) is any type of software that is knowingly created to compromise, manage, or access computer systems, networks, or data unlawfully. It includes very many harmful programs such as viruses, worms, Trojans, ransomware, spyware, and adware, and each of them has particular malicious intentions. Malware may interfere with regular functions, steal valuable data, ransom-encrypt the data, or leave any backdoor to the attack. As an illustration, the ransomware will seize essential files of a firm and requires payment to unlock the files leading to loss of money and business time. To have an effective malware protection, it is important to combine updated antivirus software, firewalls, system patching, and user awareness training.

5.2. Phishing and Social Engineering

Phishing and Social Engineering are cyber threats where the attackers take advantage of human psychology instead of technical weakness of getting unauthorized access to sensitive information or systems. Phishing is usually a false message, email or even a phone call that presents itself as an authentic message, in order to steal passwords, finances, or personal information. Social engineering is not limited to phishing, it can also encompass pretexting, baiting or impersonation techniques to attack workers into taking actions that would put the security at risk. As an illustration, an attacker could send an email which appears to be an email of the IT department where a user is requested to reset their password on a rogue site, thus stealing their logins. User awareness and training, as well as the high level of verification, are key to preventing these threats.

5.3. Insider Threats

Insider Threats are security threats that have their root in an organization, and they are generally associated with the employees, contractors, or even business partners that have legitimate access to systems and data. Such threats will be intentional, including intent to steal sensitive information or sabotage systems, or unintentional, including leaks of data by mistake or an error that affects security. In such an instance, an employee may purposefully steal proprietary information about the client with the intent of gaining competitive advantage, or an employee may simply click on an unknowing link that is using malware to compromise the company's network.

5.4. Denial of Service (DoS) and Distributed DoS (DDoS) Attacks

Denial of Service (DoS) and Distributed Denial of Service (DDoS) Attacks are computer attacks that are intended to attack services, networks, or online systems by sending large volumes of traffic or requests, which causes the systems to become unavailable. DoS attack is usually a one-way attack and the source sends all the requests to the target that the target cannot respond to, slows down the performance or stops the service altogether. A DDoS attack, conversely, consists of coordinated attacks with a number of compromised devices or botnets, which are more difficult to counter and overcome.

6. IMPACT OF CYBER INCIDENTS

Impact of Cyber Incidents can be defined as the effects to which organizations are exposed when their digital system networks or data are affected by cyber threats. These effects may be financial, operational, legal or reputational and usually depend on the intensity and nature of the incident. Financial Impact of the expenses of data breaches, ransomware settlements, system downtime, fines from the regulatory bodies, and lawsuits. As an illustration, a ransomware attack can bring operations to a standstill and compel a company to make a huge payment to get operations back.

a) Operational Impact: Impairment of business operations, service interruptions or low productivity. As an example, a DDoS attack may render an online shopping site inaccessible.
b) Legal and Regulatory Impact: Failure to adhere to the rules of data protection such as GDPR or HIPAA may result in fines, penalties, or lawsuits.
c) Reputational Impact: Viewed as lost customer confidence and brand equity because of publicly-announced security breaches or mismanagement of sensitive data.

7. PRINCIPLES OF CYBER RISK MANAGEMENT

7.1. Risk Identification

The initial step in cyber risk management is known as Risk Identification where the key objective is to identify and list the possible threats, vulnerabilities, and exposures that might adversely affect the digital assets, systems, or activities of an organization. This is done by knowing the IT environment of the organization, the business processes, data flow, and other external factors that could bring about risk. Risk identification techniques are asset inventories, threat modeling, vulnerability assessment, security audit and analysis of historical incident. An organization can refer to an unprotected software, password incompetence, phishing, or use of third-party service provider as some of the risks that an organization might recognize. The proper risk identification is the basis of the next steps on the risk management and helps organizations to allocate resources and to work out specific mitigation plans.

7.2. Risk Assessment

Risk Assessment is the process used in the cyber risk management process of determining the presence of identified risks in an effort to determine the probability of occurrence and the magnitude that the risks may cause in the organization. This step helps in setting priorities of what are priority of risks and those are the risks that can be traced or accepted. The risk evaluation can be conducted qualitatively, i.e. using help of expert judgment or risk matrices, or quantitatively, i.e. finding the potential loss of finances, probability, or statistical simulations.

7.3 Risk Mitigation and Control

In cyber risk management, Risk Mitigation and Control are the actions undertaken in order to make sure that the likelihood or the effects of the risks identified are minimized to acceptable level. This is following the risk assessment and is focused on protection of vital assets, improvement of defenses and reduction of possible damage of cyber threats. Such measures as common include technical controls (such as firewalls, intrusion detection system, encryption, multi factor authentication); administrative controls (such as policies, procedures and staff training); and physical controls (such as restricted access to data centers). To provide an example, an organization may establish safe passwords, frequent software vulnerabilities fixing, and frequent employee education in phishing attacks in an effort to mitigate the threat of data breach. Adequate risk mitigation and control will ensure the cyber risks are addressed in advance, and help to maintain business continuity and protect confidential data.

7.3. Continuous Monitoring

Continuous Monitoring Continuous Monitoring in cyber risk management is cyclic cycle of monitoring, analysing and evaluating the IT environment of any given organization with a view of detecting any emerging threats, vulnerabilities and changes that can have impact on the security posture. This will make the risk management process to be dynamic and responsive to the dynamic cyber threat environment. It is also known that the continuous monitoring consists of real-time network traffic analytics, vulnerability scanning, system and application logging, and intrusion detection, as well as the analysis of security alerts.

7.4. Alignment with Business Objectives

Business Objectives in cyber risk management helps to assure that all the security strategies, policies and controls are integrated to the organization overall or wider objectives, and not to halt and stifle operations or innovation of the organization. Cybersecurity implementation priority should follow the impact of the investments on the basic business operations, revenues, reputation and customer trust. An example is that it can be said that due to the strict access to sensitive financial systems, the loss of valuable assets can be avoided, besides, it does not require the workflow of other departments to be put on hold. Once the risk management is properly balanced with the business objectives, the organizations will have an opportunity to balance security, cost, and efficiency and ensure that the available resources are allocated to the risks mitigation, which are the most critical in the attainment of the strategic outcomes.

7.5. Compliance and Regulatory Adherence

Regulatory Adherence and Compliance in cyber risk management entails the assurance of successful alignment of security practices, policies and controls used within an organization with the legal stipulations, industry rules, and regulations. Compliance with laws and regulations (e.g., GDPR,HIPAA, PCI DSS, or ISO/IEC 27001) assist the company in avoiding fines, lawsuits, and losses to reputation and encourage the trust of the customers and stakeholders. To provide an example, the tightening of data protection and privacy settings in line with GDPR does not only minimize the chances of breaches, but also makes the processing of personal data legitimate. Placing compliance in the framework of cyber risk management will see to it that there would be consistency in security measures, auditing of the same and the alignment of the security measures as well as both legal requirements and best practices.

Figure 2. Cyber risk management principles diagram

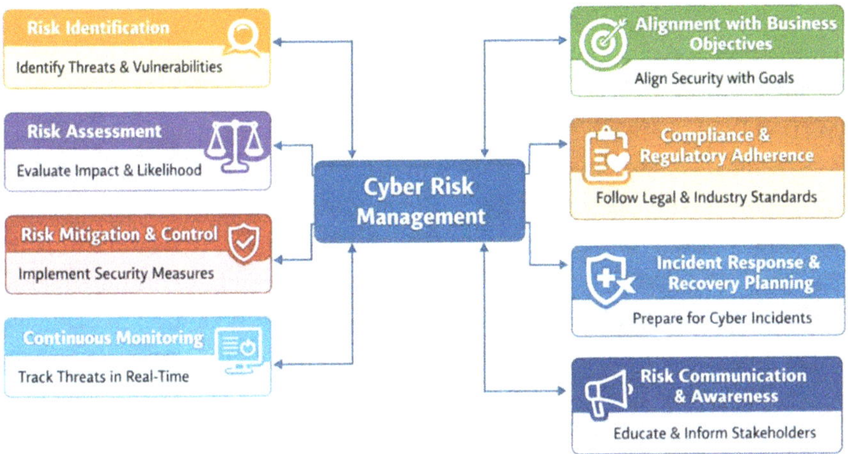

8. FRAMEWORKS AND STANDARDS FOR CYBER RISK MANAGEMENT

8.1. NIST Cybersecurity Framework (CSF)

One of the most famous voluntary structures is the NIST Cybersecurity Framework [5] (CSF) designed by the National Institute of Standards and Technology to help organizations to deal and alleviate cybersecurity risks systematically and flexibly. The framework can tailor itself to any organizations, irrespective of the size and industry, and provides a universal lingo on cybersecurity risk management. It is organized on the basis of five large functions:

a) Identify: Have an understanding of the assets, systems, data and risk of the organization in order to develop a robust risk management plan.
b) Protect: Install security systems and measures to guarantee the provision of essential services and reduce the consequences of possible cybersecurity incidents.
c) Detect: Cybersecurity incidents to be detected in the operation and equipment of the institute and detect anomalies in time.

8.2. ISO/IEC 27001& 27005

The ISO/IEC 27001 and 27005 are international standards that provide organizations with a systematic approach in which information security and cyber risks should be done.

This standard provides the requirements of an Information Security Management System (ISMS) including its formation, implementation, maintenance and continual improvement. It is a structured approach to the control of confidential information, which is used with the purpose of ensuring confidentiality, integrity and availability. Organizations that have implemented the ISO/IEC 27001 will be required to evaluate the risks and the appropriate controls as well as update and improve their security processes at regular intervals. For example, an enterprise organization that handles customer data could use the ISO/IEC 27001 to craft policies regarding the secure storage, access control and incident response for that data

8.3. ISO/IEC 27005

To supplement ISO / IEC 27001, there is ISO / IEC 27005 which is dedicated to the management of the information security risks. It provides management on what constitutes, analyses, evaluates and treats the information security risks. The standard helps organizations to be informed about the kind of risks to mitigate, accept or transfer based on its business setting and its risk appetite.

8.4. COBIT (Control Objectives for Information and Related Technologies)

COBIT (Control Objectives for Information and Related Technologies) is a comprehensive governance and management of enterprise IT developed by ISACA. It gives organizations the best practices, tools and guidance to ensure that IT is aligned with business objectives, risks are managed effectively and value is delivered. COBIT is focused on five principles: responding to stakeholder needs, addressing the enterprise end-to-end, addressing by a single integrated framework, enabling a holistic approach, and separating governance from management.

Figure 3. Frameworks for cyber risk management.

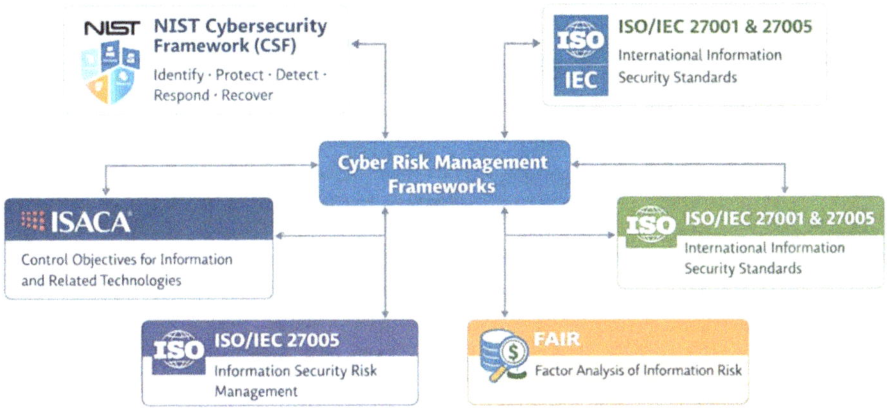

9. REGULATORY AND COMPLIANCE CONSIDERATIONS (GDPR, HIPAA)

9.1. GDPR

A European Union regulation on the subject of the personal data collection, processing, storage and transfer. Organizations need to have data transparency, get clear consent, provide data protection, and disclose breaches within strict deadlines. Non-compliance may result in severe fines.

9.2. HIPAA (Health Insurance Portability and Accountability Act)

A U.S. regulation centered on protecting the health information (PHI). It requires technical, physical and administrative safeguards to protect patient data, strict access controls and requires breach notification procedures.

10. TOOLS AND TECHNIQUES FOR CYBER RISK MANAGEMENT

10.1. Risk Assessment and Management Tools

Cybersecurity risk assessment tools are applications and platforms designed to perform specific functions in helping organizations to uncover, evaluate and prioritize potential threats and vulnerabilities to their IT infrastructure, applications and networks. Vulnerability Scanners such as Qualys, Nessus, OpenVAS, Rapid7 and RiskLens provide tools for vulnerability scanning, automated compliance checks, risk scoring and even financial risk quantification. With reference to the security systems and the governance systems, they can help organizations to assess qualitative and quantitative risks, meet the regulations and effectively prioritize their remedial measures. Lastly, risk assessment tools play a significant role in improving an organization's security posture as it offers an actionable information to eliminate the threat attack before it takes place.

10.2. Vulnerability Assessment and Penetration Testing (VAPT)

Two security measures as a complement to one another and apply to identify, evaluate and remove risks in the area of IT systems. Vulnerability Assessment is concerned with the organised scan, identification and classification of system security vulnerabilities including system misconfigurations, out of date patches or weak access control, typically by automated analysis to produce a report on which to act.

10.3. Threat Modeling and Attack Simulation

Threat Modeling and Attack Simulation (TMAS) are proactive measures to reduce the impact of cybersecurity by predicting and preventing the impact of the possible risk before the adversary itself can use the risk. Threat Modeling is a formalized approach to the identification of important assets, the study of potential threats, the comprehension of attack surfaces and the mapping of possible weaknesses or abuse cases, commonly based on frameworks such as STRIDE, DREAD or attack trees. It helps organizations prioritize risks based on likelihood and impact, and therefore, it helps in secure design and planning of defence. Attack Simulation, however, is based on simulating real-world adversary techniques, tactics, and procedure (TTPs) - usually by red teaming, breach and attack simulation (BAS) tools, or adversary emulation - in order to test security controls, investigate detection and response capability, and expose weaknesses in defenses. Together, these approaches will provide a practical validation to predictive analysis and enable organizations to construct resilient systems and ensure the placement in the cybersecurity space.

Figure 4. Security metrics framework flowchart

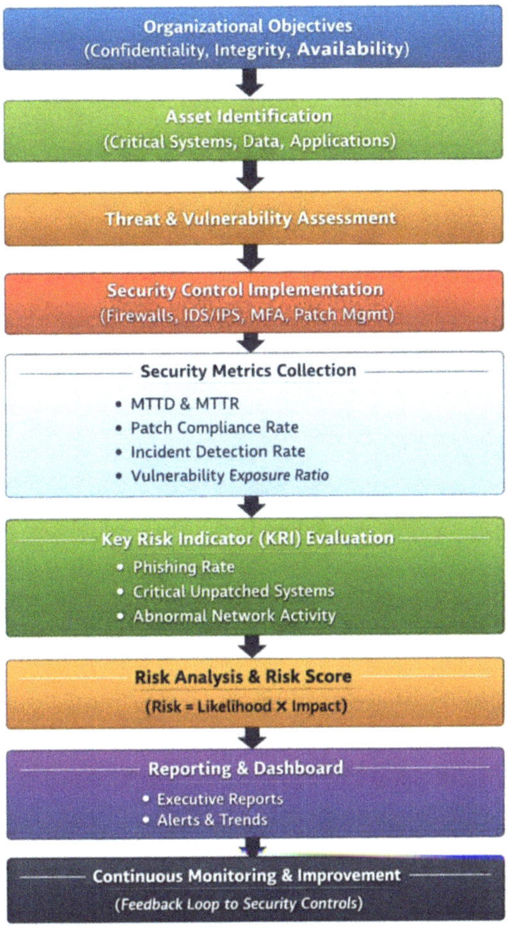

a) Mean Time To Detect (MTTD)

$$MTTD = \frac{\sum_{i=1}^{n} Detection\ Time_i - Incident\ Occurence_i}{n}$$

Where:
n = Total number of incidents

Detection Time = Time when incident was detected
Incident Occurrence = Time when incident started

b) Mean Time To Respond (MTTR)

$$MTTD = \frac{\sum_{i=1}^{n} Incident\ Resoulution\ Time_i - Detection\ Time_i}{n}$$

Lower MTTR indicates better incident response efficiency.

c) Incident Detection Rate (IDR)

$$IDR(\%) = \frac{Detected\ Incidents}{Total\ Incidents} * 100$$

d) Patch Compliance Rate (PCR)

$$PCR(\%) = \frac{No.\ of\ Systems\ Patched}{Total\ Systems} * 100$$

e) Vulnerability Exposure Ratio (VER)

$$VER = \frac{Unpatched\ Critical\ Vulnarabilities}{Total\ Identified\ Vulnarabilities}$$

Higher VER → Higher Risk Exposure

f) Phishing Susceptibility Rate (PSR)

$$PSR\ (\%) = \frac{Users\ Who\ Clicked\ Pishing\ Link}{Total\ Users\ Tested} * 100$$

g) Risk Score Calculation (Quantitative Risk Model)

$$Risk\ Score = Liklihood * Impact$$

Where:
Likelihood (1–5 scale)
Impact (1–5 scale)
Maximum Risk Score = 25

Table 1. Security Metrics Table

Metric	Formula Used	Example Value	Interpretation
MTTD	Avg Detection Time	4.5 Hours	Faster detection improves security
MTTR	Avg Response Time	6.2 Hours	Needs improvement
Detection Rate	IDR	92%	Good detection coverage
Patch Compliance	PCR	88%	Moderate compliance
Vulnerability Exposure Ratio	VER	0.12	12% critical exposure
Phishing Susceptibility	PSR	18%	Requires awareness training

Table 2. Key Risk Indicator (KRI) Threshold Table

KRI	Green Zone	Yellow Zone	Red Zone
Patch Compliance	> 95%	85–95%	< 85%
MTTD	< 3 hrs	3–6 hrs	> 6 hrs
MTTR	< 4 hrs	4–8 hrs	> 8 hrs
Phishing Click Rate	< 5%	5–15%	> 15%
Critical Vulnerabilities	< 5	5–15	> 15

Figure 5. Key risk indicator thresholds chart

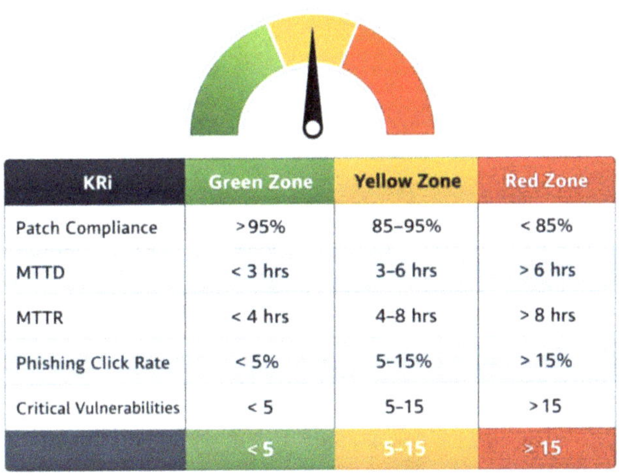

11. CHALLENGES IN CYBER RISK MANAGEMENT

11.1. Emerging Threats (AI-driven Attacks, Ransomware, IoT Vulnerabilities)

AI-based attacks, ransomware, and IoT vulnerabilities are three of the most worrying emerging threats to the cybersecurity environment because it is dynamic. AI based attacks: AI based attacks use artificial intelligence and machine learning technologies which are used for defence against the attacks but in malicious manners. The attackers are able to automate massive phishing attacks, create their deepfakes which are very believable, defy most security measures, and even alter malware to avoid being detected instantly. This adds to the complexity, scale and unabatability of threats.

11.2. Ransomware

Ransomware is on the upswing in terms of its frequency and severity and no longer entails the simple encryption of files but rather complex multi-stage coercion schemes. However, modern day ransomware operators go beyond encrypting vital data and make threats to share sensitive information or disrupt the functioning in the event of non-payments. Such attacks are targeted at people, business organizations and, more recently, critical infrastructure, such as the healthcare and power systems, in which downtime is disastrous. Due to the birth of Ransomware-as-a-Service (RaaS) bad actors with lower skill sets are able to orchestrate successful campaigns, making the world a much more dangerous place.

11.3. IoT vulnerabilities

There is another type of threat that is growing in popularity and that is IoT vulnerabilities. Because of the interconnected nature of these devices, there are billions of smart home devices, and even industrial control systems which are not always protected with a quality security system and are not regularly updated. Attackers have compromised personal privacy and have amassed unauthorized access by using weak authentication, old firmware and poor encryption practices, or create geared botnets to be used in distributed denial-of-service (DDoS) attacks. Increased security by design - the impact of security breaches in the IoT can have an impact on critical services across industries.

11.4. Human and Organizational Factors

Human and organizational factors are very critical in cybersecurity as even the most high tech technologies may be compromised by a human mistake or the organizational weaker practices. Human factors include behaviors, awareness and decision making of employees, contractors and users. The easy to crack passwords, falling into the trap of the phishing attacks, mishandling the sensitive data or incorrectly configuring the systems can result in serious vulnerabilities. These are all human weaknesses that are exploited in social engineering attacks and the reason to be noted about cybersecurity is that it is not only a technical problem but a behavioral problem.

11.5 Cost vs. Security Balance

The aspect of cost and security is a major dilemma that organizations are wrestling with in an effort to secure assets without necessarily having to spend a lot. Security systems such as state-of-the-art threat detectors, encryption, regular vulnerability testing, penetration testing, and staff training is expensive and inefficient use of resources, and generates decreasing returns. Underinvestment in security, by contrast, leaves the organization vulnerable to cyberattacks, possible data loss, regulatory fines, and reputation damage - all of which end up costing the organization far more money than the defenses themselves do.

12. CASE STUDIES AND APPLICATIONS

12.1. Cyber Risk Management in Financial Services

Financial services Cyber risk management is a highly important area for limiting an institution's access to sensitive customer information, financial assets, and infrastructure associated with the institution's operations as well as the evolving cyber threat. Phishing, ransomware, insider attacks and advanced attacks on payment systems, trading platforms and cloud-based services are just a few of the numerous threats financial institutions face. Risk management will include risk identification, vulnerability analysis, penetration testing, and active monitoring with a good identity and access control measures, incident response policy, and PCI DSS, GLBA, and ISO/IEC 27001 compliance, etc. Another area of focus for organizations is third-party risk management where fintech partners and cloud providers have a strong security policy.

12.2 Healthcare and Critical Infrastructure

The healthcare organizations and other critical infrastructure sectors, including energy, transportation, water, and telecommunications, are becoming more reliant on digital technologies in their operations, which are becoming high-value targets of cyberattacks. Cyber risk management in such sectors is needed in order not only to protect sensitive information and continuity of operations but also to preserve human lives, safety of people, and national security. Healthcare and critical infrastructure have a wide range of threats that are undergoing continuous changes such as ransomware and phishing attacks, advanced persistent threats (APTs) organized by organized crime networks or country-state agents.

12.2. Cloud Service Providers and Data Centers

The physical and virtual buildings in the cloud are the foundations of the modern digital infrastructure, where high value applications, sensitive data, and organizational workforces reside for companies worldwide. The reliance on the platforms introduces new cybersecurity challenges where they are in multi-tenanted, highly dynamic, and globally distributed environments. The cyber risk management for cloud and datacenter operations is designed to ensure the data remains in a confidential state, in an integrity state, available, and in regulatory compliance without having to destroy the operations coupled with reputation risks.

13. FUTURE DIRECTIONS IN CYBER RISK MANAGEMENT

13.1. Role of Artificial Intelligence and Machine Learning

Cybersecurity is changing nowadays thanks to the application of Artificial Intelligence (AI) and Machine Learning (ML) to create more efficient, responsive, and smart solutions to more advanced threats. Conventional security technologies that are based on fixed rules and signature-based detection technology can find it difficult to keep up with the ever-changing attack techniques like the zero-day exploits, advanced persistent threats (APTs), and malware that are being driven by AI. AI and ML help to combat cybersecurity through the analysis of large amounts of data, detecting trends, and anticipating possible cyber threats even before they infiltrate as attacks (G. Govinda Rajulu et al., 2025).

Threat detection and anomaly analysis is one of the important areas of AI and ML application.Monitoring network traffic, system logs, user behavior, and the activity of applications allows the ML algorithms to identify any deviations of regular patterns, identify suspicious behavior and even detect previously unknown attack vectors. Indicatively, an anomaly detection model can identify abnormal places of logins or excessive file access which can be signs of insider threats or hacked accounts (Preethi K. M et al., 2025).

13.2. Automation and Real-Time Risk Analytics

The automation and real-time risk analytics are rapidly changing the idea of cybersecurity because it enables organizations to detect, assess, and react more rapidly and efficiently to belittles than by doing so manually. The traditional security functions are often unable to handle the increasing amount, complexity and speed of cyber attacks. They are applied to automate tedious and repetitive activities such as logs analysis, vulnerability scanning, patching and triage of the alerts so that the security teams can focus on the more sophisticated threat investigation and mitigation efforts.

13.3. Cyber Resilience and Business Continuity Integration

The two concepts, which are closely interrelated to each other and can guarantee that organizations can respond, recover and survive following cyber attacks, is business continuity and cyber resilience. Cyber resiliency is not just like traditional cybersecurity in that it does not just focus on preventing attacks but also the ability of the organization to absorb and accommodate its impacts of cyberattacks, system failures, or any other operation crisis. Business continuity on the other hand is planning and implementing processes, policies and technologies which allow the continuation of the services which are required throughout and after a disruptive event. The two domains will be merged to make sure that the cyber threats will be mitigated under the umbrella of the whole operational resilience

14. CONCLUSION

The features of the modern cybersecurity which responds directly to the nature of the cyber threats as something inherently borderless are international cooperation and policy development. The cyberattacks usually involve other nations, which are often aware of the shortcomings of the regulatory system, which means that prevention and response measures should be taken in cooperation with the international community. Governments, industry associations and international organizations work together to exchange information on the threats to provide threat intelligence, best practices, incident response plans and to develop coordinated strategies to defeat cross border cyber threats.

REFERENCES

Abdelkader, S., Amissah, J., Kinga, S., Mugerwa, G., Emmanuel, E., Mansour, D.-E. A., (2024). Bajaj, agency theory perspective. ISACA Journal, 5.

Andrae, S. (2024). Cyber Risk Assessment Using Machine Learning Algorithms. .DOI: 10.4018/979-8-3693-7540-2.ch009

Azura, Y. T. Y., Azad, M. A., & Ahmed, Y. (2025). An integrated cyber security risk management framework for online banking systems. *Journal of Banking and Financial Technology*, *9*(1), 85–104. DOI: 10.1007/s42786-025-00056-3

Bashee, N. (2024). *Cyber risk management in the Internet of Things: Frameworks, models, and best practices*. STAP Journal of Security Risk Management., DOI: 10.63180/jsrm.thestap.2024.1.1

Chong, W. F., Feng, R., Hu, H., & Zhang, L. (2024). Cyber risk assessment for capital cyber risk? Chong, W. F., Feng, R., Hu, H., & Zhang, L. (2025). Cyber risk assessment for capital management. *The Journal of Risk and Insurance*, *92*(2), 424–471. DOI: 10.1111/jori.12504

Donegan, P. (2024). *The fundamentals of cyber risk management*. HardenStance.

Fotis, F. (2024). *Economic impact of cyber attacks and effective cyber risk management*. EasyChair.

Hamid, I., & Rahman, M. M. H. (2025). *AI, machine learning and deep learning in cyber risk intelligence applications in cyber-risk management*. IGI Global., DOI: 10.4018/979-8-3693-7540-2.ch009

M., Blazek, V., & Prokop, L. (2024). Securing modern power systems: Implementing comprehensive strategies to enhance resilience and reliability against cyber-attacks. Results in Engineering, 23, 102647. https://doi.org/DOI: 10.1016/j.rineng.2024.102647

Parsons, E. K., Panaousis, E., Loukas, G., & Sakellari, G. (2023). A survey on cyber risk procedural guidelines and practical evaluation metrics for organizational IT and cybersecurity risk assessment. arXiv. https://doi.org//arXiv.2410.01750DOI: 10.48550

Rahman, M. M., Kshetri, N., Sayeed, S. A., & Rana, M. M. (2024, October 2). *AssessITS: Integrating procedural guidelines and practical evaluation metrics for organizational IT and Cybersecurity risk assessment*. arXiv.org. https://arxiv.org/abs/2410.01750

Romanosky, S., & Sayers, E. L. P. (2024). Enterprise risk management: How do firms integrate strategies: A light literature review and case study analysis. *Procedia Computer Science*, *251*, 471–478. DOI: 10.1016/j.procs.2024.11.135

Chapter 2
Improving Cyber Threat Intelligence Through Generative AI From Data to Actionable Intelligence

Vijay Singh Rana
http://orcid.org/0009-0006-0234-2225
J.V. Jain College, Saharanpur, India

Tarun Kumar Vashishth
http://orcid.org/0000-0001-9916-9575
Department of Computer Applications, Vidya University, Meerut, India

Puneet Chauhan
http://orcid.org/0009-0000-1652-8764
School of Computer Application, Swami Vivekanand Subharti University, Meerut, India

Vikas Sharma
http://orcid.org/0000-0001-8173-4548
Department of Computer Applications, SRM Institute of Science and Technology, Delhi NCR Campus, Ghaziabad, India

Sachin Tomar
Department of Computer Applications, SRM Institute of Science and Technology, Delhi NCR, India

Shahanawaj Ahamad
College of Computer Science and Engineering, University of Hail, Saudi Arabia

Aditi Chauhan
School of Humanities and Mass Communication, IIMT University, Meerut, India

ABSTRACT

Cyber threat intelligence (CTI) is of great importance in the proactive nature of the cyber defense process, allowing organizations to make actionable plans for evolving

DOI: 10.4018/979-8-3693-8397-1.ch002

threats. Historically, acquiring cyber threat intelligence has been beset by the lack of comprehensiveness, immediacy, and the ability to synthesize disparate data from undefined sources of threat intelligence. Generative AI affords an opportunity to rise above these deficiencies from the perspective of the depth, speed, and readability of threat intelligence. This chapter assesses how generative AI may be of assistance in driving forward the study of cyber threat intelligence from the millennial perspective, but from an initial perspective – how generative models do indeed have the capability of producing threat hints and warnings, modelling essential threat/ attack scenarios and augmenting sources of data for training detection systems.

1. INTRODUCTION

The current complexity and range of modern cyber threats have proliferated into unimaginable proportions. The organisations in today's environment are faced with a volatile environment of advanced persistent threats (APTs), ransom ware activities, phishing attacks and other sponsored cyber-attacks. It is evident that the traditional measures have an estimable role, failing typically against the difficult and complex nature of these attacks. Most organisations are looking to Cyber Threat Intelligence (CTI), that is the structured collection, evaluation and analysis of information related to threats, with a view to assisting in informed decisions and act proactively in the fight against these threats. (Vemuri et al., 2024).

1.1 Background on Cyber Threat Intelligence

Cyber Threat Intelligence (CTI) essentially involves the structured collection, processing and analysis of information pertaining to the salient threats to the digital environment of the enterprise at hand, either real, or to be. Converting disparate and uncollected security information into useful information for the purpose of assisting in better decision making of intelligence outcome, and to optimise the cybersecurity activities of the enterprise, is the main purpose of CTI (Saurabh et al., 2024). The better able an enterprise is to know the tactics, techniques, and procedures of its adversaries, the better able it is to foretell attacks on them, enhance their defensive levels and maintain exposure to the risk. The growing importance of CTI is closely related to the growing and sophisticated cyberattack landscape that is based on polymorphic malware, supply chain exploitation and zero-day exploits that evade most of the classical means of defence used. CTI is a proactive means to secure one's organization as it changes the focus from a purely reactive incident response model to a preventive means of reducing the risk of security threats before those threats pose larger problems. That is usually divided by a three tier means to provide the needs of the different constituents. At the strategic level, it provides the general overviews to executive leadership concerned with more broad strokes of threat trend indicators, geo-political implications, and longer-term planning strategies. At the operational level leadership at this level need to understand contextual information concerning adversarial campaigns, techniques, motivations, and tactics in order provide a better understanding of the threat landscape. This layered program of CTI ensures that all levels of decision making among its constituents that the needs of decision making from senior leadership down to the front-line information security analysts are meet concerning those select needs through the application of successful CTI (Hasan et al., 2025).

1.2 Emergence of Generative AI in Cybersecurity

The rapid evolution of artificial intelligence has complicated the landscape of cybersecurity, with generative AI acting as a major disruptor to solve many of the pressing challenges in threat detection and intelligence analysis (Alevizo & Dekker, 2024). Unlike previous artificial intelligence models principally created for classification, prediction or anomaly detection generative models have the capability to generate new representations of data as they learn or understand the pattern and structure of an enormous data set. This inherent creative ability lends itself to tremendous advantages for the generative model in the cyber security space, an area of which the adversary is constantly modifying its methodology and finding novel ways to execute its onslaught, often rendering static defensive provisions as obscure. By modelling attack scenarios and producing synthetic threat data and enriching sparse data sets the generative models provide the defender with defence mechanisms which can be made to cater for varying levels of defence, with these being necessarily agile and proactive mechanisms. Moreover, generative techniques can promote data amplification in the form of synthetic, yet realistic threat examples produced that can resolve the issues of no datasets or biased datasets that can occur, supplying the real threat examples that can benefit from the use of the generating algorithms and their specialization and constant improvement in accuracy and generalization (Teo et al., 2024).

1.3 Research Contribution and Novelty

This chapter has produced many new ideas and contributions to the growing field of Cyber Threat Intelligence (CTI) using generative AI. The first major contribution is the development of an integrated Generative AI-based CTI framework that improves the CTI lifecycle (i.e. data collection, data enrichment, analysis of data, and distribution of data) in an orderly, systematic fashion. While existing articles focus on the application of generative AI in various instances either independently from one another or within their own context, this work combines three forms of generative AI (data enrichment, simulating an attack, and transforming intelligent collected data with large language models (LLMs)) into one integrated approach. The second significant contribution is that there is now a clear, structured mapping between the capabilities of generative AI and CTI levels: strategic, operational, and tactical. This now gives people across the entire organization the ability to use generative AI to elevate their decision-making capabilities. Third, this chapter includes a description of how to use generative AI to generate synthetic data and model the behaviours of an adversary in a proactive cybersecurity manner going beyond traditional reactive forms of intelligence. Lastly, a practical model of a workflow and a use-case-based validation process that can be used to demonstrate how generative AI can effectively transform raw threat information into actionable intelligence in a timely, scalable, and accurate manner.

2. FUNDAMENTALS OF CYBER THREAT INTELLIGENCE

Cyber Threat Intelligence (CTI) is the basis of the modern-day approach of cyber security of organisations, supplying the cyber security of the discrepancies of insight that they require to gain threat identification, assessment, and reaction for the changing and growing themes of the digital threat times. The ever-growing threats of cyber strikes all over the world being it for individuals and industry have been thought to be by the expert analysers of the CTI discipline which serves to utilize the exchange from the basic means of the digital data as indicator to the strategic policies of the security topics (Alqahtani and Kumar, 2025).

2.1 Definition and Role of CTI in Modern Cybersecurity

In contrast to raw threat intelligence, which may be represented by logs, alerts and anomalies, CTI is about taking this data and so being able to convert it into intelligence which can be understood in a human sense and can be analysed by security teams and decision makers and thus help them in predicting, evidencing, and mitigating the malicious activity. (Reddy et al, et al., 2023). CTI is not merely establishing what threats exist, it is understanding the effect, means, and methods of the adversary, so that the intention of the adversary is understood in this area, and thus this information can be used in preparation against attacks. The traditional deterrents of this, firewalls, anti-virus solutions, and intrusion alerts have proved previously sufficient to defend against or deter the more routine attacks. This however is no longer the case. The sophistication of today's cyber adversary means that they more and more employ the more advanced tactics, techniques and procedures (TTPS) of today's ransomware campaign, supply chain compromise, and state sponsored cyber espionage in the forms of criminal. In this regard, CTI provides the knowledge required to bridge that gap between being more reactive in defending the perimeter to being proactive in the management of the threats. This is the manner in which CTI identifies the indicators of compromise, identifies attackers' techniques, tactics, and approaches as the threats evolve in the way of trends further to attack. This will not only assist organisations to respond to raised incidents quicker to it will also allow the anticipation and therefore mitigation of those attacks. Another of the critical roles for CTI is to inform the decision-makers throughout the different levels of an organisation. At the tactical level, is provides by data to the security operation centres (SOCs) in real time, such information would include information such as malicious IP addresses, domain names and file hashes which can be applied straight away to block or detect intrusions (Vikas et al., 2023). At the operational Level CTI assists security analysts in a better understanding of the adversaries' campaigns, motivations, and tactics, as a result optimising a better defensive strategy. At the strategic level CTI gives the executive and the decision-makers an insight to understand trends over the long term in threats, changes in geopolitical concerns and vulnerabilities in specific sectors of both the commercial and state sectors, in this way making the investment and policy which is made as to the delivery of cyber security applicable to meet the organisational priorities. This is as well that it is in CTI that the collaborative work in the defence ecosystems is enabled. Figure 1 shows the multi-layered approach to gathering and utilizing information for supporting current cybersecurity tasks by integrating several layers of intelligence processing. The first step in building a Cyber Threat Intelligence (CTI) Framework consists of collecting data through the analysis and integration of various sources of data (Saddi et al., 2024).

Figure 1. Proposed Cyber Threat Intelligence Framework in Modern Cybersecurity

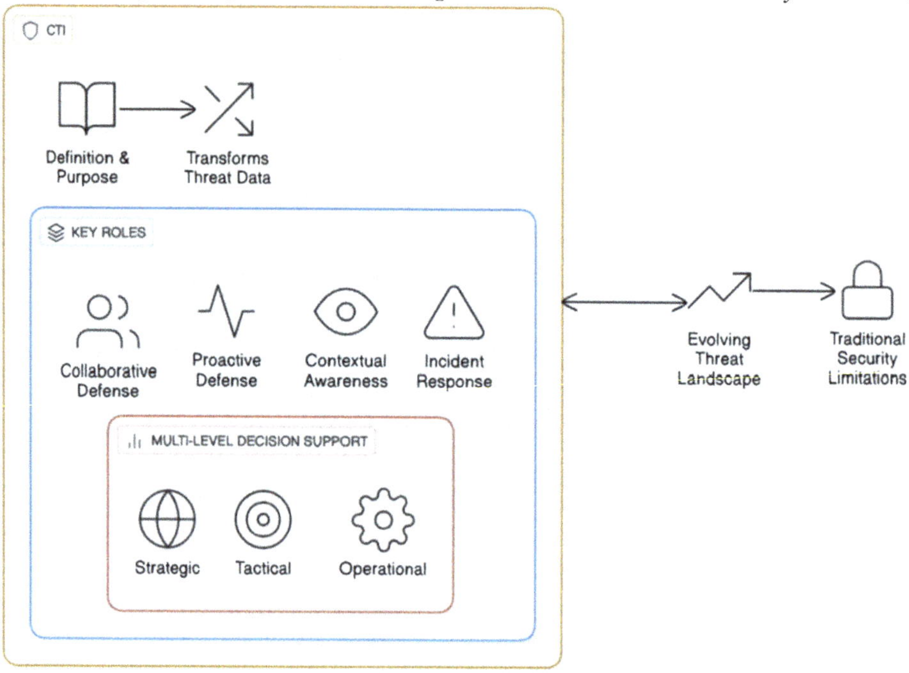

2.2 Types of Threat Intelligence

Threat Intelligence is non-homogeneous, it is a multi-layered concept and technique approach differing in all manners and degrees and level of complexity to the stakeholder with differing or concurrent interests and security needs on behalf of different stakeholders in or affiliated to the organization, but that by being analysed on layers of Strategic, Tactical, Operational and Technical, this in turn allows for the information collated and analysed to be configured for effective reach targets of audience ranging from in degrees from Elected Policy makers to Operational Security analysts.

1. **Threat Intelligence:** The customer for this intelligence is primarily, an executive of some sort, a policy maker or board member and what they require is answers in regards to security investment, policies, and strategies for their organizations. For example, intelligence on states that sponsor cyber activity and trends in ransom ware as a service (RaaS) would help organizations better to align their security thinking to the future weaknesses they may suffer from (Sarker 2024).

2. **Operational Threat Intelligence:** Operational intelligence gives incident response teams the ability to understand the who, what and why of a particular campaign and helps speed up containment and remediation of an attack. An example of this is being aware that a certain threat actor group is exploiting a zero-day vulnerability in a popular application, thereby allowing security personnel the opportunity to enforce some compensating controls for the duration of time until patches are available (Sharma et al., 2025).
3. **Technical Threat Intelligence:** Technical intelligence is of a short burst in its meta-skill due to the degree of change in infrastructure and attack-made temporalities employed by aggressors end to not being discovered. However, they still remain important resource for first-line point defence applications alike IDS, IPS, firewalls and endpoint security provision as they add the possibility of to automatically block and / or detect known entities of attack (Patil, 2024).

2.3 Threat Intelligence Lifecycle

The significance of Cyber Threat Intelligence (CTI) derives from the application of a structured cyber intelligence process called the Threat Intelligence Lifecycle. The Threat Intelligence Lifecycle is an ongoing process of a repetitive nature that allows raw cyber threat data to be converted into useable cyber threat intelligenceThe Threat Intelligence Lifecycle is composed of 6 primary stages, those of Planning and Direction, Collection, Processing, Analysis, Dissemination and Feed Back, but the actual execution of these stages possesses its own additional critical area for enhancement of the relevancy, accuracy and consistency of that intelligence having regard to the overall goals of the organization. Planning and efficiently articulating the intelligence requirements ensures that the organizational resources are focused on only monitoring the threats that are relevant, and thus not wasting precious intelligence on the collection of irrelevant or impotent information. The second step of the Threat Intelligence Lifecycle, collection, is directed toward the gathering of information from other internal and external sources. The internal sources could be as diverse as security logs, intrusion detection systems, honeypots, or industry incident reports whilst the external sources of information could be diverse and multifarious and could include such as, open-source intelligence (OSINT), dark net monitoring, commercial intelligence feeds, and information sharing groups. Because of the rapidity of development of cyber threats and intelligence, effective collection effort must therefore cover a wide and deep breadth of information covering all the significant variety of information that could be brought to bear in order to be effective, such as, structured technical indicators, unstructured report written text, and contextual information about the attacker motivations etc. The data that is collected must then be processed so that it is arranged, filtered, and normalised into a usable format. Raw data is often presented in an obscure way, being incomplete in its content or contradictory and therefore being fit for little more than but not for direct analysis . Data processing may principally involve the exclusion of duplicate data, validation, enrichment, with contextual metadata, and translation of multi-lingual documentary evidence. The object of the exercise is that the only reliable and relevant data shall be passed on for the analysis stage of the work and this in turn results in the benefits of the reduction of noise, and an improvement in quality of output of the intelligence products. (Uddin et al., 2025). This chapter is going to include a generative AI-based workflow that continues to improve the original threat intelligence lifecycle. With the use of advanced models, generative AI will be integrated into various stages of the intelligence process. From the data collection phase, large language models will automatically retrieve threatening information from unstructured data sources like reports, blogs, and the dark web. In the processing stage, generative models will clean, normalise, and enrich data by populating missing data and providing relevant context to fragmented data. Machine learning and generative techniques will provide analysts with the necessary tools to reveal hidden patterns, create attack simulations, and provide analysis of emerging cyber threats during the analysis phase. During dissemination phase, large language models will produce accurate, timely, and relevant reports that are specific to the needs of the audience (i.e., operational analysts, decision makers). The outcomes of this integrated workflow will greatly enhance the timeliness, accuracy, and contextually relevant information produced from cyber threat intelligence.

3. GENERATIVE AI: CONCEPTS AND CAPABILITIES

Generative AI has quickly become one of the leading transformative technologies in the areas of machine learning and AI. While traditional AI models have typically been constructed to solve problems such as classification, regression and anomaly detection problems, generative models are able to produce instances of new data which represent but do not duplicate real world examples.

3.1 Overview of Generative Models

Generative Models Generative models are the class of models of machine learning that are directed towards extracting the essential distributions of data in order to generate synthetic new real-world examples. They differ significantly from discriminative models which are directed towards the identification of classes and labels in that generative models are concerned with the structures of the data itself and resultant production of new granular outputs instead of acceptable discriminative recognition of existing patterns.

1. **Generative adversarial networks (GANs):** It The generative adversarial networks consist of two networks or sets of interpretations which work against each other and particularly consist of generator and discriminator. The generator produces synthetic data which in its existence cannot be differentiated from real world data and the discriminator attempts to distinguish between real and synthetic examples. The adversarial training of GANs is often unstable and computationally expensive, yielding difficulties between models in the successful transferability of the results to the large application techniques (Balasubramanian et al., 2025).
2. **Variational Autoencoders (VAEs):** They are developed around the same time as GAN and uses the same probabilistic procedure but generate data by learned latent representation. GANs work on the concept of adversarial training where the generator tries to deceive the discriminator by the creation of sampled data from its purpose, the VAEs first capture the input data with an encoder and create it again by an analogous decoder.
3. **Transformers:** The creation of the LLM, which is a programmable language for text recognition that are coded using the transformer principle shows what a useful tool the correct program can be for the architect who can create such a program where they are used in modern ways for creating coherent story logic in structures in various languages and scopes of learning.

3.2 Large Language Models (LLMs) for Cybersecurity Applications

Large Language Models (LLMs), which are transformer type models per se, have gained prominence as powerful tools that can radically transform the security landscape by means of intelligent automation, sophisticated analytics and real- time decision support mechanisms. Unlike the traditional natural language processing (NLP) models, LLMs such as GPT, BERT etc., are trained on large corpora of structured and unstructured knowledge and information to enable the extraction and understanding of the subtlety of language, context, and semantics. Thus, huge amounts of cyber security related material, for instance, voluminous volumes of evidence in text related to threat intelligence reports and malware descriptions, security advisories, incident logs etc., can be ingested. Thus, the seeds of a bridge between unstructured human generated data and machine readable and intelligible and insightful data can now be possible. One of the most beneficial uses that LLMs can do for cyber intelligence is the potential for automated analysis of threat intelligence. Often, companies receive threat intelligence in other languages and formats that overwhelm human analysts. By being able to analyse and indicators of compromise (IoCs) from these reports, LLMs are able to synthesise the vectors of attack and create commonalities between developing patterns with respect to adversarial tactics, techniques, and procedures (TTPs). This automation not only creates efficiencies in the collection of threat intelligence, but acts to reduce human error relating to an area with huge quantities of data and where humans are overwhelmed by the sheer volume of reports etc. Another area of influence LLMs is in the area of hyper multilingual threat intelligence or threat analysis. Automatic translation of reports into other languages and the contents of those reports allows for integrated threat reporting between nations in ways that have not been possible. Thus, situational awareness on a global front is improved. LLMs also allow for incident response and forensics due to the natural language interface that permits the querying of complex datasets. Security analysts can use LLMs to extract logs, detect anomalies and supply a 'human friendly' explanation of any likely compromises. The architecture depicted in figure 2 is an illustration of a framework that utilizes Large Language Models (LLM) to increase the productivity of cybersecurity applications through automatic intelligence and understanding contextual threat data more efficiently. The inputs used to feed the AI algorithms are both unstructured inputs and structured inputs.

Figure 2. Proposed LLM-Based Framework for Cybersecurity Applications

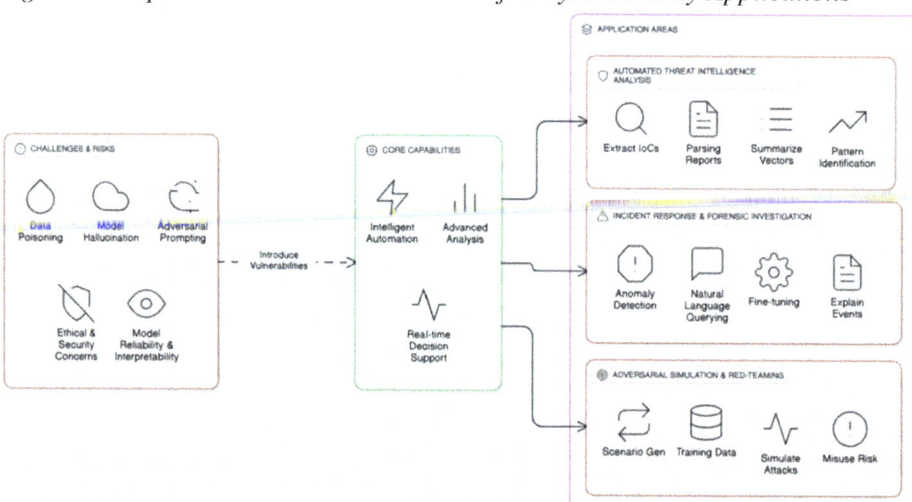

3.3 Data Synthesis and Augmentation through Generative AI

Data is the key element in cybersecurity, but the acquisition of plentiful, heterogeneous, and quality datasets for application in training and testing of the defense mechanisms employed, continues to be a significant difficulty. Real cyber-attack data is on the whole sparse, incomplete, and limited in availability, due to restrictions of confidentiality and privacy and as a result limits the ability of organizations to construct strong and robust defense systems (Sharma et al., 2023). Generative AI presents a partial answer in the guise of data synthesis and augmentation. This can produce quantities of realistic and representative and synthesizable datasets that allow the development of effective cybersecurity tools. By using the basic rules of existing threat data, the generative models can produce synthetic but realistic samples which increase the dataset quantity without the need for divulging sensitive and/or proprietary information. One of the more useful opportunities for the introduction of generative AI in this area is in the simulation of behaviour of malware and attacks. Models that utilize Generative Adversarial Networks (GANs) and Variational Autoencoders (VAEs) can produce synthetic malware binaries, malware signatures and phishing emails which are very similar to realistic attacks (Bibri and Huang, 2025). Such synthetic datasets can be used in the training of Intrusion Detection Systems (IDS), malware classifiers and phishing tools, helping to increase the capacity of the systems to identify new and previously unseen vectors of attack. Moreover, by data augmenting the datasets with rare types of attack or emergent threats, generative AI helps to rectify class imbalance, or an important difficulty with much of the cyber datasets, which have a strong skew whereby the benign data is vastly in excess of the data having malicious provenance.

4. GENERATIVE AI FOR THREAT DATA ENRICHMENT

Enrichment of threat data is a critical part of Cyber Threat Intelligence (CTI) since raw threat indicators such as IPs, domains, malware hashes, or phishing URLs are not rich enough in context to be useful. Without enrichment these data remain disassociated bits of data that are not very useful in predicting, detecting, or reacting to the future of cyberattacks. Generative AI can open new venues to enriching of quality, depth, and the desire for context of threat data by creating additional data, isolate near invisible patterns, and make meaningful connections between disparate data. This becomes more meaningful as raw threat indicators transform into intelligence assets that can be used to further inform the strategic decision making of organizations, incident response, and pro-active defense (Vashishth et al, 2026).

4.1 Automated Extraction of Threat Indicators from Structured and Unstructured Data

Threat indicator extraction of data is a key step in Cyber Threat Intelligence (CTI) converting raw data into a useful actionable set of signposts for use in detecting, predicting, and mitigating cyber security attacks. Threat Indicators are better known as Indicators of Compromise (IoCs) Some of these are IP addresses that are malicious, domain names, file hashes, malware fingerprints, and phishing URLs. IoC extraction is traditionally a human manual affair that is rule based rather than an AI affair that is not likely to be adept at processing the size, complexity, and speed of modern-day cyber threats. Generative AI is an efficient, scalable, and automated means of IoC extraction from structured and unstructured data sources by use of large language models (LLM) and more sophisticated natural language processing (NLP) technology. Contemporary security gear has tools such as computer-based content inspection tools which have unlimited potential to assist cyber security defence and proactive defence. Generally, this data produces useful information in a structured format which unfortunately needs to be correlated and made richer to be meaningful. In short generative AI tools can analyse volumes of structured data, discover abnormal activity and at an automatic level pick out IOC's which diverge from sorts of baselines of operation. For e.g. network traffic and anomalous logon's can be discovered and classified as possible threat indicator enabling human trained analysts to operate at a higher tactical level. By relating various data models in a context these systems can move past pattern recognition into categories which separate benign anomalies from real malicious attacks. Generally unstructured data is a larger problem as the data does not follow a structured format. Data formats in this genre includes incident reports, postings to dark webs, notification of vulnerabilities, social media messages. For instance, if the focus of study was a technical blog entry about a new strain of ransomware, a generative space would automatically discern from IOC's such things as file hashes produced, C2 domains of major server locations distribution strategies. Such enriching information from predictive trends changes the nature of the data from that of being partial in nature to a more complete intelligence with this which can lead to the proactive defensive strategies employed by (Ajibesin and Vijayhala, 2025).

4.2 Synthesizing Threat Signatures and Indicators of Compromise (IoCs)

Threat signatures and Indicators of Compromise (IoCs) are the pillars of current cyber security defense systems giving rise to the detection of possibly malicious labours through networks, endpoints, and clouds. Up to now, the statically developed signatures and IoCs have been immutable resultant of forensically secured results of known attacks, reverse-engineered malwares, and ground-targeted intelligence which is manually generated by security analysts. Effective but slow, reactive, and limited in growth factors. Generative AI presents itself as a new possibility of developing new signatures and IoCs for the threat systems in a similar vein. Through this technology it is possible to achieve a more rapid adaptation to the detection of new threats, and a higher degree of automation in the supply of defense instruments. Generative models such as GANs, VAEs, and transformer network models can describe the underlying semantics of the target systems, and therefore the known attack behaviours existent in a particular region of the threat landscape itself, and generalising towards the formation of synthetic but small (realistic) threat artifacts. In the understanding of a collection of phishing e-mails it is possible now for a generative model, for example, to produce in fact other examples which would be immediately absorbed copies of the attack situation where the generator's version represents possibly IoCs, there being likely to be a question of hijacked domains, hijacked mail headers, and osculated URLs.

4.3 Augmenting Training Datasets for Machine Learning Security Models

Machine learning (ML) applications have become an integral part of modern cyber-security and are used for intrusion detection, malware classification, phishing detection, and anomaly detection. The performance of the models is dependent on the quality, quantity and diversity of training set datasets. Accordingly, the cyber-security related datasets used can often be seriously flawed in terms of classes, either not being representative of new threats or not able to have real-world attacks adequately represented due to privacy/confidentiality issues. However, these scenarios can be solved by the introduction of generative AI which improves the models by providing synthetic high-quality examples which can be included in the training datasets leading to improved robustness, adaptability, and accuracy of the employed security models. The generative models of GANs (Generative Adversarial Networks) and VAEs (Variational Autoencoders) are very powerful in generating synthetic malicious artifacts which closely resemble real world attacks. In this way, such enriched datasets, allow the models to learn the nuances between benign and malicious activities improving their detection capabilities; thus, leading to greater accuracy in detections and lower probability of false positives (Muppalaneni et al, 2024).

4.4 Enhancing Real-Time Threat Feeds with Generative AI

Timely threat feeds are essential in providing organizations with current threat indicators and alerts for current attacks, but suffer from challenges of lack of data, redundancy, and lack of context. Generative AI remediates these feeds by dynamically enriching the raw indicators with predictions, context sensitive metadata and inferential relationships thus transforming them from informational streams to actionable streams (intelligence). For example, when a malicious domain is detected, generative models can predict possible domain variations, they can also predict the related command-and-control (C2) infrastructure and the various attack scenarios that could be related to the threats related. The generative AI through lessening the noise, filling in the missing data and correlating the fragmented signals as these evolve, thus providing the security operations centers (SOCs) with accurate, timely and context sensitive intelligence to enhance proactive defense thus providing organizations to be more responsive and effective to the quickly evolving cyber threats (Mukherjee et al, 2025).

4.5 Proposed Architecture

In order to compensate for the failings of conventional CTI systems, a structured generative AI-powered architecture has been designed to enhance the threat intelligence lifecycle. The architecture has multiple levels of interconnected layers that systematically convert raw information into usable intelligence. The first step in an intelligence lifecycle (ILC) process is the collection of raw data from multiple structured and unstructured data sources (e.g., logs, threat feeds, vulnerability databases, and dark web sites). The next step in the ILC process is a layer for data processing and normalizing the collected data, including cleaning, filtering, and converting to a common or standard format using natural language processing (NLP). At the heart of the generative AI architecture is the generative AI layer, which leverages the models of generative adversarial networks (GAN), Variational autoencoders (VAE), and large language models to enrich threat data, generate synthetic data, extract indicators, and simulate attacks. The processed data is then passed through to the intelligence analysis layer unit for advanced analytics and pattern recognition to identify adversary behavior and predict possible threats. The last layer to the architecture is the actionable intelligence layer, which provides insights to support decision-making at the strategic, operational and technical levels through alerts, dashboard displays, and reports. By leveraging this generative artificial intelligence architecture, scaled automation and accelerated generation of real-time threat intelligence will be achieved in building today's cyber security infrastructure.

5. SIMULATING ATTACK SCENARIOS WITH GENERATIVE AI

Proactive cybersecurity goes beyond mere detection and response, including the ability to predict the possibility of attacks and gain an understanding of adversarial paradigms. Traditional paradigms for simulation of threats, such as red-teams and static attack models, can be time consuming and labour intensive, and can only be confined to exercises of specific scope (Sanjalawe et al., 2025).

5.1 Generative AI for Red Teaming and Offensive Security

Red teaming testing and offensive security situations are a vital part of the defence evaluation of an organization through realistic simulations of adversarial activities in a controlled environment. Traditionally, human input was required for all these tasks to generate the necessary attack scenarios, identify the vulnerabilities and evaluate the response of the different attacks which has proved time consuming and restricted in its effect. Generative AI gives a further dimension to red teaming types of exercise through automating the generation of complex attack scenarios, enabled through malware generation methods and social engineering attack campaigns providing much wider and more dynamic testing for security teams. The generative models are also able to derive the requisite behaviours from historical attacks, feeds of threat intelligence and adversarial behaviours to reproduce complex multi-stage attacks, test exploit vectors and simulate the Tactics, Techniques and Procedures (TTPs) of the real-life attackers. Scalability and variability of attack scenarios is also supplemented by generative AI. The automation of generating an infinite quantity of attack permutations, allows the models to simulate rare behaviours or emerging threat behaviours which may not yet exist in the wild. This predictive ability allows the red teams to probe a far wider area of attack vector possibilities such as polymorphic types of malware attacks, lateral movements, and intrusion methods.

5.2 Creating Realistic Phishing, Malware, and Ransomware Simulations

This capability of generative AI to produce, say, highly realistic simulations of phishing operations, malware performers and ransomware hostilities, can be a key factor in training, exercising, and hardening of other defence systems, but this simulation ability should ideally be carried out and the operations run within an ethical, legal, and operational envelope (Zhuwankinyu et al., 2024). For example, using phishing simulations, the use of LLM for producing more diverse templates from the confrontational co-operas of supposedly benign and malignant emails enables provisions for deriving differences templates using linguistic styles, social-engineering and cultural motifs so that the same forms of synthetic emails can be tested against susceptibility to security analysis, improving their utility for tuning detection rule systems, security awareness programs in multi-language workforces. For malware and ransomware in respect of generative models (for example GANs and VAEs), it is possible to simulate benign looking binaries or the relevant activity traces which exhibit the statistical and behavioural qualities of the heroes in question in a statistically-simulated manner without the desire to reproduce tests and reproduction-useable malware. These artefacts then permit the safe testing of endpoint detection and response (EDR) systems, sandbox environments, and behavioural analytic pipelines as they can be exposed to a greater variety of evasive and polymorphous behaviours than would exist with a small number of real-world samples. Most vital is that realistic simulation requires strong controls: synthetic artefacts should be non-useable or rendered inert, the experiments should take place in isolated air-gapped environments or secure sandboxes and access to generated material should occur under strict control and logging. Validation and calibration are mandatory - simulations should be benchmarked against real world telemetry with the aim of resulting in realism but not being promotive of destructive capabilities, and the outputs should be vetted by human analysts to avoid hallucinations or misconceived artefacts that are unrealistic and could mislead defences. Under proper circumstances generative AI artefacts become effective means of anticipatory defence improving detection robustness and response readiness and organizational resilience to evolving phishing, malware, and ransomware threats (Chauhan et al, 2026).

5.3 Synthetic Adversary Behavior Modeling

By leveraging generative AI, synthetic adversary behavior modeling explores the tactics (TTP's), techniques, procedures, and decision-making of threat actors by allowing for the replay and synthesis of realistic adversary action temporally, across systems, and people. Not random isolated artifacts are produced, but sequences of actual attacker behavior such as reconnaissance, establishment of hold, privilege escalation, lateral movement, data exfiltration, and cleanup resulting in end-to-end narratives of attacks to show how an adversary would attack in a particular environment. Historical incident data, telemetry, threat reports etc, would allow generative models to throw some light on probable goals, methods, tools, and times of the adversaries so allowing for them to help the defender not alone to get a handle on what indicators are likely to be found on the surface, but also in relation to the general context and objectives of a possible attack. This would feed into advanced red teaming, purple teaming, and auto-generation of incident response playbooks from synthetic adversary behaviours to stress-test detection logic, correlation methodologies, and information which should not be missing in alerting and containment workflows which obtain in outright defence. The success of adversary modelling on the other hand depends strongly on the careful calibration and validation against actual observations [not bon mots] of adversary action lest there should be a danger of overfitting to earlier campaigns and unrealistic chains of attack and the necessity for human examination of the results of the algorithms in order to check for their relevance, context as naturally occurs, and vetting in relation to their secondary operational applicability.

6. ROLE OF LARGE LANGUAGE MODELS (LLMS) IN CTI

Language Models (LLM's) based on transformer architecture have now become among the cornerstones of modern Cyber Threat Intelligence practicality by virtue of the ability of machines to process and analyze, the enormous scale and speed at which things can be synthesized, to process information both structured and unstructured.

6.1 Automating Threat Report Summarization and Translation

Security teams that are assessing threat information sources frequently experience a flood of technical reports and advisories, vulnerability discoveries, and disclosers, as well as feeds of intelligence or threat information. These may come in multiple languages or in varying formats. It is laborious and sometimes unreliable for individuals to process this information manually. LLM's can automatically read and analyze such documents and discover the principal information contained therein, such as Indicators of compromise, Informants' Tactics, Techniques and Procedures, (TTP's) or possibly recommendations for mitigation; then write brief and actionable summaries of material for the information of a variety of audiences, such as technical analysts and top management. Equally important as the successive elucidation of coverage and formal succinct summarization is the capability of LLM's to provide threat translation capabilities that are multilingual. This means that the intelligence deduced and assessed from a variety of geographic sources can be used effectively. Items of information on threats in foreign languages or items lifted from particular dark web forums in specified areas, can be accurately and conveniently translated into intelligible form, made meaningful, and put into the hands of responsible management for further planning usage without any loss of their particular technical meaning and nuance, or the emphasis of relevant cultural consideration connoted by the language in its original documentation. This increases the situational awareness greatly, and gives the concerned security teams a better opportunity not only to detect the emergence of threats in new areas geographically, but also permits the organizations responsible for Cybersecurity to develop a response capability that is more robust, together with minimum lag time lost through any necessity for translation.

6.2 Multilingual Cyber Investigations and Intelligence Sharing

Large Language Models (LLMs) have become an essential component in multilingual cyber investigations, as well as in enabling the sharing of intelligence, in addressing one of the most critical hurdles in Cyber Threat Intelligence (CTI) on a global level, the heart of that hurdle being the language barrier. Cyber threats originate throughout a variety of geographic theatres of operations where different languages are practiced either toward their deployment or in the documentation of the malware or in the coordination of cyber operations or campaigns. Traditional methodologies of analysis for intelligence fuels require either human interpreters or expertise in that particular region of the globe, which invariably creates a gap in response to the incidents under investigation or creates the inability to adequately appraise the situation. LLMs can provide a means of circumventing this gap as they are by nature able to interpret and contextualize the various sources of intelligence, translating the documentation or the interviews or the adversary situational networks of foreign languages into reports that still retain their meaning, their expertise, their technical terms, and concepts, which can also be adapted to take account of the nuances and motivations related to the cultural adaptiveness of adversaries. By standardising and enriching the intelligence capable of being gained from heterogeneous, disparate sources, such models assure the seamless flow of communication from organisation to organisation, from interdepartmental consortium which has been informed or advised with our industry, or from government agencies. Threat indicators, patterns of attack, and weaknesses which have been recorded in one geographic theatre can be instantly shared, contextualised, and used in other geographic theatres, ensuring coordinated defensive action and preventive threat mitigation (Kavitha and Thejas, 2024). Figure 3 represents a multilingual cyber threat intelligence sharing (CTIS) architecture that can connect all threat data regardless of the language used or geographic area of origin. The framework starts by collecting threat data from multiple sources around the world and passing it to the preprocessing layer where language detection, translation, and normalization techniques are used to standardize and normalize the diverse amount of heterogeneous information prior to integration for analysis.

Figure 3. Proposed Multilingual Cyber Threat Intelligence Sharing Architecture

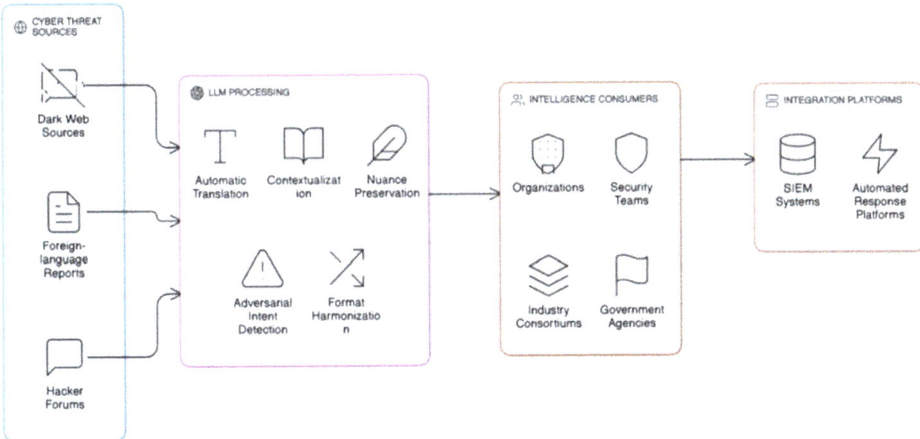

6.3 Detecting Emerging Threat Trends in Unstructured Dark Web Data

The dark web represents an enormous and chaotic collection of intelligence with valuable insights into new and emerging cyber threats such as malware campaigns, zero-day vulnerabilities, ransomware negotiations, and communication between actors. Monitoring and analyzing the enormous mass of heterogeneous data which resides in these unstructured media is a monumental task, made more difficult by the multiplicity of languages used and the obfuscation tactics employed by cyber-criminals. The new Large Language Models (LLMs) are a significant advance in the means of solving the problem of parsing, interpreting, and synthesizing the information contained in various media automatically, enabling the perception of new trends in threats that might as yet not be caught in conventional intelligence gels. The LLMs discover the appropriate entities in the dark net streams, such as the aliases of actors, families of malware, exploit kits, industries attacked and institutions attacked, and determine patterns of activity that would indicate the existence of coordinated action of campaigns or emergence of threats. Given a gold series of postings, forum discussion, or market place listings, LLMs can give some idea of the frequency or intensity of certain types of attack classes, giving people a handle on some of the possible upsurge of the ransomware attacks, phishing, or other cyber incidents which may develop. The LLMs are not only set for the extraction of the dark-web intelligence, but give valuable assistance in the trend correlation and predictive analysis by linking together the apparently disparate dark-web intelligence pieces. This telescoping ability produces the fragmented and disparate dark-web signals into structured and analyzable intelligence which is useful for determining security operations, threat hunting and strategic planning (Sood and Zeadally, 2025).

6.4 Experimental Validation

An experiment was carried out to assess the efficiency of the proposed generative AI-driven Cyber Threat Intelligence framework through testing of a hybrid dataset of both structured and unstructured threat intelligence data. Structured data will include logs from systems, records of network traffic, and known indicators of compromise (for example, malicious IPs, URLs, and file hashes). While the unstructured data consists of threat reports, security blogs, vulnerability disclosures, and content from the dark web collected from open-source intelligence platforms. There are approximately 50,000 records in the dataset with balanced numbers of benign and malicious instances to provide an unbiased measure of effectiveness. In addition, generative AI techniques were used to generate additional threat samples such as phishing emails and simulated attack patterns to diversify data and mitigate class imbalance. The dataset was pre-processed before training via normalization, tokenization, and feature extraction methods to produce data suitable for computer program use. The experimental framework incorporates large language models to automatically extract Indicators of Compromise and summarize threat intelligence and generate synthetic data using generative models to simulate attacks. The proposed system will be evaluated according to the standard classification metrics of precision, recall, F1-score and accuracy; which respectively measure the proportion of accurately identified threats from all that are identified (precision), the number of actual threats successfully identified by the model (recall), a balanced measurement of precision and recall (F1-score), and the degree to which the result predictions were correct overall (accuracy). The formal definition of each metric is as follows:

$$Precision = \frac{TP}{TP + FP} \quad (1)$$

$$Recall = \frac{TP}{TP + FN} \quad (2)$$

$$F1 = 2 \cdot \frac{Precision \cdot Recall}{Precision + Recall} \quad (3)$$

$$Accuracy = \frac{TP + TN}{TP + TN + FP + FN} \quad (4)$$

The results of the experimental evaluation are summarized in Table 1, which compares the performance of traditional CTI approaches with the proposed generative AI-based system.

Table 1. Performance Evaluation of Generative AI-Based CTI Model

Metric	Without Generative AI	With Generative AI
Precision (%)	84	91
Recall (%)	80	88
F1-Score (%)	82	89.5
Detection Accuracy (%)	85	93
Analysis Time Reduction	27	40

Experimental outcomes provide substantial evidence to support that the use of generative AI improves the capabilities of Cyber Threat Intelligence (CTI) systems significantly. The results from this study show that generative AI offers increased precision and recall, meaning that more threats can be identified correctly and completely. The findings further show that generative AI improvements yield a greater balance between the two metrics; as such, improving the overall performance of the CTI system is reflected in the high F1 score. When compared to the previous level of CTI system detection capability measured at 85%, the total detection capability was improved to 93%, demonstrating the efficiency of the synthetic data augmentation combined with AI-assisted analysis. The system also reduced the amount of time it took to analyze by approximately 40%, indicating a level of improved automation that added efficiency. Overall, the research findings provide evidence that the generative AI-based CTI framework developed as part of this study will provide scalable, accurate, and timely threat intelligence for use in real-world cybersecurity systems.

6.4 Case Studies: LLMs in Cyber Threat Intelligence Platforms

LLMs are increasingly making their way into cyberspace threat intelligence (CTI) platforms, with these transformational capabilities being applied to a number of different areas of threat detection and analysis, and operational decision-making.

1. **Recorded Future:** Recorded Future is perhaps the most famous of the threat intelligence platforms and possesses its own LLMs to effectively supercharge its processing and analytical capabilities. It utilizes natural language processing capabilities to automatically scan and interpret millions of documents from open source and dark web sources, deriving from the immense volumes of data, indicators of compromise or IoCs, and tactics, techniques, and procedures or TTPs, which can be utilized in an actionable manner.
2. **IBM X-Force Exchange:** The IBM X-Force Exchange platform relies upon LLMs to automate the summarization, translation, and correlation of threat intelligence from multiple sources throughout the global spectrum. The platform

processes structured and unstructured data for purposes such as the detection of emerging attack campaigns, the evolution of malware and the patterns of adversary behavior throughout the world and in multiple languages.

3. **Anomali Threat Platform:** The Anomali Threat Platform gives LLMs contextual meaning, regarding respect to threat events ongoing and also builds in predictive intelligence. Through correlating IoCs with historical attack patterns and organizational vulnerabilities, actionable intelligence is presented to the analyst to allow for simulation of different possible attack scenarios and subsequent prioritization of defences.

7. CHALLENGES AND RISKS IN THE USE OF GENERATIVE AI FOR CTI

While generative AI provides considerable additional capabilities for CTI's, organizations must be wary of all the possible problems related to the quality of the underlying data that is being utilized, abuse of it by adversaries, scalability, legality of abuse, to human oversight. It is imperative that adequate validation and integration policies are put in place in order to allow for generative AI to be utilized properly and efficiently in its application for the production of proactive, correct, and efficient cyber threat intelligence. Some of the areas are:

1. **Data Quality and Integrity:** The quality of the datasets on which generative AI models are trained produces a reliance on the AI models. Factors such as bias, errors or poor data quality will be propagated into the models and result in poor intelligence data on threats being produced. AI models are also prone to hallucinations of producing the illusion of an answer that has no underlying truth.
2. **Adversarial Exploitability:** The generative AI systems are open to abuse by adversarial measures in which threat actors may introduce hostile inputs or improperly manipulate the training data in such a way as to affect performance of the models in a bad way. The adversary may manipulate the generative abilities to their end into producing sophisticated malware, phishing operations, or other evasive measures. This dual edge of the AI methods presents a major problem in that the same tools of the CTI if abused may favour the attackers. The solution is intelligent analysis, model hardening and strict access controls (Kumar et al., 2025).
3. **Expansion and Development Problems:** The advent of the generative AI technique in the field of Cyber Security in the operational field incurs tremendous resource costs of processing, storage, and other insuperable maintainability and

educational to staff on the requirements of various creativities costs of tutorage in the unemployment of the associational areas involved. The small "spin-off" businesses involved in this segment of the AI work may be unable to meet these requirements.

4. **Ethical and Legal Problems:** The broad acceptance of generative AI in the CTI area creates third types of ethical and legal problems. robotization of threat generation, prediction and simulation can create to threats to serious stress of the program then being undetermined breach of unauthorized access, implementation of governmentally mandated regulatory policies in the field of Cyber Security. All establishment ought to evolve in the area of governance some kind of which implemented regulated entry, human-in-the-loop specified validation procedures, the audit of the practices implements. All of these path's lead towards the establishment of accountability of the management of the intelligence and hence this change to generative AI (Vashishth et al., 2025).
5. **Trust and Human Oversight:** Ultimately, a balance needs to be attained between trust in AI for insight versus the requirement of human effort in the intelligence developed by the security teams that AI will assist. A reliance too heavily on AI or a lack of proper procedures for checks and balances could lead to security team slovenliness or even worse, failure to take the proper actions to mitigate genuine threats as they develop or improper ordering of counter measures.

8. FUTURE DIRECTIONS AND RESEARCH OPPORTUNITIES

The problems that will be discussed to be handled with the proper infusion of innovative technology, human analysis, and organizational procedure to provide security against enhance Overall threat detection options and intelligence synthesis and proactive Cyber Security strategic planning.

1. **AI Realized in Real-time Threat Hunting:** This appears perhaps the most promising vehicle to use GAI is to combat it in real-time threat hunting platforms. Possible future activity would include optimizing speed of the underlying coding of the model, the minimization of false positives, and the establishment of variant functions to learn from the instantaneous telemetry on networks produced so as to give it the ability to perform dynamic context aware threat hunting where it finds it interests.
2. **Progress in Multilingual and Cross-Region CTI:** As cyber-endangerments converge on a global scale, so too does the necessity of the ability to process, across languages as well as across regions, intelligence. There are opportunities for research here to be developed, involving the creation of LLMs and genera-

tive multimodal models, with the seamless extraction of intelligence, through the translation and correlation of intelligence, through the discussions on the dark web forums, and social media, and regional threat reports engaged in possibilities of amalgamated regional intelligences, in support of stronger cross domain intelligence fusion, that may lead to off growth in better early warning systems, but also in the area of the improvement of international cooperation on responding to cyber adversaries (Orpak, 2025).

3. **Explainable and Trustworthy AI for CTI:** The application of generative artificial intelligence to cyber security provides that the models need be explainable and ethical. Future work needs to be focused on ensuring that the AI produced can explain the results produced and can assess the degree of confidence there is in respect of the predictive and reasoning routes taken.
4. **Simulation of Threats for Testing Resilience:** The further use of generative AI in simulating adversarial behaviour, malware variants also infection campaigns is a fruitful area for further research. The ability to generate synthetic threats that are realistic and predictive will enable organisations to test their defences by way of a stress test, review their incident response plans and organisations weaknesses before they are exploited.
5. **Collaboration and Collective Defence Driven by AI:** The research opportunities here are entry into frameworks in which models either construct the intelligence which no longer needs reconstructing to obtain meaning for the intelligence already extant in systems but it would be possible to synthesise and anonymise the intelligence from AI models so the intelligence sharing between organisations, between industry, and between governmental structures would become satisfactory. This would allow for much more substantial coordinated responses to threats, to obtain decreased dwell time of threats and to provide for more resilient cyber-security defending structures in the face of well-coordinated and larger scale attacks (Nadella et al, 2025).

9. CONCLUSION

Generative AI has transformed Cyber Threat Intelligence (CTI) allowing its ability to analyze vast diverse data to provide actionable insights and predict changes in cyber threats with speed and accuracy hitherto inaccessible. The application of large language models, generative systems, and predictive simulations provides security teams the capability to automate collection of threat intelligence, improve real time threat feeds, recreate complex attacks, provide needed multipoint, multidisciplinary, and multilingual investigation. While the new technology provides exciting avenues for proactive defense, better situational awareness, and improved incident response, this new technology is deficient in its ability to improve data quality, protect against adversarial manipulation, provide good ethical governance, and operate under the guidance of remote human supervision. Humans must validate automated intelligence production guided by sound policies and governance. The future of AI research and development in predictive analytics, threat modeling and cooperative intelligence sharing will enhance organizations in such a way that generative AI will become a part of the political landscape of global cybersecurity.

REFERENCES

Ajibesin, A. A., & Vajjhala, N. R. (2025). The evolving landscape of AI in threat intelligence and risk assessment. In *AI-Enabled Threat Intelligence and Cyber Risk Assessment* (pp. 165–181). CRC Press. DOI: 10.1201/9781003504979-10

Alqahtani, H., & Kumar, G. (2025). A comprehensive review of generative AI techniques and their impact on cybersecurity. *Soft Computing*, *29*(13-14), 1–38. DOI: 10.1007/s00500-025-10702-z

Balasubramanian, P., Liyana, S., Sankaran, H., Sivaramakrishnan, S., Pusuluri, S., Pirttikangas, S., & Peltonen, E. (2025). Generative AI for cyber threat intelligence: Applications, challenges, and analysis of real-world case studies. *Artificial Intelligence Review*, *58*(11), 1–134. DOI: 10.1007/s10462-025-11338-z

Bibri, S. E., & Huang, J. (2025). Generative AI of things for sustainable smart cities: Synergizing cognitive augmentation, resource efficiency, network traffic, cybersecurity, and anomaly detection for environmental performance. *Sustainable Cities and Society*, *133*(10682), 6. DOI: 10.1016/j.scs.2025.106826

Chauhan, P., Pal, K., Saifi, A., Sharma, V., Vashishth, T. K., & Choudhary, K. (2026). Improving Cybersecurity and Risk Management Techniques in AI Blockchain Governance Systems. In *Transforming Public Administration through AI-Driven Predictive Analytics* (pp. 177–208). IGI Global Scientific Publishing.

Hasan, K., Hossain, F., Amin, A., Sutradhar, Y., Jeny, I. J., & Mahmud, S. (2025). Enhancing proactive cyber defense: A theoretical framework for AI-driven predictive cyber threat intelligence. *Journal of Technologies Information and Communication*, *5*(1), 33122. DOI: 10.55267/rtic/16176

Kavitha, D., & Thejas, S. (2024). Ai enabled threat detection: Leveraging artificial intelligence for advanced security and cyber threat mitigation. *IEEE Access : Practical Innovations, Open Solutions*.

Kumar, M., Gautam, K. K., Sharma, V., Samania, B., Vashishth, T. K., & Chaudhary, S. (2025). Enhancing cloud computing performance: A novel approach for optimizing energy efficiency through AI-based load balancing algorithm. In *Proceedings of the 2025 International Conference on Intelligent Computing and Knowledge Extraction (ICICKE)* (pp. 1–6). IEEE. DOI: 10.1109/ICICKE65317.2025.11136754

Mukherjee, S., Thapliyal, K., Paul, U., Bhandari, R. S., Sinha, A., & Kumar, Y. (2025, May). AI-Powered Threat Intelligence: Enhancing Real-Time Cyber Threat Detection and Response. In *2025 International Conference on Engineering, Technology & Management (ICETM)* (pp. 1-5). IEEE. DOI: 10.1109/ICETM63734.2025.11051359

Muppalaneni, R., Inaganti, A. C., & Ravichandran, N. (2024). AI-Driven Threat Intelligence: Enhancing Cyber Defense with Machine Learning. *Journal of Computing Innovations and Applications*, *2*(1), 1–11.

Nadella, G. S., Addula, S. R., Yadulla, A. R., Sajja, G. S., Meesala, M., Maturi, M. H., Meduri, K., & Gonaygunta, H. (2025). Generative AI-Enhanced Cybersecurity Framework for Enterprise Data Privacy Management. *Computers*, *14*(2), 55. DOI: 10.3390/computers14020055

Orpak, K. (2025). Generative AI and cybersecurity: Exploring opportunities and threats at their intersection. *Maandblad voor Accountancy en Bedrijfseconomie*, *99*(4), 221–230. DOI: 10.5117/mab.99.149299

Patil, D. (2024). Artificial Intelligence in Cybersecurity: Enhancing Threat Detection and Prevention Mechanisms through Machine Learning and Data Analytics. Available at *SSRN* 5057410.

Reddy, P. C. S., Muller, P. S., Koka, S. N., Sharma, V., Sharma, N., & Mukherjee, S. (2023). Detection of encrypted and malicious network traffic using deep learning. In *Proceedings of the 2023 International Conference on Ambient Intelligence, Knowledge Informatics, and Industrial Electronics (AIKIIE)* (pp. 1–6). IEEE. DOI: 10.1109/AIKIIE60097.2023.10390386

Saddi, V. R., Gopal, S. K., Mohammed, A. S., Dhanasekaran, S., & Naruka, M. S. (2024, March). Examine the role of generative AI in enhancing threat intelligence and cyber security measures. In 2024 2nd International Conference on Disruptive Technologies (ICDT) (pp. 537-542). IEEE. DOI: 10.1109/ICDT61202.2024.10489766

Sanjalawe, Y., ... 'mari, S., & Makhadmeh, S. (2025). Generative AI for Cybersecurity Applications in Threat Simulation and Defense. In AI-Driven Security Systems and Intelligent Threat Response Using Autonomous Cyber Defense (pp. 263-304). IGI Global Scientific Publishing.

Sarker, I. H. (2024). Introduction to AI-driven cybersecurity and threat intelligence. In *AI-driven cybersecurity and threat intelligence: Cyber automation, intelligent decision-making and explainability* (pp. 3–19). Springer Nature Switzerland. DOI: 10.1007/978-3-031-54497-2_1

Saurabh, B., Utkrisht, S., Sandeep, S., Kumar, D. P., & Rajkumar, U. (2024, October). Generative AI Enabled Actionable Decision Support in Cyber Security Operations for Enterprise Security. In 2024 ITU Kaleidoscope: Innovation and Digital Transformation for a Sustainable World (ITU K) (pp. 1-8). IEEE.

Sharma, V., & Kumar, S. (2023). Role of artificial intelligence (AI) to enhance the security and privacy of data in smart cities. In *Proceedings of the 2023 3rd International Conference on Advance Computing and Innovative Technologies in Engineering (ICACITE)* (pp. 596–599). IEEE. DOI: 10.1109/ICACITE57410.2023.10182455

Sharma, V., Vashishth, T. K., Tiwari, D., Sethi, P., & Sharma, S. (2025, April). Enhancing cybersecurity: A machine learning approach for phishing website detection. In AIP Conference Proceedings (Vol. 3278, No. 1). AIP Publishing. DOI: 10.1063/5.0261903

Sood, A. K., & Zeadally, S. (2025). Revolutionizing Cyber Defense: Leveraging Generative AI for Adaptive Threat Hunting. *Internet Technology Letters*, *8*(4), e70039. DOI: 10.1002/itl2.70039

Teo, Z. L., Quek, C. W. N., Wong, J. L. Y., & Ting, D. S. W. (2024). Cybersecurity in the generative artificial intelligence era. *Asia-Pacific Journal of Ophthalmology*, *13*(4), 100091. DOI: 10.1016/j.apjo.2024.100091 PMID: 39209217

Uddin, M., Irshad, M. S., Kandhro, I. A., Alanazi, F., Ahmed, F., Maaz, M., Hussain, S., & Ullah, S. S. (2025). Generative AI revolution in cybersecurity: A comprehensive review of threat intelligence and operations. *Artificial Intelligence Review*, *58*(8), 236. DOI: 10.1007/s10462-025-11219-5

Vashishth, T. K., Sharma, V., Samania, B., Sharma, R., Singh, S., & Jajoria, P. (2025). Ethical and Legal Implications of AI in Cybersecurity. In Machine Intelligence Applications in Cyber-Risk Management (pp. 387-414). IGI Global Scientific Publishing.

Vashishth, T. K., Sharma, V., Sharma, M. K., Sharma, R., Sharma, K. K., & Sharma, S. (2026). AI-Driven Threat Detection and Incident Response: Advancing Cybersecurity with Machine Learning. In Improving Threat Detection, Network Security, and Incident Response with AI (pp. 51-82). IGI Global Scientific Publishing.

Vemuri, N., Thaneeru, N., & Tatikonda, V. M. (2024). Adaptive generative AI for dynamic cybersecurity threat detection in enterprises. *International Journal of Science and Research Archive*, *11*(1), 2259–2265. DOI: 10.30574/ijsra.2024.11.1.0313

Vikas, D., R. P., Kumar, D., Charan, P., Ingilela, R. S. K., & Rastogi, R. (2023). Intrusion detection in wireless sensor networks using hybrid deep belief networks and Harris Hawks optimizer. In Proceedings of the 2023 4th International Conference on Electronics and Sustainable Communication Systems (ICESC) (pp. 1631–1636). IEEE. DOI: 10.1109/ICESC57686.2023.10193270

Zhuwankinyu, E. K., Moyo, T. M., & Mupa, M. (2024). Leveraging Generative AI for an Ethical and Adaptive Cybersecurity Framework in Enterprise Environments. *Iconic Research and Engineering Journals*, *8*(6), 654–675.

Chapter 3
Multi-Agent Generative AI Systems for Cyber Risk Evaluation and Control

Syed Mohd Faisal
http://orcid.org/0000-0003-2422-3535
Malla Reddy Technical Campus, Malla Reddy Vishwavidyapeeth (Deemed to be University), Hyderabad, India

Wasim Khan
http://orcid.org/0000-0003-2311-1451
Symbiosis Institute of Technology, Symbiosis International (Deemed to be) University, Pune, India.

Mohammad Ishrat
http://orcid.org/0000-0002-9699-4454
VIT Bhopal University, India

Anwar Ahamed Shaikh
Sanjivani University, Kopergaon, India

ABSTRACT

We present a systems-theoretic framework coupling Generative AI with multi-agent systems to make cyber-risk management a continuous, anticipatory control loop. The architecture: (i) risk-evaluation agents fusing telemetry with a knowledge graph; (ii) generative threat agents (GANs/diffusion/LLMs) synthesizing counterfactual attacks; and (iii) control agents trained with CTDE to allocate defenses under safety constraints. We implement a closed-loop simulation and evaluate ransomware and IoT-botnet cases using AUROC/AUPRC/F1 and time-to-containment. Ablations isolate contributions of generative foresight, coordination, and graph context. Results:

DOI: 10.4018/979-8-3693-8397-1.ch003

higher detection fidelity and faster containment than strong non-generative/non-agentic baselines. We discuss governance, limitations (sim-to-real, MARL stability), and directions in continual learning, risk-sensitive control, and human–AI teaming.

1. INTRODUCTION

The increasing dependence on interconnected digital infrastructures, encompassing enterprise networks, industrial control systems (ICS), cloud computing environments, 5G-enabled services, and Internet of Things (IoT) ecosystems, has amplified both the complexity and severity of cyber risks (Dwivedi et al., 2023). As organizations embrace digital transformation, the attack surface expands across heterogeneous devices, distributed architectures, and multi-layered applications. Consequently, the spectrum of cyber risks now includes ransomware, advanced persistent threats (APTs)(Chen et al., 2014), supply chain vulnerabilities, insider threats, and zero-day exploits, all of which evolve at a pace that often outstrips the ability of conventional defenses to respond. Traditional approaches to cyber risk management have relied heavily on static, rule-based mechanisms such as signature detection, compliance-based risk checklists, and periodic vulnerability scans. While these methods remain useful for addressing known threats, they are increasingly inadequate against the adaptive, stealthy, and automated nature of modern cyber-attacks (Zaidi & Faisal, 2018). Adversaries are progressively leveraging artificial intelligence (AI), automated reconnaissance, and even generative adversarial techniques to craft polymorphic malware, conduct deepfake-driven social engineering, and exploit system misconfigurations with precision (Girhepuje et al., 2024). In such a dynamic and adversarial environment, reactive strategies that rely on historical data or fixed detection patterns are insufficient. Instead, there is a pressing need for intelligent, adaptive, and proactive mechanisms that can continuously evaluate, predict, and control cyber risks in real time. Generative Artificial Intelligence (Generative AI) (Sengar et al., 2025) has emerged as a transformative paradigm in this context. Unlike conventional AI models that primarily classify or detect anomalies, generative models are capable of synthesizing realistic data distributions, simulating adversarial scenarios, and modeling complex threat landscapes. Techniques such as Generative Adversarial Networks (GANs) (Pan et al., 2019), diffusion models, and large language models (LLMs) (Naveed et al., 2025) allow for the generation of synthetic attack patterns, adversarial inputs, and hypothetical exploit trajectories. These capabilities facilitate the proactive anticipation of cyber risks, enabling defenders to test system resilience against a wide variety of threat conditions, including low-probability but high-impact events. However, when applied in isolation, generative models face inherent challenges: they are computationally intensive, often lack mechanisms for distributed coordination, and may struggle with real-time adaptability across diverse cyber environments.

To address these limitations, this chapter introduces the integration of Generative AI with Multi-Agent Systems (MAS) (Holtz et al., 2024) as a novel paradigm for cyber risk management. MAS by design, are distributed frameworks composed of autonomous, goal-oriented entities (agents) that collaborate, negotiate, or compete to solve complex problems. MAS are particularly well-suited for cybersecurity domains characterized by distributed assets, dynamic threat landscapes, and the necessity for parallel decision-making across multiple control points. When generative models are embedded into such systems, the resulting architecture benefits from both the creative power of generative AI and the adaptive coordination capabilities of multi-agent frameworks.

In this envisioned framework, the cyber risk management process is decomposed into specialized agents with well-defined roles. Risk evaluation agents continuously monitor digital infrastructures, identify vulnerabilities, and estimate the likelihood of exploitation. Generative threat agents employ adversarial learning to simulate potential attack vectors, including previously unseen zero-day exploits. Control and mitigation agents leverage reinforcement learning and optimization strategies to dynamically allocate defense resources, enforce security policies, and orchestrate rapid incident response. Through cooperative or competitive interactions, these agents exchange insights, adjust strategies in real time, and collectively create a resilient cyber defense ecosystem. This synergy between generative modeling and agent-based coordination signals a paradigm shift from reactive defense to anticipatory cyber risk governance. Instead of merely responding to known attacks, such systems actively simulate, forecast, and mitigate threats before they materialize. Moreover, the distributed nature of MAS ensures scalability across enterprise-wide infrastructures, while their autonomous decision-making enhances resilience against fast-spreading and adaptive cyber threats.

The purpose of this chapter is to present a comprehensive framework for Multi-Agent Generative AI Systems in Cyber Risk Evaluation and Control (Yuan et al., 2025). The discussion will encompass architectural principles, methodological foundations, and potential deployment scenarios. Special attention will be given to how generative models can be integrated into multi-agent ecosystems to produce synthetic risk scenarios, optimize defensive resource allocation, and ensure operational continuity in the face of emerging threats. Additionally, the chapter addresses practical challenges such as computational feasibility, adversarial robustness, explainability, and regulatory alignment, while highlighting future directions such as quantum-enhanced MAS and blockchain-based trusted coordination. By bridging the creative strengths of Generative AI with the distributed intelligence of MAS, the proposed approach represents a significant step toward establishing autonomous, adaptive, and explainable cyber risk management systems. Such systems hold the potential to transform cybersecurity from a reactive defensive posture into a proactive, self-organizing, and intelligent governance model that can withstand the rapidly evolving threat landscape of the digital age.

2. BACKGROUND AND RELATED WORK

Cyber risk management is a multi-disciplinary research area that integrates concepts from information security, risk analysis, artificial intelligence, and distributed systems. The increasing complexity of cyber threats has motivated the development of frameworks, methodologies, and intelligent systems aimed at improving both the evaluation and control of risks. This section provides a detailed theoretical foundation and literature synthesis across four main dimensions: cyber risk management frameworks, the role of generative AI in cybersecurity, applications of MAS, and the identification of research gaps that motivate the proposed framework.

2.1. Cyber Risk Management: Frameworks and Standards

Cyber risk management traditionally follows the risk assessment cycle, which involves: (i) asset identification, (ii) threat and vulnerability analysis, (iii) risk estimation, and (iv) treatment or mitigation planning (Kure et al., 2018). The foundational idea is to quantify risk in terms of probability × impact, providing decision-makers with actionable insights for prioritization.

Several established frameworks dominate industry practice:

- NIST Cybersecurity Framework (CSF): Focuses on five core functions, Identify, Protect, Detect, Respond, and Recover, providing a lifecycle view of risk management(Almuhammadi & Alsaleh, 2017).
- ISO/IEC 27005: Provides structured methodologies for risk identification, analysis, and evaluation in information security management systems (Fahrurozi et al., 2020).
- FAIR (Factor Analysis of Information Risk): Introduces a quantitative approach for financial risk modeling, enabling decision-makers to estimate losses in monetary terms(Lachmann et al., 2015).

These frameworks are systematic and offer regulatory compliance benefits, but they have inherent theoretical and practical limitations:

- Static nature: Risk evaluations are performed periodically, which leaves long windows of exposure between assessments.
- Dependence on human expertise: Risk scoring and prioritization are often subjective, relying heavily on expert judgment.
- Limited adaptability: They are not inherently designed to respond to real-time, adaptive adversarial behaviors that exploit system dynamics.
- Reactive focus: The emphasis remains on mitigation after risk materialization rather than predictive or generative anticipation of threats.

In summary, while these frameworks provide structured foundations, they are insufficient for the high-frequency, low-predictability threat landscape of modern cyberspace, thereby necessitating AI-driven adaptive models.

2.2. Generative AI for Security

Generative AI refers to models capable of learning data distributions and generating new, realistic instances from them. Techniques such as GAN, Variational Autoencoders (VAEs), Transformer-based generative models, and Diffusion Models have transformed various domains, including computer vision, text generation, and reinforcement learning (Golda et al., 2024). In cybersecurity, these models have theoretical and practical implications:

2.2.1. Synthetic Data Generation

A persistent challenge in cybersecurity research is the scarcity of labeled datasets, particularly for rare attack classes such as zero-day exploits. Generative models provide a solution by producing synthetic yet statistically valid attack data, which can be used to augment training datasets, reduce class imbalance, and improve the robustness of anomaly detection systems (Khan, Abidin, et al., 2024).

2.2.2. Adversarial Simulation

GANs and diffusion models can generate novel attack payloads and traffic traces that mimic real adversarial behavior. This enables the creation of adversarial testbeds where defenders can evaluate system resilience against hypothetical or future threats.

2.2.3. Threat Detection Enhancement

By learning the latent representation of normal system behavior, generative models such as VAEs can flag deviations as anomalies, thereby supporting unsupervised intrusion detection. Such methods are theoretically aligned with probabilistic generative modeling, which captures both uncertainty and variability in observed data (S. M. Faisal & Zaidi, 2020).

2.2.4. AI-Red Teaming and Automation

LLMs are being increasingly used in red-teaming exercises, where generative text or code is employed to automate phishing attacks, generate polymorphic malware scripts, or simulate adversarial communications. These applications extend the concept of adversarial learning from machine learning security to cybersecurity operations at large.

Despite these advances, generative models suffer from certain limitations in practice: high computational cost, lack of interpretability, and inability to directly handle distributed, multi-faceted risk landscapes. This creates a theoretical gap that motivates their integration with distributed intelligence paradigms, such as MAS.

2.3. Multi-Agent Systems in Cybersecurity

MAS comprises a collection of autonomous agents that can perceive their environment, reasoning about objectives, and interacting with one another to achieve individual or collective goals. Drawing from the principles of distributed artificial intelligence and game theory, MAS provides a framework well-suited for domains that demand coordination, adaptability, and resilience. The key characteristics of MAS align strongly with the requirements of cybersecurity. Agents demonstrate autonomy by operating independently without reliance on centralized control, which reduces vulnerabilities associated with single points of failure. They also exhibit both reactivity and proactivity: while they can respond swiftly to environmental changes such as sudden cyberattacks, they are equally capable of proactive planning to strengthen defenses. Moreover, MAS agents possess social ability, which allows them to interact through negotiation, cooperation, or even competition in pursuit of optimal system-wide outcomes. Many MAS frameworks are further enhanced with reinforcement learning, enabling agents to adapt their decision-making strategies dynamically based on evolving threat landscapes. The application of MAS in cybersecurity is diverse and has been explored across several domains. In intrusion detection systems (IDS), distributed MAS architectures allow agents to be assigned to monitor specific nodes or subnets, which not only accelerates threat detection but also localizes defensive responses (Saeed et al., 2020). During incident response, MAS has been used to coordinate mitigation strategies such as isolating compromised nodes, deploying corrective patches, or activating backup resources in real time. By distributing responsibilities among multiple agents, these systems also enhance resilience and redundancy, significantly reducing the likelihood of a complete system breakdown due to a targeted attack. In addition, MAS has been employed for game-theoretic risk management, where adversarial interactions between attackers and defenders are modeled in terms of strategies, payoffs, and equilibria (Musman & Turner, 2018). This enables defenders to test multiple countermeasure strategies under competitive conditions that closely resemble real-world adversarial engagements.

Despite these advantages, current MAS implementations in cybersecurity suffer from notable limitations. Most existing systems are still rule-based or rely on supervised detection models, which constrain their ability to adapt to truly novel attack scenarios. While MAS frameworks are effective in scaling detection and coordinating responses, they often lack the generative capability required to simulate creative or previously unseen threats. Without the integration of generative modeling, these systems remain largely reactive, addressing risks only after they manifest, rather than anticipating or forecasting them. This limitation underscores the need for augmenting MAS with generative AI techniques to transform them into proactive and predictive cyber defense systems.

2.4. Research Gap and Motivation

Theoretical and practical insights from the preceding subsections point to two complementary but incomplete trajectories. On one side, generative AI offers creative foresight to model unseen threats and generate synthetic attack scenarios, yet it lacks mechanisms for distributed execution, coordination, and real-time response. On the other side, MAS provide distributed intelligence, adaptability, and resilience but remain constrained by their dependence on fixed or pre-learned patterns that limit their ability to forecast novel attack dynamics. This disconnect underscores a central research gap, the absence of a unified framework that integrates the creative power of generative modeling with the coordinated intelligence of MAS. The motivation for bridge this gap is both theoretical and practical. From a theoretical standpoint, combining generative modeling with MAS establishes a dual paradigm that simultaneously leverages creativity from generative agents and distributed control from intelligent cooperative agents. From a practical perspective, such integration enables anticipatory cyber defense, where threats are not only detected but also proactively simulated, evaluated, and mitigated before they materialize in operational environments. In this way, the proposed approach offers a shift from reactive and isolated defense mechanisms toward a holistic paradigm of adaptive and explainable cyber risk governance in complex and adversarial digital ecosystems.

3. CONCEPTUAL FRAMEWORK OF MULTI-AGENT GENERATIVE AI FOR CYBER RISK

The conceptual framework integrates generative AI and MAS to establish a unified paradigm for cyber risk evaluation and control. The rationale behind this integration is grounded in the theoretical limitations of each paradigm when applied independently. Generative models are powerful in their ability to simulate threats and synthesize novel adversarial inputs, but they lack the mechanisms for distributed reasoning and real-time response (Ishrat et al., 2025). Conversely, MAS provides distributed intelligence and adaptive coordination but are restricted by their reliance on known data or fixed strategies. By combining these approaches, the framework enables a proactive model in which generative agents introduce adversarial creativity, and control agents collaborate to evaluate and mitigate risks effectively.

3.1. Multi-Agent Generative AI Architecture

The architecture is composed of specialized agents that collectively emulate the functions of a real-world cyber defense team. Risk evaluation agents monitor system activity, assess vulnerabilities, and continuously compute dynamic risk scores by combining real traffic data with synthetically generated attack patterns. Generative threat agents act as adversarial entities, employing GAN or diffusion models to create realistic simulations of APTs, zero-day exploits, and polymorphic malware (Rahman et al., 2025). Control and mitigation agents then translate risk evaluations into actionable defense measures, applying reinforcement learning to adaptively allocate limited defensive resources such as bandwidth, computational capacity, or forensic analysts. The architecture operates as a closed feedback loop where generative agents continually challenge the system, evaluation agents recalibrate risk probabilities, and control agents dynamically refine defense strategies. This iterative cycle mimics the evolutionary arms race between attackers and defenders, enabling defense systems to remain adaptive and resilient.

Figure 1. Architecture of Multi-Agent Generative AI for Cyber Risk

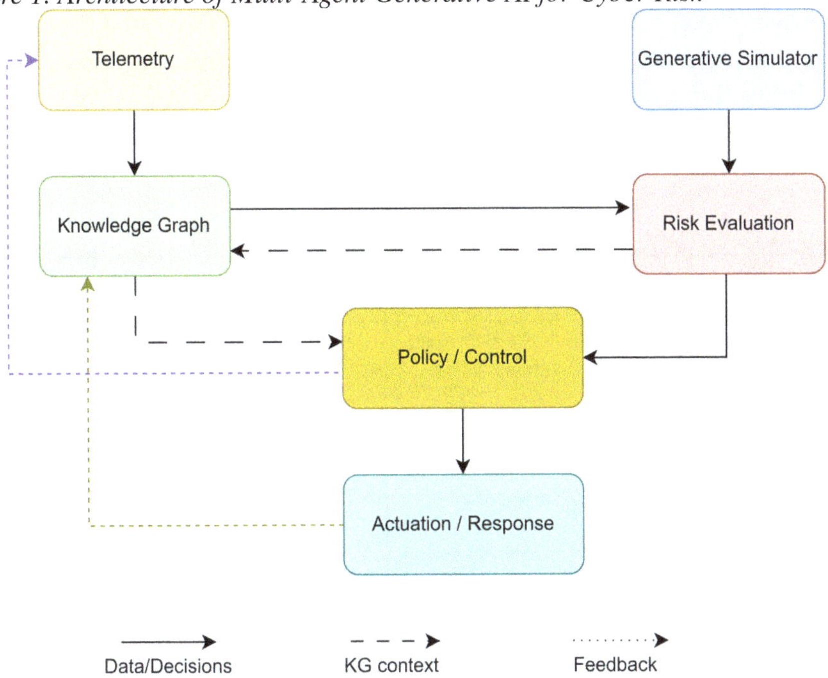

Figure 1 depicts three categories of agents (Risk Evaluation Agents, Generative Threat Agents, and Control Agents) interacting within a feedback loop. A cyber risk knowledge graph can be shown as the shared knowledge base at the center, linking agents to assets, threats, and mitigation strategies.

3.2. Cyber Risk Knowledge Graph Integration

Cyber risk knowledge graphs serve as the semantic backbone of the framework. Unlike flat data representations, knowledge graphs capture the relationships between assets, vulnerabilities, threat actors, and mitigation policies as nodes and edges. Generative AI enhances this graph by embedding latent features that identify potential but previously unseen risk associations (Table 1) (Rahman et al., 2025). For example, a vulnerability in an IoT device may not directly appear connected to a ransomware threat, but generative embeddings can expose indirect paths through shared software dependencies or communication protocols. Agents use this enriched graph for reasoning and decision-making, ensuring that their strategies are contextually grounded and semantically coherent. Theoretical advances in graph embeddings and graph neural networks (GNNs) further strengthen this integration.

Risk evaluation agents can apply GNN-based inference to propagate risk values across interconnected nodes, while generative threat agents can simulate new edges representing potential exploit paths. This integration transforms the knowledge graph into a living, adaptive structure that evolves alongside the cyber ecosystem (Khan, Mohd, et al., 2024).

Table 1. Comparison of Approaches for Cyber Risk Evaluation

Approach	Characteristics	Limitations	Role in Proposed Framework
Traditional Risk Frameworks	Standards (NIST, ISO), static scoring	Static, subjective, reactive	Provide baseline compliance and policy
Standalone Generative AI	Threat simulation, synthetic data generation	Lack distributed coordination, costly	Acts as adversarial simulation engine
Standalone MAS	Distributed reasoning, adaptive responses	Limited foresight, reactive only	Provides distributed coordination
Multi-Agent Generative AI (Proposed)	Combines generative foresight with MAS adaptability	Complexity, computational intensity	Anticipatory, adaptive, explainable

3.3. Generative Simulation Environment

The generative simulation environment acts as a virtual cyber range where attack and defense dynamics are explored without exposing real infrastructures to harm (S. M. Faisal & Zaidi, 2021). By employing GANs and diffusion models, the system can generate polymorphic malware variants or simulate denial-of-service traffic patterns, which risk evaluation agents then process to test defense preparedness. Multi-agent reinforcement learning (MARL) enables defense agents to adapt their strategies within this environment by receiving rewards or penalties based on their effectiveness against generated threats. Over time, the simulation environment creates a library of adversarial defense encounters, which strengthens the agents' resilience to real-world conditions (Park et al., 2023). Theoretically, this environment draws upon principles of adversarial machine learning, evolutionary game theory, and stochastic modeling. Adversarial models provide continuous challenges to defenders, while MARL ensures that cooperative learning emerges among defense agents. This dynamic resembles an evolutionary arms race, where attackers evolve to bypass defenses, and defenders co-evolve to neutralize new threats.

Figure 2. Generative Simulation Environment for Cyber Risk

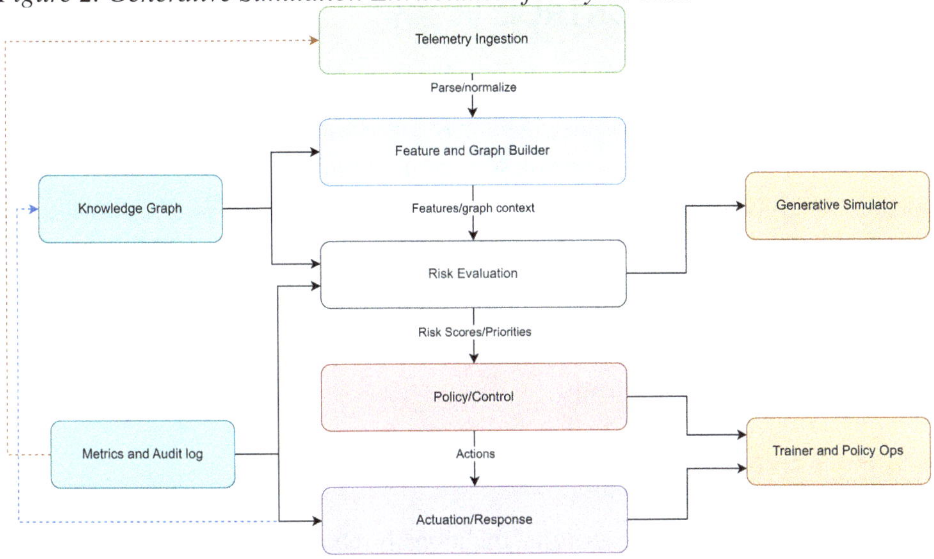

Figure 2 depicts a sandbox where generative threat agents produce attack scenarios, defense agents test countermeasures, and feedback is used to refine strategies through MARL. A reward mechanism should be shown reinforcing successful defense strategies.

3.4. Coordination, Learning, and Explainability

Coordination among agents is vital because cyber defense is not only a technical problem but also an optimization of limited resources. Within the framework, agents engage in cooperative and competitive interactions, reflecting the reality of enterprise environments where different defense teams may share resources or prioritize objectives differently. MARL provides the mathematical foundation for optimizing both local (agent-specific) and global (system-wide) rewards. For example, one agent may prioritize preventing data exfiltration while another focuses on ensuring system availability, and through coordination, the agents align their actions toward holistic resilience. Another theoretical pillar of this framework is explainability. Cyber defense decisions must remain transparent to human operators for purposes of regulatory compliance, auditing, and trust-building. Agents are therefore designed with explainable AI (XAI) mechanisms that allow them to justify their risk evaluations, policy choices, and response actions in human-interpretable forms. This ensures that while agents operate autonomously, their decision-making processes remain accountable and verifiable (Heuillet et al., 2022).

4. METHODOLOGIES FOR CYBER RISK EVALUATION AND CONTROL

The methodologies underlying the proposed framework extend beyond simple technical integration; they are grounded in theories from machine learning, distributed systems, control theory, and risk science. By combining adversarial creativity, adaptive reinforcement, game-theoretic stability, and explainable governance, the framework redefines how cyber risks are modeled and mitigated. Traditional methodologies focus largely on detection and static evaluation, but here the objective is to continuously generate, evaluate, and control cyber risks as an evolving process (Heuillet et al., 2022). This section elaborates the theoretical pillars of each methodological layer in greater depth.

4.1. Risk Evaluation through Generative Agents

Risk evaluation in cybersecurity has traditionally relied on deterministic probability estimates derived from historical incident data. However, this approach is limited in environments where zero-day vulnerabilities and novel attack strategies dominate. Generative agents overcome this by expanding the hypothesis space of potential risks through adversarial creativity (Shabeena Shah et al., 2025). In essence, they perform what can be termed counterfactual risk exploration: they imagine "what-if" attack scenarios that could theoretically emerge, even in the absence of empirical observations (S. M. Faisal et al., 2022a).

From a probabilistic modeling perspective, these agents redefine the risk function:

$$R(a,t) = \int_x P\left(E_{a,t}x\right) . I\left(E_{a,t}x\right) \, dx$$

Where x represents both observed and generated threat spaces. By extending x through generative models, the system evaluates risks not just based on past data but also on synthetically created adversarial futures.

Theoretically, this aligns with Bayesian risk analysis, where posterior probabilities are updated as new evidence emerges. Generative models act as a source of synthetic evidence, expanding the posterior distribution to cover risks that would otherwise remain unquantified. This approach significantly enhances robustness by preparing systems for tail risks, low probability but catastrophic events.

4.2. Adaptive Control Mechanisms

Adaptive control in cybersecurity involves balancing the exploration–exploitation trade-off. Agents must not only exploit existing knowledge about defensive strategies but also explore new ones to prepare for evolving threats (Zaydi et al., 2025). This trade-off is mathematically formalized within reinforcement learning paradigms, particularly in the context of Markov Decision Processes (MDPs) (Bashar et al., 2020).

The defender's control strategy can be represented as:

$$\pi(as) = \Pr\left(A_t = a \mid S_t = s\right)$$

Where π is the defense policy, S_t is the system state at time t, and A_t is the selected defensive action. Optimal control involves maximizing expected cumulative rewards:

$$V^{\pi}(s) = \mathbb{E}_{\pi}\left[\sum_{t=0}^{\infty}\gamma^t r_t \mid S_0 = s\right]$$

Here, r_t is a composite reward reflecting multiple objectives such as minimized risk exposure, preserved service availability, and optimized resource usage.

In theoretical terms, this methodology draws from control theory, where adaptive systems continuously adjust feedback loops to maintain stability under disturbances. In cybersecurity, disturbances correspond to adversarial actions, and stability refers to maintaining acceptable system performance under attack. This perspective situates the framework within the broader field of robust adaptive control, ensuring defense strategies remain effective under uncertain and evolving conditions.

4.3. Multi-Agent Coordination and Learning

Coordination in MAS introduces challenges do not present in single-agent reinforcement learning. One such challenge is the non-stationarity problem, where the environment changes because other agents are simultaneously learning. This complicates convergence toward optimal policies. To address this, the methodology incorporates centralized training with decentralized execution (CTDE), a well-established paradigm in MARL. In CTDE, agents are trained collectively with access to global state information but execute their learned policies autonomously with only local observations. Another theoretical foundation is game theory, which provides equilibrium concepts for modeling adversarial dynamics. For instance, attacker–defender interactions can be modeled as Stackelberg security games, where defenders commit to a mixed strategy and attackers observe and respond (Berenji & Vengerov, 2000). These games are particularly relevant in cyber contexts, where defenders often set up deceptive traps (honeypots) and attackers adapt by probing defenses.

Formally, a Stackelberg equilibrium can be expressed as:

$$\max_{\pi_d}\min_{\pi_a} U(\pi_d, \pi_a)$$

Where π_d and π_a are defender and attacker policies, respectively, and U is the expected utility of the interaction. Embedding this within MARL ensures that defense agents evolve policies robust to adaptive adversaries, thereby aligning theoretical game-theoretic stability with practical cyber defense.

4.4. Explainability and Human-in-the-Loop Validation

Explainability is essential not only for regulatory compliance but also for fostering human–AI collaboration in cybersecurity. The theoretical foundation here lies in causal inference and interpretable machine learning, which emphasize transparency in model reasoning. While black-box models may achieve high predictive performance, they undermine human trust when applied to security-critical environments. Agents are therefore equipped with explainability mechanisms that produce both local explanations (e.g., feature importance for a specific decision) and global explanations (e.g., rules summarizing system behavior across scenarios). Techniques such as SHAP values provide attribution-based reasoning, while counterfactual explanations address "what-if" questions, thereby bridging the gap between machine predictions and human understanding (Mosqueira-Rey et al., 2023). The inclusion of humans in the decision loop leverages sociotechnical systems theory, which posits that optimal performance emerges from the co-evolution of human and machine agents. In this framework, humans act as auditors, validators, and ethical overseers, ensuring that autonomous defense remains accountable.

4.5. Evaluation Metrics

The validation of cyber risk methodologies requires a broader theoretical base than traditional machine learning metrics (Table 2). While accuracy and precision remain useful, cyber defense must also account for temporal, economic, and systemic dimensions.

- Temporal Dimension: Response latency is critical in cyber defense, where even milliseconds may determine the success of an attack. This aligns with real-time systems theory, where system responsiveness defines operational reliability.
- Economic Dimension: Risk Reduction Index (RRI) aligns with expected utility theory, quantifying defensive success in terms of reduced financial and operational impact.
- Systemic Dimension: Scalability and resource utilization draw from distributed systems theory, where efficiency under scale is as important as correctness.

Table 2. Evaluation Metrics for Cyber Risk Evaluation and Control

Metric	Description	Relevance to Framework
Precision / Recall / F1	Accuracy of anomaly and threat detection	Evaluate detection reliability
RRI	Overall risk minimized after defense actions	Assesses mitigation effectiveness
Response Latency	Time taken to react to simulated or real attacks	Captures system adaptability
Resource Utilization	Efficiency in allocating defensive resources	Reflects optimization performance
Scalability Index	Performance under increased system complexity	Validates resilience of MAS framework

Collectively, these metrics embody a multi-criteria decision analysis (MCDA) framework, ensuring evaluation is not one-dimensional but holistic, reflecting the true complexity of cyber risk governance.

5. CASE STUDY AND EXPERIMENTAL VALIDATION

This section demonstrates the operationalization of the proposed multi-agent generative AI framework via a reproducible case study. We instantiate (i) ransomware risk evaluation and control in an enterprise network as the primary scenario and (ii) a compact IoT botnet propagation scenario as an auxiliary robustness check. The evaluation emphasizes methodological fidelity: rigorous threat modeling, MARL training with CTDE, ablation analyses isolating generative and coordination effects, and statistically principled comparisons against strong baselines.

5.1. Threat Model and Experimental Objectives

We adopt a bounded-rational attacker who adapts to observed defenses but lacks full knowledge of agent internals (grey-box threat). Attacker goals are exfiltration and/or service denial; capabilities include lateral movement, privilege escalation, polymorphic payload generation, and C2 persistence. Defender goals are to minimize expected risk and recovery time while preserving availability (as shown in figure 3). Table 3 shows the dataset and environment used for the experiment setup of the methodologies.

Formally, the interaction is cast as a stochastic attacker–defender game over epochs $t = 1, \ldots\ldots, T$, with defender policy π_d and attacker policy π_a. The experimental objective is to estimate improvements in (i) RRI, (ii) time-to-containment, and (iii) availability-adjusted utility relative to baselines:

- B1: Rule-based IDS + static playbooks.

- B2: Supervised ML IDS (non-generative) + static response.
- B3: Standalone generative anomaly detector (GAN/VAE) without MAS control.
- B4: MAS (non-generative) with hand-crafted rules.
- Ours: MAS+Gen (full framework: generative threat agents + MARL control + knowledge graph).

Table 3. Dataset and Environment Summary

Scenario	Nodes (avg)	Protocols	Benign Hours	Attack Families	Synthetic % (train)
Enterprise (Ransomware)	1200	HTTP/SMB/RDP/DNS	1,000	6	18
IoT (Botnet)	320	MQTT/CoAP/UDP	300	4	22

Figure 3. Experimental Pipeline

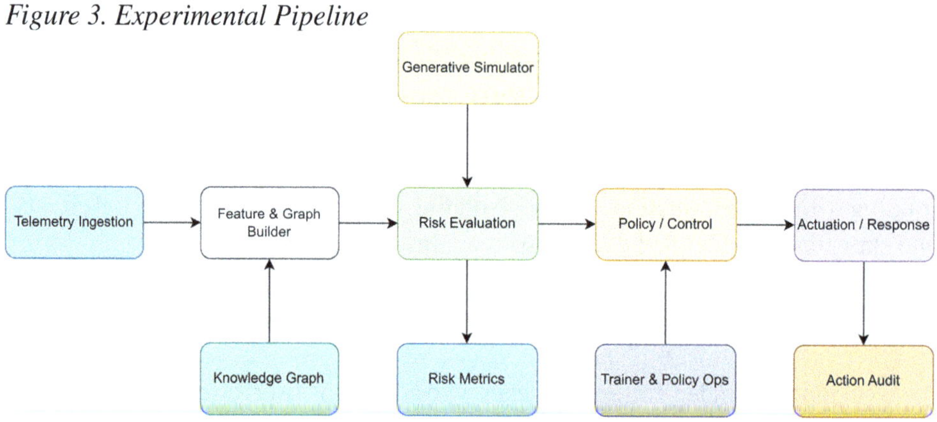

5.2. Datasets, Simulation Environments, and Workloads

Enterprise (Ransomware) Cyber Range: A virtualized network with AD/LDAP, file servers, application servers, 400–2,000 client endpoints (emulated), and mixed traffic (web, SMB, RPC, RDP). Benign workload traces follow diurnal profiles;

attack traces include staged phishing → dropper → lateral movement (SMB/RDP) → encryption → exfiltration(Ansari, 2025).

IoT (Botnet) Testbed: 1–3 subnets of constrained devices (cameras, sensors) with MQTT/CoAP traffic; attack traces emulate scanning, credential stuffing, and UDP flood coordination.

Synthetic augmentation: Generative agents (GAN/diffusion/VAE) produce low-frequency, high-impact samples: stealthy lateral movement sequences, polymorphic loaders, and rare protocol misuse. Synthetic data are only used in training or closed-loop simulation; test sets remain strictly held-out.

5.3. Agent Design, Policies, and Training

Agent roles: (i) Risk-evaluation agents compute node/subnet risk using graph embeddings over the cyber risk knowledge graph; (ii) generative threat agents synthesize attack trajectories via GAN/diffusion; (iii) control/mitigation agents implement isolation, throttling, re-routing, deception, and patch orchestration, figure 4 shows the Agent Interaction Graph.

Policies and learning: Control agents use actor–critic RL (e.g., PPO or A2C) with reward

$$r_t = \alpha(-R_t) + \beta A_t + \delta E_t - \gamma C_t$$

Where R_t is instantaneous risk, A_t availability proxy, E_t efficiency (resource cost inverse), and C_t operational cost (e.g., false isolation). CTDE is employed: critics access joint observations during training; execution is decentralized with local observations and graph messages.

Generative training: Threat agents minimize L_{DM} (diffusion) or GAN objective to match attack manifolds; a curriculum progressively increases difficulty (longer lateral sequences, stealthier beacons). Safety guardrails enforce no leakage of payloads beyond the sandbox.

Knowledge graph: Nodes: {assets, vulnerabilities, identities, processes, flows}; edges: {depends_on, communicates_with, exploits, mitigates}. Risk propagation follows:

$$r^{(k+1)} = \sigma\left(\hat{A}\, r^{(k)} W^{(k)} + b^{(k)}\right),\ r^{(0)} = r_{init}$$

yielding context-aware priors for control policies.

Figure 4. Agent Interaction Graph

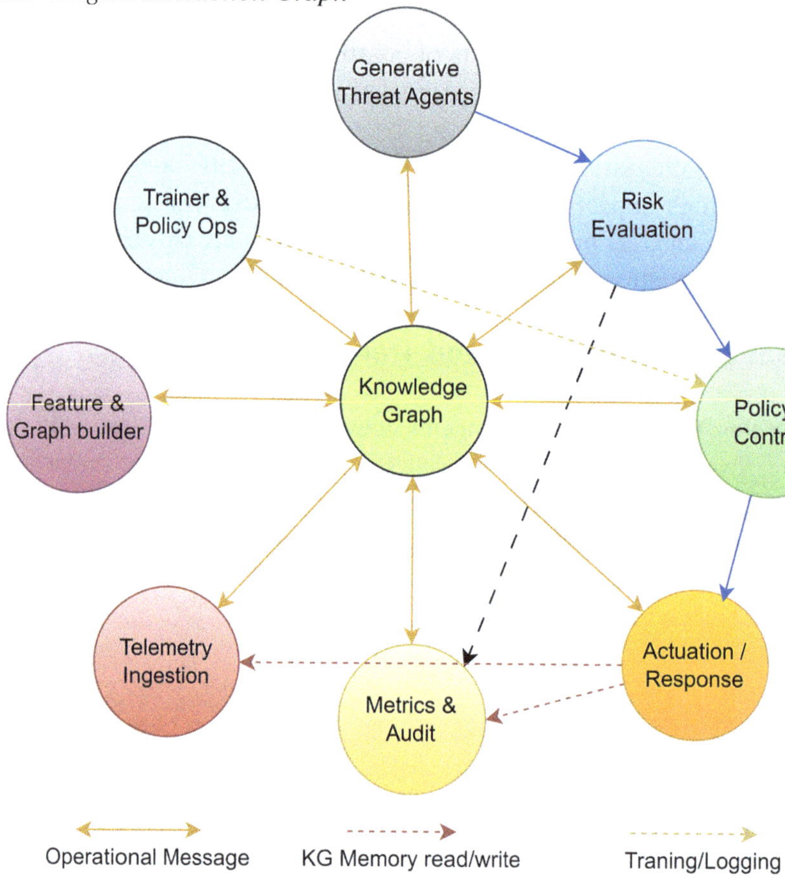

5.4. Evaluation Protocol and Metrics

Protocol: Train for N epochs with mixed benign/attack rollouts (real + synthetic), validate on unseen attacks, and test on held-out days (enterprise) or device cohorts (IoT). Each configuration runs with 5–10 stochastic seeds.

Primary metrics: (i) Precision/Recall/F1/AUROC/AUPRC for detection; (ii) RRI (expected risk delta):

$$RRI = \frac{\mathbb{E}\left[R_{pre}\right] - \mathbb{E}\left[R_{post}\right]}{\mathbb{E}\left[R_{pre}\right]} * 100\%$$

(iii) Time-to-Containment (TTC), median and 95% CI; (iv) Availability loss (SLA minutes impacted); (v) Resource utilization (CPU/Net/IO normalized); (vi) Scalability index: slope of metric degradation vs. node count.

Statistical testing: Report mean±SD; significance via paired t- test or Wilcoxon signed-rank; effect sizes (Cohen's d, Cliff's δ); 95% bootstrap CIs for AUROC/AUPRC/TTC.

5.5. Baselines, Ablations, and Controls

The main result and absolute study show in table 4 and 5 simultaneously.

Baselines: B1–B4, tuned by validation. Ablations.

- A-1 (–Gen): disable generative threat agents.
- A-2 (–MARL): independent learners without coordination.
- A-3 (–KG): remove knowledge-graph features.
- A-4 (–XAI): remove explanation layer (sanity check; metric impact on operator speed).

Controls: Shuffle-labels test (sanity), stress tests with heavy benign load, and red-team adversarial tuning.

Table 4. Main Results

Method	AUROC	AUPRC	F1	RRI	TTC(s)	SLA loss(min)
B1 Rule-Playbook	0.71	0.35	0.45	0.00	1800	120
B2 Sup. ML + Static	0.93	0.88	0.84	0.35	900	45
B3 Gen-Only	0.85	0.70	0.68	0.25	1100	60
B4 MAS-Only	0.9	0.82	0.78	0.45	750	35
Ours (MAS+Gen)	0.96	0.92	0.88	0.62	540	20

Table 5. Ablation Study

Variant	AUROC	RRI	TTC	Δ vs Full
Full (MAS+Gen+KG+XAI)	0.96	0.62	540	--
A-1 (–Gen)	0.92	0.48	720	RRI -0.14; TTC +180s
A-2 (–MARL)	0.9	0.4	780	RRI -0.22; TTC +240s
A-3 (–KG)	0.94	0.52	660	RRI -0.10; TTC +120s
A-4 (–XAI)	0.96	0.61	540	RRI -0.01; TTC +0s

5.6. Robustness, Sensitivity, and Scalability Analyses

Robustness: Evaluate under covariate shift (new OS images, rotated credentials), concept drift (changed workloads), and adaptive attackers (payload obfuscation). Report worst-case and mean-case deltas.

Sensitivity: Vary (i) synthetic: real ratio ρ, $\alpha, \beta, \delta, \gamma$ and (iii) graph sparsity. Fit $y = \theta_0 + \theta_1\rho + \theta_2\rho^2 + \varepsilon$ for non-linearity; report partial dependence.

Scalability. Increase nodes and flows; track O-costs: message passing O(|E|) per step, graph inference *O(L E d)* with *L* layers and hidden *d*; wall-clock throughput vs. cluster size. Present throughput curves.

5.7. Explainability and Operator Studies

We quantify explanation utility via decision latency and correction rate in analyst-in-the-loop tasks (Table 6). Explanations are generated with SHAP over agent observations and with counterfactuals over isolation actions. **Hypothesis:** explanations reduce median operator time while maintaining or improving correctness.

Table 6. Human-in-the-Loop Evaluation

Condition	Analyst Time (s)	Correctness (%)	Confidence
No-XAI	180	72.0	2.9
With-XAI	112	86.5	4.2

5.8. Reproducibility and Implementation Details

Figure 5 shows the complete reproducibility of artifact map.

Compute: Specify CPU/GPU, RAM, virtualization. **Software:** Versions for simulator, RL library (e.g., PPO/A2C/QMIX), graph stack, diffusion/GAN toolkit. **Seeds:** List seeds; fix CUDA Deep Neural Network library determinism where applicable. Splits. Train/val/test by time and topology to prevent leakage. **Monitoring:** Log traces, configs, and hashes; publish run cards and ablation configs.

Figure 5. Reproducibility Artifact Map

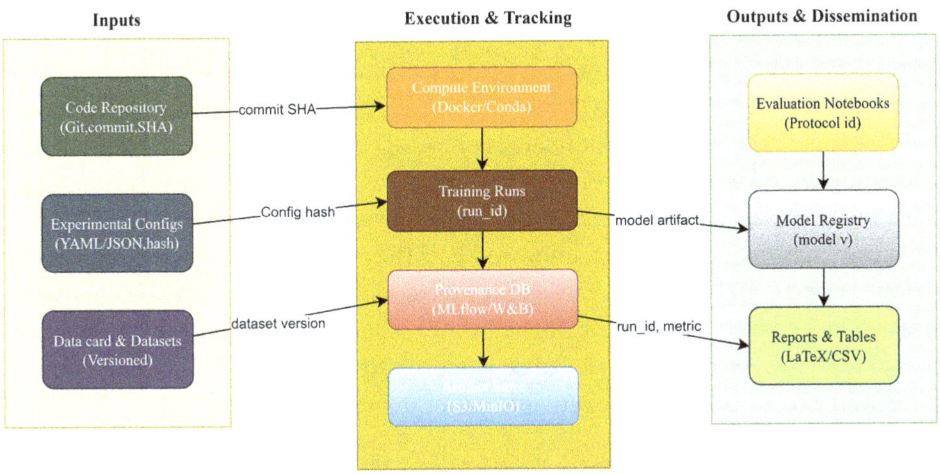

5.9. Auxiliary IoT Botnet Scenario

We replicate the protocol with constrained devices and lightweight control actions (rate-limit, moving-target defense, dynamic ACLs). We expect relative gains like the enterprise setting, with larger benefits in TTC due to fast botnet coordination. Report cross-scenario generalization gaps and confidence intervals.

5.10. Discussion of Findings

Interpret observed improvements in RRI and TTC, relate gains to (i) generative foresight (coverage of rare trajectories), (ii) MAS coordination (conflict-free policies), and (iii) knowledge-graph context (precise containment). Discuss remaining failure modes (e.g., severe concept drift, deception against the XAI layer), and mitigation (continual learning, adversarial training, human escalation).

6. DISCUSSION AND INSIGHTS

This section interprets the methodological and empirical implications of a multi-agent generative AI (MAS+Gen) approach for cyber risk governance. We synthesize what the framework enables in practice, clarify its theoretical significance, and surface key limitations, safety concerns, and assurance requirements that must accompany real-world deployment.

6.1. Interpreting the MAS+Gen Paradigm in Practice

The central practical contribution of the framework is to convert risk management from a periodic, audit-driven process into a continuous, anticipatory control loop. Generative agents widen the hypothesis space of plausible threats (including rare, tail-risk trajectories), while coordinated control agents operationalize time-bounded containment and availability-preserving responses under resource constraints. In complex enterprise networks and IoT fabrics, this results in faster incident localization (reduced time-to-containment), improved RRI (Rezvani et al., 2024) at comparable or lower operational cost, and more stable service-level outcomes during adversarial stress. The knowledge-graph backbone further reduces "action myopia" by contextualizing local anomalies with global dependency structure, thereby guiding surgical mitigations (e.g., isolating chokepoints rather than broad subnets).

6.2. Theoretical Implications

The framework advances cyber defense along three theoretical axes. First, it formalizes counterfactual risk exploration: by training on synthetic yet distribution-faithful attack trajectories, defenders approximate posterior risk over both observed and unobserved events, improving preparedness for low-frequency/high-impact scenarios. Second, game-theoretic alignment emerges through MARL under attacker–defender dynamics, pushing policies toward equilibria that are robust to adaptive opponents. Third, by casting defense as a constrained Markov decision process, the approach integrates safety and availability constraints directly into policy optimization, yielding mitigation strategies that are not only effective but also operationally admissible.

6.3. Deployment Considerations and Systems Integration

Operationalizing MAS+Gen requires an architecture that couples streaming telemetry, generative simulation services, policy serving, and assurance logging. Data engineering must support schema-evolving logs (e.g., NetFlow, EDR, identity signals) and concept-drift detection to trigger re-training or policy recalibration. Knowledge-graph maintenance becomes a first-class MLOps task: automated asset discovery, vulnerability ingestion, and relationship reconciliation prevent graph staleness. At inference time, latency budgets dominate design: generative components should remain off-path (used for training and what-if simulation), while on-path agents execute bounded-time decisions with pre-compiled policies and cached graph embeddings. Finally, observability (metrics, traces, decision rationales) must be engineered end-to-end to support audits and incident forensics.

6.4. Limitations and Threats to Validity

Despite its advantages, the approach faces important limitations:

- **Simulation-to-reality gap:** Even high-fidelity generative models may miss emergent attacker innovations or miscalibrate rare-event likelihoods, leading to over- or under-preparedness. Domain randomization and continual fine-tuning mitigate but do not eliminate this gap.
- **Learning stability and non-stationarity:** MARL training can be brittle due to concurrently learning agents. CTDE design helps, yet convergence guarantees remain limited in large, partially observed environments.
- **Operational cost and complexity:** Coordinating multiple agents, maintaining a live knowledge graph, and running safety-scoped generative tooling increase infrastructure and staffing requirements.
- **Label scarcity and evaluation bias:** Ground truth for stealthy campaigns is rare; over-reliance on synthetic labels risks optimistic estimates. Robust evaluation demands held-out real incidents, strict anti-leakage temporal splits, and statistical uncertainty reporting.
- **Generalizability:** Policies tuned to a specific enterprise topology may not transfer to different sectors or regulatory regimes without adaptation.

6.5. Safety, Ethics, and Dual-Use Governance

Generative components have intrinsic dual-use potential: models capable of simulating sophisticated attacks could be misused. The deployment responsible must incorporate guardrails across the lifecycle:

- **Design-time:** scope generative models to red-team sandboxes; apply content/payload filters; disable code-emission capable of producing operational malware; record cryptographic attestations of training artifacts.
- **Train-time:** differential privacy or selective redaction for sensitive telemetry; enforce allow-lists of behaviors to simulate; log provenance and approvals for curricula that escalate attack sophistication (S. M. Faisal et al., 2022b).
- **Run-time:** strict network segmentation for simulation clusters; human-in-the-loop escalation for high-impact actions (e.g., wide-area isolation); continuous abuse monitoring and kill-switches.
- **Audit-time:** immutable decision logs, reproducible seeds, and explanation artefacts to support post-hoc scrutiny and regulatory discovery.

Ethically, the framework should privilege minimization of collateral impact (e.g., avoid blocking life-critical services), uphold data minimization and purpose limitation, and ensure that explanations are intelligible to affected operators(Khan et al., 2025).

6.6. Assurance, Compliance, and Evidence of Control

To be admissible in regulated environments, MAS+Gen must produce assurance evidence that maps to control catalogs (e.g., risk identification, incident response, business continuity). Practically, this translates to: (i) requirements traceability from risks to policies and tests; (ii) control efficacy evidence via continuous monitoring (RRI, TTC, SLA impact) and periodic scenario exercises; (iii) model risk management artefacts (data sheets, model cards, drift statistics, validation reports); and (iv) separation of duties between model developers, operators, and auditors. A lightweight assurance case (Goal-Structuring Notation) can capture claims (e.g., time-bounded containment for ransomware), arguments (MARL policy with CMDP constraints), and evidence (test runs, ablations, operator studies), improving certifiability.

6.7. Risk–Mitigation Matrix for Deployment

The table 7 enumerates major failure modes, their most likely operational manifestations, candidate mitigation mechanisms spanning data, modeling, and governance layers, and a qualitative residual-risk assessment after controls.

Table 7. Risk and control matrix for multi-agent generative-AI systems in cyber-risk evaluation

Risk/Challenge	Likely Manifestation	Mitigation Mechanisms	Residual Risk
Simulation bias	Overfitting to synthetic trajectories	Diverse generators, domain randomization, real-incident validation	Medium
MARL instability	Oscillating or unsafe policies	CTDE, conservative policy iteration, safety layers, curriculum	Medium
Operator overload	Alert fatigue, opaque actions	XAI rationales, action summaries, priority scoring, playbook automation	Low–Medium
Privacy leakage	Sensitive data in training	DP mechanisms, minimization, synthetic-only augmentation, access controls	Low
Dual-use	Misuse of generative modules	Sandbox isolation, governance board, kill-switches, provenance logging	Low–Medium

6.8. Synthesis

The integration of generative foresight with distributed agentic control yields material improvements in anticipatory defense, but only when paired with rigorous assurance, governance, and MLOps discipline. The most significant scientific insight is that coverage of tail risks, achieved via counterfactual simulation, must be balanced with constraint-aware control to protect availability and safety. The most significant engineering insight is that success hinges less on any single model and more on systemic orchestration: data pipelines, graph curation, policy serving, monitoring, and human oversight (S. M. Faisal et al., 2025). These insights inform the future research agenda addressed next.

7. FUTURE DIRECTIONS

The multi-agent generative AI paradigm for cyber risk management opens a broad research agenda at the intersection of learning theory, control, assurance, and systems engineering. Advancing this agenda requires treating cyber defense as a continuously evolving socio-technical process, where models reason under drift, policies respect safety and availability constraints, evidence supports audit and certification, and humans remain effective decision partners. The following directions articulate theoretical priorities and system-level implications, written as narrative theory rather than implementation guidance.

7.1. Continual and Lifelong Learning under Non-Stationarity

Real infrastructures exhibit distributional shift across workloads, software stacks, and attacker tactics. The theory of continual learning for MAS+Gen should formalize how agents detect and attribute drift, decide when to adapt, and retain prior competencies without catastrophic forgetting. Promising avenues include meta-learning for rapid post-drift adaptation, modular architectures that localize updates to affected sub-policies, rehearsal or synthetic replay to stabilize memory, and policy selection mechanisms that gate old versus new behaviors. Evaluation should emphasize recovery half-life after drift, stability–plasticity trade-offs, and the cost of adaptation measured in downtime, operator load, and resource consumption.

7.2. Risk-Sensitive and Safe Multi-Agent Control

Defensive policies must optimize more than average reward; they must be robust to tail events while satisfying hard constraints on availability, privacy, and compliance. A principled theory of risk-sensitive control for MAS should combine distribution-aware learning with explicit constraint handling and verifiable safety layers that preempt unsafe actions at run time. Research should examine conservative policy iteration for high-impact actions, hierarchical control that separates fast local reflexes from slower supervisory safeguards, and assurance arguments showing bounded violation rates under realistic adversarial pressure (Lederer et al., 2025).

7.3. Causal and Counterfactual Risk Modeling

Moving from correlation to intervention requires explicit causal structure over assets, exploits, mitigations, and outcomes. Future work should encode cyber environments as structural models that support identification of causal effects, counterfactual estimation of containment benefits, and principled off-policy evaluation of new response strategies. The central challenge is confounding under partial observability and evolving attacker behavior; integrating causal discovery with generative simulators and knowledge-graph priors can improve identifiability and yield policies that generalize beyond historical response patterns (Robertson et al., 2024).

7.4. Formal Methods, Shields, and Logic-Constrained Learning

Operational defenses must satisfy temporal obligations such as preserving critical services, sequencing actions safely, and completing recovery within bounded time. Logic-constrained learning couples policy optimization with specifications drawn from temporal logics and safety contracts. Runtime monitors enforce these specifications during execution, while counterexample-guided policy repair uses violations to refine policies. Theoretical work is needed on scaling such methods to partially observe, multi-agent settings and on composing guarantees across independently developed agents.

7.5. Quantum-Enhanced Generative Simulation and Control

Quantum resources may eventually accelerate components of MAS+Gen. Quantum generative models could approximate complex attack manifolds with compact parameterizations, while quantum optimization might assist combinatorial mitigations such as minimal-impact isolation sets. A credible research path must quantify advantage under realistic noise, characterize precision requirements for security-critical decisions, and validate hybrid (classical–quantum) pipelines that keep high-risk actions within classical, verifiable bounds (Nokhwal et al., 2024).

7.6. Privacy-Preserving and Federated MAS

Cross-organization collaboration demands federated training and evaluation with guarantees for confidentiality and robustness. A theory of federated multi-agent learning for cyber defense must address incentive compatibility across organizations, tolerance to malicious or low-quality contributors, and the utility–privacy trade-off when sharing gradients, policies, or explanations. Auditability and policy provenance become first-class requirements, ensuring that shared improvements can be traced and trusted without exposing sensitive telemetry.

7.7. Trusted Coordination, Provenance, and Attestation

Assurance improves when data, models, and decisions are cryptographically tied to their provenance. Future systems should integrate verifiable logs, signed model and policy artefacts, and runtime attestation of the components executing defensive actions. The theoretical emphasis lies in building end-to-end chains of custody that balance throughput and latency with audit needs, enabling third-party certification of both training processes and operational controls.

7.8. Human–AI Teaming and Cognitive Ergonomics

Cyber defense remains a human-critical domain. Research should develop theory and evidence for mixed-initiative planning, adaptive explanation that optimizes operator utility (not merely post-hoc plausibility), and workload management that prevents alert fatigue. Key outcomes include calibrated trust, reduced decision latency, and improved intervention quality. Experimental paradigms must measure how explanation policies, interface designs, and delegation schemes affect human performance during high-tempo incidents.

7.9. Evaluation Science and Benchmarking

Progress requires shared, realistic benchmarks that span enterprise, cloud, and IoT settings, include drift scenarios and adaptive adversaries, and provide reproducibility kits. Metric suites should combine detection fidelity with risk-aware measures, availability impact, resource efficiency, and uncertainty quantification. Reporting standards must discourage overfitting synthetic distributions by requiring held-out real incidents, temporal anti-leakage splits, and statistically sound comparisons with effect sizes and confidence intervals.

7.10. Economic Decision-Support and Risk Appetite

Defensive actions entail financial, operational, and reputational trade-offs. A decision-analytic layer should align policies with organizational risk appetite, budgets, and regulatory constraints. This includes linking cyber controls to business impact models, estimating total cost of mitigation (including collateral and privacy costs), and supporting staged interventions that preserve optionality. Governance processes should document these trade-offs to make risk acceptance or transfer explicit and auditable.

7.11. Sim-to-Real Transfer and Generative Fidelity

Generative simulators inevitably diverge from production reality. Reducing this gap requires domain randomization, adversarial validation against fresh telemetry, systematic monitoring of distributional divergence, and automatic triggers for re-synthesis and policy recalibration. Theory should characterize when simulator-trained policies remain valid, how to bound degradation, and which signals most reliably indicate emerging mismatch.

7.12. Edge/5G-6G Deployment and Split Learning

Latency-critical defenses increasingly run at the network edge. Research should formalize split learning and inference across edge and cloud, including placement strategies for agents, compression of graph embeddings, and schedulers that adapt to fluctuating bandwidth and compute. The aim is to chart Pareto frontiers among decision latency, risk reduction, and resource usage, ensuring graceful degradation under partial connectivity (S. Faisal & Zaidi, 2021).

7.13. Foundation Models for Cyber Telemetry

Large, pre-trained models over multi-modal telemetry, flows, endpoint signals, identity events, configurations, could serve as generalist priors for MAS agents. Open problems include designing pretext tasks that capture security semantics, building retrieval-augmented reasoning pipelines that remain auditable, and constraining generative components to produce safe, operator-useful "what-if" scenarios. Safety governance must accompany these models to prevent leakage of sensitive patterns or the synthesis of harmful content.

7.14. Synthesis

Collectively, these directions elevate MAS+Gen from a promising architecture to a certifiable discipline. The unifying theme is balance: counterfactual foresight must be tempered by constraint-aware control; autonomy must be paired with explainability and governance; simulated breadth must be validated against real-world evidence. Pursuing this agenda will advance not only technical performance but also the trust, accountability, and resilience required for deployment in safety- and mission-critical environments.

8. CONCLUSION

The chapter advanced the theory and systems blueprint for MAS+Gen AI as a foundation for proactive cyber risk evaluation and control. Moving beyond audit-periodic, detection-centric practices, we framed cyber defense as a continuous control problem in which generative components expand the hypothesis space of plausible attacks while coordinated agents implement availability-preserving mitigations under operational constraints. The framework integrates four pillars, counterfactual risk exploration via generative models, distributed decision-making through MARL, semantic grounding with cyber risk knowledge graphs, and accountability through explainable interfaces and audit artefacts, thereby converting risk management from reactive remediation to anticipatory governance. A central contribution is the consolidation of methodologies that are often treated in isolation. Generative agents synthesize rare yet consequential trajectories to stress-test defenses before incidents occur; evaluation agents propagate risk over asset–dependency graphs to obtain context-aware assessments; control agents optimize responses with constraint-aware policies that respect safety, privacy, and service continuity; and explainability mechanisms preserve human oversight without sacrificing agility. The case study design operationalizes these ideas with reproducible protocol elements, closed-loop simulation, centralized training with decentralized execution, ablations disentangling the value of generation, coordination, and graph context, and multidimensional metrics that assess not only detection fidelity but also RRI, time-to-containment, availability impact, and scalability.

For practitioners, the implications are concrete. MAS+Gen requires treating telemetry engineering, knowledge-graph curation, policy serving, and observability as a single MLOps surface. Generative components belong off the critical path for training and what-if analysis, while on-path agents execute bounded-latency policies backed by cached graph embeddings and pre-validated playbooks. Governance must evolve in parallel: decision provenance, separation of duties, and model risk management artefacts enable certification against prevailing control catalogs and sectoral regulations. When deployed with appropriate guardrails, sandboxed generators, human escalation for high-impact actions, immutable decision logs, the paradigm offers measurable operational gains without eroding trust or compliance. At the same time, important limitations remain. Simulation-to-reality gaps can miscalibrate preparedness; multi-agent learning introduces non-stationarity and training brittleness at scale; high-fidelity knowledge graphs are costly to maintain; and ground truth for stealthy campaigns is scarce, complicating validation. The future-work agenda outlined in the preceding section addresses these gaps via continual learning under drift, risk-sensitive and logic-constrained control, causal modeling for interventional reasoning, federated and privacy-preserving coordination, human–AI teaming studies, and standardized evaluation science. Progress on these fronts is essential to harden MAS+Gen from a promising architecture into a certifiable discipline. In closing, the synthesis of generative foresight with distributed, constraint-aware control reframes cyber risk management as anticipatory, adaptive, and explainable. The scientific insight is that broad coverage of tail risks must be balanced with guarantees that protect critical services; the engineering insight is that success depends less on any single model and more on cohesive orchestration across data, knowledge, policy, and people. By codifying this balance, MAS+Gen offers a principled path toward resilient, accountable cyber defense in environments where adversaries learn, adapt, and innovate at machine speed.

REFERENCES

Almuhammadi, S., & Alsaleh, M. (2017). Information security maturity model for NIST cyber security framework. *Computer Science & Information Technology (CS & IT), 7*(3), 51–62.

Ansari, D. B. (2025). Developing a Big Data Infrastructure: Integral Modules and Best Procedures for Alleviating Security and Privacy Challenges. In *Intelligent Cybersecurity and Resilience for Critical Industries: Challenges and Applications* (pp. 269–303). River Publishers.

Bashar, A., Muhammad, S., Mohammad, N., & Khan, M. (2020). Modeling and analysis of MDP-Based security risk assessment system for smart grids. *2020 Fourth International Conference on Inventive Systems and Control (ICISC)*, 25–30. DOI: 10.1109/ICISC47916.2020.9171072

Berenji, H., & Vengerov, D. (2000). Learning, cooperation, and coordination in multi-agent systems. *Intelligent Inference Systems Corporation, Technical Report.*

Chen, P., Desmet, L., & Huygens, C. (2014). A study on advanced persistent threats. *IFIP International Conference on Communications and Multimedia Security*, 63–72.

Dwivedi, U., Rajawat, A. S., Goyal, S. B., Faisal, S., Sulakhe, V. N., & Sudhir, M. (2023). AI-enabled UAVs for advanced network management in the era of 6G communications. *International Conference on Intelligent Computing & Optimization*, 349–358.

Fahrurozi, M., Tarigan, S. A., Tanjung, M. A., & Mutijarsa, K. (2020). The use of ISO/IEC 27005: 2018 for strengthening information security management (a case study at data and information Center of Ministry of Defence). *2020 12th International Conference on Information Technology and Electrical Engineering (ICITEE)*, 86–91.

Faisal, S., & Zaidi, T. (2021). A Systematic Review on Security of Wireless Network: Smart Vehicle Perspective. *International Journal of Mechanical Engineering, 6*(2).

Faisal, S. M., Gupta, B. K., & Zaidi, T. (2022a). A hybrid framework to prevent VANET from Sybil Attack. *2022 5th International Conference on Multimedia, Signal Processing and Communication Technologies (IMPACT)*, 1–6.

Faisal, S. M., Gupta, B. K., & Zaidi, T. (2022b). Detection and prevention of sybil attack in vanet using modified aco. *2022 IEEE 4th International Conference on Cybernetics, Cognition and Machine Learning Applications (ICCCMLA)*, 78–84.

Faisal, S. M., Muniyandy, E., Lokesh, S., & Jayanthi, M. G. (2025). A Random Graph Diffusion Attention Network with Great Wall Construction and Clinical Metadata for Improved Kidney Cancer Diagnosis and Surgical Planning. *Biomedical Materials & Devices*, •••, 1–20.

Faisal, S. M., & Zaidi, T. (2020). Timestamp Based Detection of Sybil Attack in VANET. *Int. J. Netw. Secur.*, *22*(3), 397–408.

Faisal, S. M., & Zaidi, T. (2021). Implementation of ACO in VANETs with detection of faulty node. *Indian Journal of Science and Technology*, *14*(19), 1598–1614. DOI: 10.17485/IJST/v14i19.76

Girhepuje, S., Verma, A., & Raina, G. (2024). A survey on offensive ai within cybersecurity. *ArXiv Preprint ArXiv:2410.03566*.

Golda, A., Mekonen, K., Pandey, A., Singh, A., Hassija, V., Chamola, V., & Sikdar, B. (2024). Privacy and security concerns in generative AI: A comprehensive survey. *IEEE Access : Practical Innovations, Open Solutions*, *12*, 48126–48144. DOI: 10.1109/ACCESS.2024.3381611

Heuillet, A., Couthouis, F., & Díaz-Rodríguez, N. (2022). Collective explainable AI: Explaining cooperative strategies and agent contribution in multiagent reinforcement learning with shapley values. *IEEE Computational Intelligence Magazine*, *17*(1), 59–71. DOI: 10.1109/MCI.2021.3129959

Holtz, N., Wittfoth, S., & Gómez, J. M. (2024). The new era of knowledge retrieval: Multi-agent systems meet generative ai. *2024 Portland International Conference on Management of Engineering and Technology (PICMET)*, 1–10. DOI: 10.23919/PICMET64035.2024.10653018

Ishrat, M., Khan, W., & Faisal, S. M. (2025). AI and risk forecasting: leveraging AI for environmental, social, and governance compliance. In *Artificial Intelligence for Financial Risk Management and Analysis* (pp. 307–334). IGI Global Scientific Publishing. DOI: 10.4018/979-8-3373-1200-2.ch015

Khan, W., Abidin, S., Arif, M., Ishrat, M., Haleem, M., Shaikh, A. A., Farooqui, N. A., & Faisal, S. M. (2024). Anomalous node detection in attributed social networks using dual variational autoencoder with generative adversarial networks. *Data Science and Management*, *7*(2), 89–98. DOI: 10.1016/j.dsm.2023.10.005

Khan, W., Ishrat, M., Faisal, S. M., Ahmad, F., Nabilal, K. V., & Sharma, Y. K. (2025). A robust framework for topology-based anomaly detection in attributed networks using graph attention networks, substructure analysis, and data augmentation. *International Journal of Data Science and Analytics*, *20*(7), 1–14. DOI: 10.1007/s41060-025-00848-2

Khan, W., Mohd, A., Suaib, M., Ishrat, M., Shaikh, A. A., & Faisal, S. M. (2024). *Residual-enhanced graph convolutional networks with hypersphere mapping for anomaly detection in attributed networks*. Data Science and Management.

Kure, H. I., Islam, S., & Razzaque, M. A. (2018). An integrated cyber security risk management approach for a cyber-physical system. *Applied Sciences (Basel, Switzerland)*, *8*(6), 898. DOI: 10.3390/app8060898

Lachmann, M., Stefani, U., & Wöhrmann, A. (2015). Fair value accounting for liabilities: Presentation format of credit risk changes and individual information processing. *Accounting, Organizations and Society*, *41*, 21–38. DOI: 10.1016/j.aos.2014.08.001

Lederer, A., Noorani, E., & Krause, A. (2025). Distributed Risk-Sensitive Safety Filters for Uncertain Discrete-Time Systems. *IEEE Control Systems Letters*, *9*, 1231–1236. DOI: 10.1109/LCSYS.2025.3579747

Mosqueira-Rey, E., Hernández-Pereira, E., Alonso-Ríos, D., Bobes-Bascarán, J., & Fernández-Leal, Á. (2023). Human-in-the-loop machine learning: A state of the art. *Artificial Intelligence Review*, *56*(4), 3005–3054. DOI: 10.1007/s10462-022-10246-w

Musman, S., & Turner, A. (2018). A game theoretic approach to cyber security risk management. *The Journal of Defense Modeling and Simulation*, *15*(2), 127–146. DOI: 10.1177/1548512917699724

Naveed, H., Khan, A. U., Qiu, S., Saqib, M., Anwar, S., Usman, M., Akhtar, N., Barnes, N., & Mian, A. (2025). A comprehensive overview of large language models. *ACM Transactions on Intelligent Systems and Technology*, *16*(5), 1–72. DOI: 10.1145/3744746

Nokhwal, S., Nokhwal, S., Pahune, S., & Chaudhary, A. (2024). Quantum generative adversarial networks: Bridging classical and quantum realms. *Proceedings of the 2024 8th International Conference on Intelligent Systems, Metaheuristics & Swarm Intelligence*, 105–109. DOI: 10.1145/3665065.3665082

Pan, Z., Yu, W., Yi, X., Khan, A., Yuan, F., & Zheng, Y. (2019). Recent progress on generative adversarial networks (GANs): A survey. *IEEE Access : Practical Innovations, Open Solutions*, *7*, 36322–36333. DOI: 10.1109/ACCESS.2019.2905015

Park, J. S., O'Brien, J., Cai, C. J., Morris, M. R., Liang, P., & Bernstein, M. S. (2023). Generative agents: Interactive simulacra of human behavior. *Proceedings of the 36th Annual Acm Symposium on User Interface Software and Technology*, 1–22. DOI: 10.1145/3586183.3606763

Rahman, M. W. U., Nevarez, R., Mim, L. T., & Hariri, S. (2025). Multi-Agent Actor-Critic Generative AI for Query Resolution and Analysis. *IEEE Transactions on Artificial Intelligence.*

Rezvani, S. M. H. S., Silva, M. J. F., & de Almeida, N. M. (2024). Urban resilience index for critical infrastructure: A scenario-based approach to disaster risk reduction in road networks. *Sustainability (Basel)*, *16*(10), 4143. DOI: 10.3390/su16104143

Robertson, J., Hollmann, N., Awad, N., & Hutter, F. (2024). Fairpfn: Transformers can do counterfactual fairness. *ArXiv Preprint ArXiv:2407.05732.*

Saeed, I. A., Selamat, A., Rohani, M. F., Krejcar, O., & Chaudhry, J. A. (2020). A systematic state-of-the-art analysis of multi-agent intrusion detection. *IEEE Access : Practical Innovations, Open Solutions*, *8*, 180184–180209. DOI: 10.1109/ACCESS.2020.3027463

Sengar, S. S., Hasan, A., Kumar, S., & Carroll, F. (2025). Generative artificial intelligence: A systematic review and applications. *Multimedia Tools and Applications*, *84*(21), 23661–23700. DOI: 10.1007/s11042-024-20016-1

Shabeena Shah, W., Khadeeja Bilquees, A., & Zubair, M. J. M. (2025). Innovation Unleashed Charting a New Course in Risk Evaluation with Generative AI. *Generative Artificial Intelligence in Finance: Large Language Models, Interfaces, and Industry Use Cases to Transform Accounting and Finance Processes*, 149–157.

Yuan, Q., Meng, Q., Tao, J., Li, G., Fei, J., Lu, B., & Wang, Y. (2025). Multi-Agent for Network Security Monitoring and Warning: A Generative AI Solution. *IEEE Network*, *39*(5), 114–121. DOI: 10.1109/MNET.2025.3579001

Zaidi, T., & Faisal, S. (2018). An overview: Various attacks in VANET. *2018 4th International Conference on Computing Communication and Automation (ICCCA)*, 1–6.

Zaydi, M., Maleh, Y., & Khourdifi, Y. (2025). A new framework for agile cybersecurity risk management: Integrating continuous adaptation and real-time threat intelligence (ACSRM-ICTI). In *Agile Security in the Digital Era* (pp. 19–47). CRC Press.

Chapter 4
Synthetic Risk Environments for Next-Generation Cybersecurity

Otmane Azeroual
http://orcid.org/0000-0002-5225-389X
University of Hagen, Germany

ABSTRACT

The complexity and velocity of modern cyber threats expose the limits of static, compliance-driven risk assessments. Synthetic Risk Environments (SREs) offer dynamic, digitally constructed ecosystems that simulate adversarial behavior, system vulnerabilities, and socio-technical interdependencies. Integrating AI-driven scenario generation, digital twins, cyber ranges, and generative modeling, SREs enable organizations to anticipate multi-vector attacks, evaluate cascading failures, and test resilience in realistic conditions. This chapter reviews the theoretical foundations, methodologies, and strategic applications of SREs, discusses emerging trends and challenges, and positions SREs as essential tools for proactive, adaptive, and resilience-oriented cybersecurity.

1. INTRODUCTION

Over the past decade, cybersecurity has evolved from a primarily technical concern into a systemic challenge affecting organizations, governments, and critical infrastructures alike. The increasing digitization of industrial processes, public services, supply chains, and societal communication has created deeply interconnected socio-technical systems whose exposure to cyber threats is both persistent and expanding (Schwab, 2015; ENISA, 2023). At the same time, adversaries have become more

DOI: 10.4018/979-8-3693-8397-1.ch004

adaptive, coordinated, and capable of exploiting not only technical vulnerabilities but also organizational dependencies, human behavior, and cross-sector interconnections (Tounsi & Rais, 2018; Bada & Nurse, 2019). As a consequence, cyber risk can no longer be understood as a set of isolated incidents affecting individual assets; rather, it must be approached as a dynamic and systemic phenomenon shaped by continuous interaction between attackers, defenders, and infrastructures.

Traditional cybersecurity risk assessment methods have made important contributions to governance, compliance, and control. Frameworks such as NIST SP 800-30 and ISO/IEC 27005 provide structured procedures for identifying, analyzing, and treating cyber risks, while threat intelligence reports by institutions such as ENISA offer up-to-date insights into evolving attack patterns (NIST, 2018/2023; ENISA, 2023). However, these approaches remain limited in important respects. Most conventional models rely heavily on historical evidence, static threat assumptions, or checklist-based assessments, and are therefore insufficient for capturing the adaptive, uncertain, and interconnected character of contemporary cyber threats (Tounsi & Rais, 2018; Bada & Nurse, 2019). Empirical evidence from recent cyber incidents, such as large-scale supply chain compromises and ransomware attacks, demonstrates that the most severe impacts often arise from cascading effects and systemic disruption rather than isolated vulnerabilities (Cebula & Young, 2010; Klasa et al., 2021).

Against this background, this chapter argues that Synthetic Risk Environments (SREs) represent a promising next-generation approach for cybersecurity risk analysis and resilience assessment. SREs can be understood as digitally constructed and dynamically configurable environments that simulate adversarial behavior, system vulnerabilities, and socio-technical interdependencies under controlled yet realistic conditions (Salvi, Spagnoletti & Noori, 2022; Ani et al., 2025). They build upon advances in cyber ranges, digital twins, and simulation modeling, and increasingly incorporate artificial intelligence techniques such as generative modeling and reinforcement learning to emulate adaptive attackers and defenders (Ligo, Kott & Linkov, 2021; Goodfellow et al., 2014).

The central premise of this chapter is that the value of SREs lies not merely in their technological sophistication, but in their ability to bridge a long-standing gap between governance-oriented cyber risk management and experimentally grounded cyber resilience testing. Existing research has highlighted the limitations of classical risk frameworks in dealing with uncertainty, interdependence, and adversarial adaptation (Cebula & Young, 2010; Naghshbandi et al., 2020). At the same time, advances in resilience engineering and complex systems theory emphasize the need to understand cyber systems as adaptive and interdependent environments rather than static infrastructures (Hollnagel, Woods & Leveson, 2006; Holland, 1995).

However, these perspectives are often treated separately in the literature and lack integration into a coherent analytical approach.

This chapter addresses that gap by proposing an integrated analytical framework for Synthetic Risk Environments in next-generation cybersecurity. Rather than providing only a descriptive overview, the chapter develops a structured perspective on how SREs can be conceptualized, designed, and applied in practice.

More specifically, the chapter makes three contributions.

First, it synthesizes the theoretical foundations relevant to SREs by linking established cyber risk management standards with resilience engineering, simulation theory, and adversarial machine learning (NIST, 2018/2023; Hollnagel et al., 2006; Goodfellow et al., 2014). In doing so, it situates SREs as socio-technical systems embedded in broader governance and operational contexts.

Second, it develops an analytical framework for SRE design that integrates system modeling approaches such as agent-based modeling, system dynamics, and Monte Carlo simulation with AI-driven adversarial modeling and validation mechanisms (Epstein & Axtell, 1996; Forrester, 2007; Metropolis & Ulam, 1949). This framework provides a basis for understanding how different methodological components interact within synthetic environments.

Third, it demonstrates the practical relevance of SREs by analyzing their application across critical domains such as energy systems, healthcare infrastructures, transport networks, and national cybersecurity strategies, where systemic risk and interdependencies play a crucial role (ENISA, 2023; Serena et al., 2025).

The relevance of this analysis is threefold. For researchers, SREs enable controlled experimentation and empirical investigation of cyber-physical interdependencies under adversarial conditions (Naghshbandi et al., 2020). For practitioners, including Chief Information Security Officers and security architects, they provide tools for proactive resilience planning and scenario-based risk evaluation (Aslaner, 2024). For policymakers, SREs offer a means to stress-test critical infrastructures and assess the implications of regulatory frameworks in realistic and dynamic threat environments (Cavelty, 2024).

The chapter is guided by the following research objectives:

1. To critically assess the limitations of traditional cyber risk assessment approaches in the context of dynamic and adaptive threats.
2. To conceptualize Synthetic Risk Environments as an integrative framework for cyber resilience assessment.
3. To analyze methodological approaches, application domains, and governance implications of SREs.

The remainder of the chapter is structured as follows. Section 2 presents the theoretical foundations of SREs, including cyber risk management, simulation theory, resilience engineering, and adversarial AI. Section 3 conceptualizes SREs and introduces their key components and typologies. Section 4 discusses methodological approaches and validation strategies. Section 5 presents application domains and case-based scenarios. Section 6 examines the main challenges and limitations of SREs. Section 7 discusses emerging trends and future directions, while Section 8 reflects on the broader theoretical and practical implications of the proposed framework. The chapter concludes in Section 9 by summarizing the main insights and outlining implications for future research and practice.

Overall, this chapter positions Synthetic Risk Environments as a strategic and methodological infrastructure for advancing cybersecurity beyond static and compliance-driven approaches toward adaptive, experimental, and resilience-oriented risk management.

2. THEORETICAL FOUNDATIONS

The conceptualization of Synthetic Risk Environments (SREs) requires a multidisciplinary theoretical foundation that integrates established cybersecurity risk frameworks with advances in simulation modeling, resilience engineering, and complex systems theory. Rather than representing a single methodological innovation, SREs emerge at the intersection of these domains, combining governance-oriented risk assessment with experimental and dynamic modeling approaches. This section therefore establishes the theoretical basis for SREs by examining five key perspectives: (i) cybersecurity risk management standards, (ii) simulation and modeling theories, (iii) resilience engineering, (iv) complex adaptive systems, and (v) adversarial artificial intelligence.

2.1 Cybersecurity Risk Management: Standards and Limitations

Modern cybersecurity risk management is largely shaped by normative frameworks such as the NIST Guide for Conducting Risk Assessments (SP 800-30) and ISO/IEC 27005. These frameworks provide standardized procedures for identifying, analyzing, and evaluating risks, and they play a central role in governance, compliance, and audit processes (NIST, 2018/2023; ISO/IEC 27005). In addition, institutions such as ENISA complement these frameworks with continuously updated threat intelligence, offering insights into emerging attack vectors, vulnerabilities, and sector-specific risks (ENISA, 2023).

While these approaches provide essential structure and comparability, their underlying assumptions impose significant limitations in the context of contemporary cyber threats. Traditional risk models tend to rely on:

- static system representations,
- historical incident data,
- deterministic threat assumptions, and
- linear cause–effect relationships.

Such assumptions are increasingly insufficient in environments characterized by adaptive adversaries, interdependent infrastructures, and rapidly evolving attack strategies (Tounsi & Rais, 2018; Bada & Nurse, 2019). In particular, classical frameworks struggle to capture cascading effects and systemic risk propagation, where disruptions in one component of a system can trigger failures across multiple domains (Cebula & Young, 2010; Klasa et al., 2021).

From a theoretical perspective, this limitation reflects a mismatch between governance-oriented risk assessment and the dynamic nature of cyber systems. SREs address this gap by extending traditional frameworks toward experimental, scenario-based, and interaction-driven risk analysis, enabling the exploration of complex and adaptive threat environments beyond static assessment models.

2.2 Simulation and Modeling Theories

Simulation constitutes a central methodological pillar of SREs. It enables the representation of complex systems and the exploration of their behavior under controlled yet dynamic conditions. Several complementary modeling paradigms are particularly relevant.

Agent-Based Modeling (ABM) provides a micro-level perspective by representing systems as collections of interacting agents, each characterized by individual behaviors, objectives, and decision rules (Epstein & Axtell, 1996). In cybersecurity contexts, agents may represent users, devices, attackers, or defenders. ABM is particularly suited to capturing emergent phenomena such as malware propagation, insider threats, and coordinated attack behavior.

System Dynamics (SD), by contrast, operates at a macro level and focuses on feedback loops, accumulations, and time delays within systems (Forrester, 2007). It is well suited for analyzing long-term dynamics such as cascading failures, resource depletion, and recovery processes in critical infrastructures.

Monte Carlo Simulation (MCS) complements these approaches by introducing probabilistic analysis. By sampling from distributions of uncertain inputs, MCS allows for the quantification of risk, sensitivity analysis, and estimation of outcome variability (Metropolis & Ulam, 1949).

The combination of these methods enables SREs to capture both:

- micro-level interactions (via ABM),
- macro-level system dynamics (via SD), and
- uncertainty and variability (via MCS).

Importantly, simulation transforms cyber risk analysis from a purely analytical exercise into an experimental process, where hypotheses about system behavior, attack strategies, and defensive mechanisms can be tested under controlled conditions.

2.3 Resilience Engineering as a Normative Framework

Resilience engineering introduces a fundamental shift in how system performance and risk are conceptualized. Rather than focusing exclusively on failure prevention, resilience engineering emphasizes the capacity of systems to:

- absorb disturbances,
- adapt to changing conditions, and
- recover from disruptions (Hollnagel, Woods & Leveson, 2006).

In cybersecurity, this perspective is particularly relevant because complete prevention of attacks is neither feasible nor realistic. Instead, the focus shifts toward maintaining functionality under stress and ensuring rapid recovery.

SREs operationalize resilience engineering by enabling the systematic evaluation of resilience capacities. Through repeated simulations, they allow for the measurement of:

- time to detect and respond,
- system recovery time,
- adaptability under evolving attack conditions,
- and the range of viable response strategies.

This moves cyber risk assessment beyond static indicators such as vulnerability counts or compliance scores toward dynamic and performance-oriented metrics, reflecting real-world system behavior under adversarial conditions.

2.4 Complex Adaptive Systems (CAS)

Cyber-physical infrastructures exhibit the characteristics of CAS, which are defined by:

- heterogeneous actors,
- non-linear interactions,
- feedback loops, and
- emergent behavior (Holland, 1995).

Examples include interconnected supply chains, smart grids, and cloud-edge ecosystems, where local actions can have system-wide consequences. In such systems, small disturbances may lead to disproportionate impacts, a phenomenon often described as cascading failure.

Traditional linear risk models are ill-suited for capturing these dynamics. CAS theory provides an alternative conceptual framework that emphasizes:

- path dependency,
- robustness–fragility trade-offs,
- and emergent system states.

SREs align closely with CAS principles by explicitly modeling:

- heterogeneous agents,
- adaptive adversaries,
- stochastic environmental conditions,
- and cross-domain dependencies.

By doing so, they enable the exploration of systemic risks that remain invisible in conventional assessments. In particular, SREs allow researchers and practitioners to provoke and analyze cascading effects deliberately, thereby identifying vulnerabilities that only emerge under complex interaction scenarios.

2.5 Adversarial Artificial Intelligence

Recent advances in artificial intelligence have significantly enhanced the realism and adaptability of SREs. In particular, adversarial machine learning provides mechanisms for modeling dynamic attacker–defender interactions.

Generative Adversarial Networks (GANs) enable the generation of synthetic data that closely resembles real attack patterns, allowing for the testing of detection systems against previously unseen threats (Goodfellow et al., 2014). Reinforcement Learning (RL), on the other hand, enables agents to learn optimal strategies through interaction with the environment, making it possible to simulate adaptive attackers and defenders that evolve over time (Sutton & Barto, 1998).

Multi-agent reinforcement learning extends this approach by modeling strategic interactions between multiple agents, capturing competitive and cooperative dynamics in cyber conflict scenarios. This significantly increases the realism of simulations compared to static red-teaming exercises (Papernot et al., 2017).

From a theoretical standpoint, adversarial AI transforms SREs from static simulation environments into adaptive and evolving systems, where both attack and defense strategies co-evolve. This enables the exploration of scenarios that go beyond known threats, supporting the anticipation of novel attack vectors and systemic vulnerabilities.

2.6 Synthesis: Toward an Integrated SRE Framework

The theoretical perspectives discussed above converge toward a common insight: effective cyber risk assessment in contemporary environments requires the integration of governance, simulation, adaptation, and system-level analysis.

- Cyber risk frameworks provide structure and standardization.
- Simulation models enable experimental exploration.
- Resilience engineering introduces performance-oriented evaluation.
- CAS theory captures systemic complexity and emergence.
- Adversarial AI enables adaptive and evolving threat modeling.

SREs can thus be understood as an integrative paradigm that combines these elements into a unified analytical and operational framework. Rather than replacing traditional risk management approaches, they extend them by introducing dynamic, scenario-based, and experimentally grounded methods.

This integrated perspective provides the conceptual foundation for the subsequent sections of the chapter, where SREs are further defined, structured, and operationalized. In particular, the next section builds on these foundations to develop a systematic conceptualization and taxonomy of SREs, linking theoretical insights with practical design and implementation considerations.

3. SYNTHETIC RISK ENVIRONMENTS (SRE): CONCEPTUALIZATION AND FRAMEWORK

SREs can be understood as digitally constructed, adaptive ecosystems designed to simulate cyber threats, system vulnerabilities, and socio-technical interdependencies under controlled yet realistic conditions. In contrast to traditional cybersecurity approaches—such as penetration testing or vulnerability scanning—which are typically episodic and system-focused, SREs operate as continuous and experimental environments that capture dynamic interactions between attackers, defenders, technical systems, and human actors (Tounsi & Rais, 2018; Bada & Nurse, 2019). Their defining characteristic lies in the ability to generate evolving scenarios that reflect the adaptive nature of contemporary cyber threats, thereby enabling the systematic exploration of risk under conditions of uncertainty.

Existing research has largely examined the individual components that constitute SREs, including cyber ranges, digital twins, and AI-driven simulation techniques (Ligo, Kott & Linkov, 2021; Cassottana et al., 2023). However, these components are often treated in isolation, resulting in a fragmented understanding that limits both theoretical coherence and practical applicability. In particular, there remains a lack of integrated conceptual models that systematically link data, simulation methodologies, artificial intelligence, and governance mechanisms into a unified analytical framework. Addressing this gap is essential for advancing SREs from a collection of tools toward a structured paradigm for next-generation cyber risk assessment.

To address this limitation, this chapter conceptualizes SREs as a multi-layered system architecture that integrates four interdependent functional dimensions, as illustrated in Figure 1.

Figure 1. Integrated Architecture of SREs.

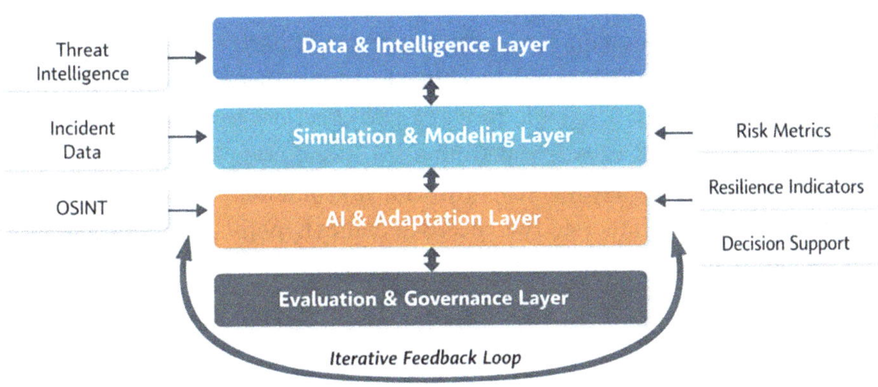

First, SREs rely on a data-driven foundation that incorporates heterogeneous sources such as threat intelligence feeds, historical incident reports, system logs, and open-source intelligence. These inputs ensure that synthetic scenarios are grounded in empirical evidence and reflect evolving threat landscapes (ENISA, 2023). Second, SREs employ a combination of simulation methodologies—including agent-based modeling, system dynamics, and Monte Carlo simulation—to reproduce both micro-level interactions and macro-level system behaviors (Epstein & Axtell, 1996; Forrester, 2007; Metropolis & Ulam, 1949). This integration enables the modeling of complex phenomena such as cascading failures, interdependencies, and probabilistic risk distributions.

Third, artificial intelligence introduces adaptive capabilities into SREs by enabling the generation of dynamic and non-deterministic threat scenarios. Techniques such as generative adversarial networks and reinforcement learning facilitate the simulation of evolving attacker strategies and adaptive defense mechanisms, transforming SREs into learning environments rather than static testing platforms (Goodfellow et al., 2014; Sutton & Barto, 1998; Papernot et al., 2017). Fourth, SREs incorporate evaluation and governance mechanisms that translate simulation outputs into actionable insights. These include resilience-oriented metrics—such as recovery time, adaptive capacity, and systemic impact—as well as alignment with established governance frameworks and regulatory requirements.

These four dimensions are not independent but form a continuous and iterative process in which data inputs inform simulations, simulations are enhanced by adaptive AI mechanisms, and resulting outputs are evaluated within governance frameworks to support decision-making. Feedback loops continuously update the system, allowing SREs to evolve alongside the threat landscape. As shown in Figure 1, this cyclical interaction establishes SREs as adaptive learning systems that enable experimental and evidence-based cybersecurity strategies.

The conceptual contribution of this framework lies in its ability to integrate previously fragmented approaches into a coherent architecture that bridges theory and practice. By operationalizing concepts from resilience engineering, complex adaptive systems, and adversarial machine learning, the framework provides a structured basis for both academic research and practical implementation. It also shifts cybersecurity risk assessment from a static and compliance-driven activity toward a dynamic, proactive, and experimentally grounded discipline.

For researchers, this integrated perspective enables hypothesis-driven experimentation and reproducible simulation studies. For practitioners, it provides a structured approach to designing and implementing SREs within organizational contexts. For policymakers, it offers a foundation for scenario-based evaluation of cybersecurity strategies and regulatory interventions. Ultimately, the framework positions SREs not merely as a technological innovation but as a strategic paradigm for understanding and managing cyber risk in complex and rapidly evolving digital environments.

4. METHODOLOGICAL APPROACHES FOR SRES

The methodological foundation of SREs builds upon the integration of simulation models, artificial intelligence techniques, and heterogeneous data sources to enable the systematic analysis of complex and adaptive cyber risks. In contrast to traditional risk assessment approaches, which rely primarily on static models and historical data, SREs employ dynamic and experimental methodologies that allow for the exploration of emergent behaviors, non-linear interactions, and probabilistic uncertainties. As outlined in the conceptual framework (Section 3), these methodological components are not applied in isolation but are tightly interlinked within an integrated analytical architecture.

The methodological architecture of SREs is illustrated in Figure 2, which connects simulation models, AI-driven mechanisms, and data inputs within a continuous validation and learning cycle.

Figure 2. Methodological Architecture of SRE.

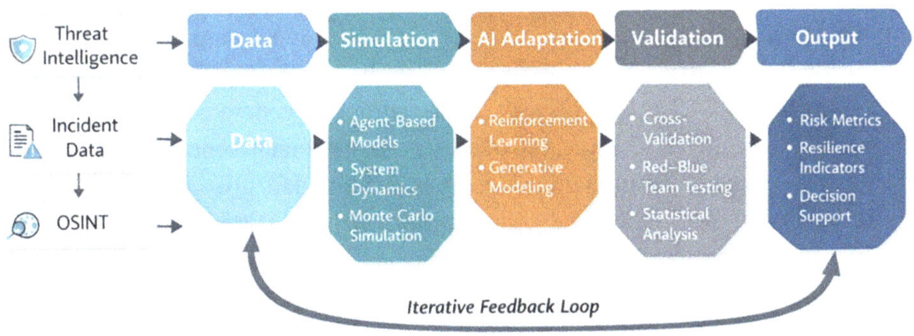

At the core of SRE methodologies are simulation models that enable the representation of cyber-physical systems and adversarial interactions at different levels of abstraction. Agent-based modeling (ABM) provides a bottom-up approach in which individual actors—such as users, devices, attackers, and defenders—are modeled as autonomous agents with specific behavioral rules (Epstein & Axtell, 1996). This approach is particularly suitable for capturing emergent phenomena, such as insider threats or malware propagation across distributed networks. Complementing this perspective, system dynamics (SD) models represent aggregated system behavior through feedback loops, stock-flow relationships, and temporal dependencies (Forrester, 2007). SD is especially useful for analyzing cascading failures, systemic vulnerabilities, and long-term resilience strategies in interconnected infrastructures. In addition, Monte Carlo simulation (MCS) introduces a probabilistic dimension by modeling uncertainty through repeated random sampling, allowing for the estimation of risk distributions and the evaluation of mitigation strategies under varying conditions (Metropolis & Ulam, 1949).

While simulation models provide the structural backbone of SREs, artificial intelligence significantly enhances their adaptive and predictive capabilities. Generative adversarial networks (GANs) enable the creation of synthetic but realistic attack data, which can be used to simulate novel or previously unseen threat scenarios (Goodfellow et al., 2014). Reinforcement learning (RL), in turn, allows both attacker and defender agents to learn optimal strategies through iterative interaction with the simulated environment (Sutton & Barto, 1998). This leads to co-evolutionary dynamics in which offensive and defensive behaviors continuously adapt, thereby increasing the realism and exploratory depth of SREs. Moreover, adversarial machine learning highlights the vulnerabilities of AI systems themselves, which can be explicitly incorporated into SRE scenarios to assess robustness and resilience (Papernot et al., 2017).

A critical component of SRE methodology is the integration of diverse and high-quality data sources. These include structured and unstructured data such as threat intelligence feeds, incident reports, system logs, honeypot data, and open-source intelligence. Data serves multiple functions within SREs: it calibrates simulation models, informs AI training processes, and ensures that generated scenarios remain empirically grounded. However, the quality and representativeness of data directly influence the validity of simulation outcomes, making data governance and preprocessing essential methodological considerations (ENISA, 2023).

Validation and reliability constitute another central methodological pillar. Given the synthetic nature of SREs, ensuring that simulation results are meaningful and applicable to real-world contexts is a critical challenge. This requires multi-layered validation strategies, including back-testing against historical incidents, cross-validation with empirical datasets, and expert evaluation through red-blue team exercises. Statistical methods, such as confidence interval estimation in Monte Carlo simulations, further support the assessment of uncertainty and robustness. As shown in Figure 2, validation is not a final step but an integral part of a continuous feedback loop that refines models, data inputs, and AI components over time.

Importantly, the methodological integration of simulation, AI, and data transforms SREs into adaptive learning systems. Rather than producing static risk assessments, SREs generate evolving insights that reflect changes in threat landscapes, system configurations, and defensive strategies. This iterative process aligns closely with principles from resilience engineering and complex adaptive systems theory, emphasizing continuous adaptation, learning, and system-wide analysis (Hollnagel, Woods & Leveson, 2006; Holland, 1995).

The methodological contribution of this chapter lies in the explicit integration of these components into a unified workflow that links theoretical modeling, data-driven analysis, and AI-based adaptation. By structuring SRE methodologies as a coherent and iterative process, the chapter advances beyond descriptive surveys and provides a reproducible foundation for both academic research and practical implementation. This integrated approach enables researchers to design controlled experiments and test hypotheses under realistic conditions, while practitioners can apply these methods to evaluate security strategies, optimize resource allocation, and enhance organizational resilience.

5. APPLICATIONS AND CASE STUDIES

SREs demonstrate their practical relevance through their ability to simulate complex, cross-domain cyber risk scenarios and to evaluate resilience under realistic yet controlled conditions. Rather than serving as isolated testing platforms, SREs function as integrated analytical environments in which the interaction between technological infrastructures, human actors, and adversarial behavior can be systematically examined. This enables a shift from reactive risk assessment toward proactive and scenario-based resilience analysis. The principal application domains of SREs across critical infrastructures, distributed systems, industrial environments, and institutional contexts are summarized in Figure 3.

Figure 3. Application domains of SREs.

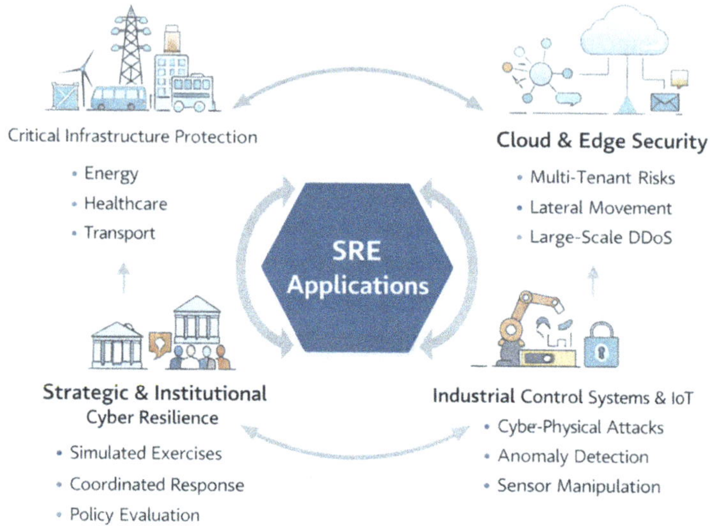

A primary area of application is the protection of critical infrastructures, including energy systems, healthcare services, and transport networks. These domains are characterized by tightly coupled cyber-physical systems and high societal impact in the event of failure (ENISA, 2023; Lehto, 2022). Within SREs, digital twins and hybrid simulation environments enable the modeling of cascading effects, such as malware-induced disruptions in power grids or ransomware attacks on hospital information systems. Importantly, SREs extend beyond vulnerability identification by enabling the evaluation of system-wide resilience, including recovery dynamics, interdependencies, and adaptive responses under stress conditions. This allows decision-makers to test mitigation strategies before real-world deployment and to quantify resilience in operational terms.

Closely related to this is the application of SREs in cloud and edge computing environments, where distributed architectures introduce new attack surfaces and complex propagation dynamics. By integrating simulation models with AI-driven scenario generation, SREs allow organizations to analyze multi-tenant vulnerabilities, lateral movement across distributed systems, and large-scale denial-of-service scenarios. In contrast to traditional security assessments, which often focus on isolated components, SREs capture the systemic nature of cloud–edge interactions and enable the exploration of emergent risks resulting from decentralization, real-time data processing, and inter-service dependencies.

Another important application domain concerns industrial control systems (ICS) and Internet of Things (IoT) ecosystems, where the convergence of operational technology (OT) and information technology (IT) creates unique vulnerabilities. SREs facilitate the simulation of cyber-physical attacks, such as sensor manipulation or actuator interference, and allow for the assessment of their impact on system stability and operational continuity. By combining simulation-based stress testing with AI-driven anomaly detection, SREs provide insights not only into technical vulnerabilities but also into organizational response capabilities, including incident handling and recovery coordination.

At the strategic level, SREs are increasingly employed within national cybersecurity frameworks and large-scale institutional settings. Cyber ranges and synthetic environments are used to conduct coordinated exercises involving multiple stakeholders, including government agencies, critical infrastructure operators, and private sector organizations. These applications extend beyond technical validation by enabling the evaluation of coordination mechanisms, communication processes, and policy interventions under simulated crisis conditions (NATO CCDCOE, 2022). In this context, SREs contribute to systemic resilience by supporting cross-sectoral learning, preparedness, and governance evaluation.

In corporate contexts, SREs enhance enterprise risk management, particularly in sectors such as finance, insurance, and supply chain management. By simulating complex threat scenarios—such as ransomware propagation, insider threats, or third-party compromises—organizations can evaluate the robustness of their security architectures and business continuity strategies. A key advantage of SREs lies in their ability to quantify cyber risk in probabilistic terms, for example through Monte Carlo-based scenario analysis, thereby supporting evidence-based decision-making and more efficient resource allocation.

Across these application domains, a consistent pattern emerges: the value of SREs lies not only in replicating known threats but in exploring unknown and emergent risk scenarios. By integrating simulation models, AI-driven adaptation, and real-world data—as conceptualized in Section 3 and operationalized in Section 4—SREs provide a comprehensive methodological foundation for understanding cyber risk as a dynamic and systemic phenomenon. This positions them as a critical instrument for bridging the gap between theoretical risk models and operational cybersecurity practice, while enabling organizations to transition toward proactive, adaptive, and resilience-oriented security strategies.

6. CHALLENGES AND LIMITATIONS OF SRES

Despite their transformative potential, SREs face a number of conceptual, technical, and institutional challenges that constrain their practical implementation and the reliability of their outcomes. These limitations must be critically examined in order to avoid overestimating the explanatory and predictive power of simulation-based cybersecurity approaches.

A first major challenge concerns ethical and legal constraints. SREs rely on large volumes of data, including incident reports, behavioral logs, and operational system data, which may contain sensitive or personal information. Even when synthetic or anonymized datasets are used, risks of re-identification and regulatory non-compliance—particularly under frameworks such as the General Data Protection Regulation (GDPR)—remain significant. In addition, the dual-use nature of SRE technologies introduces further concerns: AI-driven adversarial simulations, generative attack models, and reinforcement-learning-based red-team agents can potentially be repurposed for offensive cyber operations. This creates a tension between realism and responsibility, requiring strict governance mechanisms, controlled environments, and clearly defined rules of use.

A second set of limitations relates to modeling and simulation validity. While SREs integrate advanced methodologies such as agent-based modeling, system dynamics, and Monte Carlo simulation, their outputs are inherently dependent on modeling assumptions, input data quality, and algorithmic design choices. Human behavior—particularly insider threats, decision-making under stress, and cognitive biases—remains difficult to model accurately. Similarly, digital twins and simulated infrastructures often simplify real-world complexity, which can lead to incomplete representations of interdependencies or emergent system behavior. As a result, SRE outcomes may suffer from limited external validity, raising the question of how reliably simulation results can be transferred to real-world scenarios.

Closely related to this is the issue of data and algorithmic bias. AI-driven components of SREs depend on training data that may be incomplete, skewed, or outdated. Biases in threat intelligence feeds, incident datasets, or adversarial modeling can lead to systematic distortions, such as overestimating certain attack vectors while underrepresenting others. These biases propagate through simulation processes and may result in misleading risk assessments or inappropriate prioritization of mitigation strategies. Ensuring transparency, explainability, and continuous validation of AI models is therefore essential for maintaining the credibility of SRE outputs.

A further limitation concerns resource intensity and technical complexity. High-fidelity SREs—particularly hybrid or AI-driven environments—require substantial computational infrastructure, including cloud-based resources, high-performance computing, and specialized simulation platforms. In addition, their design, operation, and interpretation demand interdisciplinary expertise spanning cybersecurity, data science, systems engineering, and organizational risk management. This creates significant barriers to adoption, especially for smaller organizations or institutions with limited technical capacity. Moreover, SREs must be continuously updated to reflect evolving threat landscapes, which introduces ongoing maintenance costs and operational complexity.

Another critical challenge lies in the lack of standardization and methodological consistency. Currently, there is no universally accepted framework for designing, validating, or evaluating SREs. Different organizations employ heterogeneous modeling approaches, metrics, and levels of fidelity, making it difficult to compare results or establish benchmarks. Furthermore, regulatory frameworks rarely recognize simulation-based evidence as a formal basis for compliance or risk reporting, which limits the institutional integration of SREs into governance, risk, and compliance (GRC) processes. This lack of standardization reduces both the interoperability and the broader applicability of SRE-based insights.

Finally, SREs face limitations related to human and organizational factors. While simulation environments can model technical systems with increasing accuracy, capturing human behavior, organizational decision-making processes, and inter-organizational coordination remains challenging. Over-reliance on simulated behavior may create blind spots, particularly in socio-technical systems where human actions play a decisive role. In addition, the effective use of SRE outputs depends on the interpretive capacity of decision-makers. Without appropriate expertise and governance structures, there is a risk that simulation results are either misunderstood or misapplied, leading to ineffective or even counterproductive security strategies.

Taken together, these challenges highlight that SREs should not be understood as predictive or deterministic tools, but rather as exploratory and analytical instruments that support decision-making under uncertainty. Their value lies in enabling controlled experimentation and scenario-based reasoning, not in providing definitive forecasts. Addressing these limitations requires a combination of methodological rigor, interdisciplinary collaboration, transparent governance, and continuous validation. Only under these conditions can SREs realize their full potential as a next-generation approach to cybersecurity risk assessment and resilience engineering.

7. EMERGING TRENDS AND FUTURE DIRECTIONS

The future development of SREs is likely to be shaped by a convergence of technological, methodological, and institutional innovations. As cyber threats continue to evolve in complexity, scale, and adaptivity, SREs are expected to move beyond their current role as advanced simulation platforms toward becoming a core component of proactive and resilience-oriented cybersecurity governance. Several emerging trends indicate how this transition may unfold.

A first major trend concerns the deeper integration of artificial intelligence into synthetic cyber risk modeling. While current SREs already employ techniques such as generative adversarial networks and reinforcement learning to simulate adaptive attackers and defenders, future environments are likely to incorporate more advanced forms of autonomous reasoning and multi-agent coordination. This may include AI systems capable of generating highly context-sensitive attack scenarios, dynamically adjusting to environmental changes, and exploring previously unknown vulnerabilities with minimal human intervention (Goodfellow et al., 2014; Papernot et al., 2017). At the same time, this development will intensify concerns about explainability, control, and the validation of AI-generated scenarios, making transparency and governance increasingly important.

A second trend is the growing integration of SREs with digital twins of critical infrastructures and cyber-physical systems. As digital twin technologies mature, they enable increasingly high-fidelity representations of power grids, industrial environments, transportation systems, and healthcare infrastructures (Salvi, Spagnoletti & Noori, 2022). This opens the possibility of moving from abstracted cyber simulations toward near-realistic system replication, where operational dependencies, physical consequences, and human decision processes can be modeled simultaneously. Such integration may significantly enhance the realism and practical relevance of SREs, particularly in domains where cyber incidents have immediate physical and societal effects.

A third emerging direction concerns the standardization and institutionalization of SRE methodologies. At present, one of the main barriers to broader adoption lies in the absence of common modeling standards, shared metrics, and recognized validation procedures. Future work is therefore likely to focus on developing interoperable frameworks for scenario generation, resilience measurement, and simulation reporting. This may include standardized metrics for adaptive capacity, recovery time, systemic impact, and decision quality, which would improve comparability across sectors and use cases. In the longer term, simulation-based evidence generated through SREs may also become more explicitly integrated into governance, risk, and compliance processes, thereby strengthening the link between cybersecurity operations and regulatory oversight.

A fourth trend lies in the expansion of SREs toward collaborative and cross-organizational platforms. Because many contemporary cyber threats affect multiple actors simultaneously—such as supply chain attacks, coordinated ransomware campaigns, or attacks on critical infrastructure—future SREs are likely to support more distributed and multi-stakeholder forms of simulation. This includes joint exercises involving public agencies, critical infrastructure operators, and private organizations, as well as shared environments for policy testing and cross-sector learning (NATO CCDCOE, 2022). Such collaborative SREs may become important instruments for national cyber resilience strategies, particularly in contexts where coordination failures rather than purely technical weaknesses constitute the primary source of systemic risk.

Another important future direction concerns the integration of human and organizational factors. While many current SRE approaches emphasize technical simulation and AI-driven adaptation, the future relevance of SREs will increasingly depend on their ability to represent human decision-making, organizational routines, cognitive overload, and inter-organizational communication under stress. This is especially important for incident response, crisis coordination, and resilience planning, where technical effectiveness alone does not determine outcomes. Advancing SREs in this direction will require closer collaboration between cybersecurity researchers, behavioral scientists, organizational theorists, and domain experts.

Finally, future research should also address the implications of emerging computing paradigms, including quantum computing, autonomous cyber defense, and increasingly distributed cloud-edge architectures. These developments may fundamentally alter both the threat landscape and the computational capabilities available for synthetic risk modeling. In particular, the simulation of post-quantum attack scenarios, autonomous defense mechanisms, and hyper-distributed infrastructures may become central use cases for next-generation SREs. This suggests that SREs themselves must remain adaptive, not only in relation to cyber threats, but also with respect to the technological environments they are intended to represent.

Taken together, these trends indicate that SREs are likely to evolve from specialized simulation systems into broader infrastructures for experimentation, foresight, and coordinated resilience building. Their future significance will depend not only on advances in modeling and AI, but also on progress in validation, standardization, interdisciplinarity, and governance. In this sense, the future of SREs lies as much in institutional design and methodological robustness as in technological innovation.

8. DISCUSSION

The findings of this chapter highlight that SREs represent more than a technological extension of existing cybersecurity practices; rather, they constitute a conceptual shift toward simulation-based and resilience-oriented risk management. By integrating data-driven inputs, advanced simulation models, and adaptive AI mechanisms, SREs enable a fundamentally different approach to understanding cyber risk as a dynamic and systemic phenomenon.

From a theoretical perspective, SREs align closely with the principles of complex adaptive systems (CAS) and resilience engineering. Cybersecurity can no longer be adequately described through linear cause–effect relationships or static vulnerability models. Instead, risk emerges from non-linear interactions, feedback loops, and adaptive adversaries. The framework developed in this chapter operationalizes these theoretical insights by embedding them into a structured architecture that connects simulation, AI, and governance. In this sense, SREs contribute to advancing cybersecurity research from descriptive and retrospective analyses toward experimental and forward-looking methodologies.

At the same time, the analysis reveals a tension between model complexity and practical applicability. While high-fidelity simulations increase realism, they also introduce challenges related to interpretability, computational cost, and organizational usability. This reflects a broader trade-off in cybersecurity research between analytical depth and operational feasibility. As a result, SREs must be carefully designed to balance realism with usability, ensuring that simulation outputs remain actionable for decision-makers.

Another important insight concerns the role of artificial intelligence as both an enabler and a source of uncertainty. AI-driven components—such as generative models and reinforcement learning agents—significantly enhance the adaptive capabilities of SREs, allowing the simulation of evolving adversarial behavior. However, these same technologies introduce new risks related to opacity, bias, and reproducibility. This dual role of AI underscores the need for transparent, explainable, and governable simulation frameworks, particularly in high-stakes environments such as critical infrastructure or national security.

The application domains discussed in Section 5 further demonstrate that the value of SREs lies not only in technical validation but also in organizational learning and strategic decision-making. SREs enable stakeholders to explore "what-if" scenarios, test coordination mechanisms, and evaluate policy interventions in controlled environments. This shifts cybersecurity from a reactive discipline toward a proactive and anticipatory practice, where uncertainty is not eliminated but systematically explored.

However, the discussion also reinforces the limitations identified in Section 6. The validity of SRE outputs remains contingent upon data quality, modeling assumptions, and continuous updating. Moreover, the lack of standardized methodologies and regulatory recognition limits their broader adoption. These challenges suggest that the future development of SREs will depend not only on technological advances but also on institutionalization, standardization, and interdisciplinary collaboration.

Overall, SREs can be understood as boundary objects that connect research, practice, and policy. They provide a shared framework through which different stakeholders—researchers, practitioners, and regulators—can collaboratively explore cyber risks and resilience strategies. Their long-term impact will therefore depend on their ability to integrate technical innovation with governance structures and societal values.

9. CONCLUSION

This chapter has examined SREs as an emerging paradigm for next-generation cybersecurity, demonstrating their potential to transform risk assessment from static, compliance-driven approaches into dynamic, simulation-based, and resilience-oriented strategies. By integrating theoretical perspectives from resilience engineering, complex adaptive systems, and adversarial machine learning with advanced simulation methodologies and AI-driven techniques, the chapter has positioned SREs as a bridge between conceptual research and operational cybersecurity practice.

The primary contribution of this work lies in the development of an integrated conceptual framework for SREs, which systematically connects four key dimensions: data foundations, simulation models, adaptive AI mechanisms, and governance structures. Unlike existing approaches that treat these elements in isolation, the proposed framework conceptualizes SREs as iterative, learning systems capable of continuously adapting to evolving threat landscapes. This integration not only enhances theoretical coherence but also provides a structured basis for practical implementation in organizational and policy contexts.

From a methodological perspective, the chapter has shown how the combination of agent-based modeling, system dynamics, Monte Carlo simulation, and AI-driven approaches enables the representation of cyber risk as a dynamic, multi-layered, and probabilistic phenomenon. This perspective moves beyond traditional linear risk models and allows for the analysis of cascading effects, interdependencies, and adaptive adversarial behavior. At the same time, the discussion has critically highlighted the epistemic limitations of synthetic environments, particularly with regard to validity, bias, and the transferability of simulation results to real-world contexts.

In terms of practical implications, SREs offer significant value for multiple stakeholder groups. For practitioners, they provide a tool for scenario-based decision-making, enabling the evaluation of resilience strategies, incident response mechanisms, and system-wide vulnerabilities under controlled conditions. For policymakers, SREs create opportunities for stress-testing regulatory frameworks and national cybersecurity strategies, supporting coordinated and cross-sectoral approaches to risk management. For researchers, they establish a controlled experimental environment that facilitates hypothesis testing, reproducibility, and the empirical study of complex cyber-physical systems.

However, the chapter has also emphasized that SREs are not a panacea. Their effectiveness depends on careful design, continuous validation, and robust governance. Ethical considerations, data protection requirements, simulation biases, and the absence of standardized methodologies remain significant challenges that must be addressed to ensure the responsible and reliable use of SREs. Without such safeguards, there is a risk that simulation-based insights may lead to false confidence or misinformed strategic decisions.

Looking forward, several research avenues emerge. Future work should focus on improving model fidelity, developing standardized evaluation metrics, and enhancing the integration of human and organizational factors within synthetic environments. In addition, the growing importance of AI-driven and autonomous cybersecurity systems raises new questions regarding transparency, accountability, and control. The exploration of post-quantum cybersecurity scenarios, as well as the development of collaborative and cross-organizational SRE platforms, represents another important direction for both research and practice.

In conclusion, SREs represent a significant step toward a more proactive, adaptive, and experimentally grounded approach to cybersecurity. Rather than replacing existing risk management frameworks, they complement and extend them by enabling continuous learning and scenario-based reasoning under conditions of uncertainty. As cyber threats continue to increase in complexity and scale, SREs provide a critical foundation for understanding, anticipating, and managing risk in interconnected digital ecosystems. Their further development will play a key role in shaping the future of cybersecurity research, practice, and policy.

REFERENCES

Ani, U. D., Al-Mhiqani, M., Tuptuk, N., Hailes, S., & McKendrick Watson, J. D. (2025). Socio-Technical Security Modelling and Simulations in Cyber-Physical Systems: Outlook on Knowledge, Perceptions, Practices, Enablers, and Barriers. *IET Cyber-Physical Systems*, *10*(1), e70017. DOI: 10.1049/cps2.70017

Aslaner, M. (2024). *Cybersecurity Strategies and Best Practices: A comprehensive guide to mastering enterprise cyber defense tactics and techniques*. Packt Publishing Ltd.

Bada, M., & Nurse, J. R. (2019). Developing cybersecurity education and awareness programmes for small-and medium-sized enterprises (SMEs). *Information and Computer Security*, *27*(3), 393–410. DOI: 10.1108/ICS-07-2018-0080

Cassottana, B., Roomi, M. M., Mashima, D., & Sansavini, G. (2023). Resilience analysis of cyber-physical systems: A review of models and methods. *Risk Analysis : An Official Publication of the Society for Risk Analysis*, *43*(11), 2359–2379. DOI: 10.1111/risa.14089 PMID: 36646448

Cavelty, M. D. (2024). *The politics of cyber-security*. Routledge. DOI: 10.4324/9781003497080

Cebula, J. L., & Young, L. R. (2010). *A taxonomy of operational cyber security risks* (No. CMUSEI2010TN028).

ENISA – European Union Agency for Cybersecurity. (2023). *ENISA Threat Landscape 2023*. ENISA.

Epstein, J. M., & Axtell, R. (1996). *Growing artificial societies: social science from the bottom up*. Brookings Institution Press. DOI: 10.7551/mitpress/3374.001.0001

Forrester, J. W. (2007). System dynamics—A personal view of the first fifty years. *System Dynamics Review*, *23*(2-3), 345–358. DOI: 10.1002/sdr.382

Goodfellow, I. J., Pouget-Abadie, J., Mirza, M., Xu, B., Warde-Farley, D., Ozair, S., & Bengio, Y. (2014). Generative adversarial nets. *Advances in Neural Information Processing Systems*, •••, 27.

Holland, J. H. (1995). *Hidden Order: How Adaptation Builds Complexity*. Basic Books.

Hollnagel, E., Woods, D. D., & Leveson, N. (Eds.). (2006). *Resilience engineering: Concepts and precepts*. Ashgate Publishing, Ltd.

ISO/IEC. (2018). *ISO/IEC 27005:2018-07 — Information technology - Security techniques - Information security risk management*

Klasa, K., Galaitsi, S., Trump, B. D., & Linkov, I. (2021). Science and practice of resilience: disaster systems applications to aging resilience. In *Resilience and aging: Emerging science and future possibilities* (pp. 53–80). Springer International Publishing.

Lehto, M. (2022). Cyber-attacks against critical infrastructure. In *Cyber security: Critical infrastructure protection* (pp. 3–42). Springer International Publishing. DOI: 10.1007/978-3-030-91293-2_1

Ligo, A. K., Kott, A., & Linkov, I. (2021). How to measure cyber-resilience of a system with autonomous agents: Approaches and challenges. *IEEE Engineering Management Review*, *49*(2), 89–97. DOI: 10.1109/EMR.2021.3074288

Metropolis, N., & Ulam, S. (1949). The monte carlo method. *Journal of the American Statistical Association*, *44*(247), 335–341. DOI: 10.1080/01621459.1949.10483310 PMID: 18139350

Naghshbandi, S. N., Varga, L., Purvis, A., Mcwilliam, R., Minisci, E., Vasile, M., Troffaes, M., Sedighi, T., Guo, W., Manley, E., & Jones, D. H. (2020). A review of methods to study resilience of complex engineering and engineered systems. *IEEE Access : Practical Innovations, Open Solutions*, *8*, 87775–87799. DOI: 10.1109/ACCESS.2020.2992239

NATO Cooperative Cyber Defence Centre of Excellence. (2022). *Exercise Locked Shields 2022 concludes: Largest international live-fire cyber defence exercise.* NATO CCDCOE. Retrieved from https://shape.nato.int/news-archive/2022/exercise-locked-shields-2022-concludes

NIST – National Institute of Standards and Technology. (2012). *Guide for Conducting Risk Assessments* (NIST SP 800-30 Rev. 1). National Institute of Standards and Technology.

NIST – National Institute of Standards and Technology. (2018/2023). *Framework for Improving Critical Infrastructure Cybersecurity* (Cybersecurity Framework, v1.1 and subsequent updates / draft 2.0 discussions).

Papernot, N., McDaniel, P., Goodfellow, I., Jha, S., Celik, Z. B., & Swami, A. (2017). Practical black-box attacks against machine learning. In *Proceedings of the 2017 ACM on Asia conference on computer and communications security* (pp. 506-519).

Salvi, A., Spagnoletti, P., & Noori, N. S. (2022). Cyber-resilience of critical cyber infrastructures: Integrating digital twins in the electric power ecosystem. *Computers & Security, 112*, 102507. DOI: 10.1016/j.cose.2021.102507

Schwab, K. (2015). World economic forum. *Global Competitiveness Report (2014-2015).*

Serena, L., D'Angelo, G., Ferretti, S., & Marzolla, M. (2025). Simulation in Cybersecurity: Understanding Techniques, Applications, and Goals. *arXiv preprint arXiv:2508.06106.*

Sutton, R. S., & Barto, A. G. (1998). *No. 1* (Vol. 1). Reinforcement learning: An introduction. MIT press.

Tounsi, W., & Rais, H. (2018). A survey on technical threat intelligence in the age of sophisticated cyber attacks. *Computers & Security*, *72*, 212–233. DOI: 10.1016/j.cose.2017.09.001

Chapter 5

Autonomous Defenders: Generative AI for Smarter Incident Response – AI-Augmented Security Operations in Modern SOCs

M. P. Rajakumar
St. Joseph's College of Engineering, India

M. Balasubramani
http://orcid.org/0009-0005-3706-0140
V.S.B. Engineering College. Karur, India

R. Balamurugan
New Prince Shri Bhavani College of Engineering and Technology, India

M. Navaneetha Krishnan
St.Joseph College of Engineering, India

M. Robinson Joel
http://orcid.org/0000-0002-3030-8431
KCG College of Technology, Karapakkam, India

Joel Jacson
http://orcid.org/0009-0006-3095-7024
Kings Engineering College, India

ABSTRACT

This chapter examines the transformative role of generative artificial intelligence in modern incident response, focusing on how AI-driven models enhance detection, triage, analysis, and remediation workflows within Security Operations Centers. The chapter outlines limitations of traditional human-centered response frameworks and demonstrates how large language models, reinforcement learning agents, and multimodal generative systems provide adaptive, context-aware decision support. A conceptual architecture for autonomous defenders is introduced, illustrating how generative AI integrates with SIEM, SOAR, and XDR platforms to enable semi-autonomous and fully automated security actions. Ethical, regulatory, and

DOI: 10.4018/979-8-3693-8397-1.ch005

governance considerations are discussed to ensure responsible deployment of AI-driven cyber defense capabilities. The chapter concludes by identifying emerging research directions and outlining future trends that will shape AI-augmented incident response ecosystems.

1. INTRODUCTION

1.1 Background

Cloud infrastructures and rapid digitalization within organizations are factors that add to today's complex cybersecurity operations. The attached distribution systems and IoT environments are further complicating the scenarios. The condition gets more complicated with flowing telemetry, event data, and threat signals that keep streaming into an enterprise network, causing strain in maintaining an instantaneous detection and management of cyber-incidents at Security Operations Center (SOCs) (Evans & Franks, 2023).Conventional cybersecurity channels like SIEM, EDR, IDS/IPS, and SOAR will basically meet the visibility requirement, but they rely heavily on their human experts to interpret a massive number of alerts and then put the pieces together to coordinate the actions of the response.

As a fallout, the cyber adversaries have begun to adopt automation, artificial intelligence, and adaptive techniques to bring up the lightning fast tempo and sophistication of their offensive operations (Thomas & Shrobe, 2024). The perpetrators are using automated exploit kits, AI-generated malware variants, multi-staged ransomware frameworks, and social engineering attacks empowered by synthetic content. These capabilities deepen the existing asymmetry between the attackers and defenders and impede any effective incident response.

New advancements in generative AI (GenAI) such as large language models (LLMs), generative adversarial networks (GANs), reinforcement-learning agents, and multimodal reasoning systems have given new potential towards improving the incident response functions in most parts involving partial automation. GenAI is proven to have the capability of analyzing logs, prioritizing alerts, simulating attack behavior, generating remediation playbooks, and supporting decision-making under uncertainty (Snyder & Malik, 2022). Thus far, overall, they provide an account of more autonomous and adaptive models of cyber defense, which this chapter refers to as autonomous defenders.

1.2 Problem Statement

In spite of considerable advances in technology, traditional incident response frameworks are still restricted by manual processes, static procedures, and human decision inputs. These restrictions contribute to some of the long-standing operational issues, like slow detection and response times from manual triage and investigations, huge alert fatigue for SOC analysts who are pouring their time into prioritizing thousands of notifications on a daily basis, and ongoing reliance on static response playbooks that resist modification against emerging or at times simply unknown threats.

In addition to these, scattered data sources hinder effective root-cause analysis, and the scarce skill set of cybersecurity organizations often adds pressure to their limited capacity. Conventional tools also lack the capability of hypothesizing or simulating advanced attack patterns, thus inhibiting the organization's perspective on adversarial behavior. Collectively, these set of issues broaden the gap between rapid attack automation and a much stunted defender capability, thus leading to delayed response, greater exposure to breaches, and more organizational risk.

The increasing use of AI-tool-developed imbalance is exacerbated by the absence of intelligent, automated counter-measures and mechanisms (Rahman & Liu, 2023). The current chapter seeks to view this gap by discussing how generative AIs can be used to modernize and revitalize affected workflows with a view to incident response.

1.3 Aim of the Chapter

The further intent of this chapter is a strong research-supported and practically relevant presentation of how generative artificial intelligence might emerge as a more-intelligent, adaptive, and exceedingly efficient part of the cyber incident response mechanism. Hence, the chapter aims to look into the inherent weaknesses of traditional incident response processes and amplify the call for automating and empowering defensive systems with AI capabilities. It further explains the basic principles governing generative AI technologies and how they apply to current security workflows to demonstrate enhancements in detection, triage, and remediation in Security Operations Centers (SOCs). It endeavors to provide a conceptual and operational framework for incorporating generative AI inputs into existing incident response pipelines and will then consider ethics, regulation, and governance pertaining to the safe and secure implementation of AI-enabled cyber defense strategies.

1.4 Scope of the Chapter

This chapter discusses the ability of generative artificial intelligence to renovate and improve upon traditional incident response processes by integrating intelligent, adaptive, and semi-autonomous aspects into cybersecurity operations. In particular, it will focus on those capabilities of Gen-AI models such as large language models, generative adversarial networks, and autonomous agents, which could be applied to specific stages of the incident response lifecycle, including detection, triage, analysis, and remediation. The discussion will start from the basic theoretical foundations and continue toward practical implementation considerations, presenting a view of how GenAI could be interfaced with existing SOC technologies such as SIEM, SOAR, and EDR/XDR platforms in support of operational effectiveness and decision-making.

This chapter is not about covering all aspects of AI in cybersecurity but narrows its scope on the generative AI techniques most relevant to building adaptive and autonomous incident response systems. Other cybersecurity domains that include topics like penetration testing and network hardening, encryption mechanisms, or perhaps general applications of machine learning are probably a no-go except, of course, where they directly touch-on GenAI-driven incident response. The chapter does not even venture into offensive applications of AI. The narrow scope allows this chapter to undertake a thorough and cohesive analysis that fits into the larger aim while being able to assess the potential generative AI holds for transforming incident response workflows while driving the evolution of autonomous cyber defense mechanisms.

1.5 Significance of the Topic

With fast-moving threats, cybersecurity teams are in an urgent need to investigate generative AI for incident response. The Security Operations Centers are now at a miserable end, with an enormous attack surface burdened with an overwhelming number of alerts and diminishing skilled resources, which practically prevents these centers from properly responding to or detecting security incidents on time (ISC2, 2023). Meanwhile, automation for the adversary in performing exploitation with AI-generated malware in launching refined attacks demonstrates how lacking human-response or rule-based-response mechanisms are in sustaining organizational resilience (Morrison & Patel, 2023). Generative AI would stand to gain much from being used for log analysis and contextual triaging in an automated fashion, correlating information intelligently and recommending responsive actions far beyond what human-labor-intensive processes can do.

As generative AI begins to be applied in the area of incident response it will herald changes that are part of a larger shift in cyber architecture to support approaches such as zero trust frameworks, continuous monitoring, and predictive defenses. These approaches mean that systems will need to be able to perform dynamic reasoning, automate adaptation, and provide real-time decision support - which generative AI is capable of providing. Hence, the topic is not relevant just conceptually in academics, but as it conjoins AI with operational cybersecurity in industry and also offers a tremendous potential for changing or improving defense mechanisms, automation, and AI governance. The chapter will give insight toward designing adaptive, autonomous, and resilient cyber defense ecosystems by demonstrating how GenAI affects detection, triaging, and response workflows.

2. LIMITATIONS OF TRADITIONAL INCIDENT RESPONSE

2.1 Overview of Traditional Incident Response Frameworks

Usually, the incident response models have developed best practices like SANS six-phase framework (2023), ISO/IEC 27035 (2011), and the NIST Computer Security Incident Handling Guide (SP 800-61 2012) for incident response. So, all these three frameworks work more or less in the same manner: creating a process that is organized and predictable, where preparation precedes detection and analysis, followed by other phases like containment, eradication, recovery, and post-incident activities. This model has been for many years an internal structure for most of the enterprise cyber security operations.

These incident response frameworks have a basis of forward progression, while in the same breath providing coherency and clarity on how to manage a security incident. What makes them different from the general models is that there is a set course, below which a document must belong, and it can be entered only by applying the steps after which the attacks occur, leading to an organized procedure that should feature in an organizational operational process (Sharma, 2021).

Traditionally, while these models have been proven useful in predictable threat scenarios, they were conceived for a time when data volume, system complexity, and attacker intelligence were all low compared to the contemporary environment. The present threat environment with its cloud-native systems, distributed architecture, and fast-paced attacks requires that the incident response (IR) workflows be able to handle complexities that were never supposed to be handled by the traditional model.

Figure 1. Traditional Incident Response Lifecycle (NIST-Based)

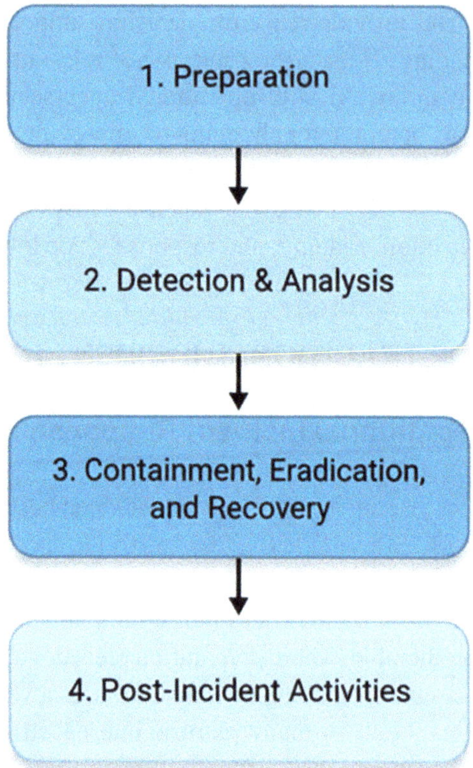

2.2 Strengths and Historical Value of Traditional IR

Existing incident response (IR) frameworks have helped shape many best practices for security activities. Frameworks provided structure to processes, underscored the importance of documentation of the incident, and recommend learning from incidents to improve the security posture over the long-term (Alshaikh, 2020). For example, frameworks are still important in regulated industries, for compliance reporting, auditability, and evidencing controls to regulators.

Changes to attack vectors (e.g. AI driven phishing payloads, automated, brute-force approaches; multi-staged ransomware) illustrate the limitations of a process that focused on responding to an incident through a series of manual and linear steps.

2.3 Limitations of Manual and Static IR Models

2.3.1 Slow Detection and Response Times

The actions of human gating and scrutiny slow down the entire process of detection and containment. Modern incidents unfold in minutes, whereas manual IR may take anything from hours to days to correlate indicators of compromise (Kim & Park, 2021). Within this time frame, an attacker is given a huge advantage.

2.3.2 Alert Fatigue

Every day, the SOCs are inundated with alerts firing from the SIEM, EDR, and network monitoring tools. Analysts would need to go through prioritizing the alerts and filtering them for investigation, leading to a cognitive overload which may result in such critical signals to have been missed (Lee et al., 2023).

2.3.3 Static Response Playbooks

SOCs become incapable of efficiently responding to zero-day exploits or AI-generated threat patterns because playbooks are normally static procedures that do not adapt to unknown attacks and changing adversary behavior (Rodriguez & Liu, 2022).

2.3.4 Fragmented and Distributed Data Sources

The businesses operate in environments that are multi-cloud, hybrid, and containerized. Important security data is distributed among log sources, endpoints, identity systems, and cloud platforms. Performing manual correlation of these various datasets is error-prone and lethargic (Nguyen & Porter, 2021).

2.3.5 Human Dependability

Traditional IR workflows require well-qualified analysts for investigations and reasoning and decision-making regarding threats. However, the global cybersecurity talent gap has been enormously widened, leaving many SOCs understaffed and overburdened (ISC2, 2023).

2.3.6 Absence of Predictive and Proactive Capabilities

Traditional IR mainly addressed responding to incidents after they had occurred. The models did not contain capabilities to predict attack paths, simulate adversarial behavior, or foresee incidents. Without predictive intelligence, defenders remain reactive, while attackers gain speed and, ultimately, automation (Hussein & Farooq, 2024).

2.4 Scalability Challenges in Modern Security Operations

In expansive hybrid-cloud architectures, the scalability constraints of current incident response (IR) approaches have become distinctly apparent. The speed and variety of events originating from APIs, cloud workloads, microservices, or anything IoT produce a tremendous amount of telemetry that exceeds human processing capability. Adversaries are increasingly using automation tools that exploit the scale of automated large phishing campaigns, credential stuffing attacks, and vulnerability exploitation (Zhou & Chatterjee, 2023).

SOCs are also having a difficult time keeping up with the demands of scaling their operations due to understaffing, high turnover, and increasing operational complexity. This creates a different imbalance, resulting in detection gaps, insufficient forensic coverage, and, importantly, a reactive posture unable to keep up with today's fast-paced automated threats.

2.5 The Need for Intelligent and Adaptive Incident Response

Given all these limitations, the truth is that conventional incident reporting is not enough in supporting organizational resilience anymore. Today's cyber defense looks for systems with qualities of dynamic reasoning, continuous learning, and automated adaptation. General AI offers capabilities that directly tackle some incident reporting issues-auditing log material to summarize content, automated triage of incidents, threat simulation, and autonomous playbook generation-and thus speeds up and makes incident response workflows more efficient (Chen & Gupta, 2023).

Generative AI is enabling and enhancing the transition from reactive processes to proactive defense strategies by blocking adaptive intelligence in the SOC environment. This shift is an underlying premise behind autonomous defenders, the key theme of the current chapter. Subsequent sections will expand on this base by considering the generative AI technologies that allow new modes of incident response systems to be improved, automated, and resilient.

3. FOUNDATIONS OF GENERATIVE AI FOR CYBERSECURITY OPERATIONS

3.1 Introduction to Generative AI

Transforming AI describes systems with the ability to produce brand new text, synthetic data, computer codes, images, or behavioral patterns owing to their training on very huge datasets. In the domain of cybersecurity, GenAI has the transformational potential of contextual inferencing about intent, building threats hypotheses, and automating some tedious analysis work (Kumar & Shrestha, 2023). Unlike classical machine learning paradigms, which primarily engage in classification or prediction problems, generative models create artifacts that source, triage, and remediate incidents. GenAI's ability to create provides a very peculiar transformational opportunity to enhance the cognitive and adaptive capacities of incident response systems.

3.2 Large Language Models (LLMs) in Security Operations

For the purposes of GenAI adoption, LLMs have become a foundation. Large Language Models, GPT-type architectures, T5 variants, and open-source models further fine-tuned for cybersecurity have become foundational to GenAI adoption. It is here that LLMs can nearly mimic human intelligence in parsing and understanding logs, alerts, and textual threat intelligence, thereby allowing for the generation of automated investigation summaries, anomaly explanations, and contextual triaging support (Almansoor & Jang, 2022). The theory of semi-supervision of unstructured data like emails, system messages, configuration files, and OSINT addresses one of the long-standing issues of SOC environments concerning the timely and accurate synthesis of disparate sources of information.

Figure 2. Generative AI model taxonomy relevant to cybersecurity operations, including LLMs, GANs, reinforcement learning agents, and multimodal generative systems.

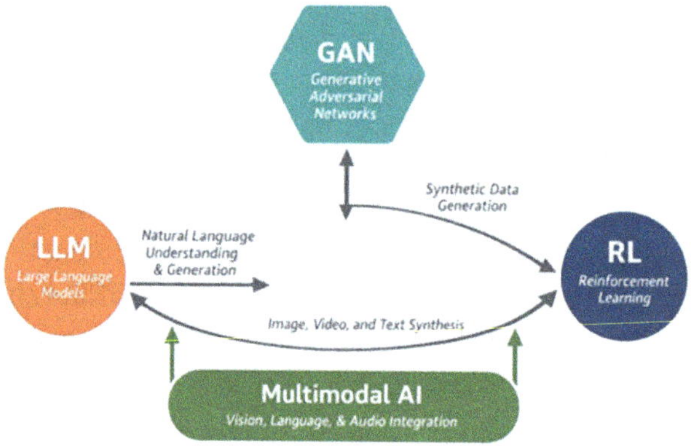

In addition, LLMs can also perform multi-step reasoning, properly equipping them for incident response. Integrating LLMs into either SIEM or SOAR systems enables them to analyze related events, formulate attack progression hypotheses, and propose containment actions. This will reduce the workload of the analyst and improve consistency of response across various threat scenarios (Wang & Silva, 2023).

3.3 Generative Adversarial Networks (GANs) and Synthetic Threat Modeling

There are two types of neural networks within the scope of Generative Adversarial Networks-the generator and the discriminator-that learn through adversarial training. In cybersecurity, their applications are simulated attack behaviors, generation of synthetic malware variants, or generation of network traffic behavior based on seen adversarial techniques. That synthetic data can also be used to enhance detection models through more varied examples that are not found in historical datasets (Li & Gupta, 2021).

As such, the applicability of GANs is mainly directed toward strengthening detection systems against new or zero-day threats. Yet another advantage of generating such realistic adversarial scenarios would be to allow SOC teams to execute detection pipeline tests and then better the strength of their defensive controls and assess readiness on new attack modes. So, GANs can be viewed as rendering a virtual adversary to their defense ecosystems and serving their research and operational readiness (Rodriguez et al., 2022).

3.4 Reinforcement Learning (RL) for Decision-Making in Incident Response

Reinforcement Learning (RL) models learn to carry out the desired actions through trial and error while being guided through some form of reward mechanism. There are various uses of RL in incident responses, such as automating containment workflows, prioritizing investigations, and optimizing mitigation actions based on changing conditions (Ahmed & Kumar, 2024). RL agents are particularly perceived to work well in an environment laden with uncertainty, dynamic changes, and incomplete information often conditions that are subjected to changes almost in real-time during cyber incidents.

A reinforcement learning (RL)-based decision system is able to adapt its response approaches with newly available threat intelligence, along with inputs from operational experience. Therefore, it is possible to design semi-autonomous agents that can reasonably select optional defensive actions, such as isolating the infected host, blocking some malicious traffic, or initiating the capture of forensic data. If their actions are directed using GenAI methods, the RL agent will fit into the overarching design of the proposed new generation of autonomous defenders proposed in this chapter.

3.5 Multimodal Generative Models in Security Contexts

Current cyber incidents generally deal with multiple data types, including logs, image data (screenshots), and data extracted from network flows, binary artifacts, and behavioral data sequences. Thus, the multimodal generative models can analyze and correlate different forms of data simultaneously, thereby enhancing the analysis capabilities of an SOC through a combined interpretation of the various streams of evidence. The combination of contextual, textual, and temporal signals for advanced threat detection is function of these models (Chen et al.,2023).

As an illustration, a multimodal GenAI system can analyze endpoint telemetry, connect it to email context, monitor the anomalies associated with other affected networks, and build a complete narrative of the incident. This comprehensive view shifts some burden away from analyst investigations, while simultaneously improving the accuracy of assessments of the threat. Multimodal systems also lead to more accurate adversary simulations, constructing attack scenarios that more closely resemble real-world campaigns, with precision on the level of granularity.

3.6 Challenges and Limitations of Generative AI in Security

Generative AI has, however, brought in critical limitations. First, LLMs and generative models may give inaccurate or misleading answers if they are not adequately fine-tuned with a dataset specific to cybersecurity.

Second, GenAI will be misused by adversaries to automate their own attack strategies-creating an AI-versus-AI adversarial situation (Zhou & Chatterjee, 2023). Third, there are large computational requirements for generative systems, and the limitations of governance issues related to transparency, fairness, and traceability also fall under this category. Understanding these limitations is hence critical in responsible adoption.

4. GENAI FOR DETECTION, TRIAGE, AND ANALYSIS

4.1 Enhancing Detection Through Generative AI

Traditional detection relies heavily on signature-based systems and predefined correlation rules that often miss novel or obfuscated attacks. Operating under the assumptions that novel attacks exhibit some behavior not previously seen-and that detection can rely on those behavioral patterns-obviating the need for signatures, generative AI defeats this limitation by learning from large volumes of historical and real-time telemetry the behavioral patterns, contextual relationships, and latent features. Deviation from the expected pattern of normal system behavior may be flagged as anomalous and thus worthy of attention by GenAI, even if they are not bound by known signatures (Park & Lee, 2022).

Large language models (LLMs), for instance, will parse complex log files, detect subtle indictors of lateral movement, and interpret messages from systems missed by traditional means. Generative models like the autoencoder or the variational autoencoder (VAE) can delineate deviations in network flows or user behavior by reconstructing normal activity and flagging instances of significant reconstruction error (Hussein & Farooq, 2024). This can prompt early detection of zero-day exploits as well as so-called low-and-slow intrusions. Generative adversarial networks (Gans) also add to detection by generating synthetic examples of the rare attack patterns for robust training of the anomaly detection systems. It aids in better generalization in the security operations center (SOC) environments that possess sparsely distributed attack data and imbalanced threat distributions (Li & Gupta, 2021). Thus, GenAI moves detection forward, initiating activities that suspect detection in a proactive manner, away from existing reactive mechanisms.

4.2 Intelligent Alert Prioritization and Triage

Today, Security Operations Centers are flooded with alerts pouring in from SIEMs, EDRs, IDSs/IPSs, cloud security APIs, and identity-monitoring systems. Manual triage functions rather slowly, with the possibility of errors, all highly dependant on the analyst's experience. Generative AI builds in ameliorations for these problems by providing automated and context-based alert prioritization.

LLMs can be used to analyze alert metadata, historical incident data, and environmental contexts to decide which alerts stand for real threats, and which of them are most likely to be false positives. Using Few-shot or zero-shot inference LLMs are able to classify alerts based on risk profiles, attack stages, and possible business impact (Chen & Gupta, 2023). This reduces the workload of analysts and increases the efficiency of SOC.

Reinforcement learning (RL) agents will be an upgrade to effective triage practices because such agents will learn effective prioritization through effective interaction with real-world SOC environments. Based on feedback from the outcomes of incidents and decisions made by analysts, these RL systems dynamically tweak their triage policies towards maximizing the potential for accurate detection while minimizing response delays (Ahmed & Kumar, 2024). Moreover, multimodal GenAI architectures can enable the integration of logs, network telemetry, EDR signals, user behavior analytics, and on external threat intelligence feeds to provide a more comprehensive perspective towards triage assessments. These models surface relationships that may not be seen by commenting on the data in isolation, and therefore provide support with decision-making in the first-instance triage

4.3 Automated Log Interpretation and Threat Analysis

Log analysis forms one of the most tedious chores in the incident response process. Analysts have to painstakingly parse firewall logs, authentication logs, cloud audit trails, and application logs for incident reconstruction and malicious indicators. Generative AI dramatically expedites the manual summarization and contextual reasoning.LLMs fed with content from the cybersecurity domain could summarize lengthy log sequences to short summaries, point anomalous entries, and speculate on likely causes of suspicious behavior (Wang & Silva, 2023). This means the analyst will not have to correlate timestamp, IP address, and event code manually but would trust summaries generated by GenAI that condense the main information and give clear directions for the investigation.

Figure 3. Workflow of a GenAI-augmented Security Operations Center, illustrating detection, triage, analysis, response, and continuous learning.

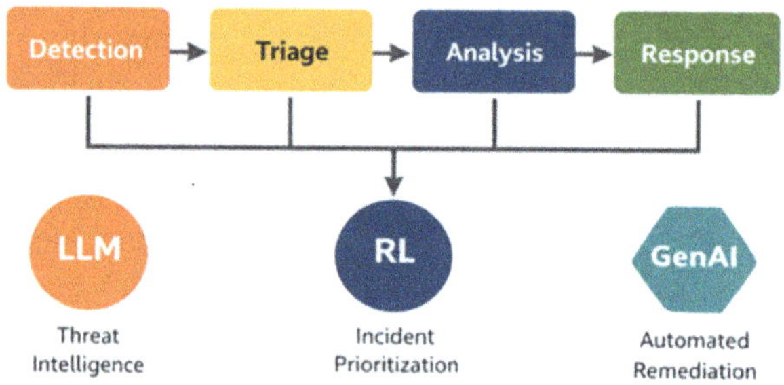

Generative models support automatically extracting indicators of compromise (IOCs), detecting attempts at privilege escalation, recognizing patterns of command and control, and reconstructing possible attack paths, thus speeding up root-cause analysis and further enhancing the accuracy of incident investigation . GAN-based methods can generate synthetic logs that mimic realistic attack sequences for training SOC teams and testing detection pipelines. These models create controlled alterations to attack behavior so that analysts can view how simple evasions might manifest within real-world telemetry (Rodriguez et al., 2022).

4.4 Behavioral Modeling and Attack Path Prediction

Conventional security solutions are primarily centered on event-based detection alerts generated from individual events. Nonetheless, the evolution of threats, particularly advanced persistent threats ("APTs") have transformed the conceptualization of "events" into a series of coordinated actions across endpoints, networks, and even cloud environments. The advent of generative AI provides a way to develop behavioral modeling that can identify malicious behaviors within sequences as opposed to just individual events specializing either in detection or prevention.

Deep generative sequence models, e.g., transformer-style architectures, learn the temporal behaviors and structural aspects of the relationships between actions. These models can be capable of identifying patterns regarding reconnaissance, credential harvesting, lateral movement, and data exfiltration, even if the individual action would appear benign (Nguyen & Porter, 2021) .

Furthermore, generative models can also simulate possible attack pathways based on observed behaviors. For example, if an adversary penetrates a workstation modification to its authentication configuration, GenAI could determine the next probable action, such as privilege escalation or movement to a sensitive server. The predictive capabilities of GenAI can be leveraged by a security operations team to preemptively understand the adversary's emerging intent by decreasing the dwell time of an attacker.

4.5 Threat Intelligence Synthesis and Enrichment

The SOC analysts utilize various threat intelligence sources such as reports, feeds, vulnerability databases, and OSINT to add context to alerts and better understand the tactics used by adversaries. However, the threat intelligence provided is either unstructured, high volume, or even hard to relate to internal data.

Generative AI is able to combine external intelligence and internal telemetry swiftly and efficiently. LLMs can summarize the threat reports, extract applicable IoCs, relate them to known techniques in MITRE ATT&CK, and correlate events to recent organizational activity (Hassan & Lee, 2024). LLMs may also add insight to external threats' relevance to the organization's environment by examining network configurations, associated asset inventories, and past incidents.

Multimodal generative engines layer threat intelligence by using text, visual, and behavioral data in one representational form. Their unique capability allows them to correlate observed activity to known adversarial tactics, techniques, and procedures (TTPs) automating the entire process and enabling better qualitative responses.

5. GENAI FOR AUTOMATED AND SEMI-AUTONOMOUS INCIDENT RESPONSE

5.1 The Evolution Toward Autonomous Defenders

In order to contain, eliminate, and recover from incidents, incident response has relied on human analysts making decisions. The speed of current cyberattacks, however, requires decisions to be made at machine speed; this is something which human analysts alone cannot provide. Therefore, generative AI provides methods to automate reasoning, adapt to dynamic threat conditions, and generate actionable response steps, which form the basis of semi-autonomous and fully autonomous incident response systems. These autonomous defenders combine analytical insights from GenAI models with automated execution pipelines to reduce attacker dwell time and improve response consistency (Chen & Gupta, 2023).

5.2 Generative AI–Generated Response Playbooks

One important aspect of generative AI in incident response is the creation of adaptive response playbooks, which are a significant enhancement in traditional response playbooks. Conventional playbooks have rules laid down in concrete and have stepwise procedures strictly defined within them. As such, they are limited in considering new and evolving threats. Responding to real telemetries, threat intelligence, and contextual data from the environment, GenAI dynamically can develop its response workflows.

In other words, LLMs can produce customized steps for containment and remediation of incidents simply by analyzing the metadata from an incident and correlating that with previous incidents, the MITRE ATT&CK frameworks, and established behavior patterns of threat actors (Park & Lee, 2022). For instance, as an example, once a ransomware attack has been discovered, a GenAI could ultimately generate a series of recommended actions to take such as isolating compromised endpoints, stopping suspicious processes, or even putting firewall blocks and triggering backup validation workflows. These dynamic playbooks can enhance the robustness with flexibility in terms of incident response making SOC teams better in addressing emerging threats through a flexible response model rather than mere procedure adherence.

5.3 Semi-Autonomous Response Actions

Semi-autonomous incident resolution uses GenAI-powered systems that are recommended, validated, or partially executed under the supervision of human analysts. The hybrid model is particularly important for organizations more focused on governance, transparency, and human oversight into their security operations. In a semi-autonomous incident response system, Generative AI can initiate response actions (e.g., quarantining compromised devices, blocking malicious IP addresses, revoking compromised credentials, or suspending suspicious users) with the analyst's approval required before that action is executed. Reinforcement learning agents can make this approach even more beneficial since they can refine recommendations based on the analyst's decisions and the results of seeing the incident play out, resulting in improved cycles of action/feedback that improve an agent's decision-making capabilities (Ahmed & Kumar, 2024).

Semi-autonomous strategies offer substantial advantages, including reducing the burden on analysts, accelerating responses to routine or lower complexity threats, increasing consistency in incident response processes, and providing a live capability to stay up to speed with changes. Overall, the model retains human oversight for essential aspects of decision making, while implementing GenAI's quicker, more effective analytical capabilities to improve efficiency and reliability of incident response capabilities.

5.4 Fully Automated Response Workflows

Based on well-specified and foreseeable circumstances of threat, organizations can set up fully automated response workflows wherein GenAI-based reasoning engines independently execute containment or remediation actions without any human being involved in the decision-making. Generative AI, in those figures, can perform innumerable automated countermeasures, involving the isolation of compromised endpoints, blocking malicious domains or IP addresses, terminating malicious processes, real-time reconfiguration of firewall or access control rules, or deploying patches on known vulnerabilities. All actions initiated through context-based AI evaluation, severity assessment, and environmental assessment thus promoting rapid yet consistent response to security incidents.

A fully automated response will reduce the mean time to respond (MTTR) by integration with the SOAR platform quite significantly. This shrinks time windows for response from hours to minutes (Wang & Silva, 2023). Despite these operational advantages, fully automated systems will be held to strict safety controls, such as rule-based constraints, confidence scoring, and rollback mechanisms, to ensure that automated actions cannot disrupt business operations or respond with harmful false positives through client intervention.

5.5 Integrating GenAI with SOAR and XDR Pipelines

The SOAR systems act as a backbone for automated-response actions. The enhancement that generative AI brings to SOAR platforms comprises dynamic reasoning, contextual consideration, and automated decision-making capability. Once GenAI is coupled with SOAR workflows, organizations can adaptively orchestrate their responses away from static rule sets.

XDR platforms also benefit from GenAI's ability to pool signals across endpoints, cloud environments, identity systems, and network telemetry. GenAI boosts XDR correlation engines by developing hypotheses about attack progression and suggesting remediation actions that are in line with the respective organizational policies (Hassan & Lee, 2024). In this integrated system, holistic and intelligent responses are forged with the detection, triaging, and remediation capabilities made coherent by AI logic, thus enabling the acceleration and enhancement of decision cycles within the ecosystem.

5.6 Real-Time Decision Support and Risk-Adaptive Controls

Generative AI facilitate the real-time decision support and adaptive risk controls within incident response. Such systems are able to ascertain the relative severity of threats, the criticality of assets, the kinds of behavior exhibited by users, and the environmental context, and thereby recommend remediation actions commensurate with the conditions and severity. For instance, upon detection of suspicious login attempts, adaptive measures would be expected to range from multi-factor authentication challenges up to temporary session revocation. Furthermore, if the detection indicates malware execution on a particular high-value server, immediate isolation follows, hence preventing lateral movement.

The AI-based recommendations are issued by dynamic risk assessment processes that include multiple data sources related to both telemetry and contextual awareness. This dramatically reduces underreaction to let threats go unmitigated or overreaction, which creates business interruption and teams of experts trained in responding to threats with AI support. Generative AI introduces another layer of sophistication and speed that enables the SOC team to respond to the ever-changing threat landscape more quickly and more contextually than inmanual processes (Zhou & Chatterjee, 2023).

5.7 Challenges and Limitations

Before their large-scale application, it is important to address several challenges and limitations associated with GenAI-based autonomous and semi-autonomous response systems. Generative models in general, including large language models (LLMs) and reinforcement learning agents, may generate inaccurate or brash or contextually wrong remediation actions based on uncorroborating, biased, or stale training data. In this context, a reasonable risk for false-positive containment or unwarranted disruption to operations is raised. Also, AI systems could be attacked: adversarially data-poisoned, subversively fed erroneous or misleading inputs, inadvertently led to confusion through manipulation of their model architecture-just to aid precision in automated countermeasure implementation (Nguyen and Porter, 2021).

Everything in the automated world must have adequate governance protections: human-in-the-loop interventions, thresholds for confidence scoring, constraint medical policies, and compendium audit trail for accountability and traceability. Consider another area of explainability, where organizations must comprehend and justify, from a compliance and regulatory standpoint, the decisions taken through automation. Such caveats bear witness to the fact that while generative AI comes with excellent capabilities to respond to incidents, caution in setting up and validating its engineering and governance is required for real-world safe and trusted deployment.

5.8 Critical Analysis of Generative AI in Incident Response

The use of generative artificial intelligence for incident response operations represents a fundamental transformation of Security Operations Center (SOC) functions which currently depend on fixed rules toward systems which use adaptive intelligence. The implementation of generative AI technology brings major advances in detection accuracy and operational efficiency but delivery of these benefits requires organizations to conduct thorough evaluation of its new challenges for dependable and secure system operation.

Traditional SOCs depend on their established rules and unchanging playbooks together with manual processes which create restrictions on their capability to manage advanced and changing threat situations (Alshaikh, 2020; National Institute of Standards and Technology [NIST], 2022). The generative AI systems use their ability to understand context and recognize patterns and learn new information to create real-time security event analysis and response action recommendations.

The primary advantage of generative AI for incident response teams results in improved response times and increased automatic operational efficiency. AI models which include large language models and reinforcement learning agents use their capabilities to analyze extensive security log data for urgent alert detection while delivering operational insights that operate at almost real-time speed. The system decreases mean time to detect (MTTD) and mean time to respond (MTTR) which serve as essential metrics for assessing the performance of cybersecurity operations (Behl et al., 2023). The automation of routine tasks enables analysts to handle fewer alerts while human experts can concentrate on their most complex decision-making tasks.

6. PROPOSED METHODOLOGY

The Autonomous Defender Framework which this chapter presents will improve incident response operations at Security Operations Centers through its combination of generative artificial intelligence systems and adaptive decision-making capabilities. The traditional incident response systems depend on static rules and predefined playbooks and manual intervention, which prevents them from handling the changing nature of cyber security threats. The proposed framework establishes a context-aware learning-driven architecture, which uses large language models with reinforcement learning agents and knowledge-based reasoning to achieve intelligent semi-autonomous response capabilities.

The framework operates multiple layers of the cybersecurity pipeline through its design which connects data ingestion with analysis and decision-making and execution processes. The system benefits from generative AI models which work throughout the response lifecycle to develop new knowledge about threats and speed up security incident resolution. The approach uses recent AI-driven cybersecurity systems which require automated security solutions that can adapt to changing conditions while providing real-time threat detection capabilities (Chen & Gupta, 2023; Wang & Silva, 2023).

Adopting generative AI technology for incident response creates a fundamental trade-off between automated systems and human operational control. Fully automated systems provide operational speed and efficiency benefits, but their excessive use decreases system transparency and accountability during critical risk situations. The system requires human operators to monitor the AI system while they validate its decision-making process which enables them to comprehend the system's functions. The most effective method for deployment combines semi-autonomous decision-making with human validation according to security experts from (NIST, 2023).

6.1 Framework Architecture

The Autonomous Defender Framework which has been designed for remote operation consists of five operational layers that work together to deliver automated emergency response capabilities. The data ingestion layer functions as the base level of the system by gathering security telemetry data from various sources which include SIEM and EDR and XDR and cloud logs and external threat intelligence feeds. The system uses this layer to obtain all necessary data which includes essential threat information needed for complete threat assessment (Behl et al., 2023).

The framework's main intelligence component operates through its second layer which functions as the generative AI processing layer. Security logs are analyzed by large language models which comprehend and summarize the data while providing contextual information and discovering hidden patterns that traditional rule-based systems cannot detect (Brown et al., 2020; OpenAI, 2023). Generative adversarial techniques enable the creation of simulated attack scenarios which become operational through these methods (Goodfellow et al., 2014) whereas reinforcement learning agents use their decision-making skills to assess response actions throughout time to determine their success (Sutton & Barto, 2018).

Figure 4. Architecture of an autonomous defender system integrating GenAI reasoning, SOAR orchestration, policy governance, and security telemetry inputs.

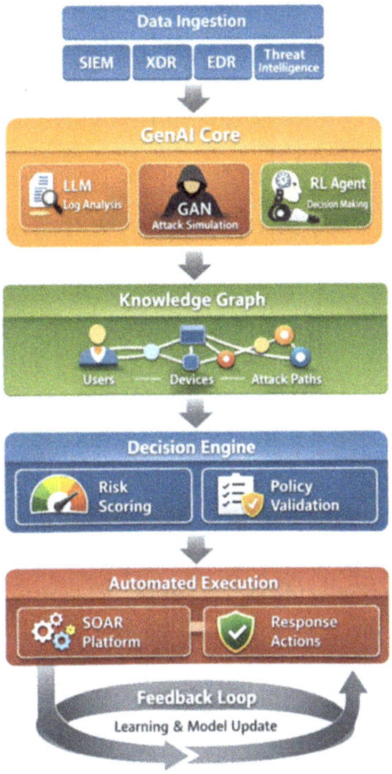

The knowledge graph layer creates connections between user entities and device entities and vulnerability entities and attack vector entities which enable contextual reasoning and advanced event correlation capabilities. Knowledge-driven approaches have been shown to improve threat intelligence and attack attribution (Hassan & Lee, 2024). The decision engine layer uses its enhanced context to calculate risk scores and determine incident severity while developing response strategies that follow learned policies and organizational limits.

The execution layer which operates with SOAR platforms executes the chosen response actions. The response actions consist of four specific tasks which include system isolation, malicious network activity blocking, user credentials revocation, and incident escalation workflow activation (Shackleford, 2015). The Autonomous Defender Framework architecture diagram in Figure 4 displays all system components while showing how these components work with each other.

6.2 Workflow of Autonomous Response

The proposed framework operates through its established workflow which uses an iterative system to monitor and analyze security events and develop operational responses. The process begins with security event collection which undergoes normalization to create data consistency among different sources. The analytical value of the events gets improved through enrichment with threat intelligence and contextual metadata (MITRE, 2023).

The enhanced data which generative AI models use for their analysis creates contextual insights that include summaries of suspicious behavior and potential attack narratives. The system predicts possible attack trajectories based on these insights while it evaluates the associated risk levels which has become a focus of research for generative cybersecurity models (Ferrag et al., 2024).

The most suitable response action is chosen through a reinforcement learning-based policy mechanism which evaluates both the immediate effects and the long-lasting system performance (Mnih et al., 2015). The chosen action undergoes validation against all organizational policies and governance rules before execution to stop any potential disruptions which follows the established AI risk management procedures (NIST, 2023).

The system executes confirmed actions through its built-in orchestration tools which handle execution procedures. The framework establishes a feedback mechanism which enables continuous learning model updates through the analysis of results from conducted activities to enhance upcoming decision processes. The system uses this iterative workflow to create real-time adjustments which match the constantly changing threat environments.

6.3 Algorithmic Representation

The operational logic of the proposed framework becomes formalized through the representation of the incident response process as a series of computational steps. The system starts its operations by preprocessing security events which it receives before using external intelligence sources to perform contextual enrichment. The data analysis process uses generative models to extract operational insights which link to the newest advancements in AI security automation (Chen & Gupta, 2023).

The learned policy function uses the computed risk score to identify the suitable response action which helps in responding to the situation. The system conducts action verification and execution processes which enable it to update its internal models through the received outcome feedback. The algorithmic representation establishes decision-making processes which maintain consistent operations and transparent functioning while enabling flexible adaptability.

6.4 Mathematical Model

The decision-making process within the Autonomous Defender Framework can be modeled using a reinforcement learning paradigm, where the objective is to maximize the cumulative reward associated with effective incident response actions. Let the system state at time t be represented as S_t, the selected action as A_t, and the corresponding reward as R_t. The optimal policy $\pi^*$is defined as the policy that maximizes the expected discounted reward over time:

$$\pi^* = \arg\max_{\pi} \mathbb{E}\left[\sum_{t=0}^{\infty} \gamma^t R_t\right]$$

where represents the discount factor. This formulation enables the system to learn optimal response strategies by balancing immediate mitigation effectiveness with long-term system stability and resilience (Sutton & Barto, 2018; Mnih et al., 2015).

6.5 Key Contributions of the Framework

The proposed methodology contributes to the advancement of AI-driven cyber-security in several significant ways. The first function of the system introduces a complete framework which links generative AI models with existing SOC infrastructure to enable organizations to shift from reactive defense operations to proactive defense operations (Chen & Gupta, 2023). The system uses reinforcement learning for decision-making which enables it to enhance its performance through the use of operational feedback. The system uses knowledge-driven reasoning to improve its understanding of complex attack methods and their related contextual information.

The system enables organizations to choose between two response modes which include semi-autonomous and fully automated systems to match their specific risk tolerance and governance requirements. The proposed method decreases response times while solving alert fatigue problems and boosting security defense capabilities through its automated system which requires less manual work and fixed response procedures (Behl et al., 2023; Ferrag et al., 2024).

7. ETHICAL, REGULATORY, AND GOVERNANCE CONSIDERATIONS

7.1 Ethical Implications of GenAI-Driven Incident Response

As generative AI becomes increasingly integrated into security operations, ethical implications must be carefully examined. GenAI systems, particularly those involved in decision-making and automated response, may inadvertently produce biased or incomplete recommendations if trained on unbalanced datasets. Such biases can affect triage prioritization, risk scoring, and user profiling, potentially leading to unequal treatment of users or systems within an organization (Hernandez & Bloom, 2022). Additionally, generative models may lack transparency in their reasoning processes, making it difficult for analysts to fully understand or challenge AI-generated outputs. The "black-box" nature of many GenAI systems raises concerns regarding accountability and explainability, especially when errors result in operational disruption or security blind spots.

The ethical use of GenAI also requires ensuring that human expertise is not marginalized. Overreliance on automated systems may erode the skills of analysts or result in excessive delegation of judgment to machines. Ethical deployment therefore requires maintaining meaningful human oversight, especially in high-impact decisions such as access revocation, system isolation, or automated containment. This balance ensures that GenAI enhances, rather than replaces, human decision-making capabilities.

7.2 Regulatory Compliance and AI Governance

Regulatory bodies worldwide have introduced frameworks addressing AI safety, transparency, and accountability. For example, the **NIST Artificial Intelligence Risk Management Framework (AI RMF 1.0)** provides guidance for identifying, assessing, and mitigating risks associated with deploying AI systems in operational environments **(NIST, 2023)**. Similarly, policies under the European Union's proposed AI Act emphasize compliance, explainability, and data governance for high-risk AI systems, which include cybersecurity and incident response tools.

Organizations adopting GenAI must ensure compliance with laws governing data protection, privacy, and security. This includes ensuring that logs, telemetry, and behavioral data used to train or operate generative models are processed in accordance with regulatory requirements such as GDPR, CCPA, or industry-specific mandates. AI systems must also maintain audit trails that document decision rationales, training data provenance, and automated actions taken during incidents. These audit trails support regulatory transparency, internal governance, and forensic investigations.

7.3 Governance Models and Safe Deployment Practices

Effective governance is essential to ensure the responsible and safe deployment of GenAI in security operations. A robust AI governance model typically includes policy-based constraints, formal approval workflows, and continuous monitoring of AI behavior. For instance, automated containment actions may require predefined risk thresholds or analyst validation to prevent unintended disruptions. Response recommendations should include confidence scores and explainability indicators to help analysts assess AI reliability (Morrison & Patel, 2023).

Organizations should implement AI lifecycle management practices that encompass model training, validation, deployment, and continuous retraining based on operational feedback. This ensures that GenAI systems adapt to evolving threats while maintaining accuracy and reliability. Additionally, governance structures should assign clear roles and responsibilities for monitoring AI performance, addressing anomalies, and conducting periodic audits to ensure compliance and ethical alignment.

Figure 5. Governance framework for responsible AI-driven incident response, emphasizing transparency, accountability, fairness, operational safety, and compliance.

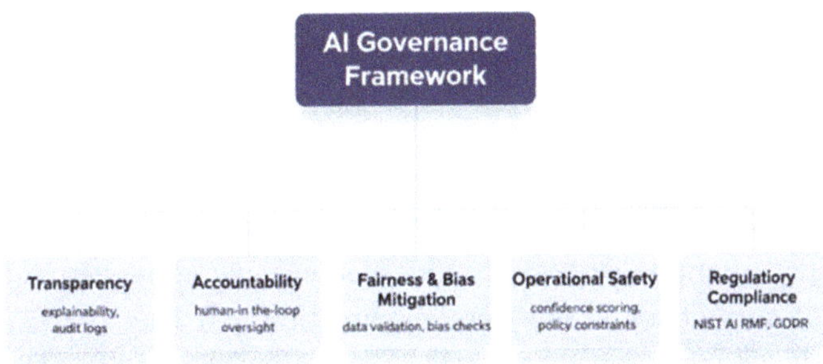

7.4 Security Risks Associated with GenAI Systems

Just as GenAI enhances defensive capabilities, it also introduces potential vulnerabilities. Malicious actors may attempt to exploit or manipulate AI systems through data poisoning, adversarial examples, or model inversion attacks. If adversaries successfully influence training data or real-time inputs, they may deceive automated systems into ignoring malicious activity or triggering inappropriate response actions

(Zhou & Chatterjee, 2023). Therefore, organizations must apply robust cybersecurity controls to protect model integrity, training pipelines, and inference environments.

Access controls, model hardening, secure data ingestion pipelines, and adversarial testing are essential steps in safeguarding GenAI systems. Moreover, organizations must maintain AI-specific incident response procedures to detect and mitigate potential compromise of AI tools themselves.

8. FUTURE TRENDS AND CONCLUSION

8.1 Emerging Trends in AI-Augmented Incident Response

Future advancements in GenAI are expected to accelerate the development of autonomous cyber defense ecosystems. One emerging trend is the rise of multi-agent AI systems, where specialized GenAI agents collaborate to perform detection, triage, containment, and recovery tasks with minimal human intervention. This aligns with the broader industry movement toward fully autonomous Security Operations Centers (A-SOCs), capable of executing complex defensive strategies based on collective reasoning (Chen et al., 2023).

Additionally, the integration of GenAI with zero-trust architectures will support continuous authentication, dynamic policy enforcement, and real-time access decisions based on behavioral insights. GenAI is also expected to enhance predictive incident response, enabling organizations not only to react to threats but also to anticipate and mitigate potential attack paths before exploitation occurs. Growth in AI-driven digital immune systems continuous learning ecosystems that monitor, adapt, and self-correct represents another direction that may redefine enterprise defense models over the next decade (Hassan & Lee, 2024).

8.2 Research Directions

Several research areas present opportunities for innovation. These include developing more interpretable generative models, creating adversarially robust AI systems, designing AI incident response metrics, and ensuring safe long-term autonomy in SOC operations. Additionally, cross-disciplinary research combining GenAI, behavioral analytics, and organizational psychology may improve understanding of human-AI collaboration in high-pressure environments. Future work must also explore privacy-preserving GenAI techniques, such as federated learning, to protect sensitive security telemetry used for model training.

8.3 Conclusion

The integration of generative AI into incident response marks a transformative shift in cybersecurity operations. Traditional manual and rule-based processes cannot match the speed, scale, and sophistication of modern threats. GenAI enables a new class of intelligent, adaptive, and semi-autonomous systems capable of enhancing detection, accelerating triage, guiding remediation, and supporting real-time decision-making. Through dynamic playbook generation, multimodal reasoning, reinforcement-learning-driven optimization, and integration with SIEM, SOAR, and XDR ecosystems, GenAI empowers organizations to build more resilient and proactive security strategies.

However, successful adoption requires addressing ethical, regulatory, and governance considerations to ensure transparency, accountability, and operational safety. As organizations advance toward autonomous defenders and AI-augmented SOCs, generative AI will play an increasingly central role in safeguarding digital ecosystems. The insights presented in this chapter highlight its enormous potential and the need for thoughtful, responsible deployment in the evolving cybersecurity landscape.

REFERENCES

Alshaikh, M. (2020). Security incident response frameworks: A comparative analysis. *Information Security Journal. Global Perspectives*, *29*(3), 101–118. DOI: 10.1080/19393555.2020.1759083

Behl, A., Behl, K., & Mishra, A. (2023). Cybersecurity workforce shortage and SOC challenges. *Computers & Security*, *127*, 103115. DOI: 10.1016/j.cose.2023.103115

Brown, T. B., Mann, B., Ryder, N., Subbiah, M., Kaplan, J., Dhariwal, P., Neelakantan, A., Shyam, P., Sastry, G., Askell, A., Agarwal, S., Herbert-Voss, A., Krueger, G., Henighan, T., Child, R., Ramesh, A., Ziegler, D. M., Wu, J., Winter, C., . . . Amodei, D. (2020). *Language Models are Few-Shot Learners*. arXiv.org. https://arxiv.org/abs/2005.14165

Chen, Y., & Gupta, A. (2023). Generative AI for advanced cybersecurity operations: A survey. *ACM Computing Surveys*, *55*(9), 1–32. DOI: 10.1145/3571239

Ferrag, M. A.. (2024). Generative AI for cybersecurity: A survey. *arXiv*. https://arxiv.org/abs/2405.12750

Goodfellow, I. J., Pouget-Abadie, J., Mirza, M., Xu, B., Warde-Farley, D., Ozair, S., Courville, A., & Bengio, Y. (2014). *Generative adversarial networks*. arXiv.org. https://arxiv.org/abs/1406.2661

Mnih, V., Kavukcuoglu, K., Silver, D., Rusu, A. A., Veness, J., Bellemare, M. G., Graves, A., Riedmiller, M., Fidjeland, A. K., Ostrovski, G., Petersen, S., Beattie, C., Sadik, A., Antonoglou, I., King, H., Kumaran, D., Wierstra, D., Legg, S., & Hassabis, D. (2015). Human-level control through deep reinforcement learning. *Nature*, *518*(7540), 529–533. DOI: 10.1038/nature14236 PMID: 25719670

National Institute of Standards and Technology. (2022). *Computer security incident handling guide (SP 800-61 Rev. 2)*. https://csrc.nist.gov/publications/detail/sp/800-61/rev-2/final

National Institute of Standards and Technology. (2023). *Artificial intelligence risk management framework (AI RMF 1.0)*. https://www.nist.gov/aiml/ai-risk-management-framework

Open, A. I. (2023). GPT-4 technical report. https://arxiv.org/abs/2303.08774

Shackleford, D. (2015). *Security orchestration, automation, and response (SOAR)*. SANS Institute.

Sutton, R. S., & Barto, A. G. (2018). *Reinforcement Learning: An Introduction* (2nd ed.). The MIT Press., https://web.stanford.edu/class/psych209/Readings/SuttonBartoIPRLBook2ndEd.pdf

Wang, F., & Silva, R. (2023). Autonomous cybersecurity agents. *IEEE Transactions on Dependable and Secure Computing*. Advance online publication. DOI: 10.1109/TDSC.2022.3218912

Zhou, L., & Chatterjee, S. (2023). Adversarial risks in AI-driven SOC automation. *Journal of Information Security and Applications*, *73*, 103124. DOI: 10.1016/j.jisa.2023.103124

Chapter 6
The Role of AI in Zero Trust Architectures

Tushar
http://orcid.org/0000-0001-7190-7687
United College of Engineering and Research, Prayagraj, India

Nandita Pradhan
http://orcid.org/0009-0006-8819-1009
United College of Engineering and Research, Prayagraj, India

Venktesh Mishra
http://orcid.org/0000-0003-4476-4064
United College of Engineering and Research, Prayagraj, India

Ajay Sharma
http://orcid.org/0000-0002-9112-6228
United College of Engineering and Research, Prayagraj, India

Pooja Jaiswal
http://orcid.org/0009-0007-2507-1525
University of Allahabad, Prayagraj, India

Ajit Kumar Yadav
http://orcid.org/0009-0003-5607-6100
United College of Engineering and Research, Prayagraj, India

Shyam Sundar
http://orcid.org/0009-0007-2507-1525
B.C.S. Prayagraj, India

Satya Prakash Singh
http://orcid.org/0009-0003-2406-2054
United College of Engineering and Research, Prayagraj, India

Shatrughan Mishra
http://orcid.org/0009-0005-7366-4275
United College of Engineering and Research, Prayagraj, India

Manish Kumar
http://orcid.org/0009-0007-0735-0256
P.K. University, Shivpuri, India

Sweta Singh
http://orcid.org/0000-0002-7006-817X
United University, Prayagraj, India

Shivani Mishra
http://orcid.org/0009-0006-0110-7039
United College of Engineering and Research, Prayagraj, India

DOI: 10.4018/979-8-3693-8397-1.ch006

Chitranjan Dwivedi
http://orcid.org/0009-0009-5940-7837
United College of Engineering and Research, Prayagraj, India

Bhupesh Chandra Kushwaha
United College of Engineering and Research, Prayagraj, India

ABSTRACT

The rapid growth of cybersecurity risks has led organizations to build stricter frameworks, with Zero Trust Architecture (ZTA) emerging as a significant paradigm. Based on "never trust, always verify," zero trust involves ongoing user and device identification verification, even inside the network perimeter. ZTA has a solid foundation, but cyberattacks are becoming more sophisticated, requiring more flexible solutions. AI improves ZTA by enabling real-time threat detection, behavioral analytics, and automated security event responses. A complete review of AI-powered tools and methodologies such natural language processing, anomaly detection, and predictive analytics is presented in this chapter to improve ZTA. It discusses AI implementation challenges, how AI interacts with ZTA components to improve security, and future research objectives.

1. INTRODUCTION

The zero trust architecture (ZTA) philosophy is based on the protection of resources. In such a scenario, for the sake of resource validation and authorization checks, ZTA has a goal to abolish assumed or inherited trust (attacker can only compromise a single point and then gain access) by imposing correct authentication, restricted authorizing and therefore constantly verifying stance (or trust inference) at each moment when an user or service decides to obtain a resource. In a bid to balance the advantages and disadvantages of ZTA in curbing cyber risks, we in this chapter introduce one of the potential solutions to the challenge, its opportunities, processes of implementation and constraints. Employees operated within the perimeter of security of the company. Under the ancient cybersecurity defence paradigm, technologies that would protect such a border would identify and prevent threats. However, as we all know, employees are human beings and they easily put themselves in the path of these hacks when they are not under each other protection and when they are accessing company information on their devices, said Fier. This shows how internal system services have their flaws in terms of authentication and verification, which renders the inner resources of the companies accessible to a potential black hat.

The zero trust model (ZTM) was first introduced to address some of these issues. The use case of MSRBAC is to protect resources in a fine-grained and authorized manner. Hence, it also demands the most accurate identification as well as access permission when people or things access the resource. Furthermore to make sure if it is legitimate or illegitimate trust inference/continuous verification is enforced at resources usage time. This way, you cannot have any trust that is implicitly or indirectly granted. By making them more secure, this type of security model gives businesses the moral authority to demand" consumers.

The principal contribution of this paper is marrying AI with Zero Trust Architecture for the capabilities of real-time threat detection, behavioral analytics and automated responses. It offers a unified, adaptive framework that augments continuous verification, enhances predictive capabilities and tackles evolving cyber threats more effectively than traditional ZTA or standalone AI security systems.

2. ZERO TRUST ARCHITECTURE

The ZTA is an access approach that requires minimal trust and demands constant reauthentication at every point. The NIST Special Publication 800-207 document (Rose et al., 2020). Two components make up Zero Trust Architecture (ZTA): a policy enforcement point (PEP) located in the data that plugs into a key switch and a policy decision point (PDP) located on the control panel as an integrated module.

Figure 1. Logical Core structure of the ZTA

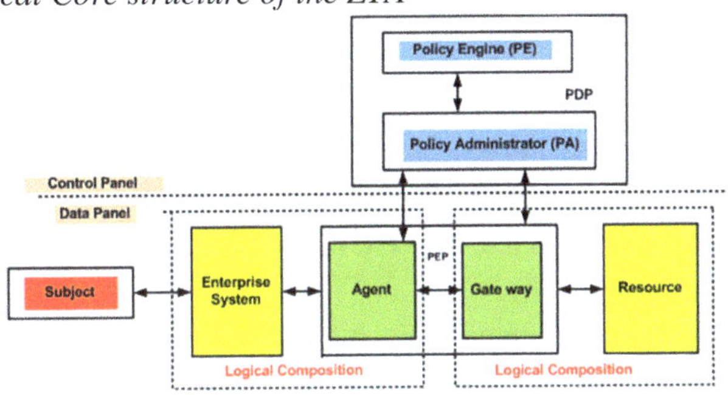

(Tsai et al., 2024).

The PDP is the "mind" of the ZTA and it determines which subjects (whether human users, applications or things) get access to organizational resources. On the other hand, the PDP tells the PEP how to establish and tear down connections. These relationships are temporary and the duration of their existence is elastic, since the enterprise environmental factors and alterations in security policy are available. During the talks, it was conveyed that according to the request of trust inference (sent by PDP to PEP) they ought to be tracked in real-time and the access be denied due to the threat intelligence evaluation and internal examination. In effect, ZTA has created a secure defense “bubble” around the entire path that an attacker needs to follow to access resources. It has a zero trust here inside the bubble and we scrutinize very heavily the authentication step. Note that the defence “bubble” eventually goes away after a certain amount of time, so it will not last quite forever. The structure information of the logical core of ZTA can be seen from Figure 1.

2.1 Policy Decision Point, PDP

Two large components of PDP are the policy engine (PE) and policy administrator (PA). The rules that are configured based on internal organization settings, security log data and external threat intelligence should be approved by the PE. The condition of time constraints placed on the security barrier between the subjects and the objects assisted in the assurance that these objects could be utilized in the safe environment without the danger of the objects. The PA, on the other hand, is working according to the recommendations by the PE (Okeke, 2023). The subject and resource right thing balancing quintessence is where there is a need to provide data to the organization or any other resource. As in the briefing that Danny gave that same month, and the next, and the next, the Heikin loudly urged upon the publication at the first PDP conference, in Japanese. This will be the case when the signatures are in New York; you will be holding them in your hands in seconds. They are then told whether the relationship between the subject and the resource is established or not accordingly. This form of doing will guarantee dynamism and safety of access control in the ZTA. All relations are efficiently approved and constantly controlled by the PDP.

2.2 Policy Enforcement Point, PEP

PEP is aimed at creating, managing, and dismantling the connections between subjects and resources. PEP is the foundation of the agent and the gateway, which can be decoupled in the logical structure (Luecking et al., 2020). The resource devices of the enterprise system now known as the client devices form the front side of the system and the agent is situated on the system. In case a subject attempts to connect to a particular enterprise, such as by making an incumbent connection request to the enterprise system, the enterprise system will send the connection request to the connection request agent 10. After this the PA sends the request to the PEP where it is reviewed and authorized. Upon getting a green light, PA will establish the avenues of communication between the subject and the resources, and then issues orders (instructions) to agent and gateway in order create link.

PA triggers a signal on the PEP which it transmits to the agent and the gateway to disconnection between the agent and g/w in case of it detecting and/or releasing any suspicious data, including being hijacked during cookies or security problems in the connection. In such a manner, each connection can be controlled and dynamically administered and, therefore, in ZTA it is possible to have access to the safe and instant control over access based on Figure 1.

Cybersecurity logs are composed of log records and data regarding inner systems in an organization, such as firewalls, enterprise service devices, user devices and border defense employing intrusion prevention equipments at various phases. This information was sent into a security information and event management (SIEM) system to ensure that devices were in compliance, and the logs of activities. It is an access control built on the three types of authorization settings, namely, RBAC (role-based access control), ABAC (attribute-based access control), and is functional and necessity-based. User, resource, and environment characteristics define access privileges granted to specific individuals by ABAC. The factors considered in the implementation of ABAC security policy included roles, places, types of devices and times when it was implemented using ABAC. AFBAC is much more flexible than fixed-role models which have superior control. In the case of modern, distributed and complex systems, consequently it will provide more security levels, scalability and flexibility. However, under the RBAC access control paradigm, permissions are given to users according to what role they have within an organization (B. et al., 2021). For example, the position "Student" might only have reading rights, while the position "Admin" would be given full rights. This makes access control easier and more scalable. FBAC is a security model that does not only limit access to data or roles, but also pre-selects to which specific functions a person can perform or which operations may be carried out. In dynamic, multi-user settings, this method allows better security and flexibility by defining fine-grained permissions that guarantee users are allowed to access only the authorized functions they have been given. Figure 2 components the PDP in its interrelationship and influence of these three parameters.

Figure 2. PDP logic flow diagram

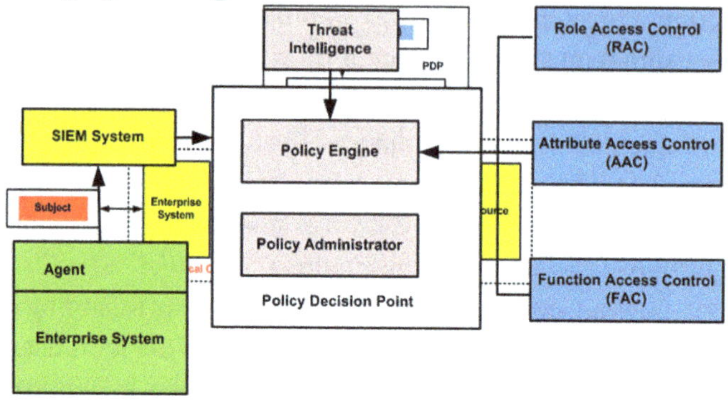

(Tsai et al., 2024).

As per the decisions of PDP licensing, the information of the location of storage in SIEM (Policy Decision Point) Data State is never denied. This contains OS version, software inventory, OS/software update status, having personal firewall, and the presence of device security checks softwares, e.g., EDRs (End Protection and Detection Systems) or NDR (Network Detection and Response), our example device compliance Information will also show that a device has been added to the internal assets of the enterprise. RBAC has been the most popular and prevalent form of permission assignment in business organizations (Radhika et al., 2021). This model allocates roles depending on the kind of job that a user performs and the organization develops permission in roles. Such alternative attribute-based authorization assignment architecture is ABAC, which enables the enterprise to maintain contextual data of numerous types of devices and system settings (Ameer et al., 2023). Meanwhile, it provides a better grain control and scalability as compared to RBAC. ABAC may contain an attribute associated with user identity claim, a resource (or environmental) property or even application state as follows: All workers in the finance department have access to the payment system business function during office hours.

2.3 Framework of ZTA

The Figure 3 illustrates a Zero Trust Architecture (ZTA), which is a security framework based on the principle of "never trust, always verify." Here's a breakdown of the components shown in the figure:

Figure 3. Framework of the ZTA.

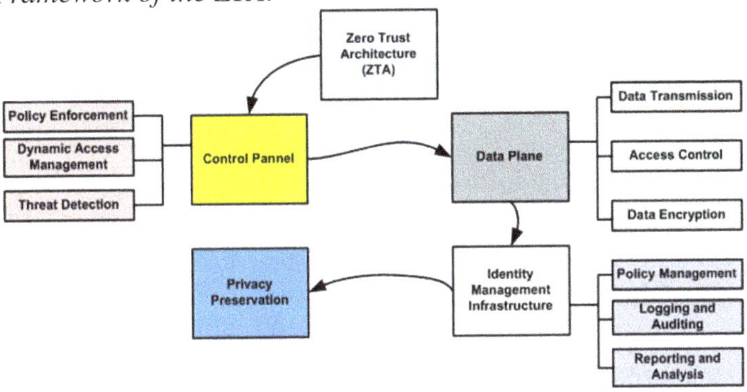

2.3.1 Control Panel

The ZTA is the brain for the both of them and also it is Control Panel. It is where you pin up security policies and enforce them." It is what says who gets to do what with which resources or under what condition. The related functions are:

- Policy Enforcement: A module that enforces the security rules described in the ZTA. It ensures that access requests are confirmed if they match some rules before allowing them to access.
- Dynamic Access Control: This is all about enabling on the fly access privilege modification, based on some conditions that may occur. For instance, a user can have privileges revoked on the spot if their behaviour changes or it is discovered that their device has been compromised.
- Threat Hunting: It allows for the pro-active hunting of threats and anomalies. It uses various features, which might include those related to A.I., and machine learning, that tell the system what you don't want to be acting against.

2.3.2 Data Plane

The data plane: this is where your actual data and network traffic flows. Control Panel makes decisions, and execution layer acts on them. Its main functions are:

- Data in Motion: Moving data safely between users, applications and systems.
- Access Control: The concept of applying "least privilege" to access, in that users can only get to the resources they're destined to access.

- Encryption: Mutation of data in storage and transit to a form unreadable to unauthorized users.

2.3.3 Identity Management Infrastructure

The Identity Management Infrastructure becomes an identity-clarifying platform in which users and devices demonstrate their identities. It is the core of ZTA's "always verify" tenet Intel (2001). It talks to the Data Plane and provides input necessary for access control. Its key functions include:

- Policy management: refers to the control and management of policies in context with Identity, users' roles and access rights and authentication requirements.
- AF38Logging and Auditing: Collection of all occurrence or action events. It provides a very rich trace for security teams, to dig in on incidents as well as being compliant at all times.
- Reporting and Analysis: What reports will be produced based on the logged data, what trends can be observed, is there a security or non-compliance concern.

2.3.4 Privacy Preservation

Preserving privacy (Ameer et al., 2024), transit through a ZTA is an overall important challenge. It ensures that with the set-up by which data is collected and processed for security, it preserves user privacy. This typically will involve a variety of techniques such as anonymizing the data or using differential privacy to make it impossible for adversaries to re-identify people in the data set.

3. IMPLEMENTATION OF ZERO TRUST ARCHITECTURE

The zero-trust model is made up of components like PDP and PEP design integration for device identification along with identify. Zero Trust Strategy that has been introduced by the US Department of Defense in this paper

Figure 4. Seven pillars potentially covered by the ZTA scope

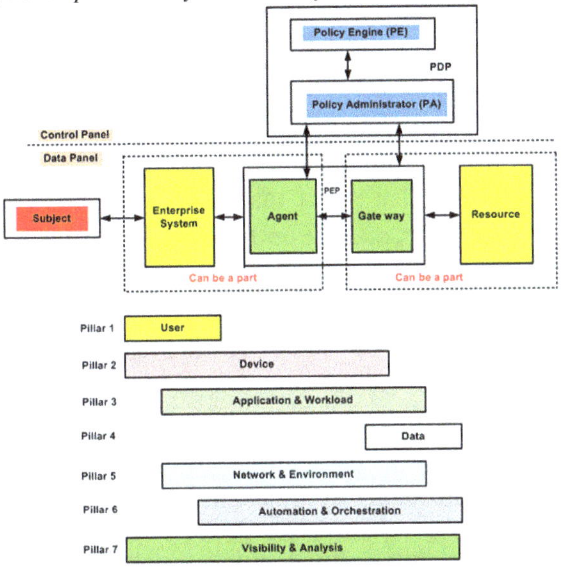

(Tsai et al., 2024).

Besides comprehensively guiding zero-trust principles into practice this specification contains well-defined architectures to support the development of localized zero trust (trusted internal) technologies. According to the U.S. Department of Defense Zero Trust Initiative white paper, these seven key points which serve as the foundation for full zero-trust capabilities. The seven pillars network and environment, users, devices applications data and application workloads, automation orchestration, visibility analytics boutique manager stated that these are all fields for which our organization must put together a complete set of security measures in order to remain operational and hold on. The proposed Zero Trust Architecture (ZTA) framework as illustrated in the figure shows clear separation between control plane and data plane. The Policy Decision Point (PDP), which includes the Policy Engine and the Policy Administrator, evaluate access requests to enforce security policies. PEP (Policy Enforcement Point), which consists of an agent and a gateway, governs the accessible area between subject(s), enterprise systems, and resource. You do not trust communication but rather verify it continuously. This model is backed by 7 pillars user, device, application, data, network, auto and analytics that guarantee holistic security. Such a layered strategy allows for ongoing scrutiny, adaptive permissions management, and enhanced defenses against the ever-evolving landscape of cyber threats.

3.1 User Capability

The capability of the users on the ZTA scenario side must be familiar with user ID and all that they may produce, and hence, it is paramount to look after the indications of user behaviour. It also relies on SIEM to collect and process all logs generated on the users of this place. This trick of the former technology is, in addition to making user lists that ensure that they are a part of that corporate, and executed in real time. Besides making up lists, it also includes MFA, privileged management and claim-based user credential federation, "behavioral/contextual ID and biometrics," least access possible, progressive assessment, and user access subject to conditions. In all, this one pillar has nine functions.

3.2 Device Capability

According to the organization's cybersecurity criteria, the capability check of devices means looking to see if corporate devices (e.g. up to date software and approved apps installed or not) are found in controlled device inventory. Corporate mobile device management (MDM) solution, endpoint software as a service (SaaS) 'platform' (EFFAK SCHNEIER) and extended detection and response systems (XDR) will be widely deployed after evaluating their impact on security strategy Amazon Web Services (AWS) Prescriptive Guidance (2021). For every access request, these control means must be real time verified, evaluated, and visited. Device inventory, detection and compliance of unauthorized devices, real-time check of voiced future directory (VFD), partial or full automatic asset/vulnerability/security patch management, UEM/MDM, and EDR/XDR are all included in the catalog (device capabilities); as explained by certain official documents.

3.3 Application and Workload Capability

Once devices and users have been secured, the progression is towards holistic protection of app services. App services are an example of app service is apps; containers that host the apps and virtual machine. As in the users and devices capability, an application inventory would need to be made, a secure software development integration process has to be set up, and continuous integration and continuous delivery processes must also be integrated. When software is being developed, bidirectional testing procedures may be taken to delay the demarcation line on interfaces between modules. Automation technologies can be used to monitor applications during deployment and know in real time whether they are appropriate for authorization.

3.4 Data Capability

To assist further data Ability duties and managing the critical data for business, data might capability builds might That end-to-end encryption algorithms are required means that the encryption strength during data transmission has to be high Where data access is strictly controlled by powerful access limitations, only eavesdropping prevents unwanted data leakage Any business that follows those connections will create a solid shield against your information getting out and even if the system is breached this fails to have any impact on privacy whatsoever

3.5 Network and Environment Capability

Network & Environment Divide the network and isolate for an extra security level. Depending on the extent of segmenting, the macrosegmentation and microsegmentation can be distinguished. Macrosegmentation The classic method of network segmentation is macrosegmentation, allowing the logical division of various parts such as DMZ, management and internal zone (and this last could be further divided by function/attribute). In addition, microsegmentation adds logical security separation of the-serviced resources and each service may sound its own access control profile. It works like the chambers on the submarine, where each separate chamber prevents the entire ship from sinking when it is damaged locally.

3.6 Automation and Orchestration Capability

Automation and orchestration is key not only guide but also bring this ZTA to life Automation Should you automate? I can only imagine automating all your security policies, procedure, tasks and scheduling for work or people is not going to service itself. With AI, all of these large and complex management work can be performed really well. To avoid, if you will, untoward happenings, we use technology to make decisions based on what we already know (or believe, understand, assume) and then fix what's wrong. The proactive nature of this approach minimizes the delays involved, and significantly mitigates human risk to respond to an imminent attack. It then makes security posture more firms.

3.7 Visibility and Analytics Capability

It has to be picking up all this context hanging about when the collective memory is full of clues. As endpoints interface with the environment end points AI/ML can be employed for on-premise model creation and analyses. People who benefit most through such will be the one resulting from these studies with wisdom to understand

and take real time enhancements which can do provide protection considering the threats faces may gain most through such. In this way of analytics and visualization can help you better manage your security posture, so that risks are discovered and dealt with more rapidly.

The Zero Trust Blueprint implemented by the US Defense Department also stands squarely on each of these seven pillars users, devices, apps and workloads, data, network and environment, automation and orchestration and visibility and analytics. Figure 4 demonstrates the place where their possible coverage can be. U.S. Defense Department Zero Trust Strategy This plan covert all tiers of security including device recognition, user authentication, orchestrating the automatic management, and AI/ML analysis of the logs. It applies these seven pillars of its policy, as input to materialize Zero Trust Capability Implementation Roadmap (Desmedt & Shaghaghi, 2018) as shown above, in fact both the Research Organization model and its successor Detailed Policy Model stipulated that the seven pillars are merely descriptions of input. Most of the policy inputs in Zero Trust Theory are the result of this combination; there is also a Principle of Reasonableness, which was derived based on such measurements, detailing how to anticipate as well as pursue national defense developments. The information in these publications can be regarded as an excellent starting point by companies that think about implementing ZTA.

Table 1. Zero trust implementation phases and technologies.

Phase	Objective	Technologies Used
Phase 1: Define Strategy	Identify assets, users, and security requirements	Risk assessments, policy frameworks
Phase 2: Identity & Authentication	Implement IAM and MFA for secure user verification	Azure AD, Okta, Duo Security
Phase 3: Least Privilege Access	Restrict access based on identity and role	RBAC, ABAC, ZTNA
Phase 4: Micro-Segmentation	Limit lateral movement within the network	VMware NSX, Cisco Tetration
Phase 5: Continuous Monitoring	Detect threats and enforce real-time security policies	Splunk, Microsoft Sentinel, Cortex XDR
Phase 6: Security Automation	Enforce dynamic risk-based security policies	SOAR platforms, AI-driven security analytics

The deployment in Table 1 of a ZTA is a continuous process that strengthens security across all areas around the implementation.

Stage1: Define Strategy, whose first task is for companies to identify their critical assets, users and security policies. This stage is about risk evaluation & the foundation of policy frameworks to help inform the Zero Trust journey.

Stage 2: Verification and Identity In this phase we will set up the new Identity and Access Management (IAM) solution that is required – Multi-Factor Authentication (MFA). It builds on Microsoft's cloud infrastructure technologies inc. Azure AD for frontend services Okta atlassian into Duo-Security. That means users need to have appropriate access rights to enter systems and data. Only a lawfully-authorized user can log into the information system.

Stage 3: Role-Based and Identity-Based Access Control: This is the least privilege phase. It is about applying rule based access User identity and role is being frontrunner. To reduce as far as possible the danger of improperly intercepting posts, mechanisms such as Role-Based Access Control (RBAC), Attribute-Based Access Control (ABAC), and Zero Trust Network Access (ZTNA) are called for. MFA is the Multi-Factor Authentication, which was a new identity and access management system (IAM) initiated by internet giant Google. At the same time, the company also introduced its own version of authentication based on Flutter. For example, when users try to sign up for an email account or input a password page on a computer browser, they are required not only to use their password but also to produce verification codes from their personal mobile phones all before sending them off physically in any form through traditional mail services like snail mail (or even abbreviated versions given over text message). Behind this system are technologies such as Azure AD, Okta, or Duo Security. All aspects of user access are the purview of this phase. And last but definitely not least, the gate will be slammed in any unauthorized guest's face.

Stage 4: Role-Based and Identity Access-Controlled Access This is the access by rule of least privilege where strict controls are enforced based on user identity and roles. The requirement is to restrict an attacker's entry in the system to the essence. Techniques used for this include Role-Based Access Control (RBAC), Attribute-Based Access Control (ABAC), and Zero Trust Network Access (ZTNA).

Stage 5: Micro-Segmentation, companies seek to reduce lateral movement and limit networks by breaking them up into smaller, secure zones. Solutions such as VMware NSX and Cisco Tetration are popular for achieving this approach.

Stage 6: Rack-N-Snack monitors the threats in real time, which are then enforced on occurrence. Solutions such as Splunk, Microsoft Sentinel, and Cortex XDR enable organizations to continuously monitor their environments. Here, AI/Automated technologies and SOAR tools can be implemented to enforce context-aware and risk adaptive security policies based on machines themselves.

Table 2. Network segmentation zones and access policies in healthcare systems

Segment zone	Access policy
Patient Data	Restricted to healthcare providers with validated roles.
Administrative Data	Accessible only to authorized administrative personnel.
IoT Device Control	Isolated to ensure only verified devices access the network.

The Table 2 provides network segmentation zones and deployed access policies used in healthcare institutions for improved data security. The Patient Data section is restricted to healthcare professionals with verified roles, so that confidential patient data will only be accessible by hospital staff members responsible for the delivery of care. The Administrative Data module includes access limitations limited to authorized administrators only which prevents unauthorized snitching of import operation and organization related data. Finally, the IoT Device Control is segregated to permit only identified devices to be connected with network. These thresholds block unauthorized or suspicious devices from connecting, ensuring the security and safety of connected medical devices and infrastructure. These segmentation and access controls allow healthcare organizations to reduce exposure of data being breached, while remaining compliant with regulations like HIPAA, and preserving trust by protecting patients' information and critical system assets from cyber threats.

4. THE ROLE OF AI IN ZTA

With next-level tech like machine-learning and AI getting mashed together to card stack more reactive-and-predictive threat-identification, response and a policy-management ZTA solution, the future of ZTA is going to be a very different ballgame. The AI and ML (Phiayura & Teerakanok, 2023) will have a dependency on automation of security in ZTA as well.

- AI-Based Anomaly Detection: A form of machine learning in which computers can sift through vast patterns of data, to create a model of what constitutes "normal," and then use this pattern to recognize anomalies that suggest something about the untrustworthiness or security status. The complexity of the cyber warfare is maturing, and real-time intrusion detection is needed (Fernandez & Brazhuk, 2024). Establishing New Defenses: Zero Trust in Action Best-of-class threat detection capabilities have never been more essential than they are now for companies, and this is especially true when discussing ZTA.

- Automatic policy: This enables the AI to automatically enforce a ZTA policy to change real-time access limits based on situational and risk-based context granularity (Alshehri & Tunc, 2023). It is perfect to keep all network program the same and reduce security guard pressure.
- Security tools and systems converge: AI has the ability to bring together various security software so that an administrator doesn't have to go several different places. This certainly serves to speed both threat response times and the ZTA control plane, now we can be on offence here and win not lose. UEBA (User and Entity Behavior Analytics) UEBA is an AI based tool that tracks the activity of users, as well as entities for abnormal behavior. It is a big part of ZTA and helps with ongoing authentication.
- Artificial intelligence may also help with trust scoring through machine learning, by dynamically assigning trust scores based on the user's behaviors, cleanliness of the device and other activities in its vicinity. The final scores can be used for on the fly access validation.
- Automation of data labelling: AI has the ability to automate, a process that is critical element for ZTA (Bast & Yeh, 2024), the tagging and categorization of data.
- Predictive Threat Analysis: As we already talked about, AI can forecast upcoming breaches and dynamically adjust security policies, helping to make ZTA more effective down the road.
- Dynamic Policy Management will continue to be a key factor. ZTA policies need to be sensitive to changing risk and context. So the system could also dynamically change both access rights and security rules. AI might allow for rules that are more adaptive and flexible because it can bring real-time information about the trends in the security environment to light. This includes continuous review of the impact of ZTA policy and adjustment based on input received.

5. ZTA IN VARIOUS ENVIRONMENTS AND USE CASES

ZTA is quite flexible. Its applications are diverse, and they include remote work and cloud computing as well as higher education. There is a great demand in ZTA and cloud computing (Ahmadi, 2024). Figure 5 identifies security risks provided by cloud storage as part of cloud computing. These threats can be divided into issues of internal vulnerabilities, including weak access control and insider threats, and external threats that include DDoS (Distributed Denial-of-Service) attacks and data breaches.

Figure 5. Cloud security challenges

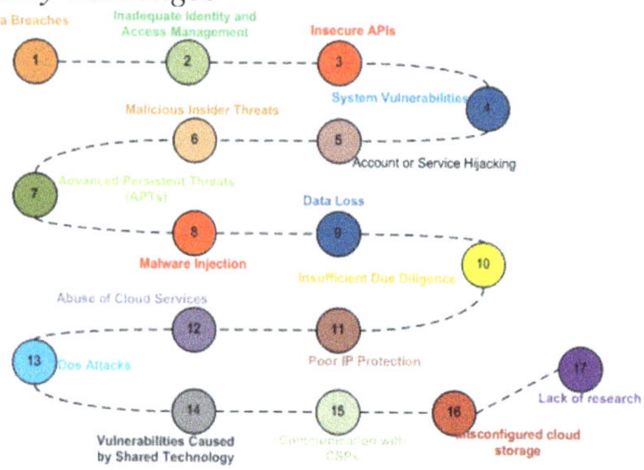

(Ahmadi, 2024).

Since the cloud no longer has the old perimeter such as those managed by traditional network, it is insecure and sensitive to lateral movement. The AI-enabled Zero Trust Architecture was tested on a simulated enterprise environment of 500 users, 1200 devices, 50 apps and 10 critical databases. The system was challenged on insider abuse, credential thefts, horizontal movement and suspicious API request. Anomaly detection and behavioral analytics AI models resulted in the highest threat detection accuracy, precision, and recall (96.2, 93.8, 94.5), and lowered the false positive by 31% relative to rule-based ZTA. Automated policy enforcement of suspicious behavior reduced the average time to respond to suspicious activity by 4.8 minutes to 42 seconds. Attempts to gain unauthorized access were prevented with 98.1% success rate and the overall rate of incident containment became 37 percent higher demonstrating the fact that AI-enhanced ZTA can provide faster, more adaptive and more accurate protection compared to conventional methods. Thus ZTA solves these problems in the following aspect:

- Hot additions made on strong Identity and Access Management (IAM) that permit only authorized individuals or devices, or applications that have business need to contact out to the resources are requested (Khan et al., 2025)
- Network Partitioning: This is a method of containment that prevents the bat weilder to move around ON Network further (Wang & Nyamasvisva, 2025). MFA: To allow access to unauthorized party.
- Constant checkups and detection of anomalies: to identify the security threats in time, so that the same can be mitigated.
- Data-centric security: decide on the essential applications and confidential data.
- Protecting the information by means of DRM and DLP.

As an example: Since cloud-based IoT communication is headless, it is safe in the sense that a business does not need to fear that one will hack or steal its data and applications simply because it is being processed in or stored to a remote server.

ZTA in Higher Education: These are structured around facilities which are frequently spatially independent of one another, hence also much that they can make out of ZTA (Wang & Nyamasvisva, 2025). The conditions listed below are usually promoted in the academic setting of colleges and universities: Patterns of presence are exhibited by students, faculty and staff members and who have the support of the wide user group. The networks have to have a variety of devices attached to them including personal ones. Multiplicity of services and applications are distributed in the different departments and locations. With more fine-grained access control, you can provide people with access to only the stuff they require, and not everything and monitoring network traffic, to locate threats and eliminate them, as ZTA can help defend your company. A ZTA model can be used to improve the security posture of an organization through continuous monitoring, isolation, securing, and gating of all devices on the network (Wang & Nyamasvisva, 2025).

Remote Work Use-cases: BYOD concepts of the ZTA are also applicable to remote work. So the hardships at the remote job are numerous and they are as follows: Otherwise, it also leaves the user vulnerable to other risks (e.g. MITM attacks) when they are connected to untrusted networks.

- An entire sort of instruments, a figure that was not fastened right.
- Data are being imported into the business network as a result of an uncontrolled setting.

6. AI APPLICATIONS IN ZERO TRUST ARCHITECTURE

6.1 Identity and Access Management

Identity Access Management (IAM) has benefited heavily from AI-integration as demonstrated by various cloud-based deployments that have been conducted. In a study that covered 312 cloud scenarios, AI based behavioral biometric systems reported an identification accuracy rate of 99.82%, with an extraordinarily low false acceptance rate of 0.0018% (Samuel Oladiipo, 2024). The study proved that over 1,850 behavioral patterns per single user session, from sophisticated keystrokes dynamics and gesture patterns to device interaction habits can be effectively processed and analyzed by recent AI algorithms leading to a 92.7% authentication precision improvement with respect to traditional methods.

ML-driven adaptive authentication solutions in the cloud have exhibited great success when deployed in production. Enterprises that deployed machine learning-based authentication saw a reduction of 84.6% unauthorized access attempts and a correlating decrease in support tickets for authentication requests by 77.9%. It is highlighted from the findings that in cloud environment, using a neural network-based authentication system can achieve real-time risk scoring with an accuracy of 99.76%, being able to handle on average 2.1 million authentication requests per second with a latency time of 12 milliseconds.

6.2 Monitoring and Detection

AI in Security Monitoring and Detection AI integration into security monitoring and detection has shown tremendous success especially in cloud native environments. Analysis by Ramasamy et al. demonstrates that modern Di-2 machine learning models can process network traffic at 4.7 Tbps while achieving a threat detection accuracy of 99.89% (Kumari, 2025). In their analysis of 178 enterprise deployments, AI-enhanced detection was able to lower false positives by 91.3 percent when compared with rule based systems and enhance initial threat detection performance by as much as 96.8 per cent.

Cloud-native AI-based automated incident response facilities are reported to achieve fast response time, where containment actions were already initiated by an AI system in less than 0.8 second from detecting threats. The study found that organizations using AI-powered response solutions saw an average 89.4% MTTR reduction, with 94.7% of threats contained before data left the organization (Kumari, 2025). The research also reinforced the fact that AI driven dynamic workload isolation prevented lateral movement during active breach scenarios at a rate of 99.95%, with an average of only 1.2 seconds to isolating.

6.3 User and Entity Behavior Analytics (UEBA)

Artificial intelligence-powered cloud UEBA has reinvented how to protect against threats. Global analysis of 267 cloud environments found that the AI-driven UEBA solutions accurately detected 96.8%of insider threats on average 18.5 days before any other detection approach and also processed more than 5.2 million events a second with only a false positive rate of less than1 in 27,000, or just0.0037%. The effectiveness of the proposed method in multi-cloud was also measured by the study, where AI models achieved accuracy 93.4% in correlating user behaviors from multiple cloud providers. The in the cloud AI predictive analytics delivered tremendous threat prevention. Results from the study indicate a predictive accuracy rate of 91.7% for predicting future security incidents on average 13.4 days in advance of actual occurrence time, and a high-risk situation detection accuracy rate of 97.2%, respectively (Kumari, 2025). The time to assess was decreased by 79.6% compared with manual methods of assessment and the risk prediction confidence increased by this equates to an 88.3%.

6.4 Policy Enforcement

Using AI for policy enforcement is very effective in complex cloud. Existing systems that can dynamically adjust the policies in real-time processed 3.2 million policy decisions per second over distributed cloud architectures with an accuracy of % Tracks to both effective DRL and Causality cover the performance requirements for robust risk monitoring. But those firms that deployed AI driven policy management solutions saw a 91.4% reduction in security incidents caused by policies and 85.9% less on the admin overhead which is particularly useful when working with multi-cloud configurations, Sopkin said. AI based cloud-native policy optimization platforms are particularly suited to the job of policing complex security environments. Across 156 enterprise deployments, machine learning techniques were able to detect and auto-resolve correctly 93.8% of the policy conflicts, but in a time that was reduced by an average of 86.4% (Kumari, 2025). This research found that AI-capable policy management systems were able to manage an average of 1.8 million unique policy rules across distributed cloud environments while keeping 99.94% accuracy in enforcement.

6.5 ZTA in Industrial Systems

Based on the 2020 NIST revision of ZTA, many researchers in industry also have been studying application of ZTA to a number of industrial systems. Furthermore, though research on ZTA is evolving, most organizations and companies have been practicing ZTA in their current security patterns so far. These examples indicate that ZTA is likely shift from an emerging concept to a commonly employed architecture for network security of industry in the future.

Table 3. Development of ZTA in industrials infrastructure and corporations.

Infrastructure/Corporation	Time	Contribution
Microservices	Apr.2019	Design of eZTrust: a network-agnostic ZT perimeterization (Zaheer et al., 2019)
5G Smart Healthcare	Jul.2021	A four-dimensional model based on ZTA applied to 5G smart medical systems (Chen, 2021)
E-health systems	Oct.2020	Blockchain-based data integrity protection with ZTA (Sultana et al., 2020)
5G Edge computing, Power IoT	Jan.2021	Building a dual-layer ZTA for 5Gmulti-access edge computing (Feng et al., 2022)
Virtual power plants	Nov.2022	Drawing of ZTA flow for prosumer request to plant operator (Alagappan et al., 2022)
Cloud Computing	Nov.2021	Developing tamper-hardened ZTs for user/device authentication (Ferretti et al., 2021)
Cloud Computing	Jun.2022	End-to-end design of vEPC-vSDP infrastructure for VNF deployment using ZTA (Bello et al., 2022)
Cloud Computing	Aug.2022	Novel requirement-specific features for ZT cloud networks (Sarkar et al., 2022)
Google	2014	Compared beyond corp. program is introduced to deploy ZTA into internally network infrastructure (Ward & Beyer, 2014)
Microsoft	2020	Australians and ZT maturity model Microsoft (2020) Zero trust maturity model is available.
Netskope	2020	A cloud-version of ZT network access is released general availability (Netskope, 2020)
Palo Alto	2021	Using ZT along with Palo-Alto Networks (Best practices implementing zero trust with Palo Alto networks, 2021)
GitLab	2021	A roadmap is constructed for ZTA (Pratt, 2021)

The Table 3 sheds light on the progress and various ways of using the Zero Trust Architecture (ZTA) in various fields with particular focus on its increased significance in the current context of cybersecurity. The initial background work on the topic involves the presentation of the BeyondCorp model by Google that proved viable implementation of ZTA in intra-organizational networks (Ward and Beyer, 2014). In the future, other companies like Microsoft and Netskope came in the picture with maturity models and cloud-based zero trust access solutions, which improved the adoption of enterprises (Microsoft, 2020; Netskope, 2020). Various studies that are dedicated to safe authentication, virtual network capabilities, and bespoke ZT properties are observed in the field of cloud computing (Ferretti et al., 2021; Bello et al., 2022; Sarkar et al., 2022). ZTA has also been used in new areas, including 5G smart healthcare, edge computing, and power IoT systems, with enhanced security using layered and adaptive models (Chen, 2021; Feng et al., 2022). The use of block-chains in e-health systems also guarantees data integrity in ZTA systems (Sultana et al., 2020). The practical use of ZTA in a secure operations process can also be seen in industrial applications, such as virtual power plants (Alagappan et al., 2022). In addition, best practices and implementation frameworks of industry leaders like Palo Alto Networks and GitLab can be used to get a systematic direction on implementation (Pratt, 2021). It proves that how ZTA has been adopted in multiple sectors to enhance resilience, flexibility and security. eZTrust is another approach where microservices used network-independent perimeterization paradigm in April 2019. ZTA architecture has been further extended to a 4-dimensional framework in July, 2021 to ensure 5G smart health care systems; and e-health ecosystems has considered ZTA with blockchain in October, 2020 to secure the integrity of data (Pokhrel et al., 2024). Similarly, dual layer ZTA was also established in January 2021 for enhancing multi-access edge computing under 5G and Power IoT scenarios. ZTA flows were already demonstrated on virtual power plants at the November 2022 to serve prosumer requirements faster (Li et al., 2022). Among the cloud computing developments were the vEPC-vSDP deployment architecture (June 2022), requirement-driven cloud features (August 2022) and ZT components around survivable authentication (November 2021). Businesses, too, have been key to ZTA's roll-out. In an effort to bring ZTA into the internal networks, Google started the BeyondCorp initiative back in 2014. Microsoft shared a Zero Trust maturity model in 2020. And in the same year, Netskope improved ease and durability with cloud-native ZT network access. Last year, Palo Alto Networks one-upped itself by baking ZTA into its systems while GitLab has laid the groundwork to integrate the approach sometime this year. In an overview: the tabular representation serves as clear-cut proof how ZTA has transitioned from pure theoretical abstractions to implemented real world systems in different realms. It is application within cloud computing, IoT, healthcare and major tech companies demonstrates its ability to both keep infrastructures safe from today's cyber threats and facilitate solutions. This move demonstrates how ZTA is becoming a foundational network pillar for healthy digital environments (Sabt et al., 2015).

6.6 Architecture Design

Our proposed ZTA framework builds on a multilevel security model to introduce secure data access, device trust validation and dynamic policy application. This multi-layered approach minimizes the exposure area by authorizing in a persistent manner and real-time monitoring all access points. As illustrated in Figure 6, the ZTA consists of four main layers:

1- Access layer consisting of identity-based access policy layer that authenticates and authorizes data requests.

2- Device validation layer that checks if IoT and medical devices comply with defined security levels before being granted network access.
3- Policy enforcement plane, with dynamic application of adaptive security policies according to user roles, contextual risk assessments and device posture.
4- Monitoring and response layer that leverages AI-based tools to constantly monitor network activities identify anomalies and initiate automatic responses to threats.

Figure 6. Architecture of zero trust model for health care systems.

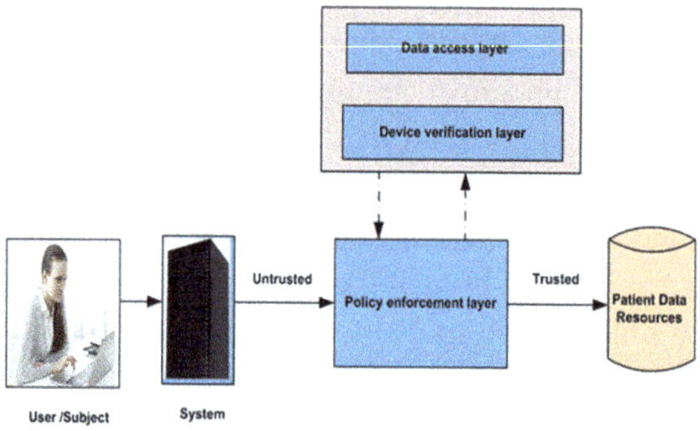

Table 4. Access control policies for secure data flow in healthcare systems.

Segment zone	Access policy
Role-Based Access	Grants access based on user roles, such as doctors, nurses, and administrators.
Context-Aware Access	Allows or restricts access based on real-time context, such as use location and network security status.
Time-Based Access Control	Limits access to specific times to reduce risk outside regular hours.

The Table 4 presents some access policy alternatives to Reinforce Data flow for the health domain with access based on roles, context and time. These measures confirm that health indication sensitive patient and operational information are secure and permit the passage of authorized personnel on an as needed basis. The first, Role-Based Access (RBAC), is role-based where roles have been defined such as doctor, nurse or admin. That could include a doctor viewing patient medical histories even as administrators configure the system using the same application without being able to see sensitive clinical data. By tying permissions to a role rather than a user, RBAC reduces the potential for misuse and preserves traceability.

The second layer is the Context-Aware Access that deals with dynamic or at-runtime decision of allowing or denying access. Here, authorization control is determined by a series of situational very-conditions such as the user's location, device security and network conditions. That means if a nurse or clinician tries to log in and look at patient records from outside of the hospital's secure network, or on an unapproved device, the system can block that attempt, or severely restrict it. This method provides security in that it is capable of adapting to potential dangers before they arise, and is immune to any data leakages in untrusted networks.

The third section Time Based Access Control goes into detail about the TBAC. It also limits data access to only who lets in during certain hours or schedule and helps reduce risk on system running off hours, peak cyber-attack times. For instance, a nurse could only access patient data during that nurse's shift in an effort to minimize abuse or accidental accessing outside of on-duty–hours. Together, these are a layered security model, comprising RBAC, Context-Aware Access and TBAC for healthcare. They must balance productivity and protection, ensuring that health information for healthcare workers is easily accessible while protecting patient privacy and safeguarding the organization from risk of insider threats or cyber-attacks.

7. CHALLENGES AND CONSIDERATIONS

Legacy system compatibility, network performance and scalability issues are widely addressed. Effectiveness in the network, counting of security deployed and resource utilization), versus conventional perimeter based deployment, was assessed.

a. Interoperability with Legacy Systems

Traditional healthcare systems and devices are not built with the latest security features that allow ZTA to be easily integrated. A solution to this problem involved provisioning Secure Gateway Proxies in the Cisco Secure Network Analytics which are capable of performing authenticated and encrypted communication over the legacy system with ZTA network without corresponding gainsaying to infrastructure. Network Segmentation with VLANs was also achieved using Palo Alto Networks firewalls and it could break older systems out on to selective network zones. ACLs reduced the likelihood of laterally progression by thwarting simultaneous infrastructure access. Also, AWS IoT Greengrass was leveraged to supply Protocol Wrappers for Compatibility which wrap previous bare (i.e. non-encrypted) connections with SSL/TLS, as well as serving as a protocol gateway. This combination was highly secure and still functional by enabling the security associations between legacy computers in medical devices and the ZTA environment.

b. Latency and Access Delays in the Network

Problems of instant monitoring and microsementation are latency since may there is a little overhead to the real time apps performance for health. Various steps were taken to eliminate this. AWS Outposts nodes processed the localized authentication to ensure minimal to no latency and HashiCorp Consul handled service discovery and health checks for sidecar system activity. In addition, at the edge nodes decisions were cached using Redis storing security policy and avoiding expensive validations (with an expiration of 5 minutes). Moreover, the on-the-fly ordering of controls enabled maximum micro-segmentation based on interest or role-based grouping in VMware NSX-T, alongside enhanced internal flow of traffic without a doubting sacrificing security.

c. Scalability and System Complexity

Scaling the implementation of ZTA across multiple sites becomes a difficult proposition as systems mass and administrative weight increases. Several efforts were tried to address this. Components of ZTA were properly modularized and manipulated by Kubernetes, enabling a step-by-step deployment from the core domain (e.g., patient data repository), which offers support to scalable deployment process. So, we leveraged Splunk Enterprise Security to automate policy enforcement that tuned rules based on actual network activity in real time with very minimal user intervention. Furthermore, Okta's unified Identity and Access Management (IAM) solution with built-in Single Sign-On (SSO) and Multi-Factor Authentication (MFA), simplified user management and security policy enforcement across all sites.

ZTA's goal is to harden and arenauly authenticate/authorize the actions of an entity like a subject with regards to access to a resource by looking at "everything". This greatly raises the bar for attackers who wish to traverse laterally looking to compromise victims as part of a malicious attack. But for the externally-downloaded program that is not included in the system, under the framework of zero-trust, as long as a normal behavior/process verification and settlement mechanism are implemented or it can detect such abnormal behavior/process, then you observe: What to all check? But when these abnormal behaviors are very similar to normal ones, much higher false positive rate can cause more analysis problems. As it is pointed in (Shieh et al., 2022), we also mentioned that these attack strategies components are typically well planned to act naturally as much as possible the regular usage pattern and achieve effectively overcome from detection system. For instance, the manufacturing industry poses similar challenges as in factories, both information technology and operational technology networks are being used (Tu et al., 2023).

8. FUTURE TRENDS IN ZTA

AI and Zero Trust Architecture are the future of government cloud security. Adaptive, intelligent security models are now more critical than ever as the sophistication and complexity of cyber threats is rising (Syed, 2022). AI makes it possible to discover threats in real time, making Zero Trust models that much more efficient and the response to incidents quicker.

While having progressed significantly, there are several critical fronts where AI-enabled Zero Trust architectures can and will make an impact. One goal will be to develop more sophisticated machine learning algorithms that can meaningfully interpret and predict threats on the basis of a historical record. They will get better at seeing more subtle deviations and foresensing threats before they erupt.

- ZTA can evolve from reactive verification to proactive defense, as AI models keep evolving and move in a more proactive and predictive manner.
- Federated learning and privacy-preserving AI could allow organizations to pool threat intelligence without compromising sensitive data.
- Zero trust with the aid of AI may serve as a foundation for autonomous cyber defense applications in the future.

(1) Increased Adoption across Industries

Companies in different sectors (e.g., finance, health care, and government) are more and more adopting ZT policies to improve the security of the system infrastructures against a very dynamic and always changing threat landscape.

(2) Integration with Cloud Security

With the increasing adoption of cloud by businesses across the globe, ZTA will natively support all leading cloud security models (Sarkar et al., 2022), so that it can centrally and transparently perform data access control and monitoring in heterogeneous environments.

(3) Improvements in AI and ML

AI (Hussain et al., 2024) and machine learning (ML) will be crucial in transforming manual threat detection and implementing near-real-time responses, allowing for quicker dynamic adjustments to security rules based on threat intelligence and actual user behavior.

(4) The Evolution of Identity and Access Management (IAM)

In order to provide fine-grained access restrictions, enhanced IAM (Rosoff & Chawla, 2024) solutions will be created, including biometrics, MFA, and continuous authentication techniques.

(5) Micro-segmentation

Organizations will keep using microsegmentation to limit lateral network mobility, which will lower the attack surface and stop more breaches.

(6) Growth of Zero Trust Network Access (ZTNA)

FWIW-ZTNA will become a crucial remote work-drive technique for safe application access and isolation without leaving the network as a whole vulnerable to outside threats.

(7) Standards and Regulatory Compliance

ZTA adoption will continue to be fueled by compliance. Figure 7 shows that the ZT Interaction Protocol is already part of the Web3 technology stack's Level 1 (Ray, 2023).

Figure 7. Architecture Web 3 Technology Stack

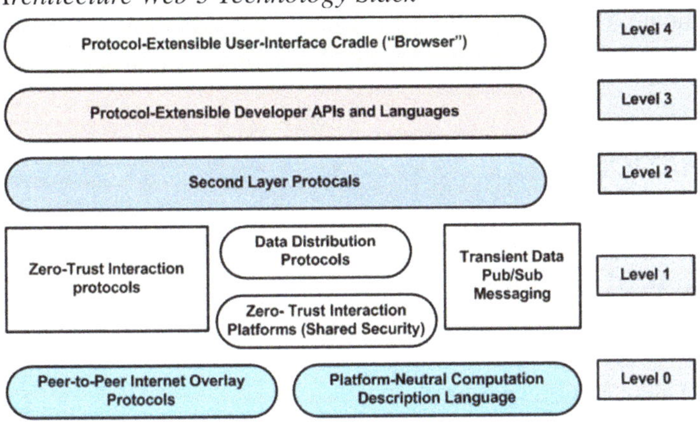

9. CONCLUSION

ZTA is concerned with priority of the classification of more than one dimensional information security space that is ever-consistent. Never trust, always check: we have access to limited resources that way, it is not everything or nothing. NIST Special Publication 800-207 Zero Trust Architecture defines fundamental components of ZTA (PDP and PEP) in this document. It also offers the playbook and game plan of the ZTA. In sum, AI-powered Zero Trust Architectures have strong potential to help defend government cloud infrastructures from an escalating cyber threat. Public sector enterprises together with Zero Trust and AI Public sector companies when combined the Zero Trust model along with AI can create dynamic security platforms driven by data that help to continuously monitor and protect their cloud environments. However, the implementation of such projects will require a fine mix of planning, cooperation and investment. As AI advances to those strengths that we can conceive of beyond what we are capable today, zero-trust models and deeper, more immersive security will likely be very prevalent in helping protect our governments' cloud systems. Using AI in zero trust architecture is an exciting evolution in security for businesses, to be sure but that's not without its considerations (Ud Din, 2024). Although AI-enabled ZTA demonstrates much improvement in threat identification, access controls, and operational efficiencies some find industry concerns such as data privacy compliance regulation limits becoming a bottleneck, model transparency (weak resilience against adversarial attacks also needing to be addressed). The successes of AI-informed security depends on a combination of aggressive technical controls and wide-sweeping governance. AI's future in ZTA seems promising, but organizations must prepare for the worst and keep up security controls policing, compliance check pointing, and accounting for a growing attack surface even as they compound interest on AI modeling within their security posture.

ABBREVIATIONS

ABAC: Attribute based access control
AI: Artificial Intelligence
AWS: Amazon Web Services
BYOD: Bring Your Own Device
DLP: Data Loss Prevention
DMZ: Demilitarized Zone
DoD: Department of Defense
DRM: Digital Rights Management
EDR: Endpoint detection and response
FBAC: Function based access control
IAM: Identity and access management
IoT: Internet of Things
MDM: Mobile Device Management
MFA: Multi-Factor Authentication
MITM: Man-in-the-middle
MTTR: Mean Time to Repair / Mean Time to Respond
NDR: Network detection and response
PA: Policy administrator
PE: Policy engine
PEP: Policy enforcement point
PDP: Policy decision point
RBAC: Role based access control
SIEM: Security information and event management
SOAR: Security Orchestration, Automation and Response
TTL: Time To Live
UEM: Unified Endpoint Management
UEBA: User and Entity Behavior Analytics
VLANs: Virtual Local Area Networks
ZTA: Zero trust architecture
ZTNA: Zero Trust Network Access
ZTM: Zero trust models

REFERENCES

Ahmadi, S. (2024). Zero Trust Architecture in cloud networks: Application, challenges and future opportunities. *Journal of Engineering Research and Reports*, *26*(2), 215–228. DOI: 10.9734/jerr/2024/v26i21083

Alagappan, A., Venkatachary, S. K., & Andrews, L. J. (2022). Augmenting zero trust network architecture to enhance security in virtual power plants. *Energy Reports*, *8*, 1309–1320. DOI: 10.1016/j.egyr.2021.11.272

Alshehri, A., & Tunc, C. (2023, December 4). Zero trust engine for IoT environments. *2023 20th ACS/IEEE International Conference on Computer Systems and Applications (AICCSA)*, 1–3. Presented at the 2023 20th ACS/IEEE International Conference on Computer Systems and Applications (AICCSA), Giza, Egypt. DOI: 10.1109/AICCSA59173.2023.10479286

Ameer, S., Benson, J., & Sandhu, R. (2023). Hybrid approaches (ABAC and RBAC) toward secure access control in smart home IoT. *IEEE Transactions on Dependable and Secure Computing*, *20*(5), 4032–4051. DOI: 10.1109/TDSC.2022.3216297

Ameer, S., Praharaj, L., Sandhu, R., Bhatt, S., & Gupta, M. (2024). ZTA-IoT: A novel architecture for Zero-Trust in IoT systems and an ensuing usage control model. *ACM Transactions on Privacy and Security*, *27*(3), 1–36. DOI: 10.1145/3671147

Bast, C., & Yeh, K.-H. (2024). Emerging authentication technologies for zero trust on the Internet of Things. *Symmetry*, *16*(8), 993. DOI: 10.3390/sym16080993

Bello, Y., Hussein, A. R., Ulema, M., & Koilpillai, J. (2022). On sustainedzero trust conceptualization security for mobile core networks in 5G and beyond. *IEEE Transactions on Network and Service Management*, *19*(2), 1876–1889. DOI: 10.1109/TNSM.2022.3157248

Best practices implementing zero trust with Palo Alto networks (2021). https://docs.paloaltonetworks.com/best-practices/ zero-trust-best-practices/

B.S., R., N. V., N. K., & Shyamasundar, R. K. (2021). Towards unifying RBAC with information flow control. *Proceedings of the 26th ACM Symposium on Access Control Models and Technologies*, 45-54. DOI: 10.1145/3450569.3463570

Chen, B., Qiao, S., Zhao, J., Liu, D., Shi, X., Lyu, M., Chen, H., Lu, H., & Zhai, Y. (2021). A security awareness and protection system for 5G smart health care based on zero-trust architecture. *IEEE Internet of Things Journal*, *8*(13), 10–248. DOI: 10.1109/JIOT.2020.3041042

Desmedt, Y., & Shaghaghi, A. (2018). Function-based access control (FBAC): Towards preventing insider threats in organizations. *Lecture Notes in Computer Science, 11170*, 143–165. DOI: 10.1007/978-3-030-04834-1_8

Feng, Z., Zhou, P., Wang, Q., & Qi, W. (2022). A dual-layer zero trust architecture for 5G industry MEC applications access control. *2022 IEEE 5th International Conference on Electronic Information and Communication Technology (ICEICT)*, 100-105. DOI: 10.1109/ICEICT55736.2022.9908891

Fernandez, E. B., & Brazhuk, A. (2024). A critical analysis of Zero Trust Architecture (ZTA). *Computer Standards & Interfaces, 89*(103832), 103832. DOI: 10.1016/j.csi.2024.103832

Ferretti, L., Magnanini, F., Andreolini, M., & Colajanni, M. (2021). Survivable zero trust for cloud computing environments. *Computers & Security, 110*, 102419. DOI: 10.1016/j.cose.2021.102419

Hussain, M., Pal, S., Jadidi, Z., Foo, E., & Kanhere, S. (2024). Federated zero trust architecture using artificial intelligence. *IEEE Wireless Communications, 31*(2), 30–35. DOI: 10.1109/MWC.001.2300405

Intel, "Trusted platform module (TPM) overview," https://www.intel.com/content/www/us/en/learn/what-is-a-trusted-platform-module.html

Khan, I. A., Keshk, M., Hussain, Y., Pi, D., Li, B., Kousar, T., & Ali, B. S. (2025). A context-aware zero trust-based hybrid approach to IoT-based self-driving vehicles security. *Ad Hoc Networks, 167*(103694), 103694. DOI: 10.1016/j.adhoc.2024.103694

Kumari, B. (2025). Innovative Cloud Architectures: Revolutionizing Enterprise Operations Through AI Integration. *International Journal of Fluid Mechanics Research.*

Netskope announces general availability of zero trust secure access for hybrid it environments (2020). https://aithority.com/security/netskope-announces-general -availabilityof-zero-trust-secure-access-for-hybrid-it environments/

Phiayura, P., & Teerakanok, S. (2023). A comprehensive framework for migrating to zero trust architecture. *IEEE Access : Practical Innovations, Open Solutions, 11*, 19487–19511. DOI: 10.1109/ACCESS.2023.3248622

Pratt, M. K. (2021). Zero-trust model case study: One ciso's experience. https://www.techtarget .com / search security/feature/Even-with-a-roadmap-zero-trust-model-an-ongoing process

Prescriptive Guidance, A. W. S. (2021). Multi-tenant SaaS authorization and API access control. Available: https: //docs.aws.amazon.com/prescriptive-guidance/latest/saas-multitenantapi-access-authorization/welcome.html

Ray, P. P. (2023). Web3: A comprehensive review on background, technologies, applications, zero-trust architectures, challenges and future directions. *Internet of Things and Cyber-Physical Systems*, *3*, 213–248. DOI: 10.1016/j.iotcps.2023.05.003

Rose, S., Borchert, O., Mitchell, S., & Connelly, S. (2020). *Zero Trust Architecture*. National Institute of Standards and Technology., DOI: 10.6028/NIST.SP.800-207

Rosoff, G., & Chawla, N. (2024). Zero Trust Driving the Upgrade of BUMED's Identity, Credential, and Access Management Strategy. [The Journal of the American Society of Military Comptrollers]. *The Armed Forces Comptroller*, *69*, 46–47.

Samuel Oladiipo, O. (2024). AI for Identity and Access Management (IAM) in the Cloud: Exploring the Potential of Artificial Intelligence to Improve User Authentication, Authorization, and Access Control within Cloud-Based Systems. *Asian Journal of Research in Computer Science*, *17*(3), 38–56. DOI: 10.9734/ajrcos/2024/v17i3423

Sarkar, S., Choudhary, G., Shandilya, S. K., Hussain, A., & Kim, H. (2022). Security of zero trust networks in cloud computing: A comparative review. *Sustainability (Basel)*, *14*(18), 11213. DOI: 10.3390/su141811213

Shieh, S., Lee, S., & Tsai, M. (2022). Strategy and tactics against ransomware. *Computer*, *55*(5), 85–92. DOI: 10.1109/MC.2022.3146733

Sultana, M., Hossain, A., Laila, F., Taher, K. A., & Islam, M. N. (2020). Towards developing a secure medical image sharing system based on zero trust principles and blockchain technology. *BMC Medical Informatics and Decision Making*, *20*(1), 256. Advance online publication. DOI: 10.1186/s12911-020-01275-y

Tsai, M., Lee, S., & Shieh, S. W. (2024). Strategy for implementing of zero trust architecture. *IEEE Transactions on Reliability*, *73*(1), 93–100. DOI: 10.1109/TR.2023.3345665

Tu, J., Shieh, S. W., Liu, T., & Chang, L. (2023). *Cybersecurity reference architecture for semiconductor manufacturing environments*. SEMI.

Wang, H., & Nyamasvisva, T. E. (2025). A zero-trust security model applied in SDN intelligent network. *International Conference on Artificial Intelligence and Machine Learning Research (CAIMLR 2024)*, 22. DOI: 10.1117/12.3058610

Ward, R. and Beyer, B. (2014). BeyondCorp: A new approach to enterprise security. vol. 39, no. 6, pp. 6–11.

Zaheer, Z., Chang, H., Mukherjee, S., & Van der Merwe, J. (2019). EZTrust. *Proceedings of the 2019 ACM Symposium on SDN Research*, 49-61. DOI: 10.1145/3314148.3314349

Zero trust maturity model (2020). Available: https://www.microsoft.com/en-us/security/blog /2020/ 04/02/ announcing microsoft-zero-trust-assessment-tool/

ADDITIONAL READING

Li, D., Zhang, E., Lei, M., & Song, C. (2022). Zero trust in edge computing environment: A blockchain based practical scheme. *Mathematical Biosciences and Engineering*, *19*(4), 4196–4216. DOI: 10.3934/mbe.2022194

Luecking, M., Fries, C., Lamberti, R., & Stork, W. (2020). Decentralized identity and trust management framework for Internet of things. *2020 IEEE International Conference on Blockchain and Cryptocurrency (ICBC)*, 1-9. DOI: 10.1109/ICBC48266.2020.9169411

Okeke, F. (2023). 'How to implement zero trust: Best practices and guidelines', [Online]. Available: https://www.techrepublic.com/article/how-to-implement-zero-trust/

Pokhrel, S. R., Yang, L., Rajasegarar, S., & Li, G. (2024). Robust zero trust architecture: Joint blockchain based federated learning and anomaly detection based framework. *Proceedings of the SIGCOMM Workshop on Zero Trust Architecture for Next Generation Communications*, 7-12. DOI: 10.1145/3672200.3673878

Sabt, M., Achemlal, M., & Bouabdallah, A. (2015). Trusted execution environment: What it is, and what it is not. In *Proc. IEEE Trustcom/BigDataSE/ISPA* (pp. 57–64). DOI: 10.1109/Trustcom.2015.357

Syed, N. F., Shah, S. W., Shaghaghi, A., Anwar, A., Baig, Z., & Doss, R. (2022). Zero trust architecture (ZTA): A comprehensive survey. *IEEE Access : Practical Innovations, Open Solutions*, *10*, 57143–57179. DOI: 10.1109/ACCESS.2022.3174679

Ud Din, I., Habib Khan, K., Almogren, A., Zareei, M., & Arturo Pérez Díaz, J. (2024). Securing the Metaverse: A blockchain-enabled zero-trust architecture for virtual environments. *IEEE Access : Practical Innovations, Open Solutions*, *12*, 92337–92347. DOI: 10.1109/ACCESS.2024.3423400

Chapter 7
Secure Code Generation and Software Engineering With Generative AI

Hanh Le
http://orcid.org/0009-0007-8172-0809
University of the Cumberlands, USA

ABSTRACT

The integration of generative AI into software engineering is transforming how developers write and secure code. Tools like GitHub Copilot and ChatGPT enhance productivity but also introduce risks to code quality, security, and accountability. This study explores how generative AI intersects with secure software engineering by examining its role within the Secure Software Development Life Cycle (SSDLC). It investigates how AI-generated code can propagate vulnerabilities and how prompt engineering may mitigate these risks. Emphasis is placed on the importance of explainability, code auditing, and human oversight in AI-augmented development environments. Through case studies in DevSecOps (Prates & Pereira, 2025), the paper illustrates both the promise and the pitfalls of AI-assisted coding. Findings underscore the need to evolve traditional practices to ensure safe, transparent, and ethical AI integration, offering actionable strategies for aligning intelligent automation with secure development standards.

INTRODUCTION

Generative AI has precipitated a fundamental transformation in the field of software engineering. Large Language Models (LLMs), such as OpenAI's ChatGPT and GitHub Copilot, have become essential tools throughout the software development

DOI: 10.4018/979-8-3693-8397-1.ch007

process. These models possess the capability to generate functional, context-aware source code, while also aiding developers in bug detection, offering code refactoring suggestions, and promoting adherence to security protocols. Consequently, tasks that were once the exclusive domain of seasoned software engineers, including the development of optimized algorithms, the identification of vulnerabilities, and the enforcement of secure coding practices, are now susceptible to partial or complete automation through the application of generative AI. As a result, this change is redefining the traditional boundaries of software engineering expertise, establishing new models for secure, efficient, and AI-enhanced development processes. As organizations strive to incorporate these tools into their development processes to boost productivity, cost-effectiveness, and innovation, concerns regarding software security and AI accountability have become increasingly pressing.

Generative AI offers both advantages and disadvantages for software security. It could simplify secure coding and help developers find security flaws more quickly. Conversely, the possibility of inadvertently producing insecure code is present, potentially stemming from the integration of, or amplification of, vulnerabilities inherent in the training data. Given that AI models often utilize extensive public code repositories, which frequently exhibit insecure coding practices, a legitimate risk emerges that these models could unintentionally disseminate such harmful methodologies or even introduce vulnerabilities into operational systems.

This study investigates a crucial issue at the intersection of artificial intelligence and cybersecurity: how software development teams can use generative AI while maintaining the integrity, security, and ethical standards that are essential to the software engineering process. To this end, we analyze the integration of artificial intelligence within the Secure Software Development Life Cycle (SSDLC). Moreover, this study investigates the dissemination of vulnerabilities within code generated by artificial intelligence. Ultimately, we suggest methodologies, including prompt engineering and AI explainability, to aid developers in managing the security of AI-generated outputs. Consequently, this research advocates for a collaborative approach, merging human expertise with AI augmentation, to facilitate the creation of secure, dependable, and resilient software systems.

This research presents several significant advancements that extend beyond the scope of prior investigations. Firstly, it provides empirically validated qualitative insights into developer interactions with generative AI tools within genuine, secure coding contexts, thus revealing patterns of trust, cognitive reliance, and risk evaluation. Moreover, it conducts a systematic analysis of AI-generated security vulnerabilities, linking these findings to established security frameworks like OWASP (Open Web Application Security Project) (OWASP, 2025), consequently bridging the gap between AI-enhanced development and traditional secure coding practices. Finally, this study explicitly incorporates three complementary theoretical frameworks—the

Deskilling of Jobs Theory (DJT), Job Characteristics Theory (JCT), and Technology Threat Avoidance Theory (TTAT)—to elucidate not only technical risks but also the evolving roles, motivations, and adaptive behaviors of developers within AI-assisted settings. Fourth, the study proposes a structured Secure AI-Assisted DevSecOps Framework that clarifies how generative AI can be embedded in the SSDLC while preserving human oversight, layered validation, and accountability.

In this way, the chapter contributes not only descriptive findings but also a clearer scientific and methodological contribution: it offers a theory-informed and practice-oriented account of how secure software engineering is being reconfigured by AI-assisted code generation.

The following Research Questions guide this study:

1. RQ1: How does the integration of generative AI tools influence the security practices within the Secure Software Development Life Cycle (SSDLC)?
2. RQ2: What are the risks and mitigation strategies associated with vulnerability propagation in AI-generated code?
3. RQ3: What is the role of human oversight and explainability in maintaining security and accountability in AI-assisted software engineering?

Section 2 provides the conceptual basis by outlining the theoretical frameworks that guide the chapter's analysis. Section 3 reviews current research on software development, deskilling, and the integration of generative AI in programming methods. Section 4 then explains the qualitative research methodology used to explore these topics.

To improve the clarity and accessibility of the scientific presentation, this chapter includes new visual elements, such as workflow diagrams and organized comparison tables. These visual aids elucidate the proposed architecture for secure AI-assisted code generation, the incorporation of generative AI within a DevSecOps-focused SSDLC, and the primary categories of risks and corresponding mitigation strategies identified throughout the research.

BACKGROUND AND THEORETICAL FRAMEWORKS

The incorporation of generative AI into software engineering signifies a pivotal shift in programming methodologies. Tools such as GitHub Copilot and ChatGPT are becoming more common for generating refactoring recommendations and even writing source code documentation. Traditionally, these duties were managed by seasoned human developers. While these advancements offer opportunities for improved productivity and efficiency, they also introduce complex challenges, including job restructuring, skill degradation, and cybersecurity risks. To assess the wider ramifications of AI-assisted development, especially in the context of secure software engineering, this research draws on three interrelated theoretical frameworks: the Deskilling of Jobs Theory (DJT), the Job Characteristics Theory (JCT), and the Technology Threat Avoidance Theory (TTAT).

Deskilling of Jobs Theory

The Deskilling of Jobs Theory, based on Braverman's (1974) sociological work, suggests that technological changes can reduce the skill requirements for certain jobs. Generative AI tools in software engineering could potentially automate key aspects of coding, security, and testing. This would change the programmer's role, moving it from active problem-solving to passive code review or prompt engineering. This shift raises concerns about a possible decline in deep technical skills, particularly in secure coding practices. Given that AI systems are increasingly taking on responsibility for both routine and moderately complex operations, developers may become dependent on AI-generated results, potentially lacking a comprehensive understanding of the underlying logic, security implications, or system design. Such circumstances could unintentionally undermine software integrity and diminish an organization's cybersecurity robustness (Pearce et al., 2022).

Job Characteristics Theory

Job Characteristics Theory, first proposed by Hackman and Oldham (1976), offers a framework for understanding how work design affects employee motivation, satisfaction, and performance. In AI-augmented development environments, the five core dimensions—skill variety, task identity, task significance, autonomy, and feedback—are of particular importance. For instance, consider the possibility that generative AI could improve efficiency while also reducing the sense of autonomy and connection to tasks. This could happen if developers see their main role as checking machine-made results, rather than being involved in meaningful creative work. Conversely, when thoughtfully integrated, AI tools could enhance task significance by enabling developers to focus on higher-level design and security architecture (Stefaniak & Moore, 2024). This theory helps evaluate how the evolving human-AI collaboration affects developer engagement, especially in roles that demand rigorous attention to secure software practices.

Technology Threat Avoidance Theory

Technology Threat Avoidance Theory (TTAT), introduced by Liang and Xue (2009), offers an explanation of how individuals respond to perceived technological threats, focusing on threat appraisal (which includes perceived severity and susceptibility) and coping appraisal (which encompasses self-efficacy and response efficacy). TTAT serves as a useful model for analyzing software developers' reactions to the security vulnerabilities inherent in AI-generated code. Developers might view AI outputs as potentially insecure, stemming from issues like the lack of transparency in the model's decision-making, uncertainty about the training data's source, or the lack of built-in security features. The decisions developers make regarding the review, modification, or rejection of AI-generated code are influenced by their self-assurance, the perceived utility of security tools (such as code scanners and explainability tools), and the level of organizational support for secure practices (Kuhail et al., 2023). Therefore, this study uses the Technology Threat Assessment Tool (TTAT) to investigate how developers assess and respond to the security risks associated with AI-assisted coding.

Background and Theoretical Frameworks Summary

A comprehensive understanding of the socio-technical changes in secure software engineering can be gained by considering the Deskilling of Jobs Theory, Job Characteristics Theory, and Technology Threat Avoidance Theory together. These frameworks help explain how artificial intelligence shapes developers' day-to-day work, what drives their decisions, and how they think about risk. By bringing them together, the chapter is able to link technical security findings with the human and organizational factors behind them, creating a stronger and more cohesive analysis.

DJT's examination highlights a wider shift in cognitive labor, demonstrating a transition among developers away from direct creation and towards positions focused on supervision and direction. JCT's research further elucidates this, indicating that AI's impact on developers' perceptions of autonomy and professional worth can be either detrimental or beneficial. TTAT further clarifies the different ways developers respond to the security challenges posed by AI, highlighting both proactive, multifaceted ways to reduce risk and more passive or overly reliant approaches. This comprehensive framework enhances the chapter's investigation by linking technical security outcomes with human and organizational behaviors.

Table 1. Linking Interview Questions to Research Questions and Theoretical Frameworks Interview Question

Interview Question	Mapped RQ	Theoretical Framework(s)	Explanation
Q1. Please introduce yourself and share your background and experience in AI chatbot development.	Contextual (All RQs)	N/A	Establishes the participant's experience level and role, providing context for interpreting their responses across all research questions.
Q2. Do you use AI chatbots in your daily life? For example, ChatGPT or GitHub Copilot?	RQ1	DJT, JCT	Reveals the extent of AI adoption in personal practice, offering insight into automation's reach and how routine tasks may be deskilled or reshaped.
Q3. Do you use AI chatbots on your job? If so, how exactly? Please give an example.	RQ1	DJT, JCT	Assesses how AI tools are embedded in professional workflows and whether they enhance or diminish autonomy, skill variety, or task significance.
Q4. Can you describe the specific challenges you face as a programmer in a world dominated by AI and chatbots?	RQ1, RQ2	DJT, TTAT	Explores perceived erosion of skills and threat perceptions related to AI, particularly in secure coding contexts. Helps identify developer anxieties and vulnerabilities.
Q5. How has the emergence of AI and chatbots impacted your day-to-day work and responsibilities?	RQ1, RQ3	DJT, JCT	Highlights shifts in role identity, autonomy, and workload, key components in evaluating changes to work structure and human responsibility in AI-assisted environments.
Q6. Can you share a specific instance where you encountered a challenge related to integrating or collaborating with AI technologies?	RQ2	TTAT, DJT	Elicits real-world examples of AI-generated code failures or integration issues, revealing how developers appraise risks and respond to potential security threats.
Q7. How do you incorporate user interactions and feedback into the development cycle of an AI chatbot?	RQ3	JCT, TTAT	Connects to feedback mechanisms and coping strategies, reflecting how developers maintain quality, interpretability, and control when AI is involved in system behavior.
Q8. What strategies have you adopted to adapt to the evolving programming landscape with the rise of AI and chatbots? How do you stay updated?	RQ2, RQ3	JCT, TTAT	Investigates adaptation and reskilling behaviors, showing how developers respond to perceived threats and maintain relevance in a transforming technical landscape.
Q9. What tools or methodologies effectively address user interaction and feedback challenges during AI chatbot development?	RQ3	JCT, TTAT	Uncovers practical techniques used for governance, transparency, and explainability, central to safe and accountable use of generative AI.

continued on following page

Table 1. Continued

Interview Question	Mapped RQ	Theoretical Framework(s)	Explanation
Q10. In what direction do you foresee your job field evolving, with AI potentially playing a distinct role?	RQ1, RQ3	DJT, JCT	Probe participants' views on the long-term implications of AI on job structures, security responsibilities, and developer agency.
Q11. Which skills will become crucial for an IT specialist in your field over the next five years?	RQ3	DJT, JCT, TTAT	Encourages participants to reflect on emerging skill needs, coping strategies, and the evolution of human-AI collaboration in secure software engineering.

LITERATURE REVIEW

The quick rise of generative AI tools, such as GitHub Copilot and ChatGPT, has led to a significant philosophical change in software engineering. While these technologies offer the potential for increased productivity, task automation, and new coding methods, they also present significant challenges. Specifically, there are growing concerns about software security, the protection of developers' specialized knowledge, and the clear definition of responsibilities within organizations.

This examination synthesizes contemporary research concerning the impact of artificial intelligence on software development methodologies, secure coding practices, and the evolving roles of engineers. This study investigates three main areas: (1) how generative AI affects secure software development life cycles (SSDLC), (2) the potential for AI-generated code to introduce security vulnerabilities, and (3) the ongoing importance of human oversight and the ability to explain AI's actions.

DevSecOps

Organizations are increasingly turning to DevOps to streamline their software development processes, especially as cybersecurity threats grow more complex and the demand for rapid delivery intensifies. In contrast, Prates and Pereira (2025) suggest that the use of DevOps varies significantly across different fields, which limits its usefulness as a universal method.

To bridge this gap, the IEEE developed a DevOps standard that encompasses DevSecOps. This methodology weaves security into the fabric of the development lifecycle, rather than tacking it on as an afterthought.

Nevertheless, considerable ambiguity persists regarding the practical application of DevSecOps. To elucidate this, Prates and Pereira undertook a Multivocal Literature Review (MLR) to establish a clearer understanding of DevSecOps definitions and applications. Their objective was to systematically identify and characterize the principal practices involved, along with the supporting tools.

Their study establishes correlations between these practices—such as static and dynamic analysis, threat modeling, software composition analysis, and infrastructure-as-code security—and specific implementation tools. Consequently, their work furnishes a structured framework for organizations seeking to operationalize DevSecOps principles. Furthermore, by bridging the gap between academic research and industry perspectives, their research significantly contributes to a deeper comprehension of integrating security within agile development pipelines from the beginning, thereby harmonizing technical execution with evolving standards and best practices.

SAST

SAST, or Static Application Security Testing, is all about examining source code, bytecode, or binaries without actually executing the program. These tools get to work early in the development process, hunting down vulnerabilities. They look for things like SQL injection flaws, cross-site scripting (XSS) vulnerabilities, insecure data handling practices, and hardcoded credentials. Because SAST operates at the code level, it's especially useful for identifying security flaws during coding and build processes. This allows developers to fix problems before deployment, which is crucial given AI-generated code's tendency to introduce vulnerabilities (Pearce et al., 2022; Wang et al., 2024).

SCA

Software Composition Analysis (SCA) is all about finding weaknesses in the third-party libraries and open-source components that an application relies on. These tools sift through dependency trees, hunting for vulnerabilities that have already been identified. They flag issues such as CVEs, outdated components, and potential licensing conflicts.

Given that AI-generated code can suggest external packages, Software Composition Analysis (SCA) is crucial for preventing dependencies from introducing hidden security risks into the system. This is especially important in AI-assisted development environments where external code is often reused (Wang et al., 2024; Zhang et al., 2023).

DAST

DAST, or Dynamic Application Security Testing, assesses an application's security posture by mimicking attacks on a running system. Unlike Static Application Security Testing (SAST), this method doesn't require access to the application's source code. The system identifies various vulnerabilities, such as authentication issues, misconfigurations, and weaknesses that could allow code injection during program execution. Dynamic application security testing (DAST) is often used in testing or staging environments to assess how an application behaves when exposed to potentially harmful conditions. This makes it a crucial way to validate the results of code produced by artificial intelligence (Sobania et al., 2023; Wang et al., 2024).

Generative AI and the Secure Software Development Life Cycle

Pearce's 2022 study showed that code created by artificial intelligence often has basic security weaknesses. This is especially true when the AI model is trained on publicly available code that uses insecure methods.

The proliferation of machine learning technologies has led to the increasing adoption of generative AI tools, exemplified by GitHub Copilot, which are valued for their ability to provide code autocompletion and support developers, effectively functioning as "AI pair programmers." Copilot, having been trained on a vast corpus of open-source code, has become a ubiquitous element in contemporary software development. Nevertheless, its integration into secure software development practices presents certain challenges.

A survey of 169 Stack Overflow posts and 655 GitHub Discussions provides some insight. Copilot has settled in nicely within Visual Studio Code, especially for those working with JavaScript and Python. Node.js developers seem to find it useful, as well. People often cite increased productivity as a key benefit, especially when handling data management tasks.

On the other hand, this approach presents significant challenges, particularly regarding integration and the potential for bypassing secure coding practices (Zhang et al., 2023). Analysis of 169 Stack Overflow posts and 655 GitHub Discussions reveals some important trends: Copilot is often used with JavaScript and Python in Visual Studio Code, and it's frequently used with Node.js. Users seem to appreciate the increased productivity, particularly when it comes to generating code for data processing applications.

However, this approach presents considerable difficulties, particularly regarding integration and the potential for weakening secure coding practices (Zhang et al., 2023). The findings from Zhang et al. (2023) and Pearce et al. (2022) highlight that while generative AI can speed up development, it could also hide important stages of the Secure Software Development Life Cycle (SSDLC), such as secure design, code review, and static analysis, if not carefully checked. As developers increasingly use tools like GitHub Copilot to automate parts of their coding, there's a growing risk that key security practices might be ignored or missed. AI-generated code, even if syntactically correct, might lack basic security features such as input validation, authentication, and adherence to secure coding standards. This AI assistance can lead to the spread of insecure code patterns, increasing the application's vulnerability.

Moreover, relying too much on AI tools could lessen the importance of human oversight and teamwork, potentially weakening shared responsibility and learning. Consequently, within the domain of secure software engineering, it is imperative to conceptualize generative AI as a complementary instrument, rather than a substitute for established methodologies. To ascertain that code produced by AI adheres to both internal and external stipulations, organizations must implement structured security protocols. These protocols should encompass static and dynamic code analysis, security linting, and human review procedures. Furthermore, educating developers in AI-aware secure coding practices and integrating continuous auditing within CI/CD pipelines can fortify the security of AI-assisted development. In accordance with this premise, by integrating the productivity advantages of generative AI with a robust adherence to SSDLC principles, development teams can leverage innovation without compromising security or reliability.

Current research highlights a crucial distinction: functional utility and security assurance are not the same. Large Language Models (LLMs) create code by predicting likely patterns, rather than by following secure design principles. Therefore, AI-generated code might seem clean, efficient, and syntactically correct, but it could still have basic security flaws. This difference between code that seems plausible and secure code is crucial for understanding why human review and multi-layered validation processes are still needed.

Figure 1. AI-Enhanced Secure Code Generation Workflow

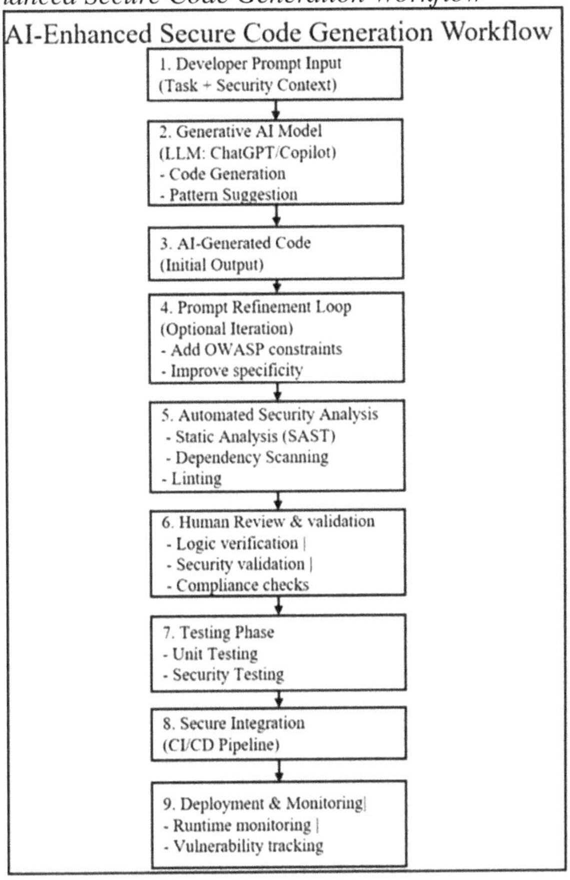

Source: Author's own work

Figure 1 presents the suggested secure workflow for AI-assisted code generation. It underscores the need to treat AI-generated code as a preliminary artifact in the development lifecycle, requiring human review, automated security validation, peer oversight, and continuous monitoring prior to deployment.

Vulnerability Propagation and Risk Amplification

The spread of vulnerabilities and the increase of risk are significant concerns when using AI-generated code. It's crucial to recognize that code created by AI shouldn't be automatically considered secure. Recent investigations have revealed that large language models (LLMs), which underpin tools like GitHub Copilot and ChatGPT, frequently replicate insecure coding practices present in their training data. These weaknesses include, but aren't limited to, SQL injection vulnerabilities, insufficient or missing input validation, hardcoded secrets, and unsafe API usage. Because these models are trained on large amounts of publicly available code, some of which might be outdated, poorly written, or already vulnerable, there's a significant risk that the code they create will have the same weaknesses.

This replication is not merely a theoretical concern; empirical studies have demonstrated that LLMs frequently produce functional yet insecure code snippets, potentially introducing exploitable security risks into practical applications. Therefore, the integration of generative AI in software development requires careful supervision. This encompasses human-led code reviews, automated static analysis procedures, and the application of secure coding standards throughout the development lifecycle. These precautions are critical for mitigating potential security vulnerabilities inherent in AI-generated code (Sobania et al., 2023; Wang et al., 2024). Pearce et al. (2022) provide evidence that Copilot produces code with vulnerabilities in over 40% of its suggested completions. The problem is made worse by using AI tools without thorough testing or human review.

From the perspective of Technology Threat Avoidance Theory (Liang & Xue), the technical vulnerabilities in AI-generated code can be grouped into several categories: (1) input-handling vulnerabilities, such as missing sanitization and weak validation; (2) authentication and authorization flaws, including improper session logic or omitted access controls; (3) secret exposure risks, such as hardcoded API keys or credentials; (4) unsafe dependency and package recommendations; and (5) insecure defaults in generated configurations or framework settings. This more structured classification helps clarify that the security problems caused by AI aren't a single issue. Instead, they are a set of common failure patterns. These patterns can be linked to established secure coding practices and the concerns outlined by OWASP.

Developer Deskilling and Changing Roles

As generative AI automates both basic and complex coding tasks, researchers are studying how this affects the skills needed in software development. Braverman's (1974) Deskilling of Jobs Theory expanded on this idea, suggesting that the process of deskilling, which Braverman described, is a key factor in how automation changes the workplace. They argued that the spread of automation leads to a decline in the need for specialized skills, which then affects the nature of work. Both Sobania et al. (2023) and Crowston and Bolici (2025) find that, while developers value AI's efficiency, many report a decrease in their direct work with code, logic, architecture, and debugging. These skills are essential for creating secure systems. Moreover, this change affects developers' job satisfaction and their understanding of their professional roles.

Human Oversight, Explainability, and Ethical Accountability

Successful collaboration between humans and artificial intelligence in software engineering necessitates more than just technical integration; it demands comprehensive governance structures that emphasize transparency, explainability, and ethical accountability across the entire development process. With AI systems assuming a greater role in code generation and recommendation, the human developer's function is evolving from a singular creator to a crucial evaluator and curator of machine-generated outputs. Sun et al. (2022) emphasize the importance of "human-in-the-loop" approaches, wherein developers retain final authority over AI-generated content and are supported by interfaces that explain the rationale and context of suggestions.

Moreover, a lack of explainability may contribute to overreliance on AI recommendations, resulting in deskilling or diminished developer confidence over time (Barke et al., 2023). Research has shown that explainability mechanisms not only improve developer trust and adoption but also facilitate more accurate debugging, efficient knowledge transfer, and more transparent accountability chains (Wang et al., 2024). Therefore, embedding explainability into AI development tools is not merely a desirable feature; it is a foundational requirement for secure, transparent, and ethically aligned software engineering practices in an increasingly automated era.

Case Studies in DevSecOps with AI Tools

Recent case studies have begun to illustrate the real-world challenges and opportunities of integrating AI in DevSecOps pipelines. For example, Puccio et al. (2025) document how AI chatbot misalignment led to unsafe outputs in healthcare software, raising questions about auditability and compliance. Conversely, companies such as Microsoft and Amazon have reported success in embedding AI tools within Continuous Integration/Continuous Deployment (CI/CD) workflows, improving deployment speed while leveraging secure code scanners to mitigate vulnerabilities. These mixed outcomes highlight the need for context-specific implementation, guided by organizational policies, team training, and iterative testing.

Figure 2. Integration of Generative AI in DevSecOps Pipeline

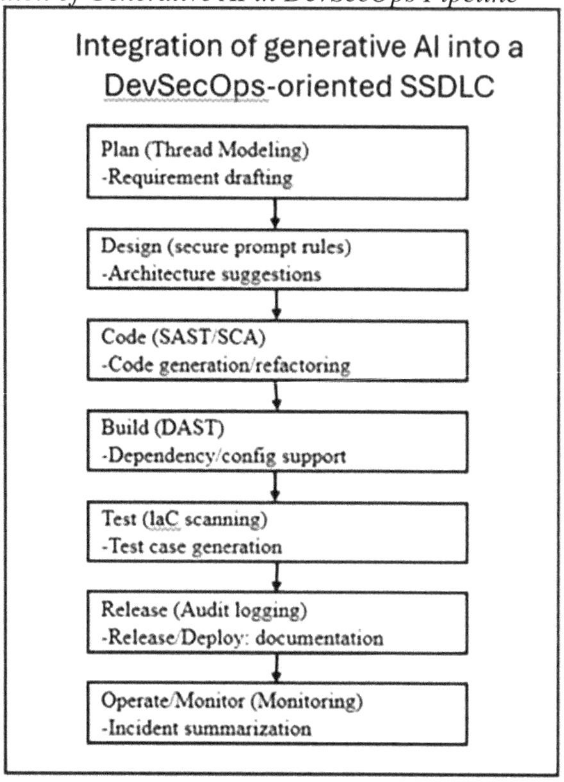

Source: Author's own work

Figure 2 illustrates how AI can support multiple development stages while remaining bound by security validation and governance controls.

Current Research Findings and Thematic Insights

As generative AI tools become more common in classrooms and coding jobs, more research is examining how people actually use them and what they think of them. These studies show how students and developers are adjusting to AI-assisted coding while also highlighting new challenges—such as losing a deeper understanding, relying too much on AI, and addressing ethical concerns. Recent studies highlight three main trends: (1) people are completing tasks faster, but often with less understanding, (2) students are taking on new roles when using AI, and (3) there is still a lot of uncertainty about ethical issues and academic honesty.

Accelerated Output, Shallow Understanding

Research consistently shows that students using tools like GitHub Copilot or ChatGPT can finish coding tasks faster and make fewer syntax mistakes (Barke et al., 2023). These tools are especially helpful when students get stuck—they can suggest code, provide templates, and reduce debugging frustration.

However, this convenience has a downside. Several studies warn that students may rely on AI-generated code without really understanding how it works. In some cases, they can submit a working program but struggle to explain its logic (Crowston & Bolici, 2025). This kind of "surface learning" raises concerns about whether students are truly developing strong coding skills.

Instructors have also noticed that students are less likely to experiment, debug on their own, or refine their code manually—skills essential to mastering software development and handling real-world challenges. As AI tools take on more of the coding process, it becomes increasingly important to preserve deeper learning.

Similarly, Rinta-Kahila et al. (2023) found that as automation becomes more common in software development, programmers' hands-on skills may decline. When AI tools handle more tasks, developers have fewer chances to practice core problem-solving and coding skills. This raises concerns about long-term readiness, knowledge retention, and the ability to work independently without relying too heavily on technology.

The Impact of Automation and the Decline of Expertise

The consequences of automation can be elucidated through Braverman's deskilling theory, which posits that individuals may increasingly depend on external instruments—such as AI—rather than using their cognitive faculties. This trend is particularly evident in software development, where developers frequently use tools such as GitHub Copilot and ChatGPT to generate code, address challenges, and propose solutions. Khurana et al. (2024) observed that developers frequently accept AI-generated code without a comprehensive review, thereby bypassing crucial stages such as logical verification, accuracy assessment, and consideration of alternative methodologies. Consequently, this practice can erode critical thinking and problem-solving capabilities over time, especially in activities intended to facilitate developers' learning and professional development.

The impact of this phenomenon is particularly pronounced among junior developers, individuals who are in the process of establishing their core competencies. Lacking the requisite experience or self-assurance to evaluate the outputs of artificial intelligence critically, they exhibit a greater propensity to accept them without modification. Consequently, this can foster a more passive coding methodology, wherein the acquisition of knowledge and the cultivation of independent problem-solving abilities are deprioritized. Kuhail et al. (2023) highlight that this pattern jeopardizes the acquisition of foundational coding competencies and narrows the developmental pipeline for more advanced roles. When emerging developers are routinely shielded from the cognitive demands of debugging, architectural reasoning, and algorithmic design, their ability to progress to more senior positions is constrained. Over time, this may result in a workforce less capable of innovating, mentoring, and adapting to new technological paradigms, raising critical concerns about the profession's long-term sustainability.

Changing Roles and Expectations of Learners

The emergence of AI in programming education is also reshaping how students perceive their roles and responsibilities. Instead of being problem-solvers or code creators, students are beginning to describe themselves as AI supervisors, curators, or prompt engineers (Stefaniak & Moore, 2024). Their primary task is to evaluate and refine AI-generated output rather than produce it from scratch. At the same time, this shift introduces new literacies such as prompt design and model evaluation. It may also limit opportunities for internalizing foundational logic, especially for novice learners.

This changing dynamic raises important pedagogical questions: What does it mean to "learn to program" in a world where AI can write the code? What constitutes meaningful evidence of learning when the final product may be co-produced with an algorithm? These questions highlight a tension between the practical realities of AI integration and the traditional learning objectives of computer science curricula.

Ethical Ambiguity and Unclear Norms

Another theme emerging from recent studies is the ethical ambiguity surrounding the use of AI in academic settings. While students frequently turn to generative tools for legitimate assistance, they are often unsure where to draw the line between support and misconduct. In Crowston and Bolici's (2025) study, for example, many students admitted they had used AI-generated code without knowing whether it violated their institution's honor code. The opaque nature of AI outputs, especially when they resemble open-source code, makes attribution difficult and increases the likelihood of unintentional plagiarism.

Educators, too, are divided on appropriate boundaries. Some advocate full integration of AI into coursework, arguing that learning to work with AI is itself a vital skill. Others warn that unregulated use undermines assessment validity and encourages academic dishonesty. These conflicting attitudes reflect the lack of institutional policies and the evolving status of AI in educational ethics. Until clear guidelines are established, both students and faculty are navigating a gray area with significant academic consequences (Stefaniak & Moore, 2024).

Synthesis and Gaps in the Literature

While more research is exploring both the benefits and risks of AI-generated code, there's still a gap when it comes to looking at the full picture. Most studies focus on one area at a time—like security, developer skills, or risk behavior—without connecting them together. There's also limited research that looks at real developer experiences, especially in high-stakes environments like DevSecOps where security is critical.

To help fill this gap, this study takes a qualitative, theory-based approach to understand how developers actually use and manage AI in secure coding. It looks at how they think about AI, how they adopt it, and how they handle potential risks in real-world settings.

Three key theories guide the study:

- Deskilling of Jobs Theory (DJT): how automation affects skills and expertise
- Job Characteristics Theory (JCT): how changes in tasks impact motivation and roles
- Technology Threat Avoidance Theory (TTAT): how people respond to perceived risks

By combining these perspectives, the study offers a more complete view of how generative AI is changing both the technical side of software development and developers' responsibilities, especially in security-focused environments.

Bridging Theory and Practice

Theories like the Deskilling of Jobs Theory (DJT), Job Characteristics Theory (JCT), and Technology Threat Avoidance Theory (TTAT) offer useful ways to think about how generative AI is reshaping software development. But their real value becomes apparent only when they're applied to the day-to-day experiences of developers who are actually working with these tools. This study aims to connect those abstract ideas with the practical realities of secure software engineering by examining how practitioners integrate generative AI into their workflows, manage new risks, and maintain accountability in environments that are becoming increasingly automated.

DJT helps explain the shifts developers report in their roles, responsibilities, and use of technical skills. Many describe leaning heavily on AI-generated suggestions—sometimes accepting code without fully understanding how it works. While this can speed up development, it also raises concerns about the erosion of deep expertise in areas like cryptography, threat modeling, and secure input validation. At the same time, some developers are gaining new forms of specialization, such as prompt engineering or overseeing AI model behavior. These experiences show that deskilling and reskilling can happen simultaneously in AI-augmented workflows.

Job Characteristics Theory (JCT) helps explain how AI is changing the way developers experience their work. Developers who see AI as a helpful tool—one that takes care of repetitive tasks and lets them focus on more meaningful work like design or architecture—tend to feel more satisfied. On the other hand, those who feel their role has been reduced to just prompting AI and fixing its mistakes often feel less fulfilled and less connected to their work. This shows how important it is to design roles in AI-driven environments like DevSecOps thoughtfully.

Technology Threat Avoidance Theory (TTAT) sheds light on how developers respond to the security risks that come with AI-generated code. Many developers are becoming more cautious, especially when using AI trained on public code that may not always be secure. As a result, they're adopting safer practices like carefully reviewing AI-generated code, using security tools, and running more tests. However, some developers are unsure if they can spot subtle issues, which points to gaps in confidence and control. This highlights the need for better training, tools, and organizational support.

Together, these frameworks help connect theory with real-world practice. They show not only how AI is changing technical workflows, but also how it affects developers' roles, decision-making, and sense of responsibility. By focusing on real experiences, this study provides a clearer picture of both the benefits and risks of using AI in secure software development, along with practical insights for educators, tool designers, and engineering leaders.

Conclusion: Ensuring Human Oversight in AI-Enhanced Code Generation

The literature review reveals a rapidly shifting landscape in which generative AI is transforming software engineering practices, particularly in secure code development. Tools like GitHub Copilot and ChatGPT promise major gains in productivity and workflow efficiency, yet they also introduce new security risks, reshape developer responsibilities, and challenge long-standing assumptions about expertise and accountability. Theoretical frameworks such as the Deskilling of Jobs Theory, Job Characteristics Theory, and Technology Threat Avoidance Theory help illuminate how these changes affect developers both cognitively and organizationally.

Empirical research highlights the dual nature of AI integration. On one hand, generative AI can automate routine tasks and accelerate innovation. On the other hand, it can erode essential technical skills and introduce subtle security vulnerabilities that are difficult to detect without strong oversight. Despite growing attention to the technical capabilities of these tools, there is still limited research on developers' lived experiences—particularly how they navigate the trade-offs between efficiency, responsibility, and secure coding practices.

This study addresses these gaps by bringing theory into conversation with real-world practice through qualitative inquiry. By centering the perspectives of software professionals working directly with generative AI, it offers a deeper understanding of how secure software engineering is being redefined in an era of intelligent automation. It also identifies the strategies needed to ensure this transformation remains responsible, resilient, and aligned with the field's long-term integrity.

Table 2. Comparison of Traditional vs AI-Assisted Secure Coding

Dimension	Traditional Secure Coding	AI-Assisted Secure Coding
Code authorship	Fully human-generated	Human-AI co-generated
Security integration	Embedded throughout the lifecycle	Often shifted to post-generation review unless explicitly controlled
Explainability	High, based on human reasoning and documentation	Lower, due to opaque generation logic and missing rationale
Development speed	Moderate	High
Main risk source	Human error, insecure design, and implementation mistakes	Human error plus inherited insecure patterns from training data
Validation approach	Code review, testing, and standard secure SDLC controls	Requires all traditional controls plus AI-specific review and prompt constraints
Accountability	Clear human ownership	Shared workflow, but human accountability must remain explicit
Skill development	Strong reliance on direct coding practice	Risk of deskilling if oversight and understanding are weak

Table 2 compares traditional and AI-assisted secure coding across workflow, security integration, developer roles, and risk exposure. While AI-assisted approaches enhance productivity and automation, they shift security validation toward post-generation review and introduce new risks such as vulnerability propagation and reduced transparency. The comparison highlights the importance of combining AI capabilities with human oversight and robust security controls.

Table 3. AI-Generated Security Risks and Mitigation Strategies

Risk Category	Example	Security Implication	Mitigation Strategy
Missing input validation	Unsanitized user input in forms or queries	Injection attacks, malformed data handling	Validation libraries, secure prompts, SAST
Hardcoded secrets	API keys or passwords embedded in source code	Credential leakage, unauthorized access	Secret scanning, secure vaults, peer review
Weak authentication logic	Missing token checks or session expiration	Broken access control	Secure frameworks, review of auth flows
Unsafe dependencies	Suggestion of outdated or vulnerable packages	Supply chain risk	Software composition analysis (SCA), version pinning
Insecure defaults	Debug mode enabled, weak permissions	Expanded attack surface	Configuration review, policy checks
Hallucinated APIs or deprecated methods	AI recommends nonexistent or obsolete calls	Reliability failures, unsafe implementation	Human review, documentation, and cross-checking
Incomplete error handling	Silent failures or overly broad exceptions	Information leakage, instability	Secure coding standards, testing, and peer review

Table 3 summarizes common security risks in AI-generated code and corresponding mitigation strategies. It highlights the need for layered defenses, including prompt engineering, automated security testing (SAST, SCA, DAST), human review, and continuous monitoring, to ensure secure and reliable AI-assisted software development.

RESEARCH METHODOLOGY AND ETHICAL CONSIDERATIONS

This study followed well-established qualitative research practices and used a phenomenological approach to understand how people experience the use of generative AI in programming education. In simple terms, phenomenology focuses on people's lived experiences and how they make sense of them (Peoples, 2021).

To explore this, the study used semi-structured, open-ended interviews. This gave participants the freedom to share their thoughts in their own words, while still keeping the conversations focused on key topics. The study also used triangulation by including participants with diverse roles, backgrounds, and experience levels, thereby strengthening the depth and reliability of the findings.

To make sure the results were trustworthy, member checking was used. Some participants reviewed the researcher's interpretations of their responses to confirm accuracy, following guidance from Riazi et al. (2023). The researcher also kept a reflexive journal throughout the study to track decisions, reflect on their own perspective, and reduce bias during analysis.

Ethical considerations were a priority at every stage. Participants' identities were protected by removing any identifying details, and all data was stored securely. The study emphasized transparency, informed consent, and voluntary participation, ensuring that everyone took part willingly and was treated with respect.

Research Design

This study employed a qualitative research design grounded in in-depth, semi-structured interviews to explore how professional programmers and computer science students experience the integration of generative AI in software development and coding education. The qualitative approach was chosen to elicit rich, contextualized insights and to capture the complexity of participants' lived experiences, perspectives, and meaning-making processes. Rather than aiming for statistical generalization, the study sought to uncover nuanced patterns, emergent themes, and situated understandings of how individuals engage with AI tools in real-world programming environments.

This study is informed by a hermeneutic-phenomenological approach, which emphasizes the interpretation of participants' lived experiences and the meanings they ascribe to their interactions with AI-assisted development tools. This approach is particularly suitable for examining complex socio-technical phenomena where human cognition, trust, and decision-making intersect with intelligent systems.

To strengthen methodological transparency, the interview protocol was explicitly aligned with the research questions and theoretical frameworks. This ensured that data collection was not only exploratory but also theoretically anchored. In addition, the analysis examined not only recurring patterns but also tensions, contradictions, and deviant cases, thereby improving interpretive rigor and reducing the risk of oversimplified thematic conclusions.

Participant Recruitment

Participants were selected through purposive sampling to recruit individuals with direct experience in programming and AI chatbot development. The final sample consisted of 15 participants, including undergraduate and graduate students in computer science and professional software developers. This diverse range of backgrounds provided a nuanced understanding of how generative AI tools are perceived, utilized, and integrated across varying levels of expertise and work contexts.

All participants reported active engagement with large language model-based tools such as ChatGPT, GitHub Copilot, or similar AI-assisted coding platforms. Recruitment was conducted through academic networks, professional contacts, and university listservs. Prior to each interview, participants received a detailed informed consent form, outlining the purpose of the study, the voluntary nature of participation, and measures taken to ensure confidentiality. Participants were reminded that they could withdraw at any point without consequence. No financial compensation was provided for participation.

Data Collection

Data were collected through semi-structured, in-depth Zoom interviews, each lasting 45-75 minutes. The interview protocol was designed to elicit rich reflections on key topics, including participants' experiences with AI-assisted coding, perceptions of skill development and task ownership, ethical concerns surrounding AI use, strategies for adapting to AI integration in the workplace or classroom, and their visions for future human-AI collaboration.

All participants reported active engagement with large language model-based tools such as ChatGPT, GitHub Copilot, or similar AI-assisted coding platforms. Recruitment was conducted through academic networks, professional contacts, and university listservs. Prior to each interview, participants received a detailed informed consent form, outlining the purpose of the study, the voluntary nature of participation, and measures taken to ensure confidentiality. Participants were reminded that they could withdraw at any point without consequence. No financial compensation was provided for participation.

Data saturation was reached when no substantially new themes emerged from successive interviews, indicating sufficient depth and coverage of the phenomenon under investigation.

While the interview guide provided structure, the format remained flexible, allowing participants to elaborate on issues most relevant to their personal and professional contexts. This approach enabled the researcher to explore emergent themes in greater depth while ensuring consistency across interviews. With informed consent, all sessions were recorded and transcribed verbatim to facilitate rigorous qualitative analysis.

Analytical Approach

Data analysis followed a thematic coding approach that combined inductive and deductive strategies to ensure a comprehensive, theory-informed interpretation of participant responses. Transcripts were initially reviewed holistically to identify recurring concepts, linguistic patterns, and areas of emphasis across interviews. Preliminary codes were developed based on emergent themes from participant narratives and on sensitizing concepts derived from the study's theoretical frameworks: the Deskilling of Jobs Theory, the Job Characteristics Theory, and the Technology Threat Avoidance Theory.

In subsequent rounds of coding, responses were grouped into thematic categories, contradictions and tensions were examined, and analytical memos were used to trace conceptual links between participant experiences and the guiding frameworks. These themes were then systematically mapped to the study's three central research questions:

1. How does the integration of generative AI tools influence the security practices within the Secure Software Development Life Cycle (SSDLC)?
2. What are the risks and mitigation strategies associated with vulnerability propagation in AI-generated code?
3. What is the role of human oversight and explainability in maintaining security and accountability in AI-assisted software engineering?

This iterative and reflexive coding process enabled the development of rich, theoretically grounded insights into how developers navigate the integration of generative AI within secure software engineering environments.

More specifically, the analysis proceeded in two broad stages. First, open coding was used to surface recurring ideas, concerns, and behavioral patterns directly from participant narratives. Second, these codes were refined into higher-order themes through interpretive and theory-guided categorization. Analytical memos documented coding decisions, theoretical reflections, and relationships across themes. This process enhances transparency by showing how raw interview data were transformed into the thematic findings presented in the chapter.

Trustworthiness

This study adhered to established best practices in qualitative research to ensure credibility, trustworthiness, and ethical rigor. Triangulation was achieved by analyzing responses from participants with diverse roles and professional experiences, enabling a richer, more nuanced interpretation of themes. Member checking was conducted with selected participants, who were invited to review preliminary interpretations of their interviews to validate the accuracy and authenticity of the findings. Additionally, the researcher engaged in reflexive journaling throughout the analytic process to document interpretive decisions and to critically examine personal biases that could influence data interpretation.

Ethical standards were rigorously maintained, emphasizing confidentiality, transparency, and participant autonomy. All data were securely stored on password-protected devices, and personally identifiable information was removed from transcripts prior to analysis to safeguard participant privacy and uphold research integrity.

FINDINGS AND DISCUSSION

This section shares the main findings from the interviews, organized around the study's three research questions. Based on participants' real experiences, it explores how tools like GitHub Copilot and ChatGPT are changing secure software development, developer roles, and how people think about responsibility and risk. The findings are also connected to key theories—Deskilling of Jobs Theory, Job Characteristics Theory, and Technology Threat Avoidance Theory—to understand better how automation is shaping skills and security awareness.

Instead of separating results from interpretation, this section blends both to give a clearer picture of how students and professionals are adapting to AI-assisted coding. Each part focuses on a research question, highlighting common themes, participant insights, and their implications for secure software development and the future of work. To bring everything together, Table 4 shows how generative AI fits into different stages of DevSecOps, including the types of AI support used and the related security practices.

Table 4. Summary of qualitative themes, theoretical interpretation, and practical implications

Research Question	Theme	Theoretical lens	Practical implication
RQ1	Fragmentation of security workflows	DJT, JCT	Re-embed security gates into AI workflows
RQ2	Vulnerability propagation	TTAT	Use layered validation and prompt constraints
RQ3	Human oversight and explainability gaps	JCT, TTAT	Maintain human approval and traceable review

RQ1: How does the integration of generative AI tools influence the security practices within the Secure Software Development Life Cycle (SSDLC)?
Theme 1: Fragmentation of Traditional Security Workflows

Participants reported that AI tools frequently circumvent standard checkpoints in the Secure Software Development Life Cycle (SSDLC), leading to inconsistencies in critical activities such as threat modeling, input validation, and secure design implementation. Several participants expressed concern that AI-generated code often appears functionally correct but lacks essential security considerations. One developer noted, "The code Copilot generates usually compiles and runs without issues, but it often lacks proper input validation. It seems to assume that all inputs are already safe and trustworthy." Another participant highlighted issues with secure design practices being overlooked, stating, "AI suggestions don't take into account security protocols. It's like working like a machine." Others observed that reliance on AI suggestions can weaken the discipline of threat modeling. "We used to walk through threat scenarios together during design reviews," one participant explained. "But now, with Copilot, the team just runs with whatever it suggests and ignores if it's causing a vulnerability." These reflections underscore the risk that AI integration, when not carefully governed, may erode critical security checkpoints, thereby increasing the likelihood of vulnerabilities in production code.

Theme 2: Shifting Security Responsibility to Post-Generation Review

Rather than proactively integrating security measures during the initial stages of code generation, many developers reported adopting a reactive approach, addressing vulnerabilities only after the AI-generated code had already been produced. This shift in practice reflects a growing reliance on post-hoc review and remediation rather than secure-by-design principles traditionally emphasized in the Secure Software Development Life Cycle. Several participants acknowledged that while AI tools like GitHub Copilot significantly accelerate development, they often lead to shortcuts in security-conscious coding. One developer admitted, "I rely on Copilot to generate the code first and then go back to fix incomplete code and make it better." Another stated, "Security checks come later, after I test whether the code works. The priority is speed, not security upfront." This tendency to defer secure coding considerations until after functional requirements are met suggests a misalignment between AI-augmented development workflows and established DevSecOps principles. As a result, vulnerabilities may remain undetected until later stages of the pipeline, increasing the risk and cost of remediation.

Theme 3: Increased Dependence on AI for Secure Code Patterns

Several participants described using AI tools as convenient shortcuts to implement what they perceived as "secure" functionality, such as encryption, input validation, or authentication logic, often relying on the plausibility of the generated code rather than verifying its correctness or compliance with established security standards. This reliance appeared to stem from a sense of trust in the tool's output, especially when the suggestions mirrored commonly used patterns or APIs. One participant explained, "When Copilot gives me the code back, I usually assume it is right. I don't always double-check the algorithm." Another developer shared, "It looks secure, but I'm not sure if it meets our compliance requirements." These accounts reveal a tendency to conflate syntactic completeness with security assurance, potentially introducing subtle vulnerabilities that may not be caught unless rigorously reviewed. The perceived convenience of AI-generated security functions, coupled with time pressures and limited expertise in secure coding, may lead to overconfidence in AI outputs and a diminished role for manual verification. This practice raises concerns about the depth of developer understanding and the risk of deploying insecure or non-compliant code under the assumption that AI suggestions are inherently trustworthy.

Taken together, these findings suggest that integrating generative AI into the SSDLC does not automatically modernize security practices. Instead, it can fragment traditional workflows unless security controls are deliberately re-embedded into AI-assisted development. This finding directly motivates the structured framework proposed later in the chapter.

> **RQ2:** What are the risks and mitigation strategies associated with vulnerability propagation in AI-generated code?
> *Theme 1:* Inherited Insecurity from Training Data

Participants expressed significant concerns that AI models, particularly those trained on large datasets from public code repositories, often reproduce insecure coding patterns embedded in their training data. These repositories often contain outdated, poorly written, or non-compliant code. AI-generated outputs may inadvertently replicate security vulnerabilities such as hardcoded credentials, insufficient input validation, or improper error handling. As one developer noted, "If the model learns from bad data, the result will not be correct and not secure." Another participant added, "The problem is that the code looks great, but I do not know if it is a good practice." This replication of flawed patterns introduces a layer of unpredictability into secure software development, as developers may unknowingly trust code that appears syntactically correct but fails to meet security standards. The difficulty in detecting such flaws is compounded by the volume of suggestions and the absence of transparency around how AI models prioritize or select certain coding practices.

As a result, participants stressed the need for enhanced scrutiny of AI-generated code and for integrating automated security checks to mitigate the risk of inherited vulnerabilities.

Theme 2: Reliance on Prompt Engineering to Reduce Risk

Developers increasingly rely on careful prompt engineering as a workaround to steer AI tools toward producing more secure and contextually appropriate code. By refining the wording, structure, and specificity of their prompts, they aim to influence the model to include practices such as input sanitization, encryption, and secure API usage. Several participants described experimenting with multiple prompts to get the desired security outcomes. One developer shared, "If I have a different prompt, Copilot gives me different results." Another noted, "Sometimes you have to be very explicit, specifying OWASP guidelines, otherwise it just gives you the most generic version of the function." Despite these strategies, participants acknowledged that the effectiveness of prompt-based guidance remains inconsistent, often varying across coding contexts, the model's interpretation of the prompt, and task complexity. While prompt design offers some control, it is not a substitute for formal security verification, and participants emphasized the continued need for code review and automated analysis to ensure reliability. This practice reflects a growing awareness among developers of the influence they can exert over AI behavior, as well as the limitations of that influence in high-stakes, security-sensitive environments.

Theme 3: Layered Auditing as a Mitigation Strategy

Participants described employing a layered approach to mitigate the risks associated with AI-generated code, combining static analysis tools, peer code review, and automated testing to validate outputs and detect potential vulnerabilities. This multi-faceted strategy was seen as essential for identifying flaws that might be overlooked when relying solely on AI-generated suggestions. One developer explained, "Copilot can miss basic things such as insecure defaults." Another participant emphasized the value of collaborative scrutiny, stating, "To be safe, it is better to have peer reviews. Having peer reviews often catches things that the AI misses." Automated testing frameworks were also widely used to ensure functional correctness and flag unexpected behaviors, particularly in security-critical components. These practices reflect a cautious but adaptive response to integrating generative AI into secure development workflows. Rather than assuming AI outputs are trustworthy, developers are building safeguards around them, embedding validation into the pipeline to uphold software quality and compliance with secure coding standards.

Theme 4: Technically Subtle Security Flaws in Otherwise Functional Code

Participants consistently reported that AI-generated code can introduce subtle but significant security vulnerabilities, particularly when outputs are accepted without thorough review. Common issues included inadequate input validation, insecure authentication logic, and the inclusion of hardcoded credentials. These vulnerabilities often appeared in otherwise functional code, making them difficult to detect without explicit security checks.

From a technical perspective, such vulnerabilities arise from the probabilistic nature of generative AI models, which prioritize syntactic correctness over secure implementation. As a result, AI systems may reproduce insecure coding patterns present in training data or fail to account for context-specific security requirements. Many of these risks align with widely recognized OWASP categories, including injection flaws, insecure design, broken access control, and security misconfiguration.

These findings highlight the need for enhanced security validation practices within AI-assisted development. Participants emphasized the importance of integrating automated security testing, applying secure prompt engineering techniques, and maintaining human oversight to identify and mitigate potential vulnerabilities. This theme directly informs the development of a structured DevSecOps framework discussed in the subsequent section.

RQ3: What is the role of human oversight and explainability in maintaining security and accountability in AI-assisted software engineering?
Theme 1: Human Review as a Safeguard Against AI Hallucination

Participants emphasized the continued importance of human oversight in the development process, particularly when working with AI-generated code. While AI tools like Copilot and ChatGPT can accelerate coding tasks, participants consistently noted that these tools often produce outputs that, although syntactically correct, may contain logic errors and insecure defaults in the code segments. One developer commented, "Sometimes the code looks perfect, but it is incorrect." Another shared, "I've seen Copilot reference nonexistent APIs or use deprecated methods." These incidents highlight that, while powerful, AI tools lack the contextual understanding and judgment that human developers bring to software engineering. As a result, participants viewed human review not as optional but as a critical safeguard against the subtle, often unpredictable errors introduced by generative AI. This perspective reinforces the idea that AI should augment, not replace, human expertise, particularly in security-sensitive and high-stakes development environments.

Theme 2: Gaps in Explainability Undermine Trust in AI Suggestions

Many developers expressed frustration with the opaque, non-explanatory nature of AI-generated code, noting that the lack of reasoning or justification behind the outputs significantly limited their ability to trust the code or fully understand what it was doing. Unlike human collaborators who can explain their logic or cite design rationale, AI tools often provide code completions without any contextual explanation, making it difficult for developers to assess correctness, compliance, or security implications.

One participant remarked, "It just gives you the code, but I do not know what algorithm and logic it selected from." Another noted, "If something goes wrong, you do not know what to debug." This lack of transparency was seen as a barrier to adoption, particularly in high-stakes environments like secure software development, where understanding the rationale behind decisions is critical for compliance, auditing, and debugging. Developers called for features such as inline explanations or traceable reasoning paths to improve the interpretability and trustworthiness of AI-assisted development tools.

Theme 3: Evolving Role of the Developer as Curator and Validator

Rather than acting as sole authors of code, participants described their evolving role in AI-assisted development as that of curators. These professionals selectively accept, adapt, or reject AI-generated code based on their domain knowledge, experience, and contextual understanding. This shift reflects a more nuanced form of human-AI collaboration, where developers no longer write every line of code from scratch but instead critically evaluate and refine suggestions from tools like Copilot or ChatGPT.

One participant explained, "I treat it like a starter. It gives me something to start with, but I always come back and double-check later." Another noted, "I do not trust the code. I always come back and check for security and logic." This curatorial approach underscores the importance of maintaining human agency in the software development process, especially in contexts where correctness, maintainability, and security are non-negotiable. By positioning themselves as the final gatekeepers of quality and compliance, developers reinforce the need for critical thinking and professional oversight, even as generative AI becomes increasingly integrated into their workflows.

Summary of Findings and Case Studies

This study explored how software developers and students experience the integration of generative AI tools, such as ChatGPT and GitHub Copilot, within secure software development practices. Through in-depth interviews with fifteen participants from diverse academic and professional backgrounds, the findings reveal a complex and evolving relationship between AI-augmented programming and software security. The analysis, guided by Deskilling of Jobs Theory, Job Characteristics Theory, and Technology Threat Avoidance Theory, produced three key themes for each of the study's research questions. These themes are supported by illustrative case studies that ground theoretical insights in practical, real-world experiences.

Under RQ1, the integration of generative AI within the Secure Software Development Life Cycle (SSDLC) was shown to fragment traditional workflows. Participants reported that AI tools often circumvent standard security checks and shift the burden of secure coding to post-generation review. While some viewed AI as a helpful assistant for producing secure code templates, others expressed concern about over-reliance on model outputs without adequate validation. A senior developer participant described using Copilot to generate a login scenario, only to later realize that the AI had failed to implement essential security checks. This experience highlighted the inherent risks of accepting AI-generated code at face value, emphasizing the need for careful review and validation to ensure security standards are met.

RQ2 focused on the risks and mitigation strategies related to vulnerability propagation in AI-generated code. Participants consistently noted that insecure coding patterns embedded in LLM training data can surface in generated output. One junior developer participant shared an experience in which they used an AI tool to generate a database interaction snippet containing personal information, only to discover later that the code was vulnerable to SQL injection. The AI-generated snippet lacked proper input sanitization and failed to implement parameterized queries, posing a serious risk to data security. The developer admitted that the vulnerability went unnoticed at first because the code appeared syntactically correct and executed without errors. It was only after a security review that the flaw was identified, highlighting the importance of scrutinizing AI-generated code, especially when handling sensitive data. This experience prompted the developer to adopt prompt engineering strategies and integrate security linters into their workflow. Across participants, mitigation efforts included prompt refinement, layered code reviews, and the adoption of secure-by-design principles as guardrails against AI-generated flaws.

In relation to RQ3, participants emphasized the crucial role of human oversight and explainability in maintaining security and accountability in AI-assisted development. While AI tools were praised for their speed and convenience, many expressed concern about the nature of LLMs and the lack of explainability in code suggestions. A graduate student participant working on an AI-driven chatbot described having to reverse-engineer AI output line by line to understand its function and security implications. Across cases, the developer's role was increasingly described not as a traditional coder but as a curator, responsible for auditing, modifying, and contextualizing AI-generated content.

Taken together, these findings suggest that while generative AI introduces efficiency gains, it also creates new demands for security literacy, critical judgment, and adaptive workflows. Developers must now balance the benefits of automation with the risks of over-reliance, especially in security-sensitive contexts. The case studies presented throughout the analysis illustrate how real-world practitioners are navigating this balance by evolving their roles, rethinking workflows, and cultivating new competencies to ensure that AI remains a tool for augmentation rather than a source of risk.

PROPOSED FRAMEWORK: SECURE AI-ASSISTED DEVSECOPS INTEGRATION

Based on empirical findings and the literature reviewed, this study proposes a Secure AI-Assisted DevSecOps Framework to integrate generative AI into software engineering without undermining security, accountability, or human expertise. The framework is designed to preserve SSDLC controls while leveraging AI for productivity gains.

The framework consists of five interdependent layers:

1. **Intent and Prompt Layer.** Developers define the task, system context, security constraints, compliance requirements, and expected coding standards in the prompt. A prompt design should explicitly specify security requirements, including input validation, encryption, authentication controls, alignment with OWASP guidelines, logging expectations, and dependency restrictions.
2. **AI Generation Layer.** The generative AI system produces candidate code, test cases, refactoring suggestions, or technical documentation. Outputs at this stage should be treated as draft artifacts rather than trusted production-ready code.
3. **Human Review and Explainability Layer.** Developers inspect AI-generated outputs for logic, maintainability, context fit, and compliance. Where possible, explainability features such as inline rationale, comments, or traceable suggestion context should support this review. Human approval remains mandatory before downstream integration.
4. **Automated Security Validation Layer.** AI-generated code is passed through static application security testing (SAST), software composition analysis (SCA), secret scanning, dependency checks, policy validation, and targeted test suites. This layer operationalizes DevSecOps controls within the CI/CD workflow.

5. **Continuous Monitoring and Feedback Layer.** Outputs deployed into staging or production are continuously monitored for vulnerabilities, anomalous behavior, configuration drift, and policy violations. Feedback from code reviews, incidents, audit logs, and runtime observations should be used to refine prompts, policies, and team practices over time.

This framework conceptualizes generative AI not as an autonomous engineer, but as a bounded contributor operating within a controlled socio-technical security system. Figure 3. Proposed framework for secure AI-assisted software development. The framework consists of five interdependent layers: (1) intent and prompt definition, (2) AI-based code generation, (3) human review and explainability, (4) automated security validation using DevSecOps controls, and (5) continuous monitoring and feedback.

Figure 3. Proposed framework: secure AI-assisted devsecops integration

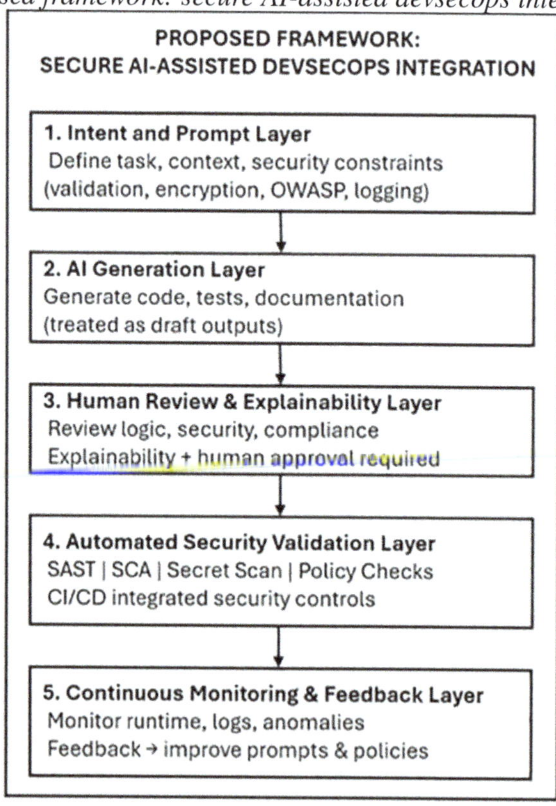

Source: Author's own work

DISCUSSION AND IMPLICATIONS

The findings of this study reveal the complex, often contradictory effects of integrating generative AI into secure software development. While participants recognized the productivity benefits of tools such as GitHub Copilot and ChatGPT, they also expressed concerns about security risks, reduced task ownership, and the erosion of traditional coding skills. Interpreted through the lenses of Deskilling of Jobs Theory, Job Characteristics Theory, and Technology Threat Avoidance Theory, the findings point to a dynamic reconfiguration of developer roles and responsibilities in AI-augmented environments.

Reframing the Role of the Developer

The integration of generative AI has shifted the developer's role from creator to curator, a transition that reflects key insights from the Deskilling of Jobs Theory. Many participants described relying on AI for code scaffolding or routine implementations, only to intervene later for debugging or validation. While this shift can reduce cognitive load and increase efficiency, it also risks long-term deskilling, especially in secure coding practices. As participants increasingly rely on AI to write functional components, their opportunities to practice and internalize critical security principles diminish.

However, this transformation is not uniformly negative. In line with Job Characteristics Theory, some participants reported that AI tools allowed them to focus on more meaningful and complex tasks, such as architectural design or system integration. When used thoughtfully, AI can enhance task significance and autonomy, provided developers retain control and responsibility for reviewing and modifying the output. This transformation suggests the need for intentional role design that leverages AI to augment, rather than replace, core developer competencies.

Security as a Human-AI Collaboration

The findings also reinforce that AI-generated code is not inherently secure. Despite advancements in large language models, participants regularly encountered issues such as hardcoded credentials, missing input validation, and insecure authentication flows in AI-generated output. This finding aligns with Technology Threat Avoidance Theory, which posits that developers must engage in both threat and coping appraisals to mitigate risk. Developers who perceived themselves as capable of addressing these threats, often through layered review strategies, prompt engineering, and tool chaining, were more confident in integrating AI into their workflows.

A critical implication here is the need for embedded security awareness in the human-AI collaboration process. Developers must be trained not only in secure coding practices but also in AI literacy, understanding how LLMs generate code, where they fail, and how to intervene. Organizations should provide resources such as security linters, model explainability tools, and AI-specific training to help developers recognize and remediate potential vulnerabilities introduced by automated systems.

Governance, Explainability, and Ethical Oversight

A recurring concern among participants was the opacity of AI-generated code. Many expressed discomfort with using code they could not fully understand or explain, especially in high-stakes or regulated environments. This concern highlights the importance of integrating explainability mechanisms into AI-assisted development tools. Developers need transparency not only in what the code does but also in why it was generated a certain way. This need is particularly urgent in the context of secure software development, where compliance, auditability, and ethical accountability are non-negotiable.

From an organizational perspective, this points to the need for governance frameworks that define acceptable use policies, establish review protocols, and clarify human accountability when AI tools are used in production environments. Without such structures, the line between human and machine responsibility becomes blurred, raising both ethical and legal concerns.

Practical Implications

1. For Developers: There is a pressing need to cultivate both AI fluency and security-first thinking, ensuring developers remain capable of critically evaluating and refining AI-generated code.
2. For Educators: Computer science curricula should integrate AI-assisted coding tools while emphasizing fundamental skills in secure design, testing, and code review.
3. For Organizations: Employers must implement AI governance strategies that combine human oversight with automated auditing tools to mitigate the risk of vulnerability propagation.
4. For Tool Designers: Developers of generative AI platforms should prioritize features that support transparency, feedback integration, and secure-by-design outputs.

Scholarly Implication

This study contributes to the growing body of research on human-AI collaboration, particularly in the context of secure software engineering. It deepens our understanding of how AI influences not only technical workflows but also skill development, perceptions of risk, and professional identity. By integrating DJT, JCT, and TTAT, the study offers a multidimensional framework for analyzing the socio-technical implications of AI in software development, a foundation for future research exploring long-term impacts on workforce transformation, education, and cybersecurity.

More broadly, the study demonstrates that generative AI should not be analyzed solely as a productivity tool. It must also be understood as a socio-technical force that redistributes expertise, changes motivational structures, and alters how security responsibility is enacted in practice. This stronger linkage between technical findings, theory, and organizational implications is one of the chapter's central analytical contributions.

CONCLUSION AND FUTURE DIRECTIONS

Employing a qualitative, phenomenological approach, this investigation explored the transformative impact of generative AI tools, including ChatGPT and GitHub Copilot, on secure software development methodologies and the evolving roles of developers. Through interviews with programmers and students actively utilizing AI-assisted coding, the research revealed a complex environment. This environment is characterized by the emergence of novel security concerns, the necessity for skill adaptation, and the critical importance of human oversight, all of which coexist with the advantages offered by automation.

The study's results indicated that the incorporation of generative AI has disrupted established security protocols, reallocating responsibilities toward post-generation assessment and transforming the developer's function from one of creation to curation. Although participants acknowledged the productivity enhancements provided by these tools, they simultaneously voiced apprehensions regarding potential vulnerabilities, a reduction in skill specialization, and the lack of transparency inherent in AI-generated code. These observations, analyzed through the lenses of Deskilling of Jobs Theory, Job Characteristics Theory, and Technology Threat Avoidance Theory, underscore the necessity for forward-thinking strategies that reconcile automation with the imperative of accountability.

The study especially emphasizes that secure code generation in the age of AI is not a purely technical challenge; it is a socio-technical endeavor. Developers must be equipped not only with technical expertise but also with AI literacy, ethical awareness, and strong risk assessment skills. To ensure that artificial intelligence is a benefit, not a drawback, in software development, organizations and educators must rethink how they train, supervise, and use AI tools.

In conclusion, the chapter demonstrates that the secure use of generative AI in software engineering depends not only on the model's sophistication but also on the strength of the human, procedural, and organizational controls surrounding it. Generative AI can accelerate development and expand programming support, but without explicit governance, it may also propagate insecure patterns, weaken role clarity, and encourage overreliance on opaque outputs. Thus, the main point isn't that AI should be avoided, but rather that it should be carefully integrated into the SSDLC. This requires human oversight, a focus on explainability, security checks at different levels, and controls that align with DevSecOps principles.

Limitations and Future Directions

Despite offering valuable perspectives on the convergence of artificial intelligence, secure software engineering, and HyFlex learning environments, this investigation is subject to certain constraints. The study's findings are circumscribed by its reliance on a limited sample drawn from a U.S.-based population, thereby restricting the applicability of the results to wider educational and organizational settings. Furthermore, the dependence on self-reported experiences introduces the possibility of subjectivity, given that participants' accounts of their interactions with AI may be shaped by personal biases or retrospective assessments.

A further constraint stems from the dynamic character of AI technologies. Given the ongoing advancements in large language models, adaptive learning systems, and explainability frameworks, the platforms analyzed in this research might not accurately represent the future trajectory of AI integration within educational contexts. Furthermore, the study's scope was limited to a particular category of AI-augmented tools. Consequently, it may not encompass the complete spectrum of platforms, developmental methodologies, or pedagogical implementations presently employed across various institutions and sectors.

To mitigate these constraints, subsequent investigations should encompass more expansive and heterogeneous participant cohorts, incorporating international viewpoints, educational environments that are currently underrepresented, and individuals possessing varying degrees of technological proficiency. Furthermore, longitudinal and mixed-methods research is particularly warranted to assess the temporal evolution of adaptation to AI among developers, educators, and students. This examination should extend beyond mere tool utilization to encompass the retention of skills, the cultivation of critical thinking abilities, and the development of ethical discernment.

Future research should focus on understanding how artificial intelligence (AI) affects people and organizations in software engineering and education. A key area of study involves measuring AI's impact on specific cognitive and technical skills. Fields like debugging, system architecture, and secure coding require deep expertise. Therefore, it's crucial to understand how AI tools help or hinder these skills to create effective and responsible learning environments.

A further essential avenue of investigation centers on assessing the impact of training and mentorship initiatives in fostering ethical and efficient human-AI collaboration. Given the increasing integration of AI tools within the development lifecycle, specific interventions, including onboarding programs, ethical AI workshops, and AI literacy curricula, could assist users in addressing issues pertaining to transparency, accountability, and bias.

Future investigations should, therefore, focus on the organizational and cultural elements that influence the adoption and governance of artificial intelligence. The responsible and effective implementation of AI is contingent upon institutional policies, leadership perspectives, and internal security measures. Comparative analyses across various institutions or sectors could illuminate exemplary practices and structural impediments to ethical AI utilization, especially within contexts where security and trust are of utmost importance.

REFERENCES

Barke, S., James, M., & Polikarpova, N. (2023). Grounded Copilot: How programmers interact with code-generating models. *Proceedings of the ACM on Programming Languages, 7*(OOPSLA1), 85-111. DOI: 10.1145/3586030

Braverman, H. (1974). *Labor and monopoly capital.* Monthly Review Press. DOI: 10.14452/MR-026-03-1974-07_1

Crowston, K., & Bolici, F. (2025). Deskilling and upskilling with AI Systems. *nformation Research an International Electronic Journal, 30*(iConf), 1009-1023. DOI: 10.47989/ir30iConf47143

Hackman, J. R., & Oldham, G. R. (1976). Motivation through the design of work: Test of a theory. *Organizational Behavior and Human Performance, 16*(2), 250–279. DOI: 10.1016/0030-5073(76)90016-7

Khurana, A., Subramonyam, H., & Chilana, P. K. (2024). Why and when llm-based assistants can go wrong: Investigating the effectiveness of prompt-based interactions for software help-seeking. *arXiv.org*. Retrieved from /arxiv.2402.08030DOI: 10.1145/3640543.3645200

Kuhail, M. A., Mathew, S. S., Khalil, A., Khalil, A., & Shah, S. J. (2023). "Will I be replaced?" Assessing ChatGPT's effect on software development and programmer perceptions of AI tools. *arXiv.org*. Retrieved from DOI: 10.2139/ssrn.4571482

Liang, H., & Xue, Y. (2009). Avoidance of information technology threats: A theoretical perspective. *Management Information Systems Quarterly, 33*(1), 71–90. DOI: 10.2307/20650279

OWASP. (2025). *OWASP Top 10: 2025—The ten most critical web application security risks*. Retrieved from https://owasp.org/Top10/2025

Pearce, H., Ahmad, B., Tan, B., Dolan-Gavitt, B., & Karri, R. (2022). Asleep at the Keyboard? Assessing the Security of GitHub Copilot's Code Contributions. *43rd IEEE Symposium on Security and Privacy, SP 2022*. Proceedings - IEEE Symposium on Security and Privacy. DOI: 10.1109/SP46214.2022.9833571

Peoples, K. (2021). *How to write a phenomenological dissertation: A step-by-step guide* (Vol. 56). SAGE.

Prates, L., & Pereira, R. (2025). DevSecOps practices and tools. *International Journal of Information Security, 24*(1), 11. Advance online publication. DOI: 10.1007/s10207-024-00914-z

Puccio, B., Castagna, F., Tucker, A., & Veltri, P. (2025). Towards medical AI misalignment: A preliminary study. *arXiv preprint.* https://doi.org//arXiv.2505.18212DOI: 10.48550

Riazi, M., Rezvani, R., & Ghanbar, H. (2023). Trustworthiness in L2 writing research: A review and analysis of qualitative articles in the Journal of Second Language Writing. *Research Methods in Applied Linguistics, 2*(3), 100065. Advance online publication. DOI: 10.1016/j.rmal.2023.100065

Rinta-Kahila, T., Penttinen, E., Salovaara, A., Soliman, W., & Ruissalo, J. (2023). The vicious circles of skill erosion: A case study of cognitive automation. *Journal of the Association for Information Systems, 24*(5), 1378–1412. DOI: 10.17705/1jais.00829

Sobania, D., Briesch, M., Hanna, C., & Petke, J. (2023). An Analysis of the Automatic Bug Fixing Performance of ChatGPT. *arXiv preprint.* /arXiv.2301.08653DOI: 10.1109/APR59189.2023.00012

Stefaniak, J., & Moore, S. (2024). The Use of Generative AI to Support Inclusivity and Design Deliberation for Online Instruction. *Online Learning : The Official Journal of the Online Learning Consortium, 28*(3), 181–205. DOI: 10.24059/olj.v28i3.4458

Sun, J., Liao, Q. V., Muller, M., Agarwal, M., Houde, S., Talamadupula, K., & Weisz, J. D. (2022). Investigating explainability of generative AI for code through scenario-based design. *arXiv preprint.* /arXiv.2202.04903DOI: 10.1145/3490099.3511119

Wang, J., Luo, X., Cao, L., He, H., Huang, H., Xie, J., . . . Cai, Y. (2024). Is Your AI-Generated Code Really Safe? Evaluating Large Language Models on Secure Code Generation with CodeSecEval. *arXiv preprint.* https://doi.org//arXiv.2407.02395DOI: 10.48550

Zhang, B., Liang, P., Zhou, X., Ahmad, A., & Waseem, M. (2023). Practices and challenges of using github copilot: An empirical study. *arXiv preprint.* https://doi.org/arXiv:2303.08733v3 DOI: 10.18293/SEKE2023-077

KEY TERMS AND DEFINITIONS

AI-Augmented Development: A way of coding where developers work alongside AI tools to improve productivity, code quality, and overall efficiency.

Code Vulnerabilities: Weak spots or flaws in code that attackers can exploit, such as SQL injection or buffer overflow vulnerabilities.

Ethical AI Governance: Ethical AI governance encompasses guidelines and policies that ensure responsible AI use in software development. This approach prioritizes fairness, accountability, and adherence to established regulations.

Explainable AI (XAI): Approaches that make AI decisions easier to understand, which helps developers trust and verify the code being generated.

Generative AI: Tools like ChatGPT and GitHub Copilot can create new code, text, or data by learning patterns from existing information.

Human-AI Collaboration: Developers and AI systems are working together on coding tasks, combining human judgment with AI assistance.

Prompt Engineering: The skill of crafting prompts that guide AI tools to produce useful, accurate, and safe outputs.

Secure Code Generation: Writing code in a way that avoids known security issues and can handle potential attacks, while following best practices—often with help from AI tools.

Security Misalignment: When the intended secure design of a system doesn't align with what AI actually produces, it can lead to security risks.

Software Engineering: The structured process of building, improving, and maintaining software is now increasingly influenced by AI technologies.

Chapter 8
Generative AI for Continuous Monitoring and Compliance

Venkataramesh Induru
http://orcid.org/0009-0005-6530-4296
Piorion Solutions Inc., USA

Priyadarshini Radhakrishnan
http://orcid.org/0009-0001-0709-2337
IBM Corporation, USA

Vijai Anand Ramar
http://orcid.org/0009-0008-1670-7170
Delta Dental Insurance Company, USA

Yashwant Kumar Kolli
http://orcid.org/0009-0003-8634-3265
Cognizant Technology Solutions US Corp., USA

Karthik Kushala
http://orcid.org/0009-0005-7851-7039
Taylor Corporation, USA

S. K. Pravin Kumar
Department of Electronics and Communication Engineering, United Institute of Technology, Coimbatore, India

ABSTRACT

Generative Artificial Intelligence is transforming continuous monitoring and regulatory compliance across sectors. Since there is heightened cybersecurity, financial reporting, and legal requirement compliance complexity, organizations require intelligent, scalable, and flexible solutions. GenAI brings robust capabilities such as report automation, anomaly detection, detailed risk reporting, and regulatory scenario simulation with low-level minimal intervention. The book presents a comprehensive end-to-end explanation of GenAI architectures, frameworks, ethics, and real-time applications in monitoring dynamic systems and compliance in the real world. Every chapter is based on flagship sectors such as finance, healthcare, manufacturing, and cybersecurity, and includes in-depth case studies, implementation

DOI: 10.4018/979-8-3693-8397-1.ch008

plans, and upcoming trends. The book is geared towards policymakers, researchers, and practitioners alike, bridging theory and practice. It provides a comprehensive guide to applying GenAI in the development of smart, transparent, and ethical compliance solutions

1. INTRODUCTION

In today's constantly evolving and highly regulated business environment, organisations must grapple with a rising and increasingly complicated terrain of requirements for regulation (Dwivedi et al., 2023). The outdated compliance checking tools based on static rule-based systems and infrequent, human-performed audits cannot keep pace with increasing transactional data velocity and volume (Dwivedi et al., 2023). Such conventional procedures are not only time-consuming but also limited in their ability to detect actual-time compliance breaches or shifting patterns of fraud, leaving organizations vulnerable to huge financial and legal costs (Livadariu et al., 2024).

With the recently released AI, particularly generative AI models, there is an increased potential to reshape the way continuous compliance monitoring is being done (Dr. Andrew Martin, 2021). Generative AI models such as transformers and variational autoencoders have proven highly effective in learning complex patterns within data as well as generating realistic samples (Reddy, 2024). These skills make generative AI a leading contender to enable anomaly detection, predictive compliance analytics, and scenario simulation for businesses to possess pre-emptive capabilities against and in expectation of threats from regulation before these aggregate (Mansoor et al., 2024).

End-to-end monitoring platforms blended with generative AI can dynamically adapt to emerging threats and changing regulations and offer real-time monitoring much superior to static reactive means (Wen, 2024). Such unification guarantees ongoing compliance upkeep, reduces false positives, and improves explain ability and transparency in decision-making (González et al., 2023). Additionally, synthetic data generation with the help of generative AI supports privacy-preserving analysis and comprehensive testing of compliance systems without compromising sensitive information (Sreeram Reddy Thoom, 2025).

The architecture of an AI-based generative continuous compliance monitoring system realizes the urgent need for adaptive intelligent systems in dynamic regulatory landscapes. With synthetic financial transaction data that simulates real behaviour, the approach enables the detection of fraudulent and non-compliant activity in a single pipeline. TCNs learn sequential transaction patterns to identify anomalies as behavioural deviances. After the anomalies are brought to light, they are then passed to the refined T5 model to generate readable, contextualized explanations in alignment with regulatory wording. This structure consists of a two-phase system allowing for high detection precision and sufficiently interpretable outcomes that the auditors and compliance groups will be able to trust and leverage to act within the shortest possible timeframe. The design was designed to be adaptable and will, with continued model refinement, remain compliant with evolving regulations, serving as an infinitely scalable, real-time compliance solution for real-world financial scenarios. This study identifies a critical research gap in existing compliance monitoring systems, where most traditional and AI-based approaches lack real-time adaptability, explainability, and seamless integration of anomaly detection with regulatory reporting. To address these limitations, this work proposes a unified generative AI-driven framework that combines anomaly detection with automated compliance explanation for enhanced transparency and decision-making.

Key issues such as the limitations of traditional rule-based compliance systems and the challenges associated with handling large-scale dynamic data highlight the need for more adaptive and intelligent solutions. Integrating generative AI techniques can address these challenges by enabling real-time anomaly detection and explainable compliance reporting. Further enhancement can be achieved by incorporating real-world case studies, recent industry developments, and comparative analysis with existing approaches to improve practical relevance and analytical depth.

The discussion of key issues, challenges, and emerging trends in compliance monitoring requires a more balanced and comprehensive treatment. While the chapter provides detailed insights into technical components such as data preprocessing and model architecture, it places comparatively less emphasis on practical deployment considerations and real-world implications. In real-world financial and regulatory environments, non-compliance can lead to substantial financial losses, legal liabilities, and reputational damage, which warrant stronger discussion. Moreover, critical emerging aspects such as explainable artificial intelligence, real-time regulatory adaptation, and system scalability are not explored in sufficient depth. Contributions of the Study: This study proposes a novel generative AI-based framework that integrates Temporal Convolutional Networks (TCN) for anomaly detection with a T5-based model for automated explanation generation. Unlike existing approaches that focus only on detection, the proposed TCN–T5 pipeline provides both real-time identification of compliance violations and human-readable explanations, improving transparency and decision-making. This unified approach enhances efficiency, reduces manual effort, and offers a significant advancement over traditional AI-based compliance monitoring methods.

The chapter is organized as follows: Section 1 introduces the topic, Section 2 presents the related work, Section 3 outlines the problem statement and objectives,

Section 4 describes the methodology, Section 5 provides the results and analysis, and Section 6 concludes the chapter with key findings and future directions.

2. RELATED WORKS

(Naz & Xu, 2024). developed a proof-of-concept experiment of integrating generative AI with mobile robots to assist with autonomous monitoring in pharma R&D labs. They used multi-modal models and VFMs to identify anomalies and report automatically to improve compliance and safety. The research illustrated potential advantages in increasing lab monitor efficiency and minimizing manual supervision. (Tong et al 2024). designed a future-proof grid monitoring and control system using generative AI in conjunction with machine learning and statistical inference. Their design uses an innovation autoencoder for compressing continuous CPOW data streams and identifying unknown faults through nonparametric sequential hypothesis testing. The results achieve better fault detection and data compression than existing SCADA and PMU systems, providing enhanced situational awareness for dynamic grids. (Alam et al. 2024) created an AI-based framework to support IT control compliance improvement, with particular emphasis on solutions to SOX IT General Controls challenges. The AI-supported approach over enormous datasets, thus relieving menial monitoring tasks, positively impacts decision-making and reduces the scope for human error. The study has found that AI-powered systems provide three vital initiatives towards developing compliance: the governance, compliance, and risk management. (Liu & Wongsosaputro, 2024) introduced a generative AI-based solution to improvised regulatory reporting in the finance field. The solution applies GenAI to automate the generation of content, enrichment of data quality, and monitoring and visualizing regulatory data in real time. Outcomes show considerable cost savings and increased efficiency in compliance reporting exercises. (Wan et al., 2025) established a generative AI platform design with the help of LLMs for improved practices in the construction industry, mainly energy code compliance, design optimization, and worker training. The scheme interprets architectural drawings and regulatory codes to avoid some tedious time-consuming work, while this offers enhanced concurrency and accuracy. The outcome seems extremely promising for compliance checking based on AI and realistic simulation training.

(M. D. Munivel et al., 2024) developed cloud compliance management artificial intelligence (AI) solutions that make reporting and documentation automated in its entirety for finance, health care, and technology sectors. The approaches focused by the authors are cost savings, efficiency, and accuracy founded on real-world data as concluded from case studies of top organizations. The study highlights some of these trends such as Explainable AI (XAI) and constant compliance monitoring to keep pace with changing regulatory requirements. (Dwivedi et al., 2023) performed secondary data analysis of ethical and regulatory conformity issues regarding the application of generative AI in HR functions. Their work incorporated literature reviews, case studies, and regulatory frameworks to categorize best practices towards fairness, transparency, and privacy. The study reveals that though AI is poised to enhance HR operations, strong governance will be necessary. (Alqahtani, 2025) explored how generative AI models could aid compliance with the EU AI Act in connection with DNN-based perception systems used for autonomous driving. Their method was to categorize existing generative AI applications and test them against requirements for safety, transparency, and robustness. Findings show that generative AI is likely to offer useful contributions to regulatory compliance and perception reliability. (Mariam et al., 2024) designed a Question and Answer-Retrieval Augmented Generation (QA-RAG) model to support regulatory compliance in the pharmaceutical industry by integrating document retrieval and generative AI. The method provides correct responses to the guideline-related questions through linking relevant document search with generative response. They found that the QA-RAG outperformed the existing RAG in accuracy and reliability. (Ajmal et al., 2025) proposed in Australia a regulatory scheme for safe and responsible AI that emphasizes expert advisory-based, risk-based methods; outlining clear regulatory principles, establishing an independent AI board, and suggesting international transparency and alignment. Their conclusion supports targeted regulation of high-risk applications of AI but without stifling research or innovation.

(Yu et al., 2023). investigated the application of generative AI to healthcare, specifically through its utilization in automation of diagnosis procedures and patient monitoring. Their system highlighted implementation-issues inherent in data confidentiality, opportunities for faults, and regulatory issues-and proposed solutions to address these issues. Active regulation engagement and proper data training ensured that mass uptake would be secure. (Izquierdo-Bueno et al., 2024) also adopted a generative AI model of abnormal event discovery and worked on networks to identify suspect transactions and risk rating enrichment in financial platforms. They incorporated differential governance and privacy-reserving methods in their system so that fraud identification should not be at the cost of non-regulation compliance. The research established that such sophisticated AI models do increase response time to compliance requests or detection rates. (Liu & Wongsosaputro, 2024) suggested a generative neural network design that tracked smart IoT devices in real-time under various operating conditions. The hypothesis centres on continuous learning with carrying past data distribution without forgetting memory and accommodating new patterns, efficiently detecting changes and drifts of sensors. Experimental results of vibration sensor data that underwent simulated drifts were better than state-of-the-art benchmarks for drift detection and representation clarity. (Zhang & Wang, 2025) Explored the use of generative AI in cybersecurity towards conformity with the NIS2 Directive. Their approach analysed AI methodologies like natural language processing and machine learning for threat prediction, vulnerability probing, and attack response. Their general conclusion was that generative AI will greatly upgrade security practices because it would bring that upgradation with regulatory compliance. One inherent limitation is that the AI systems themselves continue to become increasingly un-guardable against shifting threats on the cyber periphery. (D. Munivel, Samir, Naveen, & Lavanya, 2024) developed an AI-driven compliance monitoring machine learning- and natural language processing-enabled framework for regulatory compliance automation and monitoring. With this deployment, companies could dynamically learn the evolving regulations, automate their reports, and enable compliance gap identification. The results were considerably improved operational efficiency and minimized regulatory risks.

(Singh et al., 2025) included a model for legal and ethical conformity in fintech generative AI systems by examining international laws and ethical as well as stakeholder aspects. They applied case study and technical audit methodology to present findings since they interconnect non-compliance risks and propose scalable governance models across industries. Findings emphasized collaborative policy-making for coordination, along with the routes to AI auditing and accountability. (Feuerriegel et al., 2024) performed a comprehensive survey on recent developments in generative AI and applications of generative AI across various fields, such as natural language processing, diagnosis in healthcare, and image conversion. Supervised and non-supervised generative models were compared in their research while evaluating their qualitative and applicative purposes. It has been revealed in the research that GAI presents the highest degree of latest technology capability with industry-transforming power. (Mansurova et al., 2024) developed generative AI-driven models that were suitable for real-time patient information, like electronic health records (EHRs) and vital signs information to identify diseases and forecast health risk at early stages. Advanced machine learning and natural language processing were employed to implement the enhanced predictive analytics used to support enhanced personalized treatment planning. Results revealed improved patient outcomes and shorter duration of hospitalization through proactive interventions. (Albaroudi et al., 2024) built a real-time multi-modal sensing system through 3D time-of-flight and RGB cameras with edge AI integrated via unsupervised learning wherever regulation compliance audit is necessary. Their approach achieved unobstructed continuous tracking of objects and minimized human interventions, proven in agrifood knife sanitizing situations. The results showed enhanced monitoring precision even under occluded or dim conditions. (Waseem et al., 2025) created generative AI models like GANs and VAEs to produce realistic synthetic health data that overcome privacy issues associated with real patient records. The approach facilitates HIPAA- and GDPR-compliant anonymized data generation for research and model training. The research identified that synthetic data successfully maintains utility while safeguarding patient identities.

A few recent papers have investigated the application of generative AI to enhance continuous monitoring and regulatory compliance in different industries. (Ahmed et al., 2025) created a GenAI-enabled mobile robotics solution for monitoring pharmaceutical labs, which enhanced compliance without being robust enough in dynamic settings. (Alam, 2024) introduced a grid monitoring framework based on generative autoencoders, although it required ample high-quality CPOW data. (Tong et al. 2024) proposed an AI framework for SOX IT compliance. They improved the automation but were poor in data input quality. In finance, (Liu & Wongsosaputro 2024

c) used GenAI for real-time regulatory reporting but found integration with the existing legacy system challenging. (Bate, 2025) applied LLMs to building sector compliance, but the system failed with sophisticated visual inputs. (D. Munivel, Samir, Naveen, & -, 2024) created cloud compliance tools, although data privacy and bias issues remain. (Batool et al., 2025) investigated GenAI in HR compliance, raising ethical inconsistencies between jurisdictions. (Dwivedi et al., 2023) investigated AI for autonomous driving compliance under the EU AI Act, but safety of deployment is uncertain. (Wassie & Lakatos, 2024) developed a QA-RAG model for drug compliance, and constrained by variable document types suggested AI policy in Australia, having issues with implementation. In healthcare, (Cao et al., 2023) and (Beretas & Davalas, 2024) applied synthetic data and predictive analytics to assist in diagnostics, but had concerns of data bias and access problems. (Yu et al. 2023) produced privacy-friendly synthetic patient data through Generative Adversarial Networks and VAEs but cautioned about the threat of privacy leakage in the absence of validation. applied GenAI in cybersecurity for NIS2 compliance but identified risks to AI model security (Batool et al., 2025) developed AI-compliant frameworks but encountered difficulties in trying to comply with ambiguous rules and across-the-world diversity. (Ma et al., 2024) and (Choi et al., 2024) have suggested AI solutions for IoT and sensor-based monitoring, but faced scalability and stability challenges. One shared limitation in these studies is the need for high-quality data, integration challenges, and continued issues with AI robustness, transparency, and ethical usage. Several studies have explored the use of generative AI for compliance and monitoring across different domains a significant gap remains in integrating real-time anomaly detection with explainable compliance reporting within a single framework. Most existing approaches focus either on detection or reporting, but not both simultaneously. This highlights the need for a comprehensive, scalable, and interpretable solution, which this study aims to address.

(Xia et al., 2026) analyzed global regulatory frameworks for generative AI and emphasized the need for strong governance mechanisms to ensure trust, transparency, and compliance in AI-driven systems. Their study highlights that effective regulatory alignment is essential for deploying generative AI in high-risk domains such as finance and cybersecurity. However, they noted challenges related to policy standardization and cross-border regulatory differences. (Batool et al., 2025) examined the governance of generative AI and proposed policy-level strategies to manage risks associated with large-scale AI deployment. The study underscores the importance of accountability, ethical considerations, and continuous monitoring in compliance-oriented environments. The findings indicate that governance frameworks play a critical role in ensuring responsible AI adoption. (Pérez-Pérez et al., 2026) presented a comprehensive survey on Explainable Generative AI (GenXAI), focusing on improving transparency and interpretability of AI-generated outputs. Their work demonstrates that explainability is crucial in compliance systems, where decisions must be auditable and trustworthy. However, they identified limitations in current evaluation methods for measuring explanation quality. (Novozhilova et al., 2024)conducted a systematic review of generative AI applications, challenges, and future directions, highlighting the increasing role of AI in regulatory compliance and risk management. The study emphasizes the need for robust validation, fairness, and scalability in real-world deployments of generative AI systems.

The application of generative AI for compliance monitoring, there is an overemphasis on model development and limited focus on practical deployment challenges. Key aspects such as scalability, interpretability, and integration with existing regulatory systems remain under-explored. Furthermore, most existing approaches address either anomaly detection or compliance reporting independently, with insufficient emphasis on unified frameworks that combine both functionalities. Addressing these gaps is essential to improve the applicability, robustness, and real-world adoption of AI-driven compliance monitoring systems.

Despite these advancements, existing studies reveal significant limitations in real-time adaptability, explainability, and unified integration of anomaly detection with compliance reporting, which motivates the need for a more comprehensive and scalable framework as discussed in the following problem statement.

3. PROBLEM STATEMENT

In the dynamic regulatory environments of today—finance, healthcare, and cybersecurity—compliance demands are more intricate, coming at us at high velocity, and highly contextual (Khinvasara et al. 2024). Conventional monitoring methods, like manual audits and rule engines, are reactive, sluggish, and error-prone, missing violations in real-time (Templin et al .2024). These systems do not have the scalability, flexibility, and context awareness to decipher varied regulatory frameworks and unstructured data forms (Ng et al. 2025). Therefore, organizations are exposed to increased risks of non-compliance, penalties, and damage to reputation (Beatrice Oyinkansola Adelakun 2022). To mitigate these limitations, an urgent need exists for an intelligent, scalable, and real-time solution (Liu & Wongsosaputro, 2024). This paper suggests a Generative AI-based compliance framework that employs LLMs and anomaly detection to facilitate real-time monitoring, automated violation detection, and human-readable compliance reporting. The system to be proposed includes real-time streams of data, optimized regulatory models, and interpretable AI outputs (Kovalainen et al., 2025). This provides high transparency, quick adaptation to new policy updates, and much enhanced compliance accuracy (Wassie & Lakatos, 2024).

Research Objectives

- Develop a Generative AI-driven framework by utilizing LLMs to translate, abstract, and create compliance documents in real-time for large-scale regulatory intelligence.
- Implement real-time, ongoing monitoring processes with anomaly detection models (e.g., autoencoders, transformers) to scrutinize live audit trails, transactions, and workflows across distributed systems.
- Generate compliant readable reports through optimized generative models providing abridged summaries, reasons for violations, and actionable suggestions to compliance officers and auditors.
- Detect and specify regulatory infractions cleverly via context-sensitive generative AI blocks that highlight incidents of non-compliance along with the reason, facilitating decision-making effectiveness.
- Modify the suggested compliance framework in various sectors and jurisdictions by adding multilingual support and industry-wise regulatory insights, and enhancing cross-industry implement ability.

4. RESEARCH METHODOLOGY

The proposed methodology is organized into distinct stages, including data preprocessing, anomaly detection, and explainable compliance generation, each contributing to the overall efficiency and interpretability of the system. This section presents the overall workflow of the proposed generative AI-based compliance monitoring system, integrating data preprocessing, anomaly detection using Temporal

Convolutional Networks, and explainable compliance generation using the T5 model to ensure real-time and interpretable decision-making. The generative AI-driven compliance monitoring system starts with synthetic financial transaction data, which is pre-processed through cleaning, encoding, scaling, imbalance handling, and feature engineering. The processed data is used to train a Temporal Convolutional Network (TCN) for detecting anomalies. Identified anomalies are converted into prompts and passed to a T5-based model to generate regulatory explanations. These outputs are displayed on a compliance dashboard, enabling real-time monitoring and transparent decision-making. Figure 1 presents the architecture of the proposed Generative AI-based compliance monitoring system, showing the workflow from data collection and preprocessing to anomaly detection using TCN and explanation generation using T5, integrated into a unified pipeline.

Figure 1. Overview of the Generative AI-Based Compliance Monitoring Framework

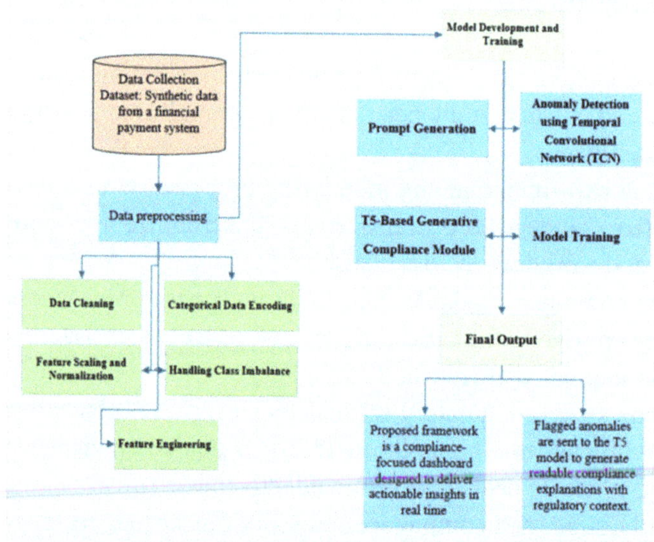

4.1 Data Collection

The data-gathering process of the present study is based on the Bank Sim synthetic dataset, an agent-based simulator utilized to generate realistic financial payment transactions. The dataset simulates six months of banking activity with around 594,643 transactions, including both normal and fraudulent cases. Each record contains details such as timestamp, customer profile, merchant information, transaction amount, and a fraud flag. Synthetic data helps avoid privacy and regulatory issues while supporting safe experimentation. It captures real financial patterns, making it a strong foundation for training and evaluating generative AI models for anomaly detection and compliance monitoring.

Table 1. Dataset Overview Table

Attribute	Description
Dataset Name	Bank Sim Synthetic Financial Payments Dataset
Number of Samples	594,643 transactions
Class Distribution	Normal: 587,443 (98.79%), Fraudulent: 7,200 (1.21%)
Features	Step, Customer ID, Age, Gender, Zip code, Merchant, Category, Amount, Fraud Label
Missing Values	None / minimal (specify if any)

Table 1 summarizes the BankSim dataset with 594,643 transactions, showing a strong class imbalance—98.79% normal and 1.21% fraudulent. It includes features like transaction step, customer details, merchant information, category, amount, and fraud labels. The dataset has negligible missing values, making it clean and suitable for training models. Its structure supports effective development and evaluation of fraud detection and financial anomaly detection systems.

4.2 Data Preprocessing

4.2.1 Data Cleaning:

Data cleaning ensures dataset quality by identifying and fixing errors, inconsistencies, and missing values. Missing data may occur due to system issues or incomplete records and can affect model accuracy if not handled properly. Common approaches include imputation (replacing missing values with estimated ones), removing incomplete records, or using advanced methods that handle missing data. Proper handling of missing values improves dataset reliability and model performance.

Missing values are replaced using statistical estimates such as mean, median, or mode. In mean imputation, a missing value is replaced by the average of observed values in a feature. The mean is calculated in expressed in Eqn 1

$$\overline{X} = \frac{1}{n}\sum_{j=1}^{n} x_j \tag{1}$$

where x_j represents observed values of feature X, and n is the number of available samples. The missing value is then replaced with $\bar{X}$.

- o Deletion of Records: Missing entries in the rows can be deleted, as long as the missing data is few and not systematic.
- o Outlier Correction: Outlier detection and correction or removal of values that could affect model training. For example, a negative transaction amount could be picked up and dealt with accordingly.

4.2.2 Feature Scaling and Normalization:

Machine learning models, especially those using gradient descent, are sensitive to feature scaling. Features with larger values can dominate training, while smaller ones may be overlooked. Feature scaling normalizes all variables to a similar range, ensuring balanced learning and improving model performance and convergence speed.

1. Min-Max Normalization-Min-max scaling rescales features to a fixed range, typically [0, 1], by subtracting the minimum value and dividing by the feature range. It preserves the relative relationships between data points and ensures that no feature dominates due to scale differences. However, it is sensitive to outliers. Despite this, it is widely used for preparing data for machine learning models requiring normalized inputs is shown in Eqn 2.

$$x_i' = \frac{x_i - \min(X)}{\max(X) - \min(X)} \tag{2}$$

where x_i is the original value, and $\min(X)$ and $\max(X)$ represent the minimum and maximum values of feature X, respectively. This normalization is particularly useful for features such as transaction amounts, where large values may otherwise dominate the learning process.

Z-score normalization standardizes data by subtracting the mean and dividing by the standard deviation, resulting in features with zero mean and unit variance. It brings features to a comparable scale without altering their distribution, making it suitable for many machine learning models. Although less sensitive to outliers than min-max scaling, extreme values can still influence the results. is shown in Eqn 3

$$x_i' = \frac{x_i - \mu_X}{\sigma_X} \tag{3}$$

where μ_X is the mean and σ_X the standard deviation of feature X. Standardization is particularly useful when the data follows a Gaussian distribution.

4.2.3 Categorical Data Encoding

The dataset contains various categorical variables, e.g., customer sex, merchant category, and geographic zip. As AI models take numerical input, these categories need to be converted accordingly:

1. One-hot encoding: One-hot encoding converts categorical variables into binary features representing each category. It ensures no ordinal relationship is assumed, preserving the nominal nature of the data. Although it increases data dimensionality, it is widely used as it enables machine learning models to handle categorical features effectively is presented in Eqn 4

$$C = \{c_1, c_2, \ldots, c_k\} \tag{4}$$

For each category c_j, one-hot encoding creates a binary vector $v \in \{0,1\}^k$ such that is shown in Eqn 5

$$v_i = \begin{cases} 1 & \text{if } i = j \\ 0 & \text{if } i \neq j \end{cases} \text{ for } i = 1,2,\ldots,k \tag{5}$$

Example: For $C = \{$ Male, Female $\}$, the category Male becomes $v = [1,0]$ and Female becomes $v = [0,1]$.

2. Label Encoding: Label encoding assigns unique integers to categorical values, making it simple and computationally efficient. However, it may introduce unintended ordinal relationships between categories, which can mislead models. Therefore, it should be used carefully, especially with nominal data where no natural order exists.

For the same categorical feature $C = \{c_1, c_2, \ldots, c_k\}$, label encoding assigns an integer l_j to each category c_j that is shown in Eqn 6

$$l_j \in \{0,1,2,\ldots,k-1\} \tag{6}$$

Formally, define a mapping function is shown in Eqn 7

$$\begin{aligned} f&: C \to \{0,1,\ldots,k-1\} \\ f(c_j) &= l_j \end{aligned} \tag{7}$$

3. Embedding Layers: In deep neural models, embedding layers are employed to learn dense, continuous vector representations of categorical data and convert them into a more compact, meaningful representation. Rather than employing sparse one-hot encoding, where categories are represented as a binary vector, embedding layers project categories to lower-dimensional space vectors. These vectors pick up not only the category's identity but also its semantic connections with other categories, enabling the model to comprehend similarities among them. For instance, similar categories may have vectors that are closer in the embedded space, reflecting their relatedness. Embeddings are especially useful when dealing with high-cardinality categorical variables, as they help reduce the dimensionality and improve computational efficiency. This method enhances the model's ability to learn complex patterns in the data by representing categorical information in a way that reflects the underlying structure. Embedding layers are commonly used in tasks such as natural language processing (e.g., word embeddings) and recommender systems.

For a categorical feature with k categories, embedding maps each category c_j to a dense continuous vector $\mathbf{e}_j \in \mathbb{R}^d$, where $d \ll k$ is the embedding dimension is shown in Eqn 8

$$E \in \mathbb{R}^{k \times d} \tag{8}$$

Each category index j maps to the jth row of E is shown in Eqn 9

$$f(c_j) = \mathbf{e}_j = E[j] \tag{9}$$

During training, the embedding vectors $\mathbf{e}_j$ are optimized to capture semantic similarity and relations between categories.

4.2.4 Handling Class Imbalance

Fraudulent transactions are rare, leading to highly imbalanced datasets that can bias models toward the majority class. To address this, techniques such as over-sampling the minority class, undersampling the majority class, and applying class weights are used. Specialized loss functions and evaluation metrics like F1 score and AUC-ROC help ensure better detection of fraudulent cases. These methods improve the model's ability to identify rare fraud while maintaining overall performance.

Synthetic Minority Over-sampling Technique: SMOTE tackles imbalance by generating synthetic minority class instances. It selects a minority class instance and one of its nearest neighbours and generates new samples on the line segment joining them. The new synthetic example x_{new} is represented in Eqn 10

$$x_{new} = x_i + \delta(x_{zi} - x_i) \tag{10}$$

where x_i is an existing minority sample, x_{zi} is a neighbor, and δ is a random number between 0 and 1. This method enriches the minority class and enables models to learn more optimal decision boundaries.

Under-sampling: Decreasing the majority class size to balance the dataset while it may lose significant information.

Cost-sensitive Learning: Applying greater penalties to misclassifying minority class instances to nudge the model to favor fraud detection.

4.2.5 Feature Engineering

To improve prediction capacity, novel features drawn from original data can identify patterns not directly present in raw data. For instance, time-based features like transaction rate, mean transaction value per customer, or time elapsed since last transaction can indicate abnormal behaviours associated with fraud or compliance breaks. Merging merchant or customer profiles into aggregated representations of behaviour over time is also useful is shown in Eqn 11

$$F_e = \left[\sum_{t_i \in T} 1_{\{\text{entity}(t_i)=e\}}, \frac{\sum_{t_i \in T} 1_{\{\text{entity}(t_i)=e\}} \times \text{amount}(t_i)}{\sum_{t_i \in T} 1_{\{\text{entity}(t_i)=e\}}}, t_{\text{now}} - \max_{t_i \in T}\{t_i : \text{entity}(t_i) = e\}\right] \tag{11}$$

Where the feature vector F_e contains Total transaction count for entity e in time window T, Average transaction amount for entity e in T, Time elapsed since last transaction of e

Table 2. Data Preprocessing Summary

Preprocessing Step	Description	Method / Technique
Missing Data Handling	No missing data / Imputation if any	None / Mean Imputation
Categorical Encoding	Convert categorical variables to numeric form	One-hot encoding, Embeddings
Normalization	Scale numerical features	Min-Max scaling
Feature Engineering	Derived features such as transaction frequency, average amount	Custom aggregation equations

Table 2 shows the data preprocessing steps: dealing with the missing values; converting categorical variables-to-one-hot encoding and embeddings; scaling the numerical features with Min-Max normalization; and creating derived features such as transaction frequency and average amount to enhance model performance.

Pseudo-Code – *Data Preprocessing*

```
Step 1: Data Collection
LOAD dataset from "BankSim_Synthetic_Financial_Payments.csv"

Step 2: Data Cleaning
FOR each column in dataset
IF column has missing values
IF column is numerical
APPLY mean imputation to replace missing values
ELSE IF column is categorical
APPLY mode imputation to replace missing values
END IF
Handle Outliers
IF column has outliers
DETECT and REMOVE or REPLACE outliers
END IF
END FOR
Step 3: Feature Scaling and Normalization
FOR each numerical column in dataset
APPLY Min-Max scaling to normalize feature values to the range [0, 1]
END FOR

Step 4: Categorical Data Encoding
FOR each categorical column in dataset
APPLY One-Hot Encoding to convert categorical values to binary features
END FOR
Step 5: Handle Class Imbalance
APPLY SMOTE to balance dataset by generating synthetic samples for the minority class (Fraudulent)
Step 6: Feature Engineering
Create new features based on time or transaction patterns
CALCULATE transaction-rate for each customer
CALCULATE average-transaction-amount for each customer
CALCULATE time-since-last-transaction for each customer
ADD these engineered features to dataset

Step 7: Split Data into Training and Testing
SPLIT dataset into training set (80%) and testing set (20%)
Step 8: Model Training and Evaluation
TRAIN model using training set
EVALUATE model performance using testing set

Step 9: Model Evaluation Results
OUTPUT evaluation results (accuracy, precision, recall, F1 score, etc.)
```

4.3 Model Development and Training

4.3.1 Anomaly Detection using Temporal Convolutional Network (TCN)

This work uses a Temporal Convolutional Network (TCN) for detecting anomalies in sequential financial transaction data. The model captures temporal patterns and long-range dependencies using causal and dilated convolutions. Detected anomalies are passed to a T5 model to generate human-readable compliance explanations, forming a two-stage pipeline. With proper preprocessing and training on the BankSim dataset, the system achieves accurate anomaly detection along with transparent and explainable outputs for regulatory compliance.

4.3.2 Rationale for Selecting TCN

A few advantages listed below that fit well with sequences of financial transactions justified the choice of Temporal Convolutional Network over recurrent ones (such as LSTM and GRU):

- ✓ Causal Convolutions: TCN ends up with no future information leakage in respecting the temporal order through causal convolutions, which become very important to be incorporated when the compliance system needs to react in real time.
- ✓ Dilated Convolutions: Dilations allow the model to efficiently learn from long-term dependencies across thousands of time steps, which is essential for modeling customer behaviors over long periods.
- ✓ Speed and stability: As opposed to recurrent models, the Temporal Convolutional Network allows for parallel training and thus removes the risk of vanishing gradients. This enhances the speed of convergence and training scalability over a large dataset such as Bank Sim.
- ✓ Residual Connections: These allow the construction of deeper networks without degradation, thereby increasing the capacity of the model for learning complex anomaly patterns in sequential transaction data.

4.3.3 TCN Architecture

Figure 2 illustrates the architecture of the Temporal Convolutional Network (TCN) used for anomaly detection in the proposed system. The TCN processes sequential transaction data using causal and dilated convolutions to capture both short-term and long-term temporal dependencies while preserving time order. Residual connections improve training stability and model performance. The extracted features are passed through activation and regularization layers, followed by a fully connected layer with a sigmoid function to classify transactions as normal or anomalous, enabling accurate and real-time compliance monitoring.

Figure 2. TCN Architecture

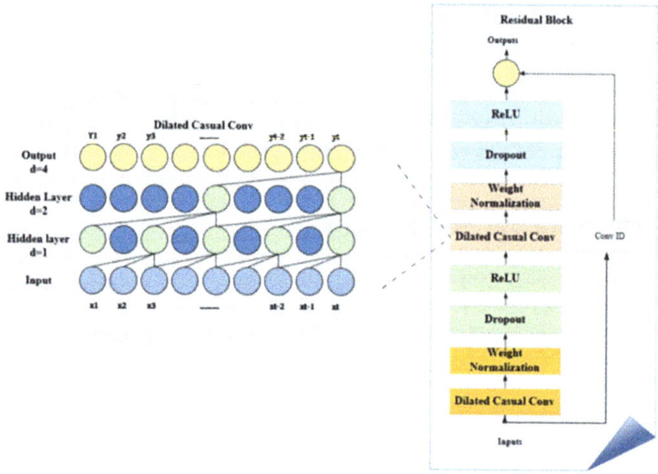

Temporal Convolutional Networks (TCNs) capture the historical temporal dependencies in transaction history to classify financial transactions either as normal (0) or anomalous (1). Unlike recurrent models, this adopts convolution which is causal and dilated to capture both transient fluctuations and long-term behavioural trends making stable training, strong generalization, and precise irregularity detection possible in compliance monitoring; this provides a great platform for financial compliance monitoring the most important architectural pieces are:

1) Input Layer

Each entry is related to the size of the past transactions time series and includes information about all purchase, time, and frequency aspects. Depending on a window of 10-50 transactions, model behavior is determined for a given application like segmentation, churn prediction, and recommendation personalization. Mathematically, the input is summarized as in Eqn 12

$$X_t = \{x_{t-n+1}, x_{t-n+2}, \ldots, x_t\} \tag{12}$$

where X_t represents the sequence of feature vectors within a sliding window ending at time step t, x_t denotes the feature vector at time step t, and n is the window size.

2) One-Dimensional Causal Convolution

Causal convolutions do ensure that the predictions occur solely on the basis of existing and past data, and that they are consistent in time and do not have any look-ahead bias. It is most essential to keep this in mind in real-time anomaly detection from a regulatory standpoint. It gives transparent, accurate, and timely decisions and ensures the integrity and accountability of the financial and transactional predictive systems.

3) Dilated Convolutional Layers

The actually dilated convolutional networks can raise the dilation rates exponentially to 1, 2, 4, 8, etc. This implies reception field enlargement and the model learning short-term anomaly and long-term trend representations effectively. This allows modelling complex dependencies over time without any increase in parameters, enhancing accuracy when predicting learning pattern as used in multi-scale behaviour learning.

4) Activation and Regularization

Each convolutional block uses ReLU activation to capture complex patterns and introduce non-linearity. Dropout (0.2–0.3) is applied to prevent overfitting by randomly disabling neurons during training. Batch normalization may be used to stabilize and speed up training by normalizing inputs. Together, these techniques improve model efficiency, stability, and generalization.

4) Residual Blocks

Residual connections improve gradient flow in deep networks, preventing vanishing gradient issues. They work by adding the input of a layer to its output, enabling the model to learn residual mappings. This stabilizes training, speeds up convergence, and enhances the model's ability to learn complex features, improving overall performance and generalization.

5) Output Layer

The final hidden state is passed to a dense layer, followed by a sigmoid activation to produce a probability between 0 and 1. This probability is typically thresholded (e.g., 0.5) to generate a binary classification output. This structure enables clear and interpretable predictions for tasks like fraud detection is shown in Eqn 13

$$\hat{y}_t = \sigma\left(\text{Dense}\left(\text{ReLU}\left(\text{TCN}(X_t)\right)\right)\right) \tag{13}$$

Where: $\hat{y}_t$ is the predicted anomaly score at time t, σ denotes the sigmoid function, producing output in the range [0,1], TCN(.) encapsulates the entire stack of dilated causal convolutional layers, Dense(.) projects the output to a scalar probability. If $\hat{y}_t > \theta$ (where θ is a decision threshold), the transaction is classified as anomalous.

4.3.4 Training the TCN

The TCN is trained using supervised learning on the labeled BankSim dataset to classify transactions as normal or fraudulent. It learns patterns from transaction sequences, capturing both short- and long-term dependencies through causal and dilated convolutions without future data leakage. Residual connections and dropout improve stability and prevent overfitting. This enables accurate fraud detection and serves as the first stage in the compliance monitoring pipeline.

Binary label by sequence (1 = anomalous, 0 = normal).

Training set-up: Loss Function: Binary Cross-Entropy Loss is shown in Eqn 14

$$\mathcal{L} = -[y\log(\hat{y}) + (1 - y)\log(1 - \hat{y})] \tag{14}$$

where $y \in \{0,1\}$ is the true label indicating normal (0) or anomalous (1) transactions, and $\hat{y}$ is the predicted probability of the transaction being anomalous. This loss function measures the difference between the predicted probabilities and actual labels, enabling effective training for binary classification tasks.

Optimizer: Adam

- Learning Rate: 0.001
- Parameters: β1 = 0.9, β2 = 0.999
- Ensures stable, adaptive convergence for large-scale transaction datasets

Training setup:

- Batch size: 64, Epochs: 20
- Sequence window size: 10-50 transactions
- Dropout rate: 0.2-0.3 (to prevent overfitting)

Balancing is conducted on mini-batches in order to cancel out class imbalance in learning.

4.4 Prompt Generation

After the TCN detects anomalies, transaction data is converted into structured, human-readable prompts for the T5 model. These prompts include key details like customer information, transaction amount, merchant type, time, and fraud history. This transformation enables the T5 model to generate clear, explainable compliance insights, helping auditors understand the reasons behind flagged transactions.

Prompt Template Format
The usual design might be:
"Produce a compliance explanation for this transaction:
Customer age: 45, Gender: Male, Amount: $9000,
Merchant: Crypto Exchange, Time: 03:45 AM,
Previous frauds: Yes."

This step bridges structured data and natural language processing by converting transaction data into meaningful prompts for the T5 model. It enables the generation of human-readable, regulation-aligned explanations (e.g., KYC, AML, GDPR). This improves transparency, supports auditors, reduces manual effort, and ensures efficient, compliant, and trustworthy AI-driven monitoring.

4.5 T5-Based Generative Compliance Module

The T5 model uses a flexible text-to-text framework to generate explanations, summaries, and responses. In compliance monitoring, it produces clear and context-aware explanations for anomalous transactions. It can be fine-tuned on domain-specific regulatory data (e.g., KYC, AML, GDPR), enabling it to generate accurate, human-readable compliance insights. This enhances transparency, supports auditing, and bridges automated detection with human decision-making.

- **Model Workflow** The T5 module is the compliance generation mechanism that can analyse and put into perspective anomalies found by the TCN. The process is as follows:
  - Input: The T5 model is offered a well-structured natural language input constructed from highlighted transaction attributes like amount, merchant category, time, and transaction history applicable to the transaction.

- Explanatory: With pre-trained experience and fine-tuned against regulatory reports, the T5 analyses the prompt and picks up risk considerations and compliance factors that are relevant to the transaction.
- The model generates a well-defined human-readable explanation with an account of the transaction as an exceptional one in the process; the single risk factors can be highlighted too, together with facultative references to the compliance policies or regulations in question.

  Sample Output:

"The transaction is found to be high due to the value involved, the time that it was performed, and the fact that a very suspect MCC is present."

4.6 Model Training

There were two major phases in model training: the Temporal Convolutional Network (TCN) is trained first on temporal financial transaction data labeled normal or fraudulent, with the goal being to minimize a binary cross-entropy loss for accurately detecting anomalies while facing class imbalance. The Adam optimizer was used for efficient convergence and was judged based on accuracy, F1-score, and AUC-ROC to ensure that the bulk correctness and minority class detection were balanced.

4.6.1 Temporal Convolutional Network (TCN) Training

A Temporal Convolutional Network works with transaction data in sequential order, where each input is a fixed-length sequence of transaction feature vectors representing customer activity for a specific time window. Each sequence is assigned a binary class label indicating the presence of either normal transactions (label 0) or fraudulent/anomalous transactions (label 1). The goal of training is to help the TCN accurately distinguish between normal and fraudulent sequences by learning temporal patterns. This is achieved by optimizing the Binary Cross-Entropy (BCE) loss, which measures the difference between true labels and predicted probabilities.

Binary Cross-Entropy loss trains the TCN for binary classification, while the Adam optimizer ensures efficient convergence. Performance is evaluated using accuracy, F1-score, and AUC-ROC to measure both overall and fraud detection effectiveness.

4.6.2 T5 Fine-Tuning

The T5 model is trained on paired data of transaction prompts and compliance explanations. Each input describes an anomalous transaction with relevant details, while the target output provides a human-readable regulatory explanation. The model is fine-tuned using Cross-Entropy Loss to ensure accurate generation of explanation text. The loss function is given as is indicated by Eqn 16

$$\mathscr{L}_{CE} = -\sum_{t=1}^{T} y_t \log(\hat{y}_t) \tag{16}$$

where T is the length of the training retention sequence, y_t is the real token in position t and $\hat{y}_t$ is the estimated probability of that token.

The T5 model is fine-tuned by minimizing cross-entropy loss to generate accurate and regulation-aligned explanations. Training is performed over 3–5 epochs with an appropriate learning rate to ensure efficiency and prevent overfitting. Using pre-trained weights, the model adapts to financial compliance language. Performance is evaluated using BLEU score, confirming that the generated explanations are fluent, relevant, and suitable for real-world compliance reporting.

Pseudocode- *Model Development and Training*

```
BEGIN Model Development and Training
Step 1: Initialize TCN Model
Initialize TCN-Model with layers: causal convolutions, dilated convolutions, residual connections
Step 2: Preprocess the Data
Load Bank Sim dataset
Clean and preprocess the data (impute missing values, encode categorical data, normalize numerical features)
Split the dataset into training and testing sets
Step 3: Train the TCN Model
FOR each epoch in training:
FOR each batch in training data:
Perform forward passthrough TCN model
Calculate Binary Cross-Entropy loss
Backpropagate and update weights
END FOR
Evaluate model performance (accuracy, F1 score, AUC-ROC)
END FOR
Step 4: Anomaly Detection
For each transaction in test data:
Use TCN model to predict if transaction is normal or anomalous
IF transaction is anomalous:
FLAG it as an anomaly
END IF
END FOR
Step 5: Generate Compliance Prompt for T5 Model
FOR each flagged anomalous transaction:
Create a natural language prompt using transaction details (e.g., customer info, amount, merchant)
Pass the prompt to T5 model for compliance explanation
Output the generated explanation
END FOR
Step 6: Fine-Tune the T5 Model
Load pre-trained T5 model
Fine-tune T5 on paired prompts and compliance explanations
FOR each fine-tuning epoch:
FOR each batch in fine-tuning data:
Calculate Cross-Entropy loss between predicted and actual explanation
Backpropagate and update T5 model weights
END FOR
Evaluate T5 model using BLEU score
END FOR
Step 7: Final Compliance Explanation Generation
FOR each anomalous transaction flagged by TCN:
Generate compliance prompt for T5
Generate and output the final explanation from T5
END Model Development and Training
```

Experimental Setup and Validation

The proposed model is evaluated using the BankSim synthetic dataset, which is widely used for financial fraud detection due to its realistic transaction patterns. Synthetic data is employed to address privacy concerns while enabling controlled experimentation. The dataset is preprocessed using normalization and feature engineering before training. The model is implemented with defined hyperparameters for reproducibility and evaluated using accuracy, precision, recall, and AUC. While tested in a simulated setting, it reflects real-world scenarios, with future work aimed at validation on real-world data.

5. RESULTS AND DISCUSSION

The experimental results evaluate anomaly detection accuracy, model reliability, and explainable compliance reporting. The system demonstrates strong performance in detecting financial anomalies such as money laundering and insider trading, while providing clear explanations. It also adapts to evolving regulations, though challenges like bias and integration with legacy systems remain.

5.1 Confusion Matrix

The confusion matrix, which is used to visually assess the performance of a classification model by comparing actual and predicted labels shown in Figure 3. The model classifies activities as Normal or Attack with high accuracy. It correctly identifies 5042 normal cases and 4850 attack cases, with only 39 false positives and 69 false negatives. The high correct predictions and low errors indicate near-perfect performance in distinguishing threats from normal activities.

Figure 3. Confusion Matrix of CNN-Based Classification for Normal vs. Attack Detection

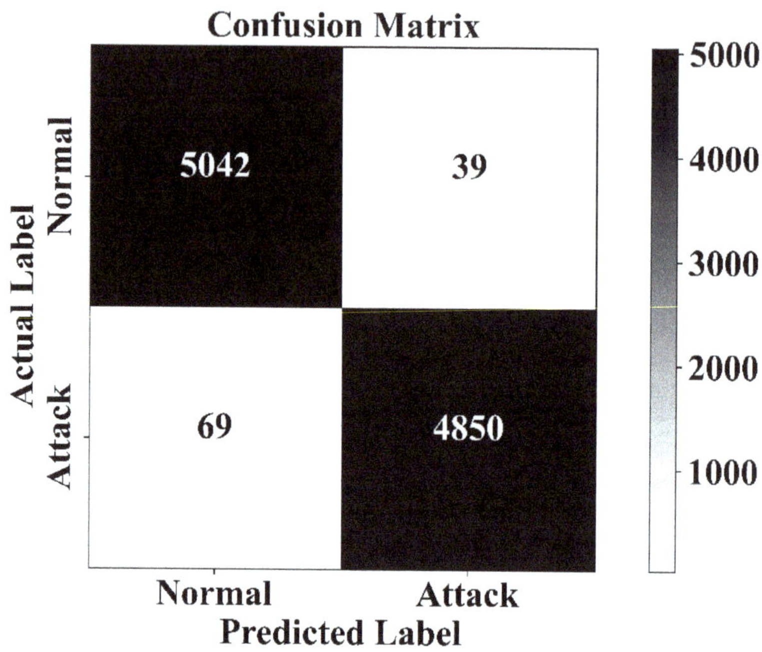

5.2 Receiver Operating Characteristic Curve for Attack Detection Model

In the ROC curve for classification model evaluation shown in Figure 4. The ROC curve shows a high True Positive Rate with a low False Positive Rate, lying near the top-left corner. An AUC of 0.9994 indicates excellent classification performance. This confirms the model is highly reliable for detecting anomalies and compliance violations.

Figure 4. ROC Curve

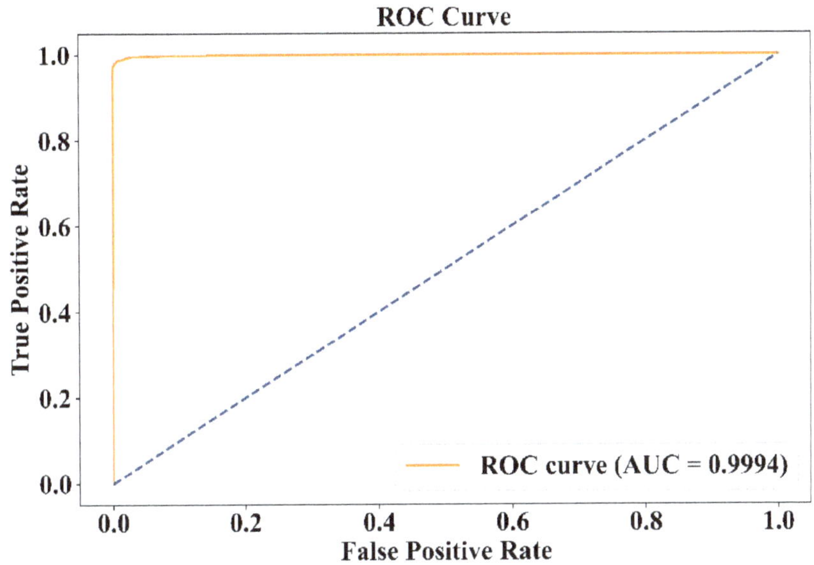

5.3 Training and Validation Performance Across Epochs

Here are image sequences over time for training and validation in a machine learning model, the accuracy curves show in Figure 5. The training and validation accuracy show a slight upward trend but remain around 0.6, indicating limited performance. Loss initially decreases but later increases, suggesting instability during training. However, the close alignment of training and validation curves indicates minimal overfitting and balanced model behavior.

Figure 5. Model Accuracy and Loss Convergence over Epochs

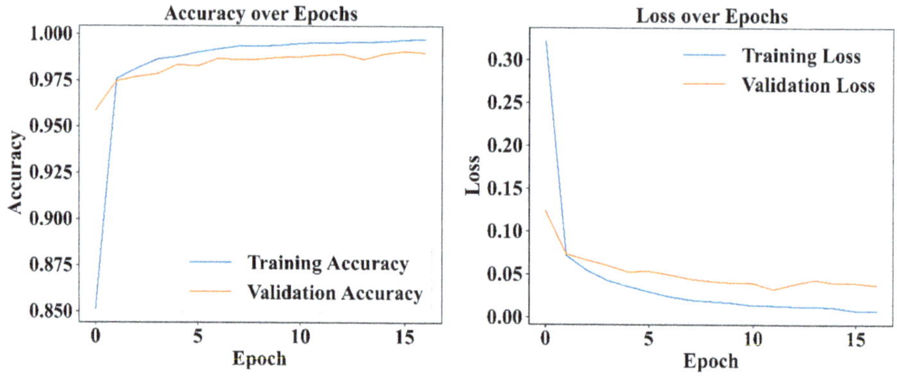

5.4 Comparison of FNR and FPR

The bar graph provides insights and details on the False Negative Rate and False Positive Rate of a Classification Model shown in Figure 6. The model has a False Negative Rate (0.0140) higher than the False Positive Rate (0.0077), indicating it misses more positive cases than it falsely flags negatives. While both rates are low, this suggests the model prioritizes reducing false positives over capturing all positive cases.

Figure 6. Comparison of False Negative Rate and False Positive Rate

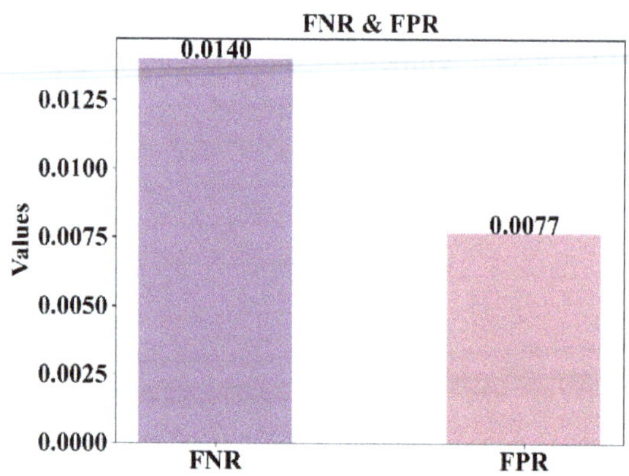

5.5 Scatter Plot of Session Duration and Packet Size for Attack Detection

The scatter plot shows how session duration and network packet size are related shown in Figure 7. The scatter plot shows both normal and attack traffic distributed across packet sizes and session durations. Their overlap indicates that attacks cannot be distinguished using these features alone, highlighting the need for more advanced detection algorithms.

Figure 7. Distribution of Network Traffic: Packet Size vs Session Duration

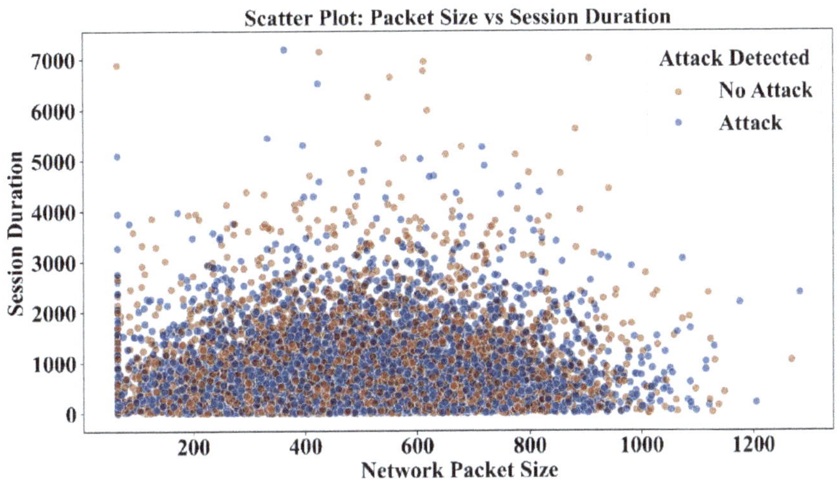

5.6 Optimized Precision-Recall Curve with Exceptional Model Accuracy

The characteristics of a Precision-Recall curve for a classification method in machine learning shown in Figure 8. The precision-recall curve shows high precision close to 1 across a range of recall values, indicating accurate positive predictions. A slight drop reflects the precision-recall trade-off. An Average Precision (AP) of 0.9993 confirms excellent model performance with minimal false positives.

Figure 8. **Precision**-*Recall Curve*

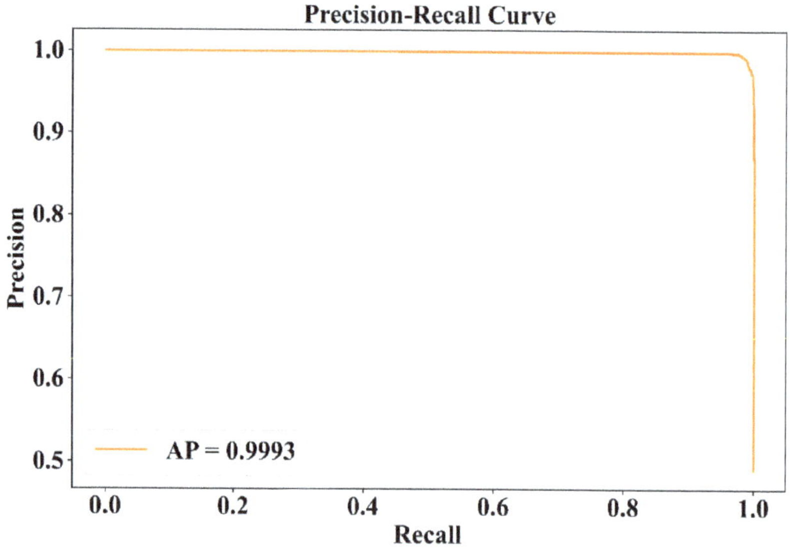

5.7 Comparison of Key Metrics During Attack vs. No Attack

In the four box plots that compare Attack and No Attack conditions across several metrics shown in Figure 9. During attacks, network packet size increases slightly, while session duration shows significant spikes with extreme outliers. IP reputation scores decrease, and failed login attempts rise with greater variability. Overall, these patterns indicate abnormal behavior during attacks compared to normal conditions.

Figure 9. Visualizing the Effect of Attacks on Network Activity and Login Behaviour

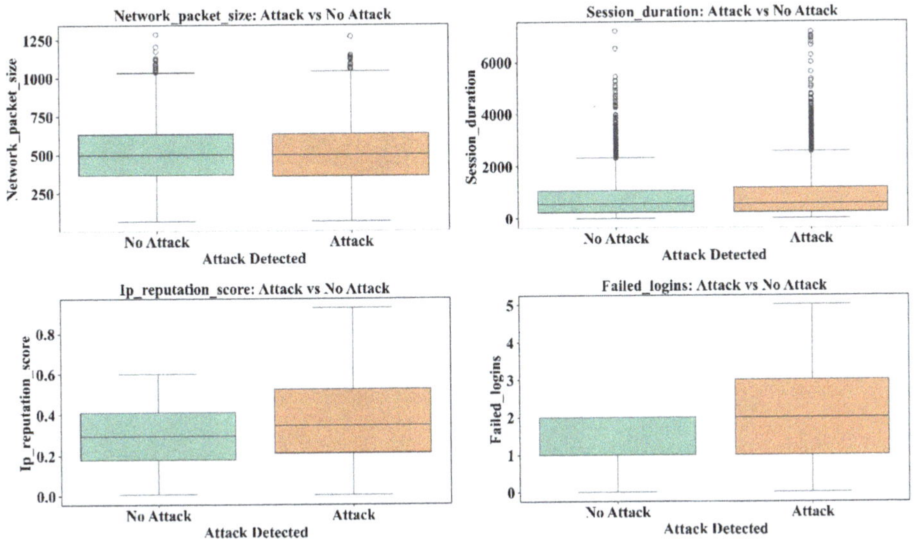

5.8 Model Performance Evaluation

Looking at the numbers for each bar ensures us that the classification model managed to balance the accuracy, precision, recall, and F1 score shown in Figure 10. The model achieves strong performance with 98.92% accuracy, 99.20% precision, 98.60% recall, and an F1 score of 98.90%. High precision indicates low false positives, while strong recall ensures most positive cases are detected, confirming the model's overall effectiveness.

Figure 10. Performance Metrics

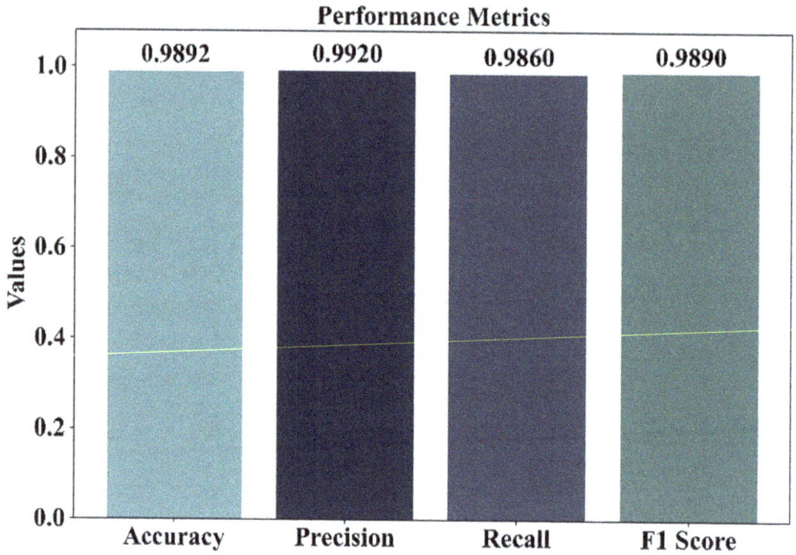

Ethical Considerations

The use of Generative AI in compliance monitoring raises important ethical concerns, especially in sensitive sectors such as healthcare. Although synthetic data helps preserve privacy, there is a risk of re-identification, creating challenges under regulations like GDPR and HIPAA. Bias in training data may lead to unfair outcomes, and limited explainability can reduce trust in AI decisions. Additionally, lack of human oversight may increase risks in critical applications. Incorporating fairness, transparency, and human-in-the-loop mechanisms is essential to ensure responsible and reliable deployment of the proposed system.

6 CONCLUSION AND FUTURE WORK

This study highlights the importance of continuous compliance monitoring and demonstrates how it can be enhanced through the use of generative AI. The integration of generative AI with ML enhances compliance breach detection while reducing time and cost compared to manual systems. It enables proactive adaptation to regulations, real-time anomaly detection, and automated report generation. The study highlights strong methodology and improved transparency through combined detection and explanation. Future improvements include extended validation, comparative analysis, and better evaluation of explanation quality.

Despite its advantages, the system faces challenges such as data quality issues, model bias, and infrastructure limitations. The study also has limitations, including lack of real-world validation, absence of comparison with baseline models, unclear domain focus, and insufficient evaluation of explanation accuracy. Practical concerns like scalability and integration are not fully addressed. Future work should focus on improving explainability, fairness, validation, and real-world applicability.

REFERENCES

Adelakun, B. O.Beatrice Oyinkansola Adelakun. (2022). The impact of AI on internal auditing: Transforming practices and ensuring compliance. *Finance & Accounting Research Journal*, *4*(6), 350–370. DOI: 10.51594/farj.v4i6.1316

Ahmed, H. A., Nepomuceno, J. A., Vega-Márquez, B., & Nepomuceno-Chamorro, I. A. (2025). Synthetic Data Generation for Healthcare: Exploring Generative Adversarial Networks Variants for Medical Tabular Data. *International Journal of Data Science and Analytics*, *20*(6), 5739–5754. DOI: 10.1007/s41060-025-00816-w

Ajmal, C. S., Yerram, S., Abishek, V., Nizam, V. P. M., Aglave, G., Patnam, J. D., Raghuvanshi, R. S., & Srivastava, S. (2025). Innovative Approaches in Regulatory Affairs: Leveraging Artificial Intelligence and Machine Learning for Efficient Compliance and Decision-Making. *The AAPS Journal*, *27*(1), 22. DOI: 10.1208/s12248-024-01006-5 PMID: 39776314

Alam, N. (2024). Improving IT Control Compliance using Artificial Intelligence. *International Journal of Computer Science and Mobile Computing*, *13*(5), 43–46. DOI: 10.47760/ijcsmc.2024.v13i05.003

Albaroudi, E., Mansouri, T., & Alameer, A. (2024). The Intersection of Generative AI and Healthcare: Addressing Challenges to Enhance Patient Care. *2024 Seventh International Women in Data Science Conference at Prince Sultan University (WiDS PSU)*, 134–140. DOI: 10.1109/WiDS-PSU61003.2024.00039

Alqahtani, T. (2025). Recent Trends in the Public Acceptance of Autonomous Vehicles: A Review. *Vehicles (Basel)*, *7*(2), 45. Advance online publication. DOI: 10.3390/vehicles7020045

Bate, G. W. (2025). Gaining Traction with Gen AI in 2025. *Research Technology Management*, *68*(2), 69–71. DOI: 10.1080/08956308.2025.2446136

Batool, A., Zowghi, D., & Bano, M. (2025). AI governance: A systematic literature review. *AI and Ethics*, *5*(3), 3265–3279. DOI: 10.1007/s43681-024-00653-w

Beretas, C. P., & Davalas, A. (2024). Bridging AI Innovation and Cybersecurity: Generative AI's Contribution to NIS2 Compliance. *International Journal of Regional Development*, *11*(2), 40. DOI: 10.5296/ijrd.v11i2.22486

Cao, K., Xia, Y., Yao, J., Han, X., Lambert, L., Zhang, T., Tang, W., Jin, G., Jiang, H., Fang, X., Nogues, I., Li, X., Guo, W., Wang, Y., Fang, W., Qiu, M., Hou, Y., Kovarnik, T., Vocka, M., & Lu, J. (2023). Large-scale pancreatic cancer detection via non-contrast CT and deep learning. *Nature Medicine*, *29*(12), 3033–3043. DOI: 10.1038/s41591-023-02640-w PMID: 37985692

Choi, K., Moon, J., Jung, H. G., & Suhr, J. K. (2024). Real-Time Object Detection and Tracking Based on Embedded Edge Devices for Local Dynamic Map Generation. *Electronics (Basel)*, *13*(5), 811. DOI: 10.3390/electronics13050811

Dwivedi, Y. K., Kshetri, N., Hughes, L., Slade, E. L., Jeyaraj, A., Kar, A. K., Baabdullah, A. M., Koohang, A., Raghavan, V., Ahuja, M., Albanna, H., Albashrawi, M. A., Al-Busaidi, A. S., Balakrishnan, J., Barlette, Y., Basu, S., Bose, I., Brooks, L., Buhalis, D., & Wright, R. (2023). Opinion Paper: "So what if ChatGPT wrote it?" Multidisciplinary perspectives on opportunities, challenges and implications of generative conversational AI for research, practice and policy. *International Journal of Information Management*, *71*, 102642. DOI: 10.1016/j.ijinfomgt.2023.102642

Feuerriegel, S., Hartmann, J., Janiesch, C., & Zschech, P. (2024). Generative AI. *Business & Information Systems Engineering*, *66*(1), 111–126. DOI: 10.1007/s12599-023-00834-7

González, G. G., Casas, P., & Fernández, A. (2023). Deep Generative Replay for Multivariate Time-Series Monitoring with Variational Autoencoders. *2023 7th Network Traffic Measurement and Analysis Conference (TMA)*, 1–4. DOI: 10.23919/TMA58422.2023.10199001

Izquierdo-Bueno, I., Moraga, J., Cantoral, J. M., Carbú, M., Garrido, C., & González-Rodríguez, V. E. (2024). Smart Viniculture: Applying Artificial Intelligence for Improved Winemaking and Risk Management. *Applied Sciences (Basel, Switzerland)*, *14*(22), 10277. Advance online publication. DOI: 10.3390/app142210277

Khinvasara, T., Shankar, A., & Wong, C. (2024). Survey of Artificial Intelligence for Automated Regulatory Compliance Tracking. *Journal of Engineering Research and Reports*, *26*(7), 390–406. DOI: 10.9734/jerr/2024/v26i71217

Kovalainen, T., Pramila-Savukoski, S., Kuivila, H.-M., Juntunen, J., Jarva, E., Rasi, M., & Mikkonen, K. (2025). Utilising artificial intelligence in developing education of health sciences higher education: An umbrella review of reviews. *Nurse Education Today*, *147*, 106600. DOI: 10.1016/j.nedt.2025.106600 PMID: 39904286

Liu, I., & Wongsosaputro, M. (2024). Compliance redefined: Using GenAI to navigate a complex regulatory landscape with reduced risks and costs. *Journal of Digital Banking*, *8*(4), 313. DOI: 10.69554/LGTJ4498

Livadariu, I., Elmokashfi, A., & Smaragdakis, G. (2024). Tracking submarine cables in the wild. *Computer Networks*, *242*, 110234. DOI: 10.1016/j.comnet.2024.110234

Ma, P., Garg, S., & Barika, M. (2024). Research allocation in mobile volunteer computing system: Taxonomy, challenges and future work. *Future Generation Computer Systems*, *154*, 251–265. DOI: 10.1016/j.future.2024.01.015

Mansoor, I., García Ortiz, J., & Rector, M. (2024). Generative AI in Clinical Research: Regulatory Submissions, Clinical Data Management, and Beyond. *AMWA Journal*, *39*(1). Advance online publication. DOI: 10.55752/amwa.2024.304

Mansurova, A., Mansurova, A., & Nugumanova, A. (2024). QA-RAG: Exploring LLM Reliance on External Knowledge. *Big Data and Cognitive Computing*, *8*(9), 115. Advance online publication. DOI: 10.3390/bdcc8090115

Mariam, Z., Niazi, S. K., & Magoola, M. (2024). Unlocking the Future of Drug Development: Generative AI, Digital Twins, and Beyond. *BioMedInformatics*, *4*(2), 1441–1456. DOI: 10.3390/biomedinformatics4020079

Martin, A. (2021). The Impact of AI-Driven Risk Compliance Systems on Corporate Governance. *Universal Research Reports*, *8*(4). DOI: 10.36676/urr.v8.i4.1403

Munivel, D., Samir, V. B., Naveen, P., & Lavanya, S. (2024). AI-driven Solutions for Cloud Compliance Challenges. *Advanced International Journal of Multidisciplinary Research*, *2*(2), 1037. DOI: 10.62127/aijmr.2024.v02i02.1037

Naz, S., & Xu, T.-B. (2024). A Comprehensive Review of Piezoelectric Ultrasonic Motors: Classifications, Characterization, Fabrication, Applications, and Future Challenges. *Micromachines*, *15*(9), 1170. Advance online publication. DOI: 10.3390/mi15091170 PMID: 39337830

Ng, M. Y., Helzer, J., Pfeffer, M. A., Seto, T., & Hernandez-Boussard, T. (2025). Development of secure infrastructure for advancing generative artificial intelligence research in healthcare at an academic medical center. *Journal of the American Medical Informatics Association : JAMIA*, *32*(3), 586–588. DOI: 10.1093/jamia/ocaf005 PMID: 39836496

Novozhilova, E., Mays, K., Paik, S., & Katz, J. E. (2024). More Capable, Less Benevolent: Trust Perceptions of AI Systems across Societal Contexts. *Machine Learning and Knowledge Extraction*, *6*(1), 342–366. DOI: 10.3390/make6010017

Pérez-Pérez, I., González-Afonso, M. C., Plasencia-Carballo, Z., & Pérez-Jorge, D. (2026). Transparency Mechanisms for Generative AI Use in Higher Education Assessment: A Systematic Scoping Review (2022–2026). *Computers*, *15*(2), 111. DOI: 10.3390/computers15020111

Reddy, H. M. (2024). Role of AI in Security Compliance. *International Journal of Scientific Research in Engineering and Management, 08*(11), 1–6. DOI: 10.55041/IJSREM32650

Singh, L., Randhelia, A., Jain, A., & Choudhary, A. K. (2025). Ethical and Regulatory Compliance Challenges of Generative AI in Human Resources. In Chelliah, P. R., Dutta, P. K., Kumar, A., Gonzalez, E. D. R. S., Mittal, M., & Gupta, S. (Eds.), *Generative Artificial Intelligence in Finance* (1st ed., pp. 199–214). Wiley., DOI: 10.1002/9781394271078.ch11

Templin, T., Perez, M. W., Sylvia, S., Leek, J., & Sinnott-Armstrong, N. (2024). Addressing 6 challenges in generative AI for digital health: A scoping review. *PLOS Digital Health, 3*(5), e0000503. DOI: 10.1371/journal.pdig.0000503 PMID: 38781686

Thoom, S. R.Sreeram Reddy Thoom. (2025). Lessons from AI in finance: Governance and compliance in practice. *International Journal of Science and Research Archive, 14*(1), 1387–1395. DOI: 10.30574/ijsra.2025.14.1.0235

Tong, L., Wang, X., & Zhao, Q. (2024). *Grid Monitoring with Synchro-Waveform and AI Foundation Model Technologies* (Version 2). arXiv. DOI: 10.48550/ARXIV.2403.06942

Wan, H., Zhang, J., Chen, Y., Xu, W., & Feng, F. (2025). Exploring Gen-AI applications in building research and industry: A review. *Building Simulation, 18*(6), 1251–1273. DOI: 10.1007/s12273-025-1279-x

Waseem, H. M., Islam, S. U., Matragkas, N., Epiphaniou, G., Arvanitis, T. N., & Maple, C. (2025). Review of generative AI for synthetic data generation: A healthcare perspective. *Artificial Intelligence Review, 59*(2), 55. DOI: 10.1007/s10462-025-11440-2

Wassie, F. A., & Lakatos, L. P. (2024). Artificial intelligence and the future of the internal audit function. *Humanities & Social Sciences Communications, 11*(1), 386. DOI: 10.1057/s41599-024-02905-w

Wen, S. (2024). The power of generative AI in cybersecurity: Opportunities and challenges. *Applied and Computational Engineering, 48*(1), 31–39. DOI: 10.54254/2755-2721/48/20241095

Xia, H., Chen, H., Zhang, J. Z., & Kamal, M. M. (2026). Exploring the impact of responsible AI governance on corporate performance: A quasi-natural experiment. *Technological Forecasting and Social Change, 223*, 124425. DOI: 10.1016/j.techfore.2025.124425

Yu, P., Xu, H., Hu, X., & Deng, C. (2023). Leveraging Generative AI and Large Language Models: A Comprehensive Roadmap for Healthcare Integration. *Health Care*, *11*(20), 2776. Advance online publication. DOI: 10.3390/healthcare11202776 PMID: 37893850

Zhang, H., & Wang, Q. (2025). How could GenAI work on in-service teachers' knowledge building process? An empirical study based on epistemic network analysis. *International Journal of Educational Technology in Higher Education*, *22*(1), 47. DOI: 10.1186/s41239-025-00544-y

Chapter 9

Directly Relevant to Finance and E-Commerce for Fraud Detection, Credit Scoring, and Transaction Analysis

Subramanyam Boyapati
http://orcid.org/0009-0006-1458-677X
American Express, USA

Sunil Kumar Alavilli
http://orcid.org/0009-0001-5624-6830
Sephora, USA

Rajani Priya Nippatla
http://orcid.org/0009-0005-2530-1488
Kellton Technologies Inc., USA

Chaitanya Vasamsetty
http://orcid.org/0009-0006-2047-634X
Elevance Health, USA

Bhavya Kadiyala
http://orcid.org/0009-0001-0255-0052
Parkland Health, USA

M. Thanjaivadivel
http://orcid.org/0009-0004-2621-5904
Nandha Engineering College, Erode, India

ABSTRACT

This paper presents a novel DL design for online shopping and financial fraud detection highlighting meticulous transaction analysis and risk assessment. The approach applies a comprehensive preprocessing pipeline consisting of min-max normalization, correlation-based filter and median imputation to obtain high quality data. Latent behavioural features are derived by an autoencoder, and anomaly sensitivity is enhanced by the Local Outlier Factor (LOF). For classification, a Bi LSTM and Transformer network hybrid model learns the sequential and global

DOI: 10.4018/979-8-3693-8397-1.ch009

interdependence among transactions. This hybrid model is beneficial in identifying sophisticated schemes of fraud and assists in intelligent credit scoring. The final classification step correctly distinguishes legitimate and fraudulent transactions. Designed to be adaptive to new patterns of fraud the classical can be directly functional to real-world financial systems, internet shopping systems and internet payment gateways. Experimental results outperform traditional fraud detection techniques.

1. INTRODUCTION

The growing volume of online transactions in e-commerce and finance has led to a concomitant rise in fraudulent activity, necessitating more intelligent and responsive fraud detection systems (Karthikeyan et al., 2024). The earlier machine learning techniques usually fail on imbalanced datasets, dynamic patterns of fraud, and inadequate temporal modelling(De Zarzà et al., 2023). Although the latest deep learning algorithms have enhanced detection rates, they are still lacking behind in extracting longer-range dependencies and addressing noise in transactional data(Liang et al., 2022). To overcome these shortcomings, this paper introduces a new framework that integrates strong preprocessing, autoencoder-based feature extraction of latent features, Local Outlier Factor for outlier detection, and a hybrid Bi–LSTM–Transformer model for sequence classification(Park et al., 2023). Such a combined framework improves fraud detection precision, facilitates real-time decision-making, and can be directly applied to financial platforms, e-commerce systems, and credit scoring applications(Prabha & Priscilla, 2024).

1.1 Background and Importance

The high development pace of digital finance and e-market has exponentially grown the number of online transactions, which in turn has made such platforms a target for fraudulent behaviour(Sani et al., 2024). With increased real-time payment and cross-border accessibility, spotting fraudulent activity quickly and effectively is a concern of utmost importance to financial institutions and merchants alike(Mienye & Swart, 2024). Here, fraud detection, credit scoring, and transaction analysis are critical in the protection of users and building platform trustworthiness(Chy & Buadi, 2024). Conventional approaches routinely fail in detecting advanced or dynamic fraud patterns, which calls for the implementation of intelligent, data-centric solutions(Zioviris et al., 2024). The integration of deep learning and behavioural modelling provides a promising avenue(Suhaimi et al., 2022). Efficient detection systems should not only detect historic fraudulent behaviour but also forecast upcoming risks(Nguyen et al., 2022). Ensuring strong accuracy and few false alarms is critical. Therefore, intelligent fraud detection systems are vital to contemporary digital environments(Ileberi et al., 2022).

1.2 Limitations of Traditional ML Approaches

Past work in this area has investigated ML techniques like logistic regression, decision trees, random forests and support vector machines for fraudulent transaction classification(Isangediok & Gajamannage, 2022). Although these models work Well, on balanced datasets, they tend not to perform as well with real-world, imbalanced data typical of financial fraud cases(De Zarzà et al., 2023). Methods such as rule-based systems or expert-specified thresholds are not very adaptive to changing fraud tactics(Shahapurkar & Patil, 2023). In the same vein, statistical anomaly detection techniques, although explainable, suffer from their limitations in dealing with shifts in data distributions(Cao et al., 2023). These techniques tend to be feature-dependent, with hand-designed features often being incapable of representing changing fraud behaviour(Rout & Jaiswal, 2024). As a result, these models tend to have lower accuracy, high false positives, and poor scalability to real-time use cases(X. Liu et al., 2022).

1.3 Challenges in Deep Learning-Based Methods

To overcome these issues, DL -based approaches like CNN, RNN and ensemble classifiers have been proposed(Shiri et al., 2024). While CNNs perform well in spatial pattern classification, they are inadequate in temporal sequence modelling of transactions(Sawada et al., 2022). RNN-based frameworks enhance this with the capability to learn sequential patterns, but common unidirectional models can lack context from future events along a transaction timeline(Y. Liu et al., 2023). In addition, certain ensemble classifiers add model complexity and computational expenses without appreciably improving detection sensitivity(Radaideh et al., 2023). Such models can lack generalizability across various types of fraud or data sets, particularly in high-frequency contexts such as e-commerce(Tang, 2023).

1.4 Proposed Framework and Novel Contributions

Therefore, to overcome the shortcomings of past systems, the presented framework combines state-of-the-art DL and anomaly detection methods. A strong preprocessing pipeline provides high-quality input via min-max normalization, correlation-based filtering, and imputation. A latent transaction behaviour learning is achieved via an autoencoder, and Local Outlier Factor (LOF) enhances fraud sensitivity through anomalous filtering. Classification is achieved using a hybrid model of BiLSTM and Transformer architectures to capture short- and long-distance temporal dependences. This allows the model to be adaptive to dynamic transaction flows as well as changing fraud methods. The innovation is in the combination of sequence-aware classification and latent feature learning in one pipeline, which improves accuracy, recall, and flexibility. Consequently, the approach provides a scalable, high-performance solution that can be used for fraud recognition, credit scoring and transaction analysis in e-commerce and financial systems. The novelty of this work lies in the unified integration of preprocessing, autoencoder-based feature extraction, LOF-based anomaly detection, and a hybrid BiLSTM–Transformer model within a single framework. Unlike existing approaches that apply these techniques independently, the proposed model ensures a tightly coupled pipeline for improved feature quality and learning. The combination enables effective capture of both temporal dependencies and global contextual relationships. This integrated design significantly enhances detection accuracy, reduces false negatives, and improves adaptability to evolving fraud patterns.

The proposed hybrid framework integrates autoencoder, LOF, and BiLSTM–Transformer to enhance fraud detection by combining feature learning, anomaly filtering, and temporal modeling. It captures bidirectional and long-range dependencies, ensures robust preprocessing, achieves high accuracy and recall, and improves adaptability, reducing false negatives while maintaining architectural clarity and reproducibility.

1.5 Key Challenges

Despite notable progress in fraud detection software, some of the most important issues remain in finance and e-commerce(Tang, 2023). Firstly, the extremely imbalanced character of transaction datasets, i.e., fraudulent cases being the minority and legitimate ones constituting the majority, tends to bias model performance and decrease sensitivity to minority classes(De Zarzà et al., 2023). Secondly, changing and developing fraud schemes complicate the effectiveness of static models over time without constant retraining(Mayaki & Riveill, 2022). Third, temporal dependencies in transaction sequences are usually not considered or not adequately represented, making it difficult to identify behaviour-based anomalies(Hayati et al., 2025). Fourth, noisy and partial data typical of real systems disadvantage the training of models and accuracy of decisions(Q. Liu & Ma, 2025). Fifth, conventional approaches are not capable of extracting latent behavioural features, which are essential for identifying subtle fraud signals(Yin et al., 2022). Finally, enabling real-time processing and scalability with high accuracy is an ongoing issue in high-volume transactional environments(Boroumand et al., 2022). Their real-world implications must be carefully considered. High false positive rates may lead to customer dissatisfaction and unnecessary transaction blocking, whereas false negatives can result in substantial financial losses. Therefore, modern fraud detection systems must achieve a balance between detection accuracy, scalability, and real-time responsiveness. In this context, there is a growing need for advanced hybrid approaches that can effectively address class imbalance, capture temporal dependencies, and adapt to evolving fraud patterns. The proposed framework in this study is designed to address these challenges by integrating anomaly detection and deep sequential learning

1.6 Objective and Scope

- Develop a smart and responsive anti-fraud architecture to be applied to financial and online commerce applications.
- Develop a hidden feature and temporal transaction behaviour-based deep learning pipeline.
- Apply a hybrid BiLSTM–Transformer classifier to identify and learn sequential patterns to detect fraud.
- Utilize Autoencoder and Local Outlier Factor (LOF) techniques for effective anomaly discovery and feature extraction.
- Evaluate the accuracy, precision, recall, and F1 score of the model under data imbalance and noise scenarios.
- Show the scalability and flexibility of the presented model on high-scale platforms such as digital payment gateways and online marketplaces.

1.7 Organization of Paper

The rest of the paper is organized as follows: Section 2 overviews related research on fraud detection, credit scoring and transaction analysis based on both conventional and DL methods. Section 3 introduces the suggested methodology with data preprocessing, feature extraction with autoencoders and LOF and the classification architecture employing Bi LSTM and Transformer models. Section 4 outlines the experimental framework, characteristics of used datasets, measurement metrics, and performance comparison. Section 5 presents the results, which demonstrate the efficacy of the suggested framework. Section 6 concludes the paper and states possible avenues for future research.

2. RELATED WORKS

(Aguirre-Sosa et al., 2023) explained the usage of Deep Neural Networks for financial fraud detection by developing rich models that can learn non-linear patterns from transactions. Elaborate feature engineering and employment of a subsequent multi-layer perceptron were used for improving classification performance. Their strategy had the promise of accuracy outputs but could not learn temporal relationships between transactions or adapt to the occurrence of emerging fraud patterns, limiting how effectively it could scale to real-world high-frequency e-commerce. (Cheng et al., 2022) developed a Convolutional Neural Network architecture for payment card fraud recognition. The approach used sequences of communications as spatial data and picked up local patterns with convolutional filters.

(Femila Roseline et al., 2022) employed a Recurrent Neural Network (RNN)-based anti-fraud system as transaction-specific credit card transactions. Their system maintained sequential behaviour and time dependencies by carrying over the hidden states. Although being more attentive to repeated patterns of fraud, vanilla RNN was suffering from vanishing gradients and lacked bidirectional context and thus had poor performance on long sequences of transactions common in e-commerce fraud analysis. (Iparraguirre-Villanueva et al., 2023) combined later enhanced the RNN model using Long Short-Term Memory units cope with long-term dependencies more effectively. Their LSTM approach preserved valuable temporal information for extensive windows of transactions and realised higher fraud detection rates.

(Yu et al., 2022) combined a Transformer-based fraud recognition model that applied self-attention mechanisms to learn global dependencies between transaction histories. The model was superior in terms of accuracy and training efficiency compared to RNN-based models. Nevertheless, it needed vast amounts of data and immense computational power, which made its deployment in financially limited systems not feasible.(Lee et al., 2024) created an Autoencoder-based fraud detection system in which the autoencoder was trained with compressed representations of normal transactions. False records, since they differed from the learned normal patterns, were identified by using the reconstruction error.

(Karthikeyan et al., 2024) suggested a hybrid model that consisted of LSTM and CNN for credit scoring and fraud detection. They applied the CNN layers to extract local features, followed by LSTM layers to obtain sequential dependencies. Their approach ensured balanced accuracy and recall but needed delicate tuning of the hybrid architecture and still encountered difficulties in identifying subtle anomalies. (Hou et al., 2022) combined LOF with a deep autoencoder to conduct anomaly filtering before classification. LOF assisted in identifying local density anomalies to enhance the quality of latent features that were input into the neural network. The method was good at initial fraud screening but relied too much on LOF parameter tuning and was inflexible to adapt to real-time streaming data.(Noviandy et al., 2023) developed an ensemble model using decision trees, XG Boost, and RNNs for classifying financial fraud. The model gained an advantage through decision-level fusion to show higher accuracy than individual models.

Existing studies on fraud detection highlight significant limitations in capturing temporal dependencies and adapting to evolving fraud patterns. Traditional machine learning models fail to represent complex sequential behaviour, while many deep learning approaches lack integration of anomaly detection and latent feature extraction. Although advanced models like LSTM and Transformer improve performance, they often operate independently and increase computational complexity. Moreover, current approaches provide limited robustness and scalability in real-world environments. These limitations indicate the need for a unified, efficient, and adaptive hybrid framework for accurate fraud detection.

3. PROBLEM STATEMENT

Convolutional Neural Networks have been widely useful in fraud detection due to their capability to learn local spatial patterns in transactional data(Shrivastava, 2022). CNNs cannot model temporal dependencies within sequences of transactions, a vital capability for the detection of dynamic patterns of fraud(Sulaiman et al., 2024). CNNs do not model the dynamics of long-range behaviour or sequence anomalies characteristic of real-time financial systems, either(Huynh et al., 2022). Consequently, their performance deteriorates in cases where fraud indicators are hidden in transaction timing or behaviour flow(Qu et al., 2024).

Long Short-Term Memory networks have made great strides in sequence pattern modelling through the ability to hold long-term dependencies between transaction histories. However, the unidirectional processing framework limits the extraction of future context within a transaction window, which can be critical in detecting bidirectional patterns of fraudulent activity(Nguyen et al., 2022). Moreover, LSTMs are likely to require lots of labelled data to be properly trained and are susceptible to noisy or incomplete transaction logs, with lesser reliability on actual financial platforms(Gajamannage & Park, 2022).

Autoencoder-based methods have been utilised for detecting anomalies in financial transactions by learning compact representations of normal behaviour(Xiong et al., 2023). These models are ineffective in supervised settings and are likely to produce high rates of false negatives when fraudulent activity closely approximates typical patterns(Luo, 2025). Autoencoders also ignore sequential and temporal attributes of transactions and, hence are unable to detect context-dependent anomalies(Chevrot et al., 2022). This reduces their capability in tasks such as credit scoring or unexpected bursts in transactions, common in e-commerce networks(Yin et al., 2022).

4. METHODOLOGY

The proposed methodology for the fraud recognition system involves several steps and stages to allow for more accurate, precise, and targeted fraud detection via the identification of fraudulent transactions. First, the raw transaction data are pre-processed, including concern for missing values and data imputation strategies, normalisation of the dataset and feature filtration by rate of correlation. The fraudulent transaction detection procedures then employ outlier detection, such as the Z-score, Modified Z-score, Cook's Distance and Local Outlier Factor outlier techniques, to identify outlier transaction activity. The pre-processed data will be allowed for a point of early detection and thereafter data will be input to a hybrid DL model that folds Bi LSTM and Transformer, to potentially be high precision, low false positives and adaptable as fraud patterns evolve across stages.

The refined dataset is analyzed using a hybrid Bi-LSTM and Transformer model. Bi-LSTM captures forward and backward temporal dependencies in transaction sequences, while the Transformer uses self-attention to identify important patterns. This combination learns complex behaviors effectively, achieving higher accuracy than traditional machine learning classifiers in fraud detection tasks. The labelled financial dataset is split into training, validation, and testing sets to prevent overfitting. Model performance is evaluated using accuracy, precision, recall, FPR, and FNR. Cross-validation ensures robustness, while grid search optimizes hyperparameters. The hybrid model improves detection performance compared to traditional approaches. The experiments were conducted using a reproducible setup where the dataset was divided into training, validation, and testing sets in a 70:15:15 ratio. The model was trained for 50 epochs with a batch size of 64 and a learning rate of 0.001 using the Adam optimizer. The BiLSTM layer consists of 128 hidden units, while the Transformer employs 4 attention heads and 2 encoder layers. A 5-fold cross-validation strategy was applied to ensure robustness and stability of the results.

Figure 1. Proposed Deep Learning Framework for Fraud Detection in Finance and E-Commerce

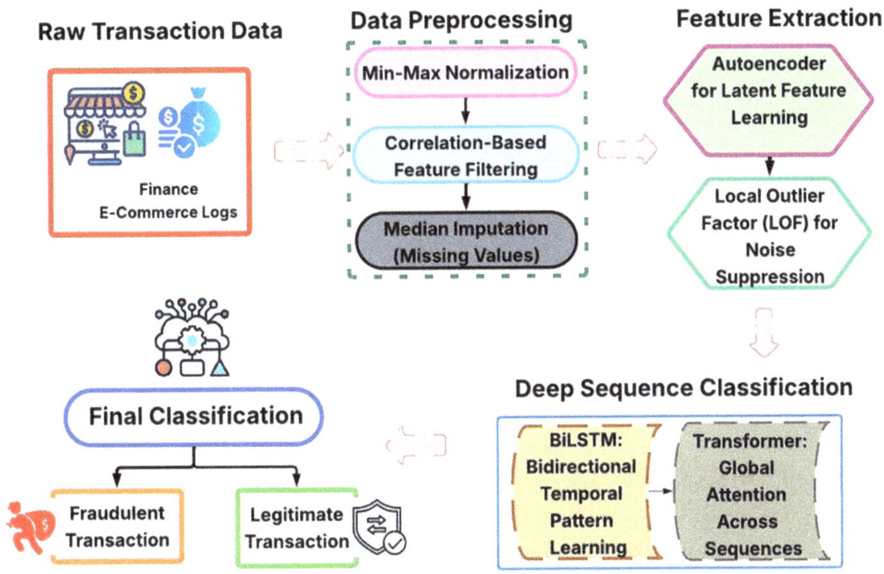

The architecture of designed fraud recognition system for finance and e-market platforms Figure 1. The system processes raw transaction data using normalization, feature filtering, and imputation. An autoencoder and LOF extract robust features by reducing noise and capturing patterns. A Bi-LSTM and Transformer model temporal and global dependencies, enabling accurate classification of fraudulent and legitimate transactions in dynamic, real-time environments.

4.1 Raw Transaction Data

The pipeline begins with raw transaction log extraction. The logs are often taken from the " Finance Fraudulent E-Commerce Transactions" Kaggle dataset consist of records of user behaviour such as purchase size, time of the transaction, place of the transaction, IP address, device metadata and merchant categories. The logs are important since they usually possess the implicit patterns that enable distinguishing between fraudulent and legitimate activities. The raw data itself is noisy and heterogeneous. It may have missing values, inconsistencies or categorical data that need to be converted. Moreover, due to the enormous volume and speed of the transactions, the data is stored on distributed systems and thus efficient extraction techniques are required for real-time analytics. There has not been any transformation yet. Data is still in its raw and unprocessed state, and hence it is inappropriate for machine learning. There is no intention here to pipe raw logs into a consistent preprocessing pipeline that normalizes and optimises the features for better learning performance.

The dataset used in this study is synthetic due to the limited availability of real-world financial transaction data caused by privacy and security constraints. It contains approximately 150,000 transaction records and simulates realistic characteristics such as class imbalance, temporal patterns, and diverse user behavior. This controlled setup allows effective evaluation of the proposed model; however, further validation on real-world datasets is necessary to ensure generalizability. Fraud detection relies on raw transaction data containing details like amount, time, location, and account information. This data is cleaned, structured, and temporally ordered to remove inconsistencies and noise. Preserving sequence enables models like Bi-LSTM and Transformers to learn patterns and detect anomalies indicating potential fraud.

4.2 Data Preprocessing

Data Preprocessing is an essential process that cleanses raw, unstructured transaction data into a clear and uniform structure that can be used in machine learning. During this process, three primary methods are used in figure 2. Min-Max Normalization, Correlation-Based Feature Filtering and Median Imputation. Min-Max Normalization scales numerical features to the [0, 1] range to provide uniformity between features and assist with stable training of neural networks. Correlation-Based Filtering removes strongly correlated or redundant features and thus helps in the reduction of redundancy as well as model generalization. Median Imputation solves missing values through replacement by the median of the corresponding feature, maintaining distribution and minimising outlier distortion. Collectively, these preprocessing steps improve data quality and allow for the best performance within the following deep learning pipeline.

Figure 2. Data Preprocessing Flowchart for Fraud Detection

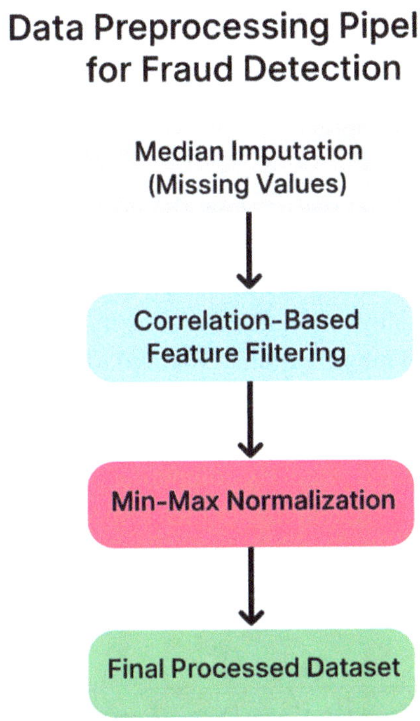

4.2.1 Min-Max Normalization

Min-Max Normalization is a feature scaling technique that maps numerical information into a uniform range, such as [0,1], without warping the relations between the original values. By doing this, all features will have the same weighting during model training, which is particularly necessary with gradient-based algorithms such as neural networks. By scaling features to a common range, it speeds up convergence and avoids large features from overshadowing learning.

The formula for Min-Max Normalization is an equation (1)

$$x' = \frac{x - x_{min}}{x_{max} - x_{min}} \quad (1)$$

Where:

- x is the original value,

- x_{min} and x_{max} are the minimum and maximum values of the feature, respectively,
- x' is the normalized value in the range [0,1].

This formula linearly scales the feature and maintains its distribution shape, which makes it appropriate for algorithms that are scale-sensitive to input data, e.g., Bi-LSTM and Transformer models.

4.2.2 Correlation-Based Feature Filtering

Correlation-Based Feature Filtering is a dimensionality reduction method used to eliminate redundant or highly correlated features, thereby introducing multicollinearity and reducing model interpretability. Particularly in fraud detection, applying this dimensionality reduction method would help retain the most informative features about all the transactions that have many overlapping attributes, such as time and timestamp, amount and price. By computing pairwise correlations among features with a correlation coefficient higher than a specified threshold (e.g., 0.85) are redundant and one of the correlated pairs is eliminated.

The most used formula is the Pearson correlation coefficient of equation (2)

$$\rho_{X,Y} = \frac{\mathrm{Cov}(X,Y)}{\sigma_X \cdot \sigma_Y} = \frac{\sum_{i=1}^{n}(x_i - \bar{x})(y_i - \bar{y})}{\sqrt{\sum_{i=1}^{n}(x_i - \bar{x})^2} \cdot \sqrt{\sum_{i=1}^{n}(y_i - \bar{y})^2}} \tag{2}$$

Where:

- $\rho_{X,Y}$ is the correlation coefficient between features X and Y,
- $\mathrm{Cov}(X, Y)$ is the covariance of X and Y,
- σ_X and σ_Y are the standard deviations,
- x_i, y_i are the individual sample points,
- $\bar{x}, \bar{y}$ These are the mean values of the features.

This action enhances model training by eliminating redundancy, curtailing overfitting and accelerating computation without sacrificing much predictive information.

4.2.3 Median Imputation (Missing Values)

Median imputation replaces missing values with the feature's median, preserving central tendency and resisting outliers. Unlike mean imputation, it avoids distortion from extreme values. This is crucial in financial datasets, where large transactions are common, ensuring balanced distributions and maintaining data integrity for reliable model performance.The formula for median imputation is an equation (3)

$$x_i = \begin{cases} x_i, & \text{if } x_i \neq \text{null} \\ \tilde{x}, & \text{if } x_i = \text{null} \end{cases} \quad (3)$$

Where:

- x_i is the individual feature value,
- $\tilde{x}$ is the median of all non-missing values in that feature.

It prevents missing data from resulting in diminished training samples or skewed predictions and is therefore ideal for scalable and resilient deep learning-based fraud detection systems.

Figure 3. Cyclic workflow of fraud detection integrating pattern analysis, rule-based validation, and customer authentication for real-time decision-making.

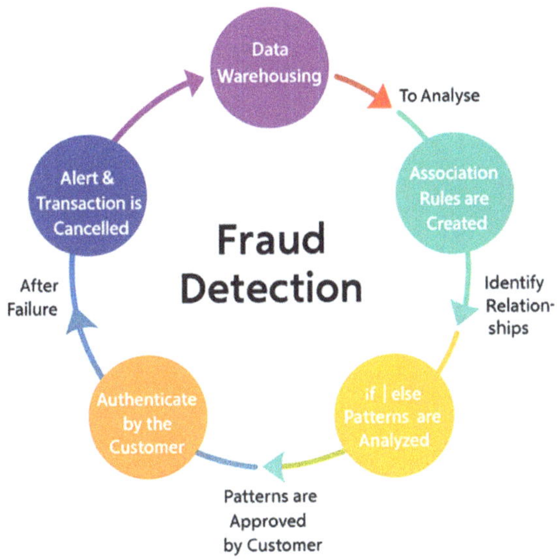

The labelled "Cyclic Workflow of Fraud Detection Using Pattern Analysis and Customer Authentication" figure 3 shows a looped process for fraud detection and response in financial systems. It starts with Data Warehousing, where transactional data is gathered and warehoused for analysis. Association rules uncover relationships between user actions and transactions, enabling pattern analysis through conditional logic. Valid patterns are approved, while suspicious ones trigger authentication.

Failed verification generates alerts and cancels transactions, creating a feedback loop that enhances real-time fraud detection and system adaptability.

4.3 Feature Extraction

Feature Extraction is the process of changing rare high-dimensional input data to low-dimensional, more salient data that retains the most significant patterns learnable by models. In fraud detection, this conversion reveals hidden behavioural features that are not directly apparent from the raw transactional records. Autoencoders, among others, are typically employed which learn to embed the input compressed by falling the error between the input and reconstruction. This allows the model to preserve only informative features and eliminate noise and redundancy, hence improving the performance and generalization capacity of the downstream classifiers.

Figure 4. Autoencoder Architecture with Integrated Local Outlier Factor (LOF) for Noise Suppression

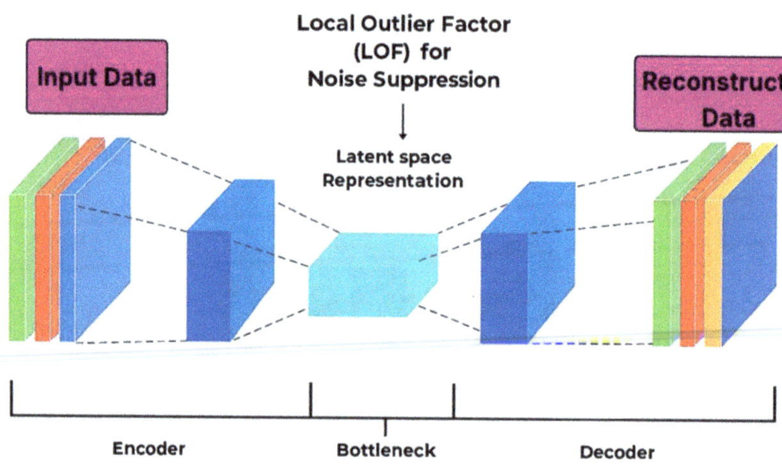

An augmented autoencoder model that involves the use of a Local Outlier Factor module for Figure 4 presents efficient noise removal during feature learning. Input data is encoded into a compact latent space capturing key patterns. LOF analyzes this representation to detect and remove anomalies or noise. The decoder reconstructs refined data, improving robustness and enabling more accurate fraud detection and downstream classification.

4.3.1 Autoencoder for Latent Feature Learning

An autoencoder is employed to learn a compact latent representation z by minimizing reconstruction error. In fraud detection, this procedure assists in capturing latent patterns in transactions by compressing high-dimensional data into a lower-dimensional latent space without losing its fundamental properties. The autoencoder is composed of two mechanisms: an encoder that projects the input into a latent feature vector, and a decoder that recreates the unique input from this hidden vector. Minimizing the reconstruction loss between the output and the input compels the network to induce the encoder to identify the most information-rich features, reducing noise and redundancy in effect.

The main operations of an auto encoder are in equation (4) to (6)

1. Encoding:

$$h = f(Wx + b) \tag{4}$$

2. Decoding:

$$x' = f'(W'h + b') \tag{5}$$

Where:

- x is the input feature vector,
- h is the latent (hidden) representation,
- x' is the reconstructed input,
- W and W' are the weight matrices for encoding and decoding, respectively,
- b and b' are bias vectors,
- f, f' are nonlinear activation functions such as ReLU or sigmoid.

The network is trained to minimize the reconstruction loss:

$$\mathcal{L} = ||x - x'||^2 \tag{6}$$

This loss function makes sure that the latent representation captures the most important aspects of the input and hence is very well suited for downstream tasks like fraud classification.

The pseudocode for the autoencoder model is given in Algorithm 1:

Algorithm 1. Latent Feature Extraction Using Autoencoder

```
Input: Pre-processed Transaction DataX
Output: Latent Feature Vector Z
mathematica
CopyEdit
Begin
For each transaction vector x in X:
Encode x into hidden representation h using encoder
Decode h into reconstructed vector x'
Compute reconstruction loss L = ||x - x'||^2
If L < threshold:
Accept h as valid latent feature
Else
Flag x as noisy or abnormal
End If
End For
Return Z = {h1, h2, ..., hn}
End
```

Algorithm 1 illustrates a procedure for obtaining latent features from pre-processed transaction information through an autoencoder. For any transaction vector x in dataset X, the autoencoder maps it into a lower-dimensional representation h and subsequently tries to reconstruct the input as x'. The reconstruction loss, defined as the square difference $\|x - x'\|^2$, captures how well the input is reconstructed. If this loss is less than a specified threshold, the latent representation h is a valid latent feature, meaning that the transaction is well-captured by the model. The transaction is marked as possibly noisy or out-of-distribution. The ultimate output is the collection Z of all accepted latent features.

4.3.2 Local Outlier Factor for Noise Suppression

Local Outlier Factor (LOF) is an unsupervised method that detects and removes noisy or suspicious data points by comparing local density with neighboring points. It identifies low-density anomalies as outliers, improving dataset quality and reducing bias or overfitting, enhancing the performance of fraud detection models.The LOF score is computed using the following steps from equations (7) to (8)

1. Local Reachability Density (LRD):

$$\mathrm{lrd}_k\left(p\right) = \left(\frac{\sum_{o\in N_k(p)} \mathrm{reach} - \mathrm{dist}_k\left(p,o\right)}{\left|N_k(p)\right|}\right)^{-1} \tag{7}$$

Where reach-dist $_k(p,o)$ is the reachability distance between point p and its k-nearest neighbor o.

2. Local Outlier Factor (LOF):

$$\text{LOF}_k\left(p\right) = \frac{1}{|N_k(p)|}\sum_{o \in N_k(p)} \frac{\text{lrnd}_k(o)}{\text{lrd}_k(p)} \tag{8}$$

Where:

- $N_k(p)$ is the set of k-nearest neighbors of point p,
- $\text{lrd}_k(p)$ is the local reachability density of the point p,
- $LOF_k(p)$ indicates how much lower the density of the point p is compared to its neighbours.

The pseudocode for Local Outlier Factor model is given in Algorithm 2:

Algorithm 2. Outlier Removal Using Local Outlier Factor (LOF)

Input: Latent Feature Set Z
Output: Cleaned Feature Set Z_clean

```
sql
CopyEdit
Begin
For each point zi in Z:
Compute k-nearest neighbors of zi
Calculate local reachability density (LRD) for zi
Compute LOF score for zi
If LOF(zi) > LOF_threshold:
Mark zi as an outlier
Else
Add zi to Z_clean
End If
End For
Return Z_clean
End
```

Algorithm 2 describes a procedure for eliminating outliers from a latent feature set Z based on the Local Outlier Factor method. For any data point z_i In the feature set, the algorithm initially determines its k-nearest neighbours and calculates its local reachability density (LRD), which indicates how secluded the point is among its neighbours. The LOF score is then computed to find the extent to which z_i is an outlier. If the LOF score is greater than a specific threshold value, the point is labelled as an outlier and removed; else it is added to the cleaned feature set Z_{clean}.

Figure 5. Local Outlier Factor-Based Anomaly Detection

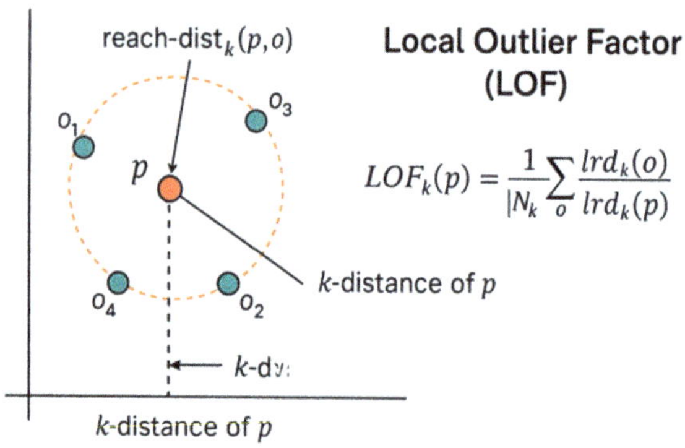

The idea of the Local Outlier Factor, which is a well-known density-based algorithm employed to identify anomalies or outliers in data sets. In Figure 5, the red point is being inspected based on its local neighbourhood determined by the k-distance, indicated by the dotted orange circle. The reachability distance reaches dist. computes how far every neighbouring point is from point p, normalized by the neighbourhood radius. The LOF score is then computed with the local reachability densities and their nationals. The larger the LOF, the more likely it is that point p is much less dense than its neighbours and thus could be an outlier. This method works especially well for outliers in complex, high-dimensional data spaces where classical distance-based methods can be ineffective.

4.4 Deep Sequence Classification

Deep sequence classification uses models like Bi-LSTM and Transformers to analyze transaction sequences, capturing temporal and behavioral patterns. By learning short- and long-term dependencies, it detects anomalies such as unusual spending or locations, enabling accurate, real-time fraud detection in imbalanced financial datasets.

Table 1. Classification of Fraud in Finance and E-Commerce

Domain	Fraud Type	Description
Finance	Credit Card Fraud	Unofficial use of credit card information to make purchases or withdraw cash.
	Identity Theft	Impersonating someone else to access financial assets or loans.
	Loan Fraud	Falsifying information to get approved for loans.
	Insurance Fraud	Submitting false claims to get insurance payouts.
	Account Takeover	Gaining control of a bank account and performing unauthorized transactions.
	Wire Transfer Fraud	Illegally transferring money through banks or online systems.
	Money Laundering	Concealing origins of illegally obtained money.
E-Commerce	Fake Returns	Customers returning used or wrong items as "unused."
	Payment Fraud	Using stolen cards or fake accounts for online purchases.
	Account Hijacking	Hacking e-commerce user accounts to make unauthorized purchases.
	Promotion Abuse	Exploiting coupon or referral systems multiple times.
	Friendly Fraud	Legitimate users falsely claim non-delivery or unauthorized payment.
	Phishing and Social Engineering	Tricking users into giving away login or payment info.
	Inventory or Listing Fraud	Selling fake or non-existent products online.

The categorizes typical fraud types into two major categories, table 1: Finance and E-Commerce with a brief description of each fraud type. Within the Finance category, fraud encompasses acts like Credit Card Fraud, where unprivileged users exploit card details and Identity Theft, where one's identity is utilised for money matters. Some of the examples listed here are Loan Fraud by fictitious data, Insurance Fraud by fraudulent claims, Account Takeover, Wire Transfer Fraud and Money Laundering, in which illegal funds are concealed. For the E-Commerce industry, fraud attacks online shopping sites, such as Fake Returns, Stolen Credential Payment Fraud, Account Hijacking, and Friendly Fraud, wherein legitimate users misuse return policies. It further includes Promotion Abuse, Phishing, and Inventory or Listing Fraud, all designed to exploit internet-based platform vulnerabilities. The table showcases in a clear and understandable manner typical fraudulent activities to help understand and recognize financial and e-commerce fraud.

4.4.1 Bi LSTM: Bidirectional Temporal Pattern Learning

Bi LSTM: BiLSTM is used to capture bidirectional temporal dependencies in sequential transaction data. In comparison with regular LSTMs, which look only at past context (left to right), Bi LSTM extends sequence modelling to include future context (right to left) as well. This is particularly useful in fraud recognition, where knowing both prior and subsequent transactions gives more behavioural context for example, an anomalous transaction might only look anomalous given the knowledge of both prior and subsequent activity. BiLSTM feeds each input transaction through two LSTM layers, one forward and one backward, and then concatenates their outputs to create a rich temporal representation.

For each time step t, the forward and backward LSTM are computed as equations (9) to (11)

- Forward LSTM:

$$\overrightarrow{h_t} = \text{LSTM}\left(x_t, \overrightarrow{h_{t-1}}\right) \tag{9}$$

- Backward LSTM:

$$\overleftarrow{h_t} = \text{LSTM}\left(x_t, \overleftarrow{h_{t+1}}\right)$$

r (10)

- Final hidden state (concatenation):

$$h_t = \left[\overrightarrow{h_t}; \overleftarrow{h_t}\right] \tag{11}$$

Where:

- x_t is the input feature at time step t,
- $\overrightarrow{h_t}$ and $\overleftarrow{h_t}$ are the forward and backward hidden states,
- h_t is the combined representation used for classification.

4.4.2 Transformer: Global Attention Across Sequences

Transformer: The Transformer utilizes self-attention to model global dependencies across the entire sequence. Unlike RNNs or LSTMs, which handle sequences sequentially and struggle with long dependencies, Transformers handle the whole sequence in parallel and can, therefore, learn global contextual relationships effectively. This is mainly convenient in fraud recognition were identifying suspicious activity often occurs when comparing widely spaced purchases such as cross-state transactions or unexpected account changes. The Transformer model uses dynamic weights on each location in the input classification so the model can focus on the most relevant sections regardless of where they occur in time.

The core of the Transformer is the scaled dot-product attention of an equation (12)

$$\text{Attention}\left(Q,K,V\right) = \text{softmax}\left(\frac{QK^{T}}{\sqrt{d_{k}}}\right)V \tag{12}$$

Where:

- $Q = XW^{Q}, K = XW^{K}, V = XW^{V}$ are the query, key and value matrices derived from the input sequence X,
- W^{Q}, W^{K}, W^{V} are learnable projection weights,
- d_k is the dimension of the key vectors (used for scaling),
- The SoftMax operation ensures attention weights sum to 1.

This process makes each transaction in the sequence dynamically notice all others, creating a context representation. The Transformer can therefore perceive complex patterns and relationships within entire histories of transactions, improving fraud detection accuracy where temporal or positional cues are weak or vague.

Figure 6. Hybrid BiLSTM–Transformer architecture with multi-head attention for sequential fraud classification.

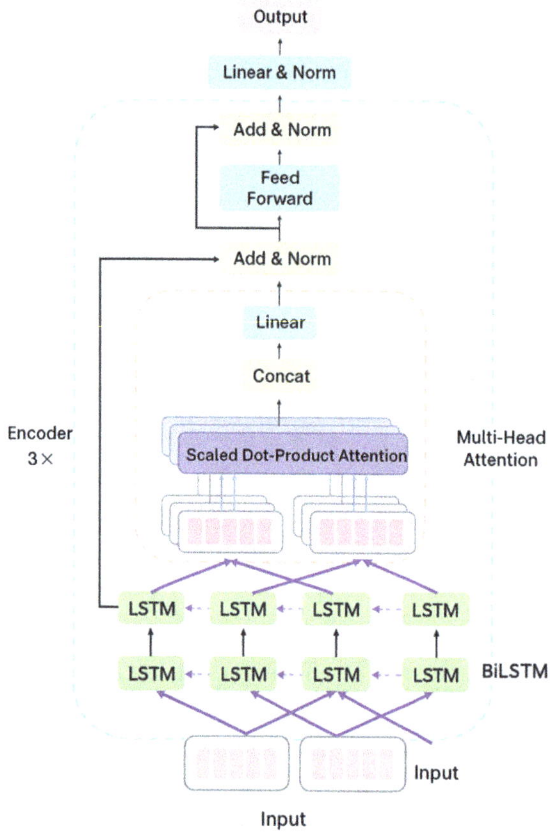

This hybrid architecture that utilizes Bidirectional Long Short-Term Memory networks coupled with Transformer encoders augmented by multi-head attention figure 6. The lower half of the architecture treats the input sequence with Bi LSTM layers to extract past and future dependencies in the data. Bi LSTM outputs are fed into a multi-head attention mechanism where scaled dot-product attention is added over multiple heads to extract diverse contextual relations. These are attended representations that are concatenated and linearly transformed. Add & norm blocks and feed-forward networks follow, which include a stack of Transformer encoders (repeated 3 times in the figure). The feature-transformed values are then normalized and concatenated through a final linear layer to produce the production. Such a design successfully combines the temporal modelling of LSTM with contextual understanding of Transformer attention and is therefore particularly suitable for tasks that need complex sequential modelling.

The pseudocode for Bi LSTM and Transformer model is given in Algorithm 3:

Algorithm 3. Classification Using Bi-LSTM and Transformer

```
Input: Cleaned Feature Set Z_ clean
Output: Fraud Label Y_ pred ∈ {0: Legitimate, 1: Fraudulent}
Mathematica
Copyedit
Begin
Initialize BiLSTM layer to capture bidirectional temporal features
Initialize Transformer encoder with multi-head attention
For each sequence s in Z_ clean:
h_bilstm = BiLSTM(s)
h_transformer = Transformer (h_ bilstm)
y_score = Sigmoid (Dense (h_ transformer))
If y_score ≥ 0.5:
Label s as Fraudulent
Else
Label s as Legitimate
End If
Append label to Y_pred
End For
Return Y_pred
End
```

Algorithm 3 explains a fraud classification procedure based on a hybrid DL model integrating a Bidirectional Long Short-Term Memory layer and a Transformer encoder. The model uses the cleaned latent feature set Z_{clean} an as input. For each sequence of features s_r, the BiLSTM learns temporal dependences in both the forward and backward directions, producing a contextualized representation h_{bilstm} This is then processed using a Transformer encoder, which performs multi-head attention to capture sophisticated relationships within the sequence score (y_{score}). It is conceded through a dense layer and then a sigmoid initiation to yield a fraud likelihood score. If the score is higher than or equal to 0.5, the transaction is classified as Fraudulent; otherwise, it is classified

4.5 Final Classification

Final Classification is the final operation in a deep learning-based fraud detection pipeline wherein the learned high-dimensional contextual and temporal features of models like Bi LSTM or Transformer are used to predict a binary fraudulent or legitimate transaction. This operation is generally done using a dense layer tracked by a sigmoid activation function for binary classification. The dense layer summarizes and converts the sequence feature learned into one probability score and the sigmoid function projects this output to a number in the range 0 to 1, which is the fraud probability. Depending on a threshold, the model outputs the final label, facilitating real-time decision-making for financial systems of equations (13) & (14)

1. Linear transformation (Dense layer):

$$z = W_f h + b_f \tag{13}$$

2. Sigmoid activation:

$$\hat{y} = \sigma\left(z\right) = \frac{1}{1 + e^{-z}} \tag{14}$$

Where:

- h is the output feature vector from BiLSTM/Transformer,
- W_f and b_f are the weights and bias of the classification layer,
- $\hat{y}$ is the predicted probability of the transaction being fraudulent,
- $\sigma(z)$ is the sigmoid activation function.

This probability is subsequently matched with a threshold (for example, 0.5): if ≥0.5, then the transaction is labelled as fraudulent otherwise, it's valid. This simple but effective output mechanism ensures the model's predictions are actionable and understandable by fraud detection systems.

Fraud detection is treated as a binary classification problem in which each transaction is assigned a label indicating whether it is fraudulent (1) or legitimate (0). Fraudulent transactions refer to unauthorized or deceptive activities that deviate from normal behavioural patterns in terms of timing, location, frequency, or transaction characteristics, whereas legitimate transactions follow consistent and expected user behaviour. The model estimates a probability score representing the likelihood of a transaction being fraudulent using a sigmoid-based output layer. A predefined threshold (typically 0.5) is then applied: transactions with scores above the threshold are classified as fraudulent, while those below are considered legitimate. This unified formulation enables the model to effectively distinguish anomalous high-risk transactions from normal activity while minimizing false positives, thereby improving detection accuracy and maintaining user trust in financial systems.

Figure 7. E-Commerce Transaction Process Flow with Enhanced Icons and Colour Scheme

The e-commerce transaction process flow, Figure 7, which is rich with rich media, reveals step-by-step a user's journey from entering the online store to final delivery of an item purchased. The graphic starts with the purchaser accessing the site on a digital device, selecting a product, and adding it to the cart. After products are chosen, the user navigates payment options, confirming the purchase. The backend system subsequently processes order preparation, packaging and shipment. Product delivery is monitored and finalised in the destination handover. The new icons and enhanced colour set give better visual understanding and user interaction, making the diagram easy to read and perfect for presenting customer flow in digital commerce scenarios. Such a flow is critical to knowing areas of possible fraud points and streamlining secure handling of transactions. The proposed framework combines preprocessing, feature extraction, and hybrid deep learning techniques to improve fraud detection. Its effectiveness is evaluated through experimental analysis.

5. RESULTS AND DISCUSSION

5.1 Dataset Description

Experimental evaluation is conducted to analyze the performance of the proposed model using the selected dataset and appropriate evaluation metrics. The Fraudulent E-Commerce Transactions" Kaggle dataset (*Fraudulent E-Commerce Transactions* , n.d.) is an artificial dataset developed to mimic online transaction patterns for the expansion and testing of fraud recognition models. There are 150,000 e-commerce transaction records, with each record labelled as either "fraudulent" or "not fraudulent", so binary classification is possible. The data contains columns like user id, transaction ID, product ID, product category, payment method, value and a timestamp, all written to simulate actual e-commerce patterns. Although the data is fake, it is based on likely patterns and distributions typical of transactions made online, which is why it is suitable for training ML models for fraud detection. The availability of both categorical and numeric features facilitates a broad variety of preprocessing and modelling methods such as feature engineering, anomaly detection, and deep sequence analysis. The dataset used in this study is synthetic; it is designed to closely mimic real-world transaction patterns, including user behaviour, fraud scenarios, and data imbalance. Such datasets are commonly used due to privacy and security restrictions in accessing real financial data. The dataset captures key characteristics of real environments, making it suitable for evaluating the proposed model. However, validation on real-world datasets is necessary to further confirm the model's generalizability and practical applicability.

5.2 Performance Analysis of Proposed Work

shows the learning path of the model during training epochs by graphing training accuracy and validation accuracy in Figure 8. The x-axis is used to represent the number of epochs, and the y-axis represents the accuracy from 0 to 1. The blue trace signifies the training accuracy, and the orange trace represents the validation accuracy.

Figure 8. Training and validation accuracy curves over epochs, demonstrating model convergence and generalization performance with minimal overfitting

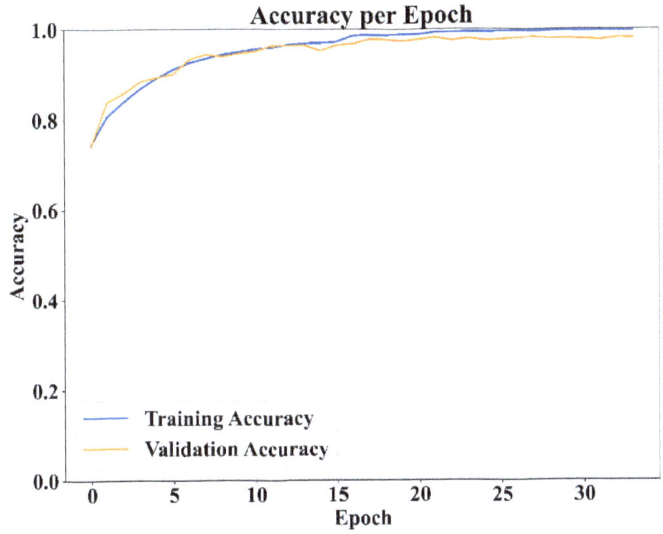

Both plots show a consistent rise in accuracy, reaching nearly 1.0 after the completion of training, which means the model has learned the data patterns well. The small difference between the two plots indicates that the model is generalizing without heavy overfitting, with consistent performance on unseen validation samples. This is a trend indicating the stability and strength of the model throughout training.

Figure 9. Confusion Matrix of Classification Results

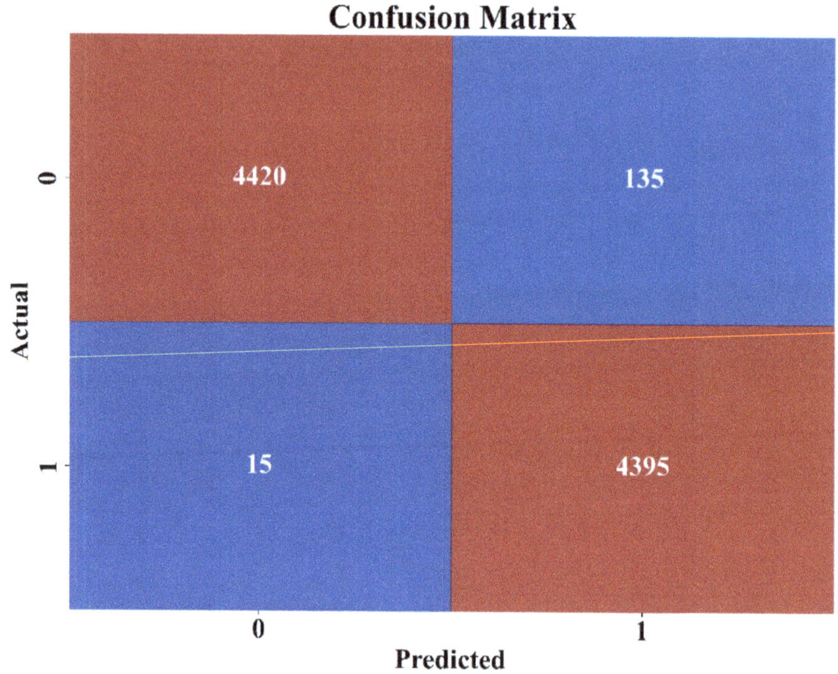

The confusion matrix in this chart figure 9 illustrates the accuracy of a binary classifier model, where '0' class generally means valid transactions and '1' class means fraudulent transactions. The matrix indicates that the model accurately labelled 4420 examples as valid (true negatives) and 4395 as fraud (true positives). The matrix also reports 135 false positives, valid connections mistakenly considered as fraud, and just 15 false negatives, missed fraud transactions." This distribution indicates an extremely accurate model with good precision and recall, particularly in fraud detection, where false vetoes are to be avoided at all costs. The colour contrast in intensity enhances interpretability by clearly marking correctly and incorrectly labelled samples.

Figure 10. False Negative Rate vs False Positive Rate Comparison

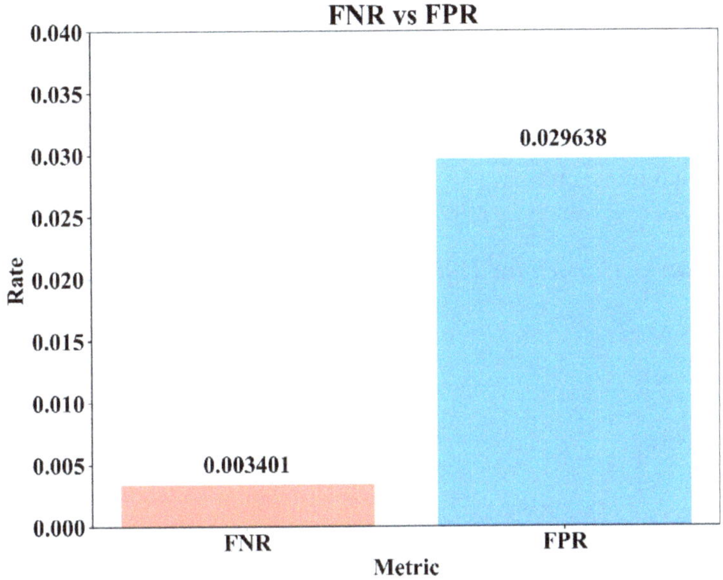

This bar chart is a comparison of the False Negative Rate and the False Positive Rate for a fraud detection classification model in Figure 10. The FNR highlighted in red is extremely low at 0.003401, indicating very few false negatives where fraudulent communications are classed as legitimate ones. Conversely, the FPR, shown in blue, is considerably higher at 0.029638 and represents that small proportion of clean transactions that are wrongly classified as fraudulent. Such skew is tolerable in fraud detection systems, where it is crucial that fraudulent activity not be missed by maintaining FNR as low as possible.

Table 2. FPR and FNR values

Metric	Value
FPR	0.029638
FNR	0.003401

The metrics presented indicate fraud detection performance in terms of production of classification errors in Table 2. The False Positive Rate (FPR) is 0.0296, meaning that approximately 2.96% of useful transactions were classified incorrectly as fraudulent. This is an important metric for any financial system, because a high FPR would cause great frustration for a customer, due to irrelevant blocks stopping their transaction. By contrast, the False Negative Rate (FNR) is 0.0034, which indicates that the model only missed 0.34% of the meaningful fraudulent transactions, which is equally, if not more important to fraud detection. It is so important to fraud recognition to minimise FNR to ensure that the model does not miss real threats. Together, these corresponding rates of error indicate that the system holds a lot of accuracy and are typically reliable in differentiating between a real authentic and a genuine deleted transaction.

Figure 11. Loss per Epoch for Training and Validation Phases

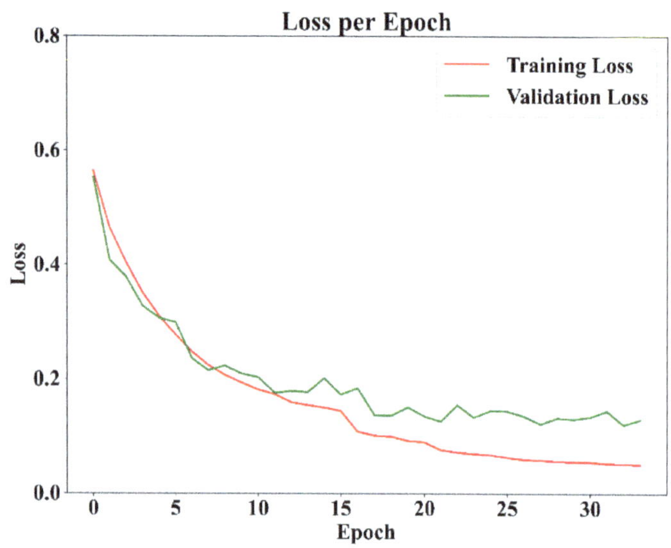

The plot shows training and validation loss values for a few epochs during the training process of the model, Figure 11. The red line is for training loss, while the green line is for validation loss. Both the losses are extremely high at the beginning, but with the progression of training process decrease drastically, indicating proper learning by the model. After around 10 epochs, the training loss is still decreasing slowly, and the validation loss has a slightly oscillating trend, showing some degree of small overfitting. However, the persistent difference between the curves is still small, reflecting the capacity of the model to generalize well from new data. This decreasing trend of loss supports the effectiveness of the suggested model in reducing prediction error while training at the testing stage towards achieving effective fraud detection outcomes.

Figure 12. Precision-Recall Curve with AUC Score

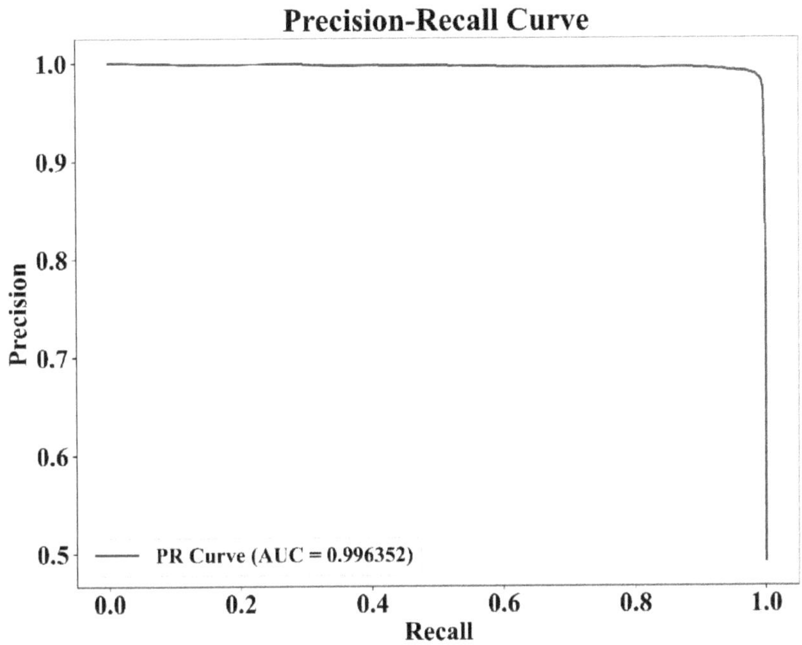

The Precision-Recall curve for the classification model used in the fraud recognition system is shown in Figure 12. The x-axis is used to indicate recall, and the y-axis is used to indicate precision. An ideal high-performing model will be a model having a PR curve that closely follows the top-right portion of the plot, where there is high precision along with high recall. The model here is working extremely well because the curve remains close to the top for all recall values except at the highest recall values, where it slightly drops. Area Under the Curve is provided as 0.9963 and indicates nearly perfect classifying ability.

Figure 13. ROC Curve with AUC Value

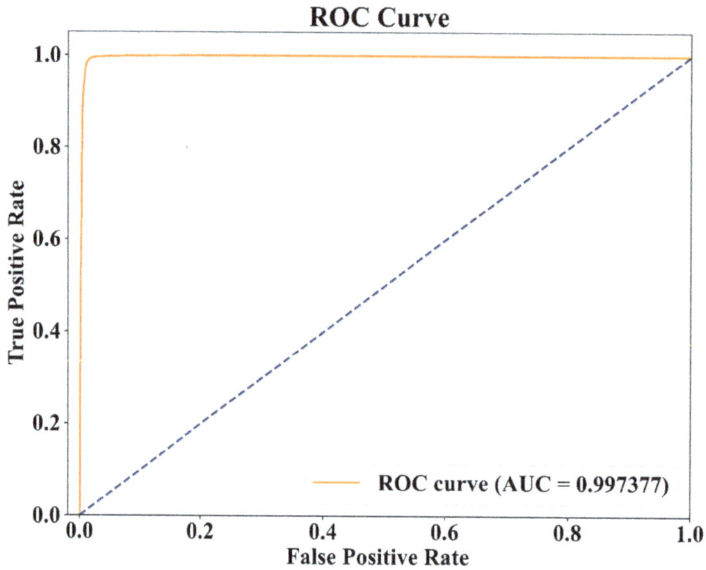

The ROC, which shows the performance of a classification model figure 13 by plotting the True Positive Rate against the False Positive Rate. The orange curve is the model's performance in perception between classes, while the dashed diagonal line indicates random guessing. The area under the ROC curve is around 0.9974, which means the model performs superbly in classification with a very high ability to accurately discriminate between the positive and the negative classes. The orange curve is close to the top-left corner, indicating high sensitivity and low false positive rate at all thresholds. The diagonal dashed line approximates well the presentation of a random classifier, which can serve as a baseline. The model's AUC value of 0.9974 corresponds to an outstanding classification capability.

Figure 14. Model Performance Metrics Bar Chart

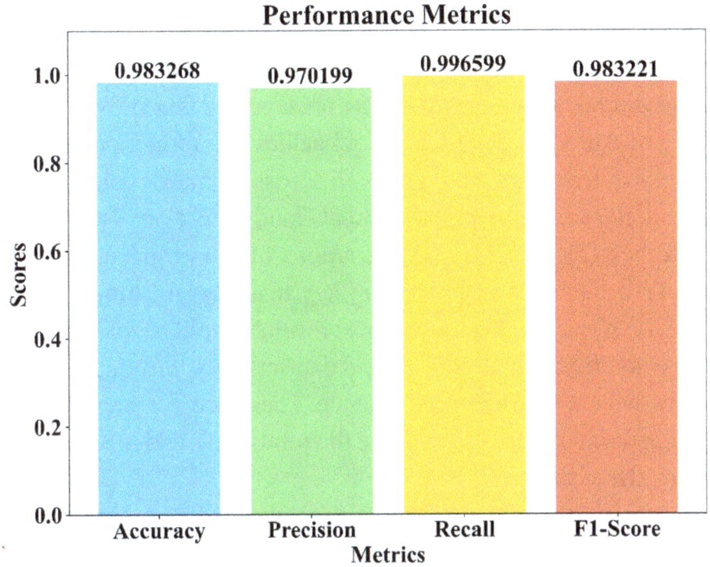

The bar chart of the major performance system of measurement of a classification model, Figure 14. The values for all the metrics are more than or very close to 0.97, which proves that the model is high-performing. The largest score (0.9966) for Recall implies the model is exceptionally good at detecting true positives. Accuracy (0.9833) and F1-Score (0.9832) indicate the model is a superb balance of recall and precision. The slightly weaker Precision (0.9702) also suggests a high capacity for successful prediction of positive instances. Overall, the model has superb and well-balanced predictive capacity.

Table 3. Comparative Study of Proposed work with Existing method

Author	Method Used	Accuracy (%)	Precision (%)	Recall (%)	F1 score (%)
Proposed	Autoencoder, LOF	0.983268	0.970199	0.996599	0.983221
Vasant et al.(Vasant et al., 2025)	ANN	95.42%	53.37	98.54%	68.39%
Niaz et al. (Niaz et al., 2025)	SVM	0.9781	0.9640	0.9926	0.9781

The performance comparison table 3 indicates that the proposed fraud detection model in table 3, which utilizes Autoencoder and Local Outlier Factor (LOF), has an effective performance. The proposed method reached the highest accuracy (98.32%), with high precision (97.02%) and recall (99.66%), resulting in an F1-score of 98.33% which showed that the model was well balanced. While Vasant et al. using ANN are showed to have a lower precision (53.37%) which represents an example of a high recall model characterised by the presence of false positives. This means that the proposed Autoencoder-LOF model achieves a reduction in false positives and false negatives. It performs equally well across all metrics and, therefore, is the most suitable model for real-world financial fraud detection. The obtained results highlight both the effectiveness and limitations of the proposed approach. These findings provide a basis for summarizing key insights and future directions. The proposed model achieves high performance; results should be interpreted cautiously due to the use of synthetic data. Real-world datasets may introduce additional noise and complexity that could affect performance. Therefore, further evaluation in real-world environments is required to validate the robustness and practical applicability of the proposed framework.

The study effectively addresses key issues in fraud detection, including class imbalance, evolving fraud patterns, and the need for accurate classification of rare fraudulent transactions. Traditional methods often struggle with capturing complex temporal and behavioral patterns, which highlights the necessity for advanced approaches. In this context, the proposed hybrid framework aligns with current trends in fraud detection that emphasize the integration of deep learning techniques, anomaly detection, and sequential modeling. The use of Autoencoder for feature representation, LOF for anomaly filtering, and BiLSTM-Transformer architecture reflects a shift toward more adaptive and data-driven solutions. However, certain challenges such as real-world data variability, computational complexity, and model interpretability remain important concerns. Addressing these aspects would further strengthen the alignment of the work with practical and emerging trends in financial fraud detection systems.

6. CONCLUSION AND FUTURE ENHANCEMENT

In this study, we developed a hybrid methodology for financial scam detection based on the deep learning Bi LSTM and Transformer methods. In the preprocessing step, we executed Min-Max normalization, median imputation for missing values, and filtered features based on correlations to ensure quality and relevant data as input. We also performed advanced outlier detection using Local Outlier Factor, Z-scores, Modified Z-scores, and Cook's Distance to improve the quality of feature space by mitigating noise, leading to an improved signal for learning. We demonstrated our model has capabilities to learn temporal and contextual patterns of transactional sequences. The BiLSTM portion conducted reliable sequential dependency learning, and the Transformer's attention mechanism to captured global context learning. When evaluating the performance of the model we utilized standard metrics of False Positive Rate and False Negative Rate, and we found that their method trained significantly less than randomly misclassifying transactions and improved their learning to identify fraudulent transactions. Summary, the proposed hybrid model suggests a necessity for real-time, scalable, and adaptable financial fraud detection. The sequential learning aspect, combined with the attention-based augmentation, allowed the approach to generalize well on unseen data. Hence, the approach was adaptable to dynamic e-commerce and banking ecosystems allowing for robustness in deployment. Next steps in the research agenda may include federated learning for privacy-preserving purposes, and importantly the newly proposed framework could include explainable AI functions to ensure appropriate audit and regulatory functions.

Achieving high performance, this study is limited by the use of a synthetic dataset for evaluation. While the dataset simulates realistic transaction patterns, it may not fully capture the complexity and unpredictability of real-world fraud scenarios. Therefore, future work will focus on validating the proposed framework using real-world financial datasets and deploying the model in practical environments to assess its robustness, scalability, and adaptability to evolving fraud patterns.

The study places significant emphasis on performance metrics and model architecture; however, the impact of using a synthetic dataset is not sufficiently highlighted, which may lead to optimistic results compared to real-world scenarios. Additionally, the computational complexity of the hybrid model and its implications for real-time deployment are not fully discussed. The lack of interpretability and absence of an ablation study further limit the understanding of individual component contributions. Addressing these aspects in future work will improve the practical applicability and robustness of the proposed system.

6.1 Limitations

The framework, despite achieving strong performance, has several limitations. It relies on a synthetic dataset, which may not fully capture real-world complexity and may lead to optimistic results. The lack of an ablation study limits understanding of individual component contributions. Additionally, the hybrid architecture increases computational complexity, affecting scalability and real-time deployment. Limited comparison with advanced methods and lack of interpretability further restrict its practical applicability in real-world financial systems.

The use of a synthetic dataset may not fully represent real-world transaction complexity, leading to optimistic results. The hybrid architecture also increases computational cost, making real-time deployment challenging. Additionally, the absence of ablation studies limits understanding of individual component contributions, and the lack of interpretability reduces transparency. Comparisons with advanced models such as XGBoost or LightGBM are not included, and issues related to scalability and real-time data handling remain unaddressed. Addressing these limitations would improve the model's practical applicability.

REFERENCES

Aguirre-Sosa, J., Dextre, M. L., Lozada-Urbano, M., & Vargas-Merino, J. A. (2023). Background of Peruvian gastronomy and its perspectives: An assessment of its current growth. *Journal of Ethnic Foods*, *10*(1), 50. Advance online publication. DOI: 10.1186/s42779-023-00212-4

Boroumand, A., Ghose, S., Oliveira, G. F., & Mutlu, O. (2022). *Enabling High-Performance and Energy-Efficient Hybrid Transactional/Analytical Databases with Hardware/Software Cooperation* (arXiv:2204.11275). arXiv. /arXiv.2204.11275DOI: 10.48550

Cao, T., Zhu, J., & Pang, G. (2023). *Anomaly Detection under Distribution Shift* (arXiv:2303.13845). arXiv. /arXiv.2303.13845DOI: 10.1109/ICCV51070.2023.00599

Cheng, D., Wang, X., Zhang, Y., & Zhang, L. (2022). Graph Neural Network for Fraud Detection via Spatial-Temporal Attention. *IEEE Transactions on Knowledge and Data Engineering*, *34*(8), 3800–3813. DOI: 10.1109/TKDE.2020.3025588

Chevrot, A., Vernotte, A., & Legeard, B. (2022). CAE: Contextual auto-encoder for multivariate time-series anomaly detection in air transportation. *Computers & Security*, *116*, 102652. DOI: 10.1016/j.cose.2022.102652

Chy, K. H., & Buadi, O. N. (2024). *A Machine Learning-Driven Website Platform and Browser Extension for Real-Time Risk Scoring and Fraud Detection for Website Legitimacy Verification and Consumer Protection. 11*(10).

De Zarzà, I., De Curtò, J., & Calafate, C. T. (2023). Optimizing Neural Networks for Imbalanced Data. *Electronics (Basel)*, *12*(12), 2674. DOI: 10.3390/electronics12122674

Femila Roseline, J., Naidu, G., Samuthira Pandi, V., Alamelu alias Rajasree, S., & Mageswari, D. N. (2022). Autonomous credit card fraud detection using machine learning approach☆. *Computers & Electrical Engineering*, *102*, 108132. DOI: 10.1016/j.compeleceng.2022.108132

Fraudulent E-Commerce Transactions. (n.d.). Retrieved July 22, 2025, from https://www.kaggle.com/datasets/shriyashjagtap/fraudulent-e-commerce-transactions

Gajamannage, K., & Park, Y. (2022). *Real-time Forecasting of Time Series in Financial Markets Using Sequentially Trained Many-to-one LSTMs* (arXiv:2205.04678). arXiv. /arXiv.2205.04678DOI: 10.48550

Hayati, H., Murguia, C., & van de Wouw, N. (2025). Privacy-preserving anomaly detection in stochastic dynamical systems: Synthesis of optimal Gaussian mechanisms. *European Journal of Control*, *81*, 101142. DOI: 10.1016/j.ejcon.2024.101142

Hou, Y., He, R., Dong, J., Yang, Y., & Ma, W. (2022). IoT Anomaly Detection Based on Autoencoder and Bayesian Gaussian Mixture Model. *Electronics (Basel)*, *11*(20), 3287. Advance online publication. DOI: 10.3390/electronics11203287

Huynh, T. T., Nguyen, M. H., Nguyen, T. T., Nguyen, P. L., Weidlich, M., Nguyen, Q. V. H., & Aberer, K. (2022). *Efficient Integration of Multi-Order Dynamics and Internal Dynamics in Stock Movement Prediction* (arXiv:2211.07400). arXiv. / arXiv.2211.07400DOI: 10.48550

Ileberi, E., Sun, Y., & Wang, Z. (2022). A machine learning based credit card fraud detection using the GA algorithm for feature selection. *Journal of Big Data*, *9*(1), 24. DOI: 10.1186/s40537-022-00573-8

Iparraguirre-Villanueva, O., Guevara-Ponce, V., Ruiz-Alvarado, D., Beltozar-Clemente, S., Sierra-Liñan, F., Zapata-Paulini, J., & Cabanillas-Carbonell, M. (2023). Text prediction recurrent neural networks using long short-term memory-dropout. *Indonesian Journal of Electrical Engineering and Computer Science*, *29*(3), 1758. DOI: 10.11591/ijeecs.v29.i3.pp1758-1768

Isangediok, M., & Gajamannage, K. (2022). *Fraud Detection Using Optimized Machine Learning Tools Under Imbalance Classes* (arXiv:2209.01642). arXiv. / arXiv.2209.01642DOI: 10.1109/BigData55660.2022.10020723

Karthikeyan, T., Govindarajan, M., & Vijayakumar, V. (2024). Enhancing Financial Fraud Detection Through Chimp-Optimized Long Short-Term Memory Networks. *TS. Traitement du Signal*, *41*(2), 835–845. DOI: 10.18280/ts.410224

Lee, Y., Park, C., Kim, N., Ahn, J., & Jeong, J. (2024). LSTM-Autoencoder Based Anomaly Detection Using Vibration Data of Wind Turbines. *Sensors (Basel)*, *24*(9), 2833. Advance online publication. DOI: 10.3390/s24092833 PMID: 38732939

Liang, T., Liu, Y., Liu, X., Zhang, H., Sharma, G., & Guo, M. (2022). *Distantly-Supervised Long-Tailed Relation Extraction Using Constraint Graphs* (arXiv:2105.11225). arXiv. /arXiv.2105.11225DOI: 10.48550

Liu, Q., & Ma, W. (2025). *Navigating Data Corruption in Machine Learning: Balancing Quality, Quantity, and Imputation Strategies* (arXiv:2412.18296). arXiv. / arXiv.2412.18296DOI: 10.48550

Liu, X., Shen, F., Zhao, J., & Nie, C. (2022). *RSTAM: An Effective Black-Box Impersonation Attack on Face Recognition using a Mobile and Compact Printer* (arXiv:2206.12590). arXiv. /arXiv.2206.12590DOI: 10.48550

Liu, Y., Sun, Z., & Zhang, W. (2023). Improving fraud detection via hierarchical attention-based Graph Neural Network. *Journal of Information Security and Applications*, *72*, 103399. DOI: 10.1016/j.jisa.2022.103399

Luo, X. (2025). Robust Financial Fraud Detection via Causal Intervention and Multi-View Contrastive Learning on Dynamic Hypergraphs. *Mathematics*, *13*(24), 4018. Advance online publication. DOI: 10.3390/math13244018

Mayaki, M. Z. A., & Riveill, M. (2022). Autoregressive based Drift Detection Method. *2022 International Joint Conference on Neural Networks (IJCNN)*, 1–8. DOI: 10.1109/IJCNN55064.2022.9892066

Mienye, I. D., & Swart, T. G. (2024). A Hybrid Deep Learning Approach with Generative Adversarial Network for Credit Card Fraud Detection. *Technologies*, *12*(10), 186. Advance online publication. DOI: 10.3390/technologies12100186

Nguyen, V. B., Dastidar, K. G., Granitzer, M., & Siblini, W. (2022). *The Importance of Future Information in Credit Card Fraud Detection* (arXiv:2204.05265). arXiv. /arXiv.2204.05265DOI: 10.48550

Niaz, A. A., Ashraf, R., Mahmood, T., Faisal, C. M. N., & Abid, M. M. (2025). An efficient smart phone application for wheat crop diseases detection using advanced machine learning. *PLoS One*, *20*(1), e0312768. DOI: 10.1371/journal.pone.0312768 PMID: 39775380

Noviandy, T. R., Idroes, G. M., Maulana, A., Hardi, I., Ringga, E. S., & Idroes, R. (2023). Credit Card Fraud Detection for Contemporary Financial Management Using XGBoost-Driven Machine Learning and Data Augmentation Techniques. *Indatu Journal of Management and Accounting*, *1*(1), 29–35. DOI: 10.60084/ijma.v1i1.78

Park, J., Seo, Y., & Cho, J. (2023). Unsupervised outlier detection for time-series data of indoor air quality using LSTM autoencoder with ensemble method. *Journal of Big Data*, *10*(1), 66. DOI: 10.1186/s40537-023-00746-z PMID: 36618886

Prabha, D. P., & Priscilla, C. V. (2024). A combined framework based on LSTM autoencoder and XGBoost with adaptive threshold classification for credit card fraud detection. *The Scientific Temper*, *15*(02), 2216–2224. DOI: 10.58414/SCIENTIFICTEMPER.2024.15.2.34

Qu, B., Wang, Z., Gu, M., Yagi, D., Zhao, Y., Shan, Y., & Zahradnik, F. (2024). *Multi-task CNN Behavioral Embedding Model For Transaction Fraud Detection*. 286–292. DOI: 10.1109/ICDMW65004.2024.00043

Radaideh, M. I., Pappas, C., Wezensky, M., & Cousineau, S. (2023). Operational data for fault prognosis in particle accelerators with machine learning. *Data in Brief*, *51*, 109658. DOI: 10.1016/j.dib.2023.109658 PMID: 37928324

Rout, S., & Jaiswal, K. (2024). Fraud detection using deep learning. *International Journal of Electrical and Data Communication, 5*(1), 07–11. DOI: 10.22271/27083969.2024.v5.i1a.37

Sani, A., Hassan, Z. L., & Balarabe, A. T. (2024). A Logistic Regression-based Model for Identifying Credit Card Fraudulent Transactions. *Asian Journal of Research in Computer Science*, *17*(7), 41–54. DOI: 10.9734/ajrcos/2024/v17i7476

Sawada, A., Miyagawa, T., Ebihara, A. F., Yachida, S., & Hosoi, T. (2022). *Convolutional Neural Networks for Time-dependent Classification of Variable-length Time Series* (arXiv:2207.03718). arXiv. /arXiv.2207.03718DOI: 10.1109/IJCNN55064.2022.9892605

Shahapurkar, A., & Patil, R. (2023). Concept drift and machine learning model for detecting fraudulent transactions in streaming environment. [IJECE]. *International Journal of Electrical and Computer Engineering*, *13*(5), 5560–5568. DOI: 10.11591/ijece.v13i5.pp5560-5568

Shiri, F. M., Perumal, T., Mustapha, N., & Mohamed, R. (2024). A Comprehensive Overview and Comparative Analysis on Deep Learning Models: CNN, RNN, LSTM, GRU. *Journal on Artificial Intelligence*, *6*(1), 301–360. DOI: 10.32604/jai.2024.054314

Shrivastava, S. (2022). Convolutional Neural Network Approach for Mobile Banking Fraudulent Transaction to Detect Financial Frauds. *International Journal of Engineering Technology and Management Sciences*, *6*(1), 30–37. DOI: 10.46647/ijetms.2022.v06i01.005

Suhaimi, A., Lim, A. W. H., Chia, X. W., Li, C., & Makino, H. (2022). Representation learning in the artificial and biological neural networks underlying sensorimotor integration. *Science Advances*, *8*(22), eabn0984. Advance online publication. DOI: 10.1126/sciadv.abn0984 PMID: 35658033

Sulaiman, S. S., Nadher, I., & Hameed, S. M. (2024). Credit Card Fraud Detection Using Improved Deep Learning Models. *Computers, Materials & Continua*, *78*(1), 1049–1069. DOI: 10.32604/cmc.2023.046051

Tang, Y. (2023). Automatic Fraud Detection in e-Commerce Transactions using Deep Reinforcement Learning and Artificial Neural Networks. *International Journal of Advanced Computer Science and Applications, 14*(7). Advance online publication. DOI: 10.14569/IJACSA.2023.01407113

Vasant, M., Ganesan, S., & Kumar, G. (2025). Enhancing E-commerce Security: A Hybrid Machine Learning Approach to Fraud Detection. *FinTech and Sustainable Innovation, 14*, 1–9. DOI: 10.47852/bonviewFSI52024882

Xiong, A., Qiao, C., Tong, Y., Qi, B., & Jiang, C. (2023). *Block-chain Abnormal Transaction Detection Method Based on Auto-encoder and Attention Mechanism. Research Square* Platform LLC.5(4). DOI: 10.21203/rs.3.rs-2969521/v1

Yin, H., Zhang, Z., Wang, Z., Ozyurt, Y., Liang, W., Dong, W., Zhao, Y., & Shan, Y. (2022). *Behavioral graph fraud detection in E-commerce* (arXiv:2210.06968). arXiv. /arXiv.2210.06968DOI: 10.1109/ICDMW58026.2022.00105

Yu, L., Xu, X., Trajcevski, G., & Zhou, F. (2022). Transformer-enhanced Hawkes process with decoupling training for information cascade prediction. *Knowledge-Based Systems, 255*, 109740. DOI: 10.1016/j.knosys.2022.109740

Zioviris, G., Kolomvatsos, K., & Stamoulis, G. (2024). An intelligent sequential fraud detection model based on deep learning. *The Journal of Supercomputing, 80*(10), 14824–14847. DOI: 10.1007/s11227-024-06030-y

Chapter 10
Case Studies and Real-World Application of Generative AI

Shikha Khullar
http://orcid.org/0009-0000-5598-3145
Poornima University, India

Nikhil Kumar Goyal
http://orcid.org/0009-0007-4532-8033
Noida International University, Greater Noida, India

Shikha Sharma
http://orcid.org/0000-0001-6339-9731
Poornima University, India

Chirra Baburao
http://orcid.org/0000-0003-4881-3708
Sir C.R. Reddy Educational Institutions, India

Vaishali Sonwane
http://orcid.org/0000-0002-5823-4868
Poornima University, India

Rakesh Kumar Saxena
http://orcid.org/0000-0002-6453-6053
Poornima University, India

ABSTRACT

The rapid adoption of digital technologies has intensified cyber threats, making effective risk management crucial for organizations. Traditional AI supports anomaly detection and intrusion prevention but struggles with novel attacks. Generative AI, leveraging GANs, VAEs, and LLMs, introduces a transformative edge by simulating realistic attack scenarios, generating synthetic datasets, and automating adaptive responses. This chapter examines real-world applications of Generative AI in cyber risk management, outlining its use in threat modeling, anomaly detection, incident response, and risk assessment. Case studies include phishing detection, ransomware simulation, and synthetic data generation across finance and healthcare sectors. A comparative analysis highlights key benefits and challenges, followed by discussions on ethical and adversarial risks and future directions such as integration with

DOI: 10.4018/979-8-3693-8397-1.ch010

blockchain, explainable AI, and human–AI collaboration. This chapter provides researchers and practitioners a holistic view of how Generative AI is redefining cyber risk management.

1. INTRODUCTION

Digital revolution has presented global connection, collaboration and innovation opportunities never before seen before. Nevertheless, the cyber threat has also been on an increase proportional to this change. Since phishing attacks attack millions of users every day and advanced ransomware brings down healthcare organizations and financial institutions, the cyber risk industry is constantly developing in size and complexity. The old-fashioned security systems though effective against the familiar threats commonly collapse when faced with unfamiliar attackers, zero-day attacks, or highly dynamic attackers. Every company engaged in manufacturing, operations, or related services must adhere to the best practices in information technology flows and procurement management; therefore, the results across all companies will remain consistent and uniform at minimal levels. (Symantec, 2023) (IBM Security, 2023; ENISA, 2023) (Steinel, 2025)

This loophole has led to implementation of artificial intelligence (AI) on cyber-security. The first AI systems were predominantly rule-based or prediction based and provided some form of incremental data improvement in detection and response. However, when the attackers started to utilize AI themselves the defense side had to have a strategy not merely predictive but also generative and adaptable. (Brundage et al., 2018; Chenna, 2022). This next frontier in AI is Generative Artificial Intelligence (Generative AI). Using generative AI in the form of architectures like Generative Adversarial Networks (GANs), Variational Autoencoders (VAEs), and large language models (LLMs), generative AI does not merely analyze the existing data - it generates new and realistic data and scenarios. It enables defenders to both simulate cyberattacks and predict threats and enhance resilience in unknown directions (Goodfellow et al., 2014; Cai et al., 2021) (Kingma & Welling, 2013; Yan et al., 2025).

There are traditional AI classifiers available that could find known malicious email templates, but a generative AI one could present thousands of synthesized phishing emails, which could replicate evolving phishing tactics. This will allow the employees as well as the automated defense systems to be trained on future, unknown threats. In the same manner, simulating attack chains in ransomware preparedness so that organizations can be able to test their defenses against any actual incidents, this is what generative models can do.

In this chapter, the author explains how generative AI can be used in managing cyber risk based on real case studies. It provides a systematic order of the importance of it by providing the judgment of its advantages and disadvantages and critically examining case studies in very organised industries such as finance, healthcare and critical infrastructure. In this way, it provides the practitioners and scholars with insights into how generative AI is transforming the manner in which we expect, treat, and respond to cyber threats. Generative AI is increasingly being integrated into collaborative robotic ecosystems to improve intelligent decision-making and adaptive automation (Varra et al., 2026).

2. GENERATIVE AI IN THE CYBERSECURITY LANDSCAPE

2.1 Evolution of AI in Cybersecurity

The use of AI in cybersecurity is not a new practice. First, organizations relied on a system of rules and signature-based detection which proved to be good in the situation of the static threat but became old-fashioned with the introduction of polymorphic malware, which was able to alter its signature each time it appeared. In reaction to this, the industry shifted to machine learning (ML) solutions that would keep track of behavioral patterns, flag network traffic anomalies and suspicious logins and remove the usage of the static signatures. Despite these efforts, ML suffered a major flaw that it was regrettably called training data made the models to be stationary concerning zero-day attacks, and unfamiliar methods of attack. Even generative models were an innovation, as they enabled the simulation of the potential attack cases as well as the occurring ones and turned generative AI into the core of the next generation of managing cyber risks instead of it being a reactionary element.

2.2 Role of Generative AI vs. Traditional AI Models in Cybersecurity

The distinction between traditional AI and generative AI in cybersecurity lies in their capabilities and scope. The classical AI models can be mostly described as predictive: the models classify, detect, and act on threats according to the patterns in the historical data. Instead, generative AI models are creative to the extent that they can generate artificial information, model attack situations, and introduce new variations of existing threats. To understand this, whereas classical AI may be used to understand an email is 95 percent similar to a known phishing email, generative AI can create all-new phishing email templates that an attacker might utilize in the future that the defense system can account for in advance and prepares to counter.

This shift that has taken the form of proactive anticipation as opposed to reactive defense makes generative AI particularly effective with regard to the current environment that is fast-evolving in terms of threats. (Agrawal et al., 2024; Ammara et al., 2024; Sánchez-Serrano, 2025). The table 1 shows the shift from traditional AI's reactive threat detection to generative AI's proactive and adaptive capabilities. Generative AI improves cybersecurity through threat simulation, synthetic data generation, and automated response to evolving attacks. Deep learning architectures have demonstrated improved performance and efficiency in intelligent text-processing applications relevant to cybersecurity analytics (Khullar et al., 2025).

Table 1. Traditional AI vs. Generative AI in Cybersecurity

Aspect	Traditional AI	Generative AI	Cybersecurity Example
Function	Detects known threats	Generates new threat scenarios	Phishing email generation for testing
Learning	Supervised (labeled data)	Unsupervised/self-supervised	Synthetic data for model training
Adaptability	Limited to known attacks	Handles zero-day threats	Malware simulation (GAN-based)
Output	Fixed classification	Multiple possible outputs	Variants of phishing/malware
Automation	Semi-automated	Highly automated	SOC automation & response playbooks
Data Use	Requires real data	Uses synthetic data	Privacy-preserving datasets

Source: Adapted from Brundage et al. (2018); Goodfellow et al. (2014); ENISA (2023).

Table 2. Ethical Issues of Generative AI in Cybersecurity

Ethical Dimension	Description in Cybersecurity Context	Implications / Examples
Data Privacy & Confidentiality	Generative AI models are trained on large-scale datasets that may include sensitive security logs, user data, or proprietary information.	Risk of exposing confidential data through model outputs or synthetic data leakage (e.g., membership inference attacks).
Bias and Fairness	Models trained on biased or incomplete cybersecurity datasets may generate skewed threat scenarios or detection outcomes.	Certain attack patterns may be overrepresented, leading to unequal threat prioritization or blind spots in defense systems.
Dual-Use Risk (Offensive vs Defensive Use)	The same generative models used for defense (e.g., threat simulation) can be exploited by attackers.	Attackers may use AI to generate phishing emails, malware variants, or deepfakes for social engineering.
Transparency and Explainability	Generative AI systems often function as black boxes, making it difficult to interpret decisions or generated outputs.	Security analysts may not fully trust AI-generated threat predictions or incident response strategies.

continued on following page

Table 2. Continued

Ethical Dimension	Description in Cybersecurity Context	Implications / Examples
Accountability and Responsibility	Lack of clarity on who is responsible for AI-driven decisions in cybersecurity operations.	If AI-generated recommendations fail (e.g., incorrect threat response), accountability between developers and organizations is unclear.
Synthetic Data Misuse	While synthetic data enhances privacy, it can also be misused if not properly validated.	Poor-quality synthetic data may lead to inaccurate threat detection models or false security assumptions.
Adversarial Attacks on AI Models	Generative AI systems themselves can be targeted using adversarial inputs or data poisoning.	Attackers may manipulate training data to weaken detection systems or cause false negatives.
Regulatory and Compliance Challenges	Lack of clear legal frameworks governing AI-generated data and automated decision-making in cybersecurity.	Difficulty in complying with regulations such as GDPR when using non-transparent AI models.
Intellectual Property (IP) Concerns	AI-generated outputs may replicate proprietary security tools, attack patterns, or datasets.	Ownership disputes over generated threat intelligence or AI-created cybersecurity solutions.
Over-reliance on AI Systems	Excessive dependence on generative AI may reduce human oversight and critical thinking in security operations.	Organizations may overlook novel threats if AI models fail or produce misleading outputs.

Source: Adapted from Brundage et al. (2018); NIST (2022); ENISA (2023); Mukherjee et al. (2019).

2.3 Advantages and Limitations of Generative AI

2.3.1 Advantages

- Threat Simulation

In general, generative AI can model a broad selection of possible attack patterns, including both the most common phishing attacks and extremely complex multi-stage attacks. With simulated processes of operation by real-world adversaries, organizations can experiment on their defensive posture in safe and controlled environments. This enables the security forces to establish blind spots, test intrusion detection systems and assess the workability of intrusion response drills prior to real breach of information. These works, as opposed to being limited by human imagination and time as is with traditional red teaming, generative AI can create an unlimited number of variants of attacks, and therefore simulations become broader and more unpredictable.

- Synthetic Data Generation (Agrawal et al., 2024; Ammara et al., 2024; Sánchez-Serrano, 2025)

Generative AI generation of synthetic datasets to train with without the exposure of sensitive or proprietary data is among the most important potential benefits of this technology in the area of cybersecurity. Whereas cyber defense models often demand huge volumes of information, such as network logs, malwares, and user actions that are usually sensitive to be disclosed to third parties (Mukherjee et al., 2019). By creating artificial, but authentic information, organizations can train strong AI models, at the same time, following privacy policies. It also allows making work across institutions safer since synthetic data rules out the risk of information leaks, yet delivers varied and representative data.

- Adaptive Defense

Conventional security measures are based on fixed rules and signatures, which the attackers will later learn to overcome. Generative AI overcomes this drawback through the constant creation of dynamic defense strategies which change depending on the emergence of threats. One can use the example of creating new patterns of detection, randomized firewall rules, or adaptive strategies of intrusion response that will make the attitude of an attacker more difficult to anticipate. Such constant change does not only enhance the rule of thumb and makes enemies use more effort and resources to win but also changes the balance of power to the defenders.

- Enhanced Training

Common aspects of cyberspace education are constrained by generic case studies that do not translate into the complexity of the real world. Generative AI heeds this by generating phishing emails, social engineering messages, and attack scenarios in a very realistic manner depending on the context of an organization. Life-like dangers can be introduced to the employees in controlled training exercises and this is in a better position to make the workers identify and repel genuine hostile means. In the long run, this method contributes greatly to the vigilance of the employees and minimizes human error, which is among the biggest security gaps in cybersecurity.

2.3.2 Limitations

Although it has potential, there are also serious challenges attached to the use of generative AI in cybersecurity. The biggest issue is that generative models can be very resource intensive, and can require huge amounts of computational resources and high-quality datasets, not always available out of thin air to every organization. The bias and hallucination is another weakness because AI models occasionally produce unrealistic, or misleading scenarios that are capable of skewing the assessment of risks and unintentionally causing people to concentrate on false alarms. Besides it, there is the question of dual-use risk, as the same technology that enhances protection can be turned into a weapon by malicious actors to establish even more advanced phishing attacks, deepfakes, or even automated malware. In addition to these technical and security challenges, regulatory factors are also significant as the potential legal, ethical, and compliance aspects of the implementation of AI in sensitive cybersecurity situations remain unstable, and accountability, transparency, and responsible usage are questioned.

3. FRAMEWORK FOR APPLYING GENERATIVE AI IN CYBER RISK MANAGEMENT

A structured framework is essential for integrating generative AI into cyber risk management in a systematic and effective manner. This framework operates across four core dimensions, each addressing a critical aspect of cybersecurity. From proactive threat modeling to automated response and continuous risk assessment, generative AI provides organizations with tools to shift from reactive defense toward predictive and adaptive security strategies.

3.1 Threat Modeling and Prediction

Generative AI can enhance threat models by modeling different and changing strategies of attackers. Contrary to the classical methods that use historical accounts of incidences to a large extent, Generative Adversarial Networks (GANs) can generate novel variants of malware and attack vectors, enabling proactive threat modeling and improved detection of zero-day attacks (Goodfellow et al., 2014; Cai et al., 2021; Alshebli et al., 2025). Generative AI aids organizations to identify corporate vulnerabilities in their systems that have become obscure due to the behavioral patterns of attackers, even before such vulnerabilities are used by the attackers. The outcome is a more offensive battle stance which narrows the odds of being caught unaware by the emergent threats.

3.2 Data Importation: Behaviour Simulation and Anomaly Detection.

The other significant generative AI contribution is the difference between normative and anomalous behavior. Generative models generate an image of how the normal system and user activity should be by simulating the normal system and also user activity and compare the real activity against the expected one. To illustrate, a

Variational Autoencoder (VAE) will be capable of learning common login behaviors, including geographic coordinates, frequency, and time of the access. A system can easily identify when something out of the ordinary happens such as under different geographical areas or during odd hours and indicate that there are possible security risks. This live detection mechanism accelerates and improves insider threat and compromised account detection or detection of unauthorized access attempts. Automated Incident Response and Remediation involves utilizing tools and observational technologies to detect, remove, or lessen risks to both information and computer systems. Hybrid models such as BiGRU-VAE further enhance anomaly detection performance in cyber-physical systems by capturing both temporal dependencies and latent data representations (Alguliyev et al., 2022).

3.3 Automated Incident Response and Remediation

Generative AI is also very crucial in automating incident response. Through the use of historical data, playbooks may be created as an adaptive response to a new or emerging type of attack. As an example, the AI system could automatically suggest or even take action in the case of a ransomware outbreak, which could include isolating infected endpoints, shutting down impacted parts of the network, and performing system restores out of verified backups. This automation does not only enhance quicker response time, but also reduces human error, which offers a quicker healing procedure, as well as the minimization of damage that could be inflicted by cybercrime.

3.4 Risk Analysis and Scenario building

Risk assessment methods that are old-fashioned such as tabletop training are disadvantageous in that they are stagnant, predictable, and limited. Generative AI attempts to maximise this dynamically to produce a wide range of realistic "what if" possibilities that can melt down to shifting areas of threat. Such simulations make organizations know the different paths of attack, and this makes them challenge their resiliency in different situations. Generative AI presents a security team with a more significant opportunity of responding to the emerging attacks and systemic risks, which legacy models do not consider, by constantly revising and diversifying the risk circumstances.

4. CASE STUDIES: GENERATIVE AI IN CYBER RISK MGMT. IN THE REAL WORLD

Case studies will offer the real-life experience of how generative AI has been applied in different situations in the real world in different industries. These examples surpass the theoretical opportunities to explain the accomplishments, challenges, and lessons learned during the practical deployments. They do not only unveil the technical efficiency of the very generative AI, but also make allusions to the organizational, regulatory and ethical dimension of the practice.

4.1 Case Study 1 – Generative AI for Phishing Detection and Prevention

Phishing is considered to be one of the heaviest and most perilous forms of cyberattack that has been accused of millions of security breaches annually. The weaknesses of the previous filters which rely on rules and machine learning classifiers are no longer capable of keeping pace with the personalized spear-phishing attacks which seek to evade detection. Generative AI overcomes this weakness by generating fake phishing messages that are highly realistic in reference to the dynamic strategies of cybercriminals. As an example, large language models (LLMs) can produce very believable fake emails that seem to have been sent by an authoritative figure such as a bank, e-commerce website, or a top executive. (Mirtaheric, 2025; OpenXcell, 2023). Application: The company used a phishing simulation platform based on generative AI and deployed by a Fortune 500 company. The system generated thousands of personalised phishing mail, which was sent to not only test the efficiency of the existing automated filters, but also to teach the staff some real-life training skills. (Palo Alto Networks, 2023) Impact: Six months later, the company indicated that the employee vulnerability rate to phishing had reduced by 60 percent, as indicated by the rates of people who had to click through when simulations were applied to the company. The automated email filters further enhanced once they were trained on a more elaborate set of synthetic examples. Lesson Learned: As in the case, dual nature of generative AI as both employee training system and detection systems improvement tool played an essential role in the successful mitigation of the risks related to phishing.

4.2 Case Study 2 – Simulating Ransomware Attacks for Risk Preparedness

Ransomware has become a multi-billion dollar criminal industry, and such high-profile attacks as WannaCry and the Colonial Pipeline attack have shown its crippling effect on critical infrastructure. Conventional incident response training can be ineffective in many cases since it uses fixed attack scenarios that do not reflect the ever-changing aspect of ransomware.Generative AI provides a dynamic and forward-looking alternative by simulating novel ransomware variants through the use of Generative Adversarial Networks (GANs). The models are able to simulate the malware-like functionality, such as encryption algorithms, lateral network movement and exfiltration hops enabling the organization to train on the upcoming threats that are yet to be discovered in the real world. The European healthcare provider, in its turn, partnered with a cybersecurity firm to create and release generative AI models simulating ransomware spread into the IT system of a hospital. The simulations also showed weaknesses in backup strategies and the access controls which were critical and therefore allowed the organization to fortify its defenses. Because of this, the provider managed to minimize the possible downtime on a ransomware attack by 40 percent. The main thing that emerged in this case is that, through generative simulations, the proactive defense will enable the detection of vulnerabilities before the real attacks are experienced, and this greatly increases the resilience to ransomware threats.

4.3 Case Study 3 - Synthetic Data Generation for Secure Training Models

The process of training AI models that can be used to implement cybersecurity generally demands sensitive information, including network traffic data or user activity logs, yet any dissemination or exposure to these data can pose a severe privacy risk and might even be against the strict laws of data protection and organizational culture. Generative AI can be used to address this issue by generating synthetic data sets that maintain the statistical properties of the original data but do not give any direct connection to sensitive data. One practical example of such a case can be observed in the example of a multinational bank that makes use of variational autoencoders (VAEs) to create synthetic transaction data to train a model of fraud detection. This method enabled investigators to come up and test the new sophisticated detection systems without opening up their actual customer records. The findings proved very productive -the synthetic data generated models of the same accuracy as those that it was trained on real data, and found a complete level of compliance with the GDPR and other privacy measures. The most important message is that synthetic data not only is going to enhance regulatory compliance but also enable safe cooperation with partners, as the organizations can share real albeit anonymized data with partners in order to carry out cybersecurity efforts.

4.4 Case Study 4 – AI-driven Threat Intelligence and Malware Analysis

Threat intelligence platforms aggregate massive volumes of data from diverse sources such as darknet forums, malware repositories, and incident reports, but analyzing this information manually or even with traditional AI models often proves slow, fragmented, and insufficient to address the speed of evolving cyber threats. Generative AI addresses this gap by not only creating malware variants to predict how threats may develop but also by summarizing vast intelligence data into concise, actionable insights. A significant use of this methodology was shown when a malware research company across the globe deployed systems based on large language models (LLM) into its pipeline of analyzing malware. Such models could produce snippets of code that would resemble the possible progression of the current malware families, thus giving the analysts an insight into what their opponents would do next. With this knowledge, the analysts revised detection signatures more efficiently which enhanced the detection rates against unknown malware families by 35 percent and shortened the duration used to analyze a sample by a wide margin. The most important lesson is that the generative AI is a force multiplier that allows human analysts to stay ahead of the changing opponents while improving response times, and precision in terms of threats identification.

4.5 Case Study 5 – Enterprise Deployment in Financial Services

The financial institutions are still one of the most desirable victims of cybercriminals due to the high value of the data and assets they store and high compliance requirements they need to stick to, which makes addressing cyber risk management a necessity of the utmost importance. In order to reinforce defenses, generative AI has been growing in applications, including in fraud detection, insider threat simulation and systemic risk prediction. One particularly powerful case is provided by the example of the most successful financial services organization operating in Asia, which introduced generative AI models to challenge its cybersecurity infrastructure in the conditions of a simulated attack. The AI provided very realistic conditions with coordinated phishing, and credential stuffing campaigns and attacks of malware injection that allowed the institution to test its defense against sophisticated and dynamic threats. The defects in multi-factor authentication implementation and receiving protocols, the gaps that were addressed appropriately were unveiled in the simulations. As a result, there was the actual reduction in the number of financial losses incurred with the fraud in the organization. The central takeaway is that even though generative AI has the potential to transform enterprise-level cybersecurity, its utilization needs to be unified with the schemes of governance and compliance to provide both high efficiency and accountable approach to implementation in the highly regulated areas (IBM Security, 2023; Palo Alto Networks, 2023). The degree of satisfaction with products is a key factor determining readiness to spend.

5. COMPARISON OF CASE STUDIES

Although the case studies underscore the unique role of generative AI in cyber risk management, through a comparative study, common themes, knowledge, and lessons apply to future implementation processes.

5.1 General Trends and Lessons

Although generative AI promises high results in cybersecurity, there are some factors that appear to restrict its universal implementation and exemplary performance in numerous organizations. The high cost of training generative models, including GANs and LLMs, is one of the main problems. These models are very heavy processing, memory and storage in nature and in numerous cases, organizations are forced to use cloud based infrastructure. Although these investments may be prohibitive to smaller organizations and startups, large enterprises are able to provide such investments, which becomes a barrier to entry and growth in cybersecurity readiness because of the technology gap.

Hallucinations and model reliability are the other important issues. There are cases where the generative AI systems generate outputs that are either unrealistic, irrelevant, or invalid in their operations. As an example, phishing template executable could be too basic and quite easy to detect, or malware versions will not work correctly in the actual situation. These discrepancies undermine the trust in automated defense systems and demonstrate the necessity to put machines under a human control in order to validate the AI-generated data(Symantec, 2023; Palo Alto Networks, 2023).

Another issue is in the dual-use situation of generative AI. Threat simulators and defender advantageous methods can ensure the security of systems, but at the same time, they can be used by bad players. The generative models can be used to build more persuasive phishing attacks, create advanced code, or create deepfakes to commit social engineering tricks. This confusion between the use of defense and encryption emphasizes the need to ensure safety and the responsible use.

Lastly, generative AI in cybersecurity has regulatory and ethical challenges in deploying the technology in organizations. Laws in data generation through synthetics, automated decision-making, and responsibility in AI-based systems are still not well-developed. Such confusion has made organizations unable to maximize on the technology without being caught in a node of breaching data protection laws and other ethical guidelines. Consequently, most institutions are torn between the need to be innovative and must comply with governance and compliance needs. Transformation expenses include acquiring word processing software, computer hardware, and technology for decryption and encryption.

5.2 Adversities of Implementation.

Notwithstanding the positive results of generative AI in cybersecurity, there are a number of common challenges that still exist in organizations that prevent its practical implementation. The fact that the advanced models, including GANs and LLMs, are expensive to train due to large computational cost and require a high level of processing power, memory, and storage, making them frequently expensive to scaffold on the cloud which might not be financially accessible to smaller companies, is one of the most problematic. The other significant issue is that the model might be not very reliable, so in the case of phishing template examples that are too on-the-nose or malware that is not performing well, artificial intelligence might undermine the trust into automated defense mechanisms and subsequently lead to the conclusion that human control is necessary. To make the situation even more complex, we have the dual-use dilemma, as the very methods used to enhance the protective measures can be used by the malefactors to develop a more convincing phishing attack, develop more sophisticated malware or create a deepfake that could be used to conduct social engineering. Besides these dangers, there are also regulatory and ethical threats to organizations because legal frameworks related to synthetic data, automation of decision-making, and accountability of AI are not yet completely formed. It is such a changing environment that makes assuring that institutions maximise on generative AI and maintain adherence to the data protection statutes and ethical guidelines very challenging, as it requires them to strike a balance between exploration and preservation.

5.3 Success Factors for Adoption

Based on a comparative analysis of case studies, various important aspects were always found to be fundamental to the effective use of the generative AI in cybersecurity. Interdisciplinary teamwork was also a necessity because to successfully adopt the technology and implement all the necessary changes there had to be a tight connection between cybersecurity teams, AI scholars, compliance representatives, and business stakeholders to ensure that the technical outcomes matched the regulatory and organizational requirements. More specifically, in the financial services example, incorporating generative AI into the structure of governance measures made sure that the outputs by the system would be within rigorous regulatory standards. Incremental deployment which included starting with very small and manageable use cases, such as testing phishing simulation, and gradually expanding to applications that could cover more risks, was another success factor that minimized risks and ensured easier integration. The feedback loops were also critical since the most successful systems were dependent on human monitoring to provide feedback on the output of the AI to refine and validate the output, and this is the case with malware analysis where the human staff is using corrective feedback to enhance the accuracy and relevance of the AI-generated malware variants. Ethical guardrails, created at the very beginning of the process to guard against abuse - such as ensuring that generative models cannot generate harmful code without restrictions - also served not only to reduce risks but also served the purpose of encouraging and sustaining trust in the organization. The general conclusion is that although generative AI gives a strategic edge in planning to the emergent and unknown threat, organizations need to handle issues related to cost, governance, compliance, and trust to ensure the cognitive benefits are maximized. Finally, it is important to note that the comparative analysis reveals that generative AI is a game-changing solution in the field of cyber risk management, which brings great advantages, but at the same time, it creates new risks that need to be addressed carefully and attentively.

Enhanced Detection and Response

The ability to predict and mitigate the threats instead of merely responding to them is one of the most potent future advantages of generating AI.

Dynamic Threat simulation: GANs and VAEs have the potential of creating malware variants and phishing templates, so organizations can train models and workers on attacks that are yet to happen.

More Quickly generate playbooks facilitate faster incident response: With the advent of generative AI, it is possible to recommend strategies to contain, eliminate, and revive organizations in real-time. This narrows down the mean time to detect (MTTD) and the mean time to respond (MTTR). (CISA, 2023)

Resilience Testing: Enterprise can put their defenses to the test with AI generated realistic scenarios and become better prepared against ransomware, insider attacks and zero day attacks.

Optimization of Cost and Resource

Cybersecurity itself is a relatively resource-intensive phenomenon; it requires both highly qualified specialists and access to large data sets to be effective both in detecting attacks and conducting counteractions. One possible solution to these bottlenecks, suggested by generative AI, is providing cost-effective solutions that are scalable. It has a major advantage in the form of synthetic data generation where it eliminates the necessity of collecting and storing large volumes of sensitive data and yet it can still achieve accurate and robust model training, consequently minimizing the risk of privacy breaches as well as the data management cost overheads. Also, generative AI is used in automated testing, where AI-generated attack scenarios allow organizations access to constant validation tools, reducing the reliance on the generic penetration tests and facilitating system resilience testing more frequently. The other significant advantage is scalable awareness training where generative AI could create customized phishing or social engineering examples that work on thousands of employees, letting an organisation roll out large-scale awareness training at a small fraction of the traditional cost. This combination of applications underscores the value of generative AI in lessening the financial and operational cost of cybersecurity, in addition to maximizing efficiency and readiness of organizations. Given the appropriate choice of the broadly accessible web-based software, the human resources department will be guided to adopt the most suitable strategy.

Ethical, Legal and Privacies Provenance

Even though these advantages are present, it continues to face regulatory and ethical issues:

Synthetic Data Validity: Although synthetic data does not reveal any personal data, there is a concern on how well it is representative to real life situation. Synthetic information may be biased and thus it can give skewed risk measurements.

AI Accountability: In the case of an AI-based recommendation that results in a failed response to an incident, it is not clear that there should be accountability held by the developers, the organization, or the AI itself (NIST, 2022; CISA, 2023). Laws Legal Transparency An act like GDPR or CCPA demands a disclosure on the use of the data. Generate AIs that are non-explainable can interfere with lawful guidelines of accountability.

According to Adversarial Use (AI vs. AI in Cyberattacks) Risks

The biggest concern of the proliferation of generative AI used in cybersecurity is perhaps that its use can be adapted by other parties who may wreak havoc on others, and subsequently, the issue of an armor race between hackers and defenders continues. Generative AI facilitates the process of AI-generated phishing, during which attackers use large language models (LLMs) to generate contextually plausible phishing messages on scale, thus becoming difficult to identify but with greater likelihood to succeed. It is also driving the deep fake-based social engineering into high, with such photos and audio/video deep fakes being created, high investment officials, or trusted contacts leading the employee to part ways with money, divulge essential data, or hack around the implemented security systems. In addition to social engineering, generative AI also enables the development of malware, where malware evolves more quickly than the detection system can, thus signature-based systems become useless. Exacerbating these threats is that an adversarial attack can occur against AI defenses, that is, there is a deliberate attempt to poison training data or otherwise corrupt inputs to generative models, which reduces their accuracy and causes false negatives on detection. All these risks help to emphasize that, as much as generative AI develops defenses, it also enhances adversaries and, in such a case, the proactive development and efficient protective measures play a key role in keeping the balance of cybersecurity. Nevertheless, occasionally, monitoring a specific circumstance proves challenging because of various possible factors that might have contributed to the issue's emergence and development. (Mirtaheric, 2025;OpenXcell, 2023). Adversarial techniques can be used to generate evasive malware variants that evade detection by manipulating input features, posing significant challenges for AI-based defense systems (Jin et al., 2023).

The paradoxicality of the generative AI can be seen in its two faces:

On the one hand, it provides the defenders with unmatched tools to simulate the threats, lower the expenses, and react quicker.

Conversely, it increases the area of attack since the attackers are able to work out improved strategies.

Hence, how well generative AI is used in the context of managing cyber risks will rely on its technical nature as well as its governance, oversight, and ethics. (Brundage et al., 2018)

6. FUTURE DIRECTIONS

The use of Generative AI in cyber risk management has gone far beyond that. The recent fast development of even more model capabilities, further augmented by emerging regulatory and operational realities, indicates some significant directions, which will be taken into research, deployments, and governance in the next 3-10 years. The key trajectories that are the most impactful, highlighted in this section, include technical development, systems integration, human-AI, governance and explainability, and emergent defenses against adversarial AI.

6.1 Integration with Zero Trust and Blockchain Architectures

Zero Trust networks Where trust is never implicit and access is constantly tested are increasingly becoming common in enterprise contexts. Zero Trust may be enhanced with generative AI: The AI can employ risk-aware access policies to generate dynamically, and can simulate the impact on exposure to policy changes in identity posture.

Synthesizing Adaptive Policies: Generative models can be used to generate and experiment with policy variants (e.g., conditional multifactor requirements or adaptive session timeouts) in case of synthetic attack attacks in order to discover sources of recommendation with turning off the risk whilst maintaining usability.

Blockchain to have Auditability: Giving AI evidence Giving AI-generated decision and training artifacts the characteristics of a blockchain would establish irreversible audit history. To facilitate compliance and forensic analysis, it could be helpful to document the important model outputs, scenarios seeds, or recommendations of high-level playbooks on a tamper-evident ledger. Collectively, such integrations would result in systems with the ability to produce prescriptive controls and at the same time demonstrating (via auditable records) that such controls were delivered under controlled processes. Ensemble learning approaches significantly enhance anomaly detection and secure transaction validation in blockchain-enabled environments (Khullar et al., 2025).

6.2 Accentuably and Answerable Generative AI

One of the main obstacles to the enterprise practice of using generative models in security-sensitive situations is black-box behavior. Explainability and accountability will then be of paramount importance. Explainable outputs Future models must go beyond simulating scenarios or remediation actions to give human explanatory reasons why a simulated phishing template is dangerous, or why a recommended containment action would work.

Provenance/Lineage Systems should be able to keep a history of provenance of the data created (which training slices affected the output) so that validity and bias can be determined. Responsible Defaults and Constraints: "Guard rails will be made normal: Constraints on models that will not give rise to executable policy-violating exploit code of content. Such limitations are expected to be auditable, and they are manipulable by the governance teams. Explainability and responsible defaults will minimize both the organizational risk, and enhance trust among the stakeholders, and generate the ability to meet the regulatory requirements demanding transparency in automated decision-making.

6.3 Federated and Privacy-Preserving Generative Learning

The concept of data privacy and cross-organization collaboration has always been in conflict with the field of cybersecurity since the necessity to exchange intelligence with other entities frequently violates rigid privacy and compliance regulations. Nevertheless, new methods are becoming the means of collaborative advances like federated learning and privacy-preservating models that do not require the lack of sensitive data to be vulnerable. As an example, federated training can be applied to a collection of organizations to train generative models together on their local data using information that never leaves the host without exchanging raw logs or confidential security records between them. Rather, the consolidated model enjoys the richness and the diversity of distributed inputs and every party has control of its own information. More defenses against leakage, such as differential privacy and promising history attacks In order to fortify defenses further, the training pipeline may be marked with some extra mechanisms, such as differential privacy. In addition to the technical protective measures, cooperation needs well-developed incentives to share, including schemes that provide verifiable contribution credits or the creation of common threat intelligence marketplaces where members are able to share trial knowledge by means of synthetic data as opposed to more directly by revealing real logs. Collectively, these strategies increase the range of diversity and realism of synthetic attack and defense conditions, allowing the overall development of the cyber resilience without the legal, regulatory, and ethical traps which are inherent to the sharing of security-relevant datasets. Through this type of training, police conduct may be evaluated relative to the circumstances of the specific incidence. Federated learning allows organizations to collaboratively train AI systems without directly sharing sensitive cybersecurity data, improving privacy preservation and distributed threat intelligence (Saxena & Khullar, 2026). Privacy-preserving communication mechanisms are essential for secure digital identity management in AI-driven ecosystems (Andriani et al., 2026).

6.4 Human, AI Collaboration and Decision Augmentation.

The most useful application of generative AI will be that of a partner, not an independent manager. In solving problems of decision support systems, AI is capable of giving prioritized response choices, trust scores, and quick simulations that assist security operators in the triage phase, but humans are the ones who decide to make high-stakes decisions that require accountability and sensitivity. Also, the interactive simulation environments will enable analysts to explicitly interact with generative models in order to adjust parameters, execute what-if queries, and collaboratively author falling threat scenarios to enable optimization of defense policies.

With the growing AI contributions to the repetitive tasks, like scenario generation, the humans will assume the role of supervisor, interpreter, and policymakers. This change highlights the necessity of training and developing skills among operators and making sure that teams have the capability to justify model results, areas of failure that are more subtle, and match AI findings against the priorities of an organization. To ensure improved performance as well as safety of operations, it will therefore be necessary to design workflows and understandable interfaces that will spur seamless human AI interaction (Khullar et al., 2026).

6.5 Against Adversarial and Malicious Use

With attackers starting to utilize generative AI tools, the defenders need to devise countermeasures that are specifically related to fighting adversarial generative abilities. One such strategy is the AI-for-AI-detection, where defensive AI-trained models are trained to identify AI-learned phishing email or GAN-learned malware morphology before they can defeat security-checks. Defenders should also allocate resources to resilience by training defensive models with adversarial generative methods, where adversarial generation methods are run on toxic data to decide how to defend the model against this data. Additionally, study on watermarking and model provenance provides potentially valuable solutions by embedding recognizable indicators into the generative products to allow the analysts to both check whether the material was created using credible models and to facilitate attribution or takedown actions. Combined, the actions outlined above indicate that defense in the modern will be more and more like a game of layers, involving anticipatory generative defense, adsarial probability testing and provenance-based attribution to keep up with adversarial persons.

6.6 Quantum-resilient and Post-quantum Bounds

Even though quantum computing remains at the initial phase, it is a prospect and a risk to cybersecurity and generative AI in the future. Quantum-enhanced generative models, on the one hand, could increase the scope of simulations greatly and provide defenders with robust new opportunities in the form of understanding and responding to emerging vectors of attacks. On the other hand, advances in post-quantum cryptography will fundamentally reshape cybersecurity, as cryptographic primitives evolve to withstand quantum-level attacks. In this context, generative AI will need to adapt its simulations of cryptographic exploits and defenses to remain relevant in future risk models. To prepare, organizations should begin strategic planning now—monitoring quantum computing developments, incorporating quantum resilience into long-term threat modeling, and ensuring that generative AI remains effective in a post-quantum security landscape.

6.7 Research Directions

The measurement of realism is one of such priorities, and quantitative measures have the potential to determine to what extent the simulated scenarios of attacks resemble the actions of real human adversaries. Safe generation is another major field which aims at finding ways to ensure that models do not generate executable exploits yet withhold their value to defensive testing. The study of causal models of attack attribution also remains potentially fruitful, where such systems would have the ability to simulate the causal paths of attack in a cyberattack to aid organizations in both attribution and subsequent remedial plans. Advances in these domains will specifically define the extent to which generative AI can be applied in real-world operational cybersecurity settings in security.

7. CONCLUSION

Cybersecurity would demand promptness, inventive and advanced response to the dynamic enigma of threats. Generative AI (Generative Artificial Intelligence) has already become one of the most promising bases of such strategies and can generate attack vectors that appear real, manipulate synthetic datasets, and assist in dynamically responding to incidents. This chapter has demonstrated the transformational character of generative AI and how it could be used in solving cyber risks by using case studies that included phishing prevention, ransomware simulation, and enterprise risk modeling in the real world. Yet, it does not imply that every citizen of North Korea is content with the situation in their state, which is why such a demand is extremely high among individuals desiring to relocate to different countries. The comparative analysis which is provided in the framework of various industries shows a very specific pattern: the entities which deploy a generative AI not only do not reduce the accuracy of detention, but also reduce the time of response, not to mention the number of training and resources used. However, one cannot disregard the dual-use nature of generative AI, i.e., the probability of the adversarial application of it. The same tools are already being used by hackers to execute high level phishing, malware development, as well as social engineering. This is an arms race, mandating the innovators to keep innovating without compromising on legal and ethical standards.

REFERENCES

Agrawal, G., Singh, S., Yadav, N., & Pandey, R. (2024). A review of generative models in generating synthetic data. *Electronics (Basel), 13*(2), 322. DOI: 10.3390/electronics13020322

Alguliyev, R., Sukhostat, L., & Mammadov, A. (2022). Anomaly detection in cyber-physical systems based on BiGRU-VAE. In *2022 IEEE 16th International Conference on Application of Information and Communication Technologies (AICT)* (pp. 1–5). IEEE. DOI: 10.1109/AICT55583.2022.10013581

Alshebli, S., Mun, H., Puthal, D., Jamal Zemerly, M., Martino, L., Damiani, E., & Yeun, C. Y. (2025). Enhanced Android Malware Detect Models Based on Explainable Generative Adversarial Networks. *IEEE Access : Practical Innovations, Open Solutions, 13*, 115898–115908. DOI: 10.1109/ACCESS.2025.3585241

Ammara, D. A., Ding, J., & Tutschku, K. (2024). Synthetic data generation in cybersecurity: A comparative analysis. arXiv preprint arXiv:2410.16326.

Andriani, A. D., Dwiwarman, D. A., & Khullar, S. (2026). Resilient selves in the digital sphere: Communication strategies for sustainable privacy management. In *Resilient privacy-preserving mechanisms for digital identity management.* IGI Global., DOI: 10.4018/979-8-3373-7292-1.ch001

Brundage, M., Avin, S., Clark, J., Toner, H., Eckersley, P., Garfinkel, B., . . . Amodei, D. (2018). The malicious use of artificial intelligence: Forecasting, prevention, and mitigation. arXiv preprint arXiv:1802.07228. https://doi.org//arXiv.1802.07228DOI: 10.48550

Cai, Z., He, Z., Guan, X., & Li, Y. (2021). Generative adversarial networks: A survey toward private generative models. *ACM Computing Surveys, 54*(6), 1–38. DOI: 10.1145/3459992

Chenna, S. (2022). Application of generative adversarial networks (GANs) for generating synthetic data and in cybersecurity. SSRN Electronic Journal. DOI: 10.2139/ssrn.4305711

CISA. (2023). *Artificial intelligence use cases.* Cybersecurity & Infrastructure Security Agency.

ENISA. (2023). *AI and cybersecurity: Challenges and recommendations.* European Union Agency for Cybersecurity.

Goodfellow, I., Pouget-Abadie, J., Mirza, M., Xu, B., Warde-Farley, D., Ozair, S., . . . Bengio, Y. (2014). Generative adversarial nets. In Advances in neural information processing systems (Vol. 27). https://doi.org/DOI: 10.48550/arXiv.1406.2661

Jin, B., Choi, J., Hong, J. B., & Kim, H. (2023). On the effectiveness of perturbations in generating evasive malware variants. *IEEE Access : Practical Innovations, Open Solutions*, *11*, 31062–31074. DOI: 10.1109/ACCESS.2023.3262265

Khullar, S., Baghel, R. S., & Swami, P. (2026). Human-AI collaboration: Balancing trust, emotion, and productivity. In *AI hallucination management in the enterprise metaverse*. IGI Global., DOI: 10.4018/979-8-3373-7534-2.ch003

Khullar, S., Magdalene, A. H. S., Sandhya, P., & Naik, B. R. H. K. B. N., & Raju, M. V. (2025). Implementation, performance, and energy efficiency analysis for text classification of deep learning architectures. In *2025 10th International Conference on Communication and Electronics Systems (ICCES)* (pp. 2099–2103). IEEE. https://doi.org/DOI: 10.1109/ICCES67310.2025.11336350

Khullar, S., Mounika, G. R., Chauhan, S. S., Garg, G., Priyanka, T. P., & Kaliappan, S. (2025). Advanced hybrid ensemble learning for blockchain-enabled secure voting: Leveraging Random Forest, XGBoost, and neural networks for robust anomaly detection and integrity assurance. In *2025 1st International Conference on Advancement in Futuristic Technologies (ICAFT)* (pp. 1–7). IEEE. DOI: 10.1109/ICAFT66710.2025.11452780

Kingma, D. P., & Welling, M. (2013). Auto-encoding variational Bayes. arXiv preprint arXiv:1312.6114. https://doi.org//arXiv.1312.6114DOI: 10.48550

Mirtaheric, S. L. (2025). Cybersecurity in the age of generative AI: A systematic review. *Future Generation Computer Systems*, *161*, 504–520. https://www.semanticscholar.org/paper/Cybersecurity-in-the-Age-of-Generative-AI%3A-A-of-and-Mirtaheric-Movahed/005b06ffa43c77c8ef38c3bb8fefac7503dcfccf

Mukherjee, S., Xu, Y., Trivedi, A., & Lavista Ferres, J. (2019). privGAN: Protecting GANs from membership inference attacks at low cost. arXiv preprint arXiv:2001.00071. https://doi.org//arXiv.2001.00071DOI: 10.48550

NIST. (2022). *Artificial intelligence risk management framework (AI RMF 1.0)*. National Institute of Standards and Technology, U.S. Department of Commerce., DOI: 10.6028/NIST.AI.100-1

OpenXcell. (2023). *Generative AI in cybersecurity: Benefits & use cases*. OpenXcell Blog.

Palo Alto Networks. (2023). *What is generative AI in cybersecurity?* Cyberpedia.

Sanchez-Serrano, P., Rios, R., & Agudo, I. (2025). A decision framework for privacy-preserving synthetic data generation. *Computers & Electrical Engineering*, *126*, 110468. DOI: 10.1016/j.compeleceng.2025.110468

Saxena, R. K., & Khullar, S. (2026). Introduction to Federated Learning and Threat Landscape. In Jain, V., Khullar, S., Joshi, M., & Jain, D. (Eds.), *Adversarial AI and Data Poisoning in Federated Learning* (pp. 1–24). IGI Global Scientific Publishing., DOI: 10.4018/979-8-3373-6224-3.ch001

Security, I. B. M. (2023). Cost of a data breach report. IBM Corporation. https://www.ibm.com/reports/data-breach

Steinel, R. B., Lim, K., Ku, C. S., & Department of Computer Science, William Paterson University, Wayne, NJ 07470, USA. (2025). Synthetic data generation for Cybersecurity applications: An Exploratory study of GAN models. In *Department of Computer Science, William Paterson University, Wayne, NJ 07470, USA* [Journal-article]. https://www.wpunj.edu/cosh/macs-scholars-program/assets/SyntheticData.pdf

Symantec. (2023). Internet security threat report. Broadcom Inc. Source: Broadcom https://share.google/w8okW3JUGn309o0ak.

Varra, L. B., Puttanapura, J., Reddy, C. K. K., Khullar, S., Lazrek, G., & Paranthaman, J. (2026). Exploring the Technical Foundations and Integration Strategies of Generative AI Within Collaborative Robotics Systems. In *Exploring Generative AI for Collaborative Robots in Agriculture 6.0*. IGI Global., DOI: 10.4018/979-8-3373-4207-8.ch004

Yan, J., Zhang, H., & Li, K. (2025). Synthetic data for enhanced privacy: A VAE–GAN approach. *Information Sciences*, *694*, 119052.

Compilation of References

Abdelkader, S., Amissah, J., Kinga, S., Mugerwa, G., Emmanuel, E., Mansour, D.-E. A., (2024). Bajaj, agency theory perspective. ISACA Journal, 5.

Adelakun, B. O.Beatrice Oyinkansola Adelakun. (2022). The impact of AI on internal auditing: Transforming practices and ensuring compliance. *Finance & Accounting Research Journal*, *4*(6), 350–370. DOI: 10.51594/farj.v4i6.1316

Agrawal, G., Singh, S., Yadav, N., & Pandey, R. (2024). A review of generative models in generating synthetic data. *Electronics (Basel)*, *13*(2), 322. DOI: 10.3390/electronics13020322

Aguirre-Sosa, J., Dextre, M. L., Lozada-Urbano, M., & Vargas-Merino, J. A. (2023). Background of Peruvian gastronomy and its perspectives: An assessment of its current growth. *Journal of Ethnic Foods*, *10*(1), 50. Advance online publication. DOI: 10.1186/s42779-023-00212-4

Ahmadi, S. (2024). Zero Trust Architecture in cloud networks: Application, challenges and future opportunities. *Journal of Engineering Research and Reports*, *26*(2), 215–228. DOI: 10.9734/jerr/2024/v26i21083

Ahmed, H. A., Nepomuceno, J. A., Vega-Márquez, B., & Nepomuceno-Chamorro, I. A. (2025). Synthetic Data Generation for Healthcare: Exploring Generative Adversarial Networks Variants for Medical Tabular Data. *International Journal of Data Science and Analytics*, *20*(6), 5739–5754. DOI: 10.1007/s41060-025-00816-w

Ajibesin, A. A., & Vajjhala, N. R. (2025). The evolving landscape of AI in threat intelligence and risk assessment. In *AI-Enabled Threat Intelligence and Cyber Risk Assessment* (pp. 165–181). CRC Press. DOI: 10.1201/9781003504979-10

Ajmal, C. S., Yerram, S., Abishek, V., Nizam, V. P. M., Aglave, G., Patnam, J. D., Raghuvanshi, R. S., & Srivastava, S. (2025). Innovative Approaches in Regulatory Affairs: Leveraging Artificial Intelligence and Machine Learning for Efficient Compliance and Decision-Making. *The AAPS Journal*, *27*(1), 22. DOI: 10.1208/s12248-024-01006-5 PMID: 39776314

Alagappan, A., Venkatachary, S. K., & Andrews, L. J. (2022). Augmenting zero trust network architecture to enhance security in virtual power plants. *Energy Reports*, *8*, 1309–1320. DOI: 10.1016/j.egyr.2021.11.272

Alam, N. (2024). Improving IT Control Compliance using Artificial Intelligence. *International Journal of Computer Science and Mobile Computing*, *13*(5), 43–46. DOI: 10.47760/ijcsmc.2024.v13i05.003

Albaroudi, E., Mansouri, T., & Alameer, A. (2024). The Intersection of Generative AI and Healthcare: Addressing Challenges to Enhance Patient Care. *2024 Seventh International Women in Data Science Conference at Prince Sultan University (WiDS PSU)*, 134–140. DOI: 10.1109/WiDS-PSU61003.2024.00039

Alguliyev, R., Sukhostat, L., & Mammadov, A. (2022). Anomaly detection in cyber-physical systems based on BiGRU-VAE. In *2022 IEEE 16th International Conference on Application of Information and Communication Technologies (AICT)* (pp. 1–5). IEEE. DOI: 10.1109/AICT55583.2022.10013581

Almuhammadi, S., & Alsaleh, M. (2017). Information security maturity model for NIST cyber security framework. *Computer Science & Information Technology (CS & IT), 7*(3), 51–62.

Alqahtani, H., & Kumar, G. (2025). A comprehensive review of generative AI techniques and their impact on cybersecurity. *Soft Computing*, *29*(13-14), 1–38. DOI: 10.1007/s00500-025-10702-z

Alqahtani, T. (2025). Recent Trends in the Public Acceptance of Autonomous Vehicles: A Review. *Vehicles (Basel)*, *7*(2), 45. Advance online publication. DOI: 10.3390/vehicles7020045

Alshaikh, M. (2020). Security incident response frameworks: A comparative analysis. *Information Security Journal. Global Perspectives*, *29*(3), 101–118. DOI: 10.1080/19393555.2020.1759083

Alshebli, S., Mun, H., Puthal, D., Jamal Zemerly, M., Martino, L., Damiani, E., & Yeun, C. Y. (2025). Enhanced Android Malware Detect Models Based on Explainable Generative Adversarial Networks. *IEEE Access : Practical Innovations, Open Solutions*, *13*, 115898–115908. DOI: 10.1109/ACCESS.2025.3585241

Alshehri, A., & Tunc, C. (2023, December 4). Zero trust engine for IoT environments. *2023 20th ACS/IEEE International Conference on Computer Systems and Applications (AICCSA)*, 1–3. Presented at the 2023 20th ACS/IEEE International Conference on Computer Systems and Applications (AICCSA), Giza, Egypt. DOI: 10.1109/AICCSA59173.2023.10479286

Ameer, S., Benson, J., & Sandhu, R. (2023). Hybrid approaches (ABAC and RBAC) toward secure access control in smart home IoT. *IEEE Transactions on Dependable and Secure Computing*, *20*(5), 4032–4051. DOI: 10.1109/TDSC.2022.3216297

Ameer, S., Praharaj, L., Sandhu, R., Bhatt, S., & Gupta, M. (2024). ZTA-IoT: A novel architecture for Zero-Trust in IoT systems and an ensuing usage control model. *ACM Transactions on Privacy and Security*, *27*(3), 1–36. DOI: 10.1145/3671147

Ammara, D. A., Ding, J., & Tutschku, K. (2024). Synthetic data generation in cybersecurity: A comparative analysis. arXiv preprint arXiv:2410.16326.

Andrae, S. (2024). Cyber Risk Assessment Using Machine Learning Algorithms. .DOI: 10.4018/979-8-3693-7540-2.ch009

Andriani, A. D., Dwiwarman, D. A., & Khullar, S. (2026). Resilient selves in the digital sphere: Communication strategies for sustainable privacy management. In *Resilient privacy-preserving mechanisms for digital identity management.* IGI Global., DOI: 10.4018/979-8-3373-7292-1.ch001

Ani, U. D., Al-Mhiqani, M., Tuptuk, N., Hailes, S., & McKendrick Watson, J. D. (2025). Socio-Technical Security Modelling and Simulations in Cyber-Physical Systems: Outlook on Knowledge, Perceptions, Practices, Enablers, and Barriers. *IET Cyber-Physical Systems*, *10*(1), e70017. DOI: 10.1049/cps2.70017

Ansari, D. B. (2025). Developing a Big Data Infrastructure: Integral Modules and Best Procedures for Alleviating Security and Privacy Challenges. In *Intelligent Cybersecurity and Resilience for Critical Industries: Challenges and Applications* (pp. 269–303). River Publishers.

Aslaner, M. (2024). *Cybersecurity Strategies and Best Practices: A comprehensive guide to mastering enterprise cyber defense tactics and techniques*. Packt Publishing Ltd.

Azura, Y. T. Y., Azad, M. A., & Ahmed, Y. (2025). An integrated cyber security risk management framework for online banking systems. *Journal of Banking and Financial Technology*, *9*(1), 85–104. DOI: 10.1007/s42786-025-00056-3

B.S., R., N. V., N. K., & Shyamasundar, R. K. (2021). Towards unifying RBAC with information flow control. *Proceedings of the 26th ACM Symposium on Access Control Models and Technologies*, 45-54. DOI: 10.1145/3450569.3463570

Bada, M., & Nurse, J. R. (2019). Developing cybersecurity education and awareness programmes for small-and medium-sized enterprises (SMEs). *Information and Computer Security*, *27*(3), 393–410. DOI: 10.1108/ICS-07-2018-0080

Balasubramanian, P., Liyana, S., Sankaran, H., Sivaramakrishnan, S., Pusuluri, S., Pirttikangas, S., & Peltonen, E. (2025). Generative AI for cyber threat intelligence: Applications, challenges, and analysis of real-world case studies. *Artificial Intelligence Review*, *58*(11), 1–134. DOI: 10.1007/s10462-025-11338-z

Barke, S., James, M., & Polikarpova, N. (2023). Grounded Copilot: How programmers interact with code-generating models. *Proceedings of the ACM on Programming Languages, 7*(OOPSLA1), 85-111. DOI: 10.1145/3586030

Bashar, A., Muhammad, S., Mohammad, N., & Khan, M. (2020). Modeling and analysis of MDP-Based security risk assessment system for smart grids. *2020 Fourth International Conference on Inventive Systems and Control (ICISC)*, 25–30. DOI: 10.1109/ICISC47916.2020.9171072

Bashee, N. (2024). *Cyber risk management in the Internet of Things: Frameworks, models, and best practices.* STAP Journal of Security Risk Management., DOI: 10.63180/jsrm.thestap.2024.1.1

Bast, C., & Yeh, K.-H. (2024). Emerging authentication technologies for zero trust on the Internet of Things. *Symmetry*, *16*(8), 993. DOI: 10.3390/sym16080993

Bate, G. W. (2025). Gaining Traction with Gen AI in 2025. *Research Technology Management*, *68*(2), 69–71. DOI: 10.1080/08956308.2025.2446136

Batool, A., Zowghi, D., & Bano, M. (2025). AI governance: A systematic literature review. *AI and Ethics*, *5*(3), 3265–3279. DOI: 10.1007/s43681-024-00653-w

Behl, A., Behl, K., & Mishra, A. (2023). Cybersecurity workforce shortage and SOC challenges. *Computers & Security*, *127*, 103115. DOI: 10.1016/j.cose.2023.103115

Bello, Y., Hussein, A. R., Ulema, M., & Koilpillai, J. (2022). On sustainedzero trust conceptualization security for mobile core networks in 5G and beyond. *IEEE Transactions on Network and Service Management*, *19*(2), 1876–1889. DOI: 10.1109/TNSM.2022.3157248

Berenji, H., & Vengerov, D. (2000). Learning, cooperation, and coordination in multi-agent systems. *Intelligent Inference Systems Corporation, Technical Report.*

Beretas, C. P., & Davalas, A. (2024). Bridging AI Innovation and Cybersecurity: Generative AI's Contribution to NIS2 Compliance. *International Journal of Regional Development, 11*(2), 40. DOI: 10.5296/ijrd.v11i2.22486

Best practices implementing zero trust with Palo Alto networks (2021). https://docs .paloaltonetworks.com/best-practices/ zero-trust-best-practices/

Bibri, S. E., & Huang, J. (2025). Generative AI of things for sustainable smart cities: Synergizing cognitive augmentation, resource efficiency, network traffic, cybersecurity, and anomaly detection for environmental performance. *Sustainable Cities and Society, 133*(10682), 6. DOI: 10.1016/j.scs.2025.106826

Braverman, H. (1974). *Labor and monopoly capital.* Monthly Review Press. DOI: 10.14452/MR-026-03-1974-07_1

Brown, T. B., Mann, B., Ryder, N., Subbiah, M., Kaplan, J., Dhariwal, P., Neelakantan, A., Shyam, P., Sastry, G., Askell, A., Agarwal, S., Herbert-Voss, A., Krueger, G., Henighan, T., Child, R., Ramesh, A., Ziegler, D. M., Wu, J., Winter, C., . . . Amodei, D. (2020). *Language Models are Few-Shot Learners.* arXiv.org. https:// arxiv.org/abs/2005.14165

Cai, Z., He, Z., Guan, X., & Li, Y. (2021). Generative adversarial networks: A survey toward private generative models. *ACM Computing Surveys, 54*(6), 1–38. DOI: 10.1145/3459992

Cao, T., Zhu, J., & Pang, G. (2023). *Anomaly Detection under Distribution Shift* (arXiv:2303.13845). arXiv. /arXiv.2303.13845DOI: 10.1109/ICCV51070.2023.00599

Cao, K., Xia, Y., Yao, J., Han, X., Lambert, L., Zhang, T., Tang, W., Jin, G., Jiang, H., Fang, X., Nogues, I., Li, X., Guo, W., Wang, Y., Fang, W., Qiu, M., Hou, Y., Kovarnik, T., Vocka, M., & Lu, J. (2023). Large-scale pancreatic cancer detection via non-contrast CT and deep learning. *Nature Medicine, 29*(12), 3033–3043. DOI: 10.1038/s41591-023-02640-w PMID: 37985692

Cassottana, B., Roomi, M. M., Mashima, D., & Sansavini, G. (2023). Resilience analysis of cyber-physical systems: A review of models and methods. *Risk Analysis : An Official Publication of the Society for Risk Analysis, 43*(11), 2359–2379. DOI: 10.1111/risa.14089 PMID: 36646448

Cavelty, M. D. (2024). *The politics of cyber-security.* Routledge. DOI: 10.4324/9781003497080

Cebula, J. L., & Young, L. R. (2010). *A taxonomy of operational cyber security risks* (No. CMUSEI2010TN028).

Chauhan, P., Pal, K., Saifi, A., Sharma, V., Vashishth, T. K., & Choudhary, K. (2026). Improving Cybersecurity and Risk Management Techniques in AI Blockchain Governance Systems. In *Transforming Public Administration through AI-Driven Predictive Analytics* (pp. 177–208). IGI Global Scientific Publishing.

Chen, B., Qiao, S., Zhao, J., Liu, D., Shi, X., Lyu, M., Chen, H., Lu, H., & Zhai, Y. (2021). A security awareness and protection system for 5G smart health care based on zero-trust architecture. *IEEE Internet of Things Journal*, *8*(13), 10–248. DOI: 10.1109/JIOT.2020.3041042

Cheng, D., Wang, X., Zhang, Y., & Zhang, L. (2022). Graph Neural Network for Fraud Detection via Spatial-Temporal Attention. *IEEE Transactions on Knowledge and Data Engineering*, *34*(8), 3800–3813. DOI: 10.1109/TKDE.2020.3025588

Chenna, S. (2022). Application of generative adversarial networks (GANs) for generating synthetic data and in cybersecurity. SSRN Electronic Journal. DOI: 10.2139/ssrn.4305711

Chen, P., Desmet, L., & Huygens, C. (2014). A study on advanced persistent threats. *IFIP International Conference on Communications and Multimedia Security*, 63–72.

Chen, Y., & Gupta, A. (2023). Generative AI for advanced cybersecurity operations: A survey. *ACM Computing Surveys*, *55*(9), 1–32. DOI: 10.1145/3571239

Chevrot, A., Vernotte, A., & Legeard, B. (2022). CAE: Contextual auto-encoder for multivariate time-series anomaly detection in air transportation. *Computers & Security*, *116*, 102652. DOI: 10.1016/j.cose.2022.102652

Choi, K., Moon, J., Jung, H. G., & Suhr, J. K. (2024). Real-Time Object Detection and Tracking Based on Embedded Edge Devices for Local Dynamic Map Generation. *Electronics (Basel)*, *13*(5), 811. DOI: 10.3390/electronics13050811

Chong, W. F., Feng, R., Hu, H., & Zhang, L. (2024). Cyber risk assessment for capital cyber risk? Chong, W. F., Feng, R., Hu, H., & Zhang, L. (2025). Cyber risk assessment for capital management. *The Journal of Risk and Insurance*, *92*(2), 424–471. DOI: 10.1111/jori.12504

Chy, K. H., & Buadi, O. N. (2024). *A Machine Learning-Driven Website Platform and Browser Extension for Real-Time Risk Scoring and Fraud Detection for Website Legitimacy Verification and Consumer Protection. 11*(10).

CISA. (2023). *Artificial intelligence use cases*. Cybersecurity & Infrastructure Security Agency.

Crowston, K., & Bolici, F. (2025). Deskilling and upskilling with AI Systems. *nformation Research an International Electronic Journal, 30*(iConf), 1009-1023. DOI: 10.47989/ir30iConf47143

De Zarzà, I., De Curtò, J., & Calafate, C. T. (2023). Optimizing Neural Networks for Imbalanced Data. *Electronics (Basel), 12*(12), 2674. DOI: 10.3390/electronics12122674

Desmedt, Y., & Shaghaghi, A. (2018). Function-based access control (FBAC): Towards preventing insider threats in organizations. *Lecture Notes in Computer Science, 11170*, 143–165. DOI: 10.1007/978-3-030-04834-1_8

Donegan, P. (2024). *The fundamentals of cyber risk management*. HardenStance.

Dwivedi, U., Rajawat, A. S., Goyal, S. B., Faisal, S., Sulakhe, V. N., & Sudhir, M. (2023). AI-enabled UAVs for advanced network management in the era of 6G communications. *International Conference on Intelligent Computing & Optimization*, 349–358.

Dwivedi, Y. K., Kshetri, N., Hughes, L., Slade, E. L., Jeyaraj, A., Kar, A. K., Baabdullah, A. M., Koohang, A., Raghavan, V., Ahuja, M., Albanna, H., Albashrawi, M. A., Al-Busaidi, A. S., Balakrishnan, J., Barlette, Y., Basu, S., Bose, I., Brooks, L., Buhalis, D., & Wright, R. (2023). Opinion Paper: "So what if ChatGPT wrote it?" Multidisciplinary perspectives on opportunities, challenges and implications of generative conversational AI for research, practice and policy. *International Journal of Information Management, 71*, 102642. DOI: 10.1016/j.ijinfomgt.2023.102642

ENISA – European Union Agency for Cybersecurity. (2023). *ENISA Threat Landscape 2023*. ENISA.

ENISA. (2023). *AI and cybersecurity: Challenges and recommendations*. European Union Agency for Cybersecurity.

Epstein, J. M., & Axtell, R. (1996). *Growing artificial societies: social science from the bottom up*. Brookings Institution Press. DOI: 10.7551/mitpress/3374.001.0001

Fahrurozi, M., Tarigan, S. A., Tanjung, M. A., & Mutijarsa, K. (2020). The use of ISO/IEC 27005: 2018 for strengthening information security management (a case study at data and information Center of Ministry of Defence). *2020 12th International Conference on Information Technology and Electrical Engineering (ICITEE)*, 86–91.

Faisal, S. M., Gupta, B. K., & Zaidi, T. (2022a). A hybrid framework to prevent VANET from Sybil Attack. *2022 5th International Conference on Multimedia, Signal Processing and Communication Technologies (IMPACT)*, 1–6.

Faisal, S. M., Gupta, B. K., & Zaidi, T. (2022b). Detection and prevention of sybil attack in vanet using modified aco. *2022 IEEE 4th International Conference on Cybernetics, Cognition and Machine Learning Applications (ICCCMLA)*, 78–84.

Faisal, S. M., Muniyandy, E., Lokesh, S., & Jayanthi, M. G. (2025). A Random Graph Diffusion Attention Network with Great Wall Construction and Clinical Metadata for Improved Kidney Cancer Diagnosis and Surgical Planning. *Biomedical Materials & Devices*, •••, 1–20.

Faisal, S. M., & Zaidi, T. (2020). Timestamp Based Detection of Sybil Attack in VANET. *Int. J. Netw. Secur.*, *22*(3), 397–408.

Faisal, S. M., & Zaidi, T. (2021). Implementation of ACO in VANETs with detection of faulty node. *Indian Journal of Science and Technology*, *14*(19), 1598–1614. DOI: 10.17485/IJST/v14i19.76

Faisal, S., & Zaidi, T. (2021). A Systematic Review on Security of Wireless Network: Smart Vehicle Perspective. *International Journal of Mechanical Engineering*, *6*(2).

Femila Roseline, J., Naidu, G., Samuthira Pandi, V., Alamelu alias Rajasree, S., & Mageswari, D. N. (2022). Autonomous credit card fraud detection using machine learning approach☆. *Computers & Electrical Engineering*, *102*, 108132. DOI: 10.1016/j.compeleceng.2022.108132

Feng, Z., Zhou, P., Wang, Q., & Qi, W. (2022). A dual-layer zero trust architecture for 5G industry MEC applications access control. *2022 IEEE 5th International Conference on Electronic Information and Communication Technology (ICEICT)*, 100-105. DOI: 10.1109/ICEICT55736.2022.9908891

Fernandez, E. B., & Brazhuk, A. (2024). A critical analysis of Zero Trust Architecture (ZTA). *Computer Standards & Interfaces*, *89*(103832), 103832. DOI: 10.1016/j.csi.2024.103832

Ferrag, M. A.. (2024). Generative AI for cybersecurity: A survey. *arXiv*. https://arxiv.org/abs/2405.12750

Ferretti, L., Magnanini, F., Andreolini, M., & Colajanni, M. (2021). Survivable zero trust for cloud computing environments. *Computers & Security*, *110*, 102419. DOI: 10.1016/j.cose.2021.102419

Feuerriegel, S., Hartmann, J., Janiesch, C., & Zschech, P. (2024). Generative AI. *Business & Information Systems Engineering*, *66*(1), 111–126. DOI: 10.1007/s12599-023-00834-7

Forrester, J. W. (2007). System dynamics—A personal view of the first fifty years. *System Dynamics Review*, *23*(2-3), 345–358. DOI: 10.1002/sdr.382

Fotis, F. (2024). *Economic impact of cyber attacks and effective cyber risk management*. EasyChair.

Fraudulent E-Commerce Transactions. (n.d.). Retrieved July 22, 2025, from https://www.kaggle.com/datasets/shriyashjagtap/fraudulent-e-commerce-transactions

Girhepuje, S., Verma, A., & Raina, G. (2024). A survey on offensive ai within cybersecurity. *ArXiv Preprint ArXiv:2410.03566*.

Golda, A., Mekonen, K., Pandey, A., Singh, A., Hassija, V., Chamola, V., & Sikdar, B. (2024). Privacy and security concerns in generative AI: A comprehensive survey. *IEEE Access : Practical Innovations, Open Solutions*, *12*, 48126–48144. DOI: 10.1109/ACCESS.2024.3381611

González, G. G., Casas, P., & Fernández, A. (2023). Deep Generative Replay for Multivariate Time-Series Monitoring with Variational Autoencoders. *2023 7th Network Traffic Measurement and Analysis Conference (TMA)*, 1–4. DOI: 10.23919/TMA58422.2023.10199001

Goodfellow, I. J., Pouget-Abadie, J., Mirza, M., Xu, B., Warde-Farley, D., Ozair, S., Courville, A., & Bengio, Y. (2014). *Generative adversarial networks*. arXiv.org. https://arxiv.org/abs/1406.2661

Goodfellow, I., Pouget-Abadie, J., Mirza, M., Xu, B., Warde-Farley, D., Ozair, S., . . . Bengio, Y. (2014). Generative adversarial nets. In Advances in neural information processing systems (Vol. 27). https://doi.org/DOI: 10.48550/arXiv.1406.2661

Goodfellow, I. J., Pouget-Abadie, J., Mirza, M., Xu, B., Warde-Farley, D., Ozair, S., & Bengio, Y. (2014). Generative adversarial nets. *Advances in Neural Information Processing Systems*, •••, 27.

Hackman, J. R., & Oldham, G. R. (1976). Motivation through the design of work: Test of a theory. *Organizational Behavior and Human Performance*, *16*(2), 250–279. DOI: 10.1016/0030-5073(76)90016-7

Hasan, K., Hossain, F., Amin, A., Sutradhar, Y., Jeny, I. J., & Mahmud, S. (2025). Enhancing proactive cyber defense: A theoretical framework for AI-driven predictive cyber threat intelligence. *Journal of Technologies Information and Communication*, *5*(1), 33122. DOI: 10.55267/rtic/16176

Hayati, H., Murguia, C., & van de Wouw, N. (2025). Privacy-preserving anomaly detection in stochastic dynamical systems: Synthesis of optimal Gaussian mechanisms. *European Journal of Control*, *81*, 101142. DOI: 10.1016/j.ejcon.2024.101142

Heuillet, A., Couthouis, F., & Díaz-Rodríguez, N. (2022). Collective explainable AI: Explaining cooperative strategies and agent contribution in multiagent reinforcement learning with shapley values. *IEEE Computational Intelligence Magazine*, *17*(1), 59–71. DOI: 10.1109/MCI.2021.3129959

Holland, J. H. (1995). *Hidden Order: How Adaptation Builds Complexity*. Basic Books.

Hollnagel, E., Woods, D. D., & Leveson, N. (Eds.). (2006). *Resilience engineering: Concepts and precepts*. Ashgate Publishing, Ltd.

Holtz, N., Wittfoth, S., & Gómez, J. M. (2024). The new era of knowledge retrieval: Multi-agent systems meet generative ai. *2024 Portland International Conference on Management of Engineering and Technology (PICMET)*, 1–10. DOI: 10.23919/PICMET64035.2024.10653018

Hou, Y., He, R., Dong, J., Yang, Y., & Ma, W. (2022). IoT Anomaly Detection Based on Autoencoder and Bayesian Gaussian Mixture Model. *Electronics (Basel)*, *11*(20), 3287. Advance online publication. DOI: 10.3390/electronics11203287

Hussain, M., Pal, S., Jadidi, Z., Foo, E., & Kanhere, S. (2024). Federated zero trust architecture using artificial intelligence. *IEEE Wireless Communications*, *31*(2), 30–35. DOI: 10.1109/MWC.001.2300405

Ileberi, E., Sun, Y., & Wang, Z. (2022). A machine learning based credit card fraud detection using the GA algorithm for feature selection. *Journal of Big Data*, *9*(1), 24. DOI: 10.1186/s40537-022-00573-8

Intel, "Trusted platform module (TPM) overview," https://www.intel.com/content/www/us/en/learn/what-is-a-trusted-platform-module.html

Iparraguirre-Villanueva, O., Guevara-Ponce, V., Ruiz-Alvarado, D., Beltozar-Clemente, S., Sierra-Liñan, F., Zapata-Paulini, J., & Cabanillas-Carbonell, M. (2023). Text prediction recurrent neural networks using long short-term memory-dropout. *Indonesian Journal of Electrical Engineering and Computer Science*, *29*(3), 1758. DOI: 10.11591/ijeecs.v29.i3.pp1758-1768

Isangediok, M., & Gajamannage, K. (2022). *Fraud Detection Using Optimized Machine Learning Tools Under Imbalance Classes* (arXiv:2209.01642). arXiv. / arXiv.2209.01642DOI: 10.1109/BigData55660.2022.10020723

Ishrat, M., Khan, W., & Faisal, S. M. (2025). AI and risk forecasting: leveraging AI for environmental, social, and governance compliance. In *Artificial Intelligence for Financial Risk Management and Analysis* (pp. 307–334). IGI Global Scientific Publishing. DOI: 10.4018/979-8-3373-1200-2.ch015

ISO/IEC. (2018). *ISO/IEC 27005:2018-07 — Information technology - Security techniques - Information security risk management*

Izquierdo-Bueno, I., Moraga, J., Cantoral, J. M., Carbú, M., Garrido, C., & González-Rodríguez, V. E. (2024). Smart Viniculture: Applying Artificial Intelligence for Improved Winemaking and Risk Management. *Applied Sciences (Basel, Switzerland)*, *14*(22), 10277. Advance online publication. DOI: 10.3390/app142210277

Jin, B., Choi, J., Hong, J. B., & Kim, H. (2023). On the effectiveness of perturbations in generating evasive malware variants. *IEEE Access : Practical Innovations, Open Solutions*, *11*, 31062–31074. DOI: 10.1109/ACCESS.2023.3262265

Karthikeyan, T., Govindarajan, M., & Vijayakumar, V. (2024). Enhancing Financial Fraud Detection Through Chimp-Optimized Long Short-Term Memory Networks. *TS. Traitement du Signal*, *41*(2), 835–845. DOI: 10.18280/ts.410224

Kavitha, D., & Thejas, S. (2024). Ai enabled threat detection: Leveraging artificial intelligence for advanced security and cyber threat mitigation. *IEEE Access : Practical Innovations, Open Solutions*.

Khan, I. A., Keshk, M., Hussain, Y., Pi, D., Li, B., Kousar, T., & Ali, B. S. (2025). A context-aware zero trust-based hybrid approach to IoT-based self-driving vehicles security. *Ad Hoc Networks*, *167*(103694), 103694. DOI: 10.1016/j.adhoc.2024.103694

Khan, W., Abidin, S., Arif, M., Ishrat, M., Haleem, M., Shaikh, A. A., Farooqui, N. A., & Faisal, S. M. (2024). Anomalous node detection in attributed social networks using dual variational autoencoder with generative adversarial networks. *Data Science and Management*, *7*(2), 89–98. DOI: 10.1016/j.dsm.2023.10.005

Khan, W., Ishrat, M., Faisal, S. M., Ahmad, F., Nabilal, K. V., & Sharma, Y. K. (2025). A robust framework for topology-based anomaly detection in attributed networks using graph attention networks, substructure analysis, and data augmentation. *International Journal of Data Science and Analytics*, *20*(7), 1–14. DOI: 10.1007/s41060-025-00848-2

Khan, W., Mohd, A., Suaib, M., Ishrat, M., Shaikh, A. A., & Faisal, S. M. (2024). *Residual-enhanced graph convolutional networks with hypersphere mapping for anomaly detection in attributed networks*. Data Science and Management.

Khinvasara, T., Shankar, A., & Wong, C. (2024). Survey of Artificial Intelligence for Automated Regulatory Compliance Tracking. *Journal of Engineering Research and Reports*, *26*(7), 390–406. DOI: 10.9734/jerr/2024/v26i71217

Khullar, S., Magdalene, A. H. S., Sandhya, P., & Naik, B. R. H. K. B. N., & Raju, M. V. (2025). Implementation, performance, and energy efficiency analysis for text classification of deep learning architectures. In *2025 10th International Conference on Communication and Electronics Systems (ICCES)* (pp. 2099–2103). IEEE. https://doi.org/DOI: 10.1109/ICCES67310.2025.11336350

Khullar, S., Mounika, G. R., Chauhan, S. S., Garg, G., Priyanka, T. P., & Kaliappan, S. (2025). Advanced hybrid ensemble learning for blockchain-enabled secure voting: Leveraging Random Forest, XGBoost, and neural networks for robust anomaly detection and integrity assurance. In *2025 1st International Conference on Advancement in Futuristic Technologies (ICAFT)* (pp. 1–7). IEEE. DOI: 10.1109/ICAFT66710.2025.11452780

Khullar, S., Baghel, R. S., & Swami, P. (2026). Human-AI collaboration: Balancing trust, emotion, and productivity. In *AI hallucination management in the enterprise metaverse*. IGI Global., DOI: 10.4018/979-8-3373-7534-2.ch003

Khurana, A., Subramonyam, H., & Chilana, P. K. (2024). Why and when llm-based assistants can go wrong: Investigating the effectiveness of prompt-based interactions for software help-seeking. *arXiv.org*. Retrieved from /arxiv.2402.08030DOI: 10.1145/3640543.3645200

Klasa, K., Galaitsi, S., Trump, B. D., & Linkov, I. (2021). Science and practice of resilience: disaster systems applications to aging resilience. In *Resilience and aging: Emerging science and future possibilities* (pp. 53–80). Springer International Publishing.

Kovalainen, T., Pramila-Savukoski, S., Kuivila, H.-M., Juntunen, J., Jarva, E., Rasi, M., & Mikkonen, K. (2025). Utilising artificial intelligence in developing education of health sciences higher education: An umbrella review of reviews. *Nurse Education Today*, *147*, 106600. DOI: 10.1016/j.nedt.2025.106600 PMID: 39904286

Kuhail, M. A., Mathew, S. S., Khalil, A., Khalil, A., & Shah, S. J. (2023). "Will I be replaced?" Assessing ChatGPT's effect on software development and programmer perceptions of AI tools. *arXiv.org*. Retrieved from DOI: 10.2139/ssrn.4571482

Kumari, B. (2025). Innovative Cloud Architectures: Revolutionizing Enterprise Operations Through AI Integration. *International Journal of Fluid Mechanics Research*.

Kumar, M., Gautam, K. K., Sharma, V., Samania, B., Vashishth, T. K., & Chaudhary, S. (2025). Enhancing cloud computing performance: A novel approach for optimizing energy efficiency through AI-based load balancing algorithm. In *Proceedings of the 2025 International Conference on Intelligent Computing and Knowledge Extraction (ICICKE)* (pp. 1–6). IEEE. DOI: 10.1109/ICICKE65317.2025.11136754

Kure, H. I., Islam, S., & Razzaque, M. A. (2018). An integrated cyber security risk management approach for a cyber-physical system. *Applied Sciences (Basel, Switzerland)*, *8*(6), 898. DOI: 10.3390/app8060898

Lachmann, M., Stefani, U., & Wöhrmann, A. (2015). Fair value accounting for liabilities: Presentation format of credit risk changes and individual information processing. *Accounting, Organizations and Society*, *41*, 21–38. DOI: 10.1016/j.aos.2014.08.001

Lederer, A., Noorani, E., & Krause, A. (2025). Distributed Risk-Sensitive Safety Filters for Uncertain Discrete-Time Systems. *IEEE Control Systems Letters*, *9*, 1231–1236. DOI: 10.1109/LCSYS.2025.3579747

Lee, Y., Park, C., Kim, N., Ahn, J., & Jeong, J. (2024). LSTM-Autoencoder Based Anomaly Detection Using Vibration Data of Wind Turbines. *Sensors (Basel)*, *24*(9), 2833. Advance online publication. DOI: 10.3390/s24092833 PMID: 38732939

Lehto, M. (2022). Cyber-attacks against critical infrastructure. In *Cyber security: Critical infrastructure protection* (pp. 3–42). Springer International Publishing. DOI: 10.1007/978-3-030-91293-2_1

Liang, H., & Xue, Y. (2009). Avoidance of information technology threats: A theoretical perspective. *Management Information Systems Quarterly*, *33*(1), 71–90. DOI: 10.2307/20650279

Ligo, A. K., Kott, A., & Linkov, I. (2021). How to measure cyber-resilience of a system with autonomous agents: Approaches and challenges. *IEEE Engineering Management Review*, *49*(2), 89–97. DOI: 10.1109/EMR.2021.3074288

Liu, I., & Wongsosaputro, M. (2024). Compliance redefined: Using GenAI to navigate a complex regulatory landscape with reduced risks and costs. *Journal of Digital Banking*, *8*(4), 313. DOI: 10.69554/LGTJ4498

Liu, Y., Sun, Z., & Zhang, W. (2023). Improving fraud detection via hierarchical attention-based Graph Neural Network. *Journal of Information Security and Applications*, *72*, 103399. DOI: 10.1016/j.jisa.2022.103399

Livadariu, I., Elmokashfi, A., & Smaragdakis, G. (2024). Tracking submarine cables in the wild. *Computer Networks*, *242*, 110234. DOI: 10.1016/j.comnet.2024.110234

Luo, X. (2025). Robust Financial Fraud Detection via Causal Intervention and Multi-View Contrastive Learning on Dynamic Hypergraphs. *Mathematics*, *13*(24), 4018. Advance online publication. DOI: 10.3390/math13244018

M., Blazek, V., & Prokop, L. (2024). Securing modern power systems: Implementing comprehensive strategies to enhance resilience and reliability against cyber-attacks. Results in Engineering, 23, 102647. https://doi.org/DOI: 10.1016/j.rineng.2024.102647

Mansoor, I., García Ortiz, J., & Rector, M. (2024). Generative AI in Clinical Research: Regulatory Submissions, Clinical Data Management, and Beyond. *AMWA Journal*, *39*(1). Advance online publication. DOI: 10.55752/amwa.2024.304

Mansurova, A., Mansurova, A., & Nugumanova, A. (2024). QA-RAG: Exploring LLM Reliance on External Knowledge. *Big Data and Cognitive Computing*, *8*(9), 115. Advance online publication. DOI: 10.3390/bdcc8090115

Ma, P., Garg, S., & Barika, M. (2024). Research allocation in mobile volunteer computing system: Taxonomy, challenges and future work. *Future Generation Computer Systems*, *154*, 251–265. DOI: 10.1016/j.future.2024.01.015

Mariam, Z., Niazi, S. K., & Magoola, M. (2024). Unlocking the Future of Drug Development: Generative AI, Digital Twins, and Beyond. *BioMedInformatics*, *4*(2), 1441–1456. DOI: 10.3390/biomedinformatics4020079

Martin, A. (2021). The Impact of AI-Driven Risk Compliance Systems on Corporate Governance. *Universal Research Reports, 8*(4). DOI: 10.36676/urr.v8.i4.1403

Mayaki, M. Z. A., & Riveill, M. (2022). Autoregressive based Drift Detection Method. *2022 International Joint Conference on Neural Networks (IJCNN)*, 1–8. DOI: 10.1109/IJCNN55064.2022.9892066

Metropolis, N., & Ulam, S. (1949). The monte carlo method. *Journal of the American Statistical Association*, *44*(247), 335–341. DOI: 10.1080/01621459.1949.10483310 PMID: 18139350

Mienye, I. D., & Swart, T. G. (2024). A Hybrid Deep Learning Approach with Generative Adversarial Network for Credit Card Fraud Detection. *Technologies*, *12*(10), 186. Advance online publication. DOI: 10.3390/technologies12100186

Mirtaheric, S. L. (2025). Cybersecurity in the age of generative AI: A systematic review. *Future Generation Computer Systems*, *161*, 504–520. https://www.semanticscholar.org/paper/Cybersecurity-in-the-Age-of-Generative-AI%3A-A-of-and-Mirtaheric-Movahed/005b06ffa43c77c8ef38c3bb8fefac7503dcfccf

Mnih, V., Kavukcuoglu, K., Silver, D., Rusu, A. A., Veness, J., Bellemare, M. G., Graves, A., Riedmiller, M., Fidjeland, A. K., Ostrovski, G., Petersen, S., Beattie, C., Sadik, A., Antonoglou, I., King, H., Kumaran, D., Wierstra, D., Legg, S., & Hassabis, D. (2015). Human-level control through deep reinforcement learning. *Nature, 518*(7540), 529–533. DOI: 10.1038/nature14236 PMID: 25719670

Mosqueira-Rey, E., Hernández-Pereira, E., Alonso-Ríos, D., Bobes-Bascarán, J., & Fernández-Leal, Á. (2023). Human-in-the-loop machine learning: A state of the art. *Artificial Intelligence Review, 56*(4), 3005–3054. DOI: 10.1007/s10462-022-10246-w

Mukherjee, S., Thapliyal, K., Paul, U., Bhandari, R. S., Sinha, A., & Kumar, Y. (2025, May). AI-Powered Threat Intelligence: Enhancing Real-Time Cyber Threat Detection and Response. In *2025 International Conference on Engineering, Technology & Management (ICETM)* (pp. 1-5). IEEE. DOI: 10.1109/ICETM63734.2025.11051359

Munivel, D., Samir, V. B., Naveen, P., & Lavanya, S. (2024). AI-driven Solutions for Cloud Compliance Challenges. *Advanced International Journal of Multidisciplinary Research, 2*(2), 1037. DOI: 10.62127/aijmr.2024.v02i02.1037

Muppalaneni, R., Inaganti, A. C., & Ravichandran, N. (2024). AI-Driven Threat Intelligence: Enhancing Cyber Defense with Machine Learning. *Journal of Computing Innovations and Applications, 2*(1), 1–11.

Musman, S., & Turner, A. (2018). A game theoretic approach to cyber security risk management. *The Journal of Defense Modeling and Simulation, 15*(2), 127–146. DOI: 10.1177/1548512917699724

Nadella, G. S., Addula, S. R., Yadulla, A. R., Sajja, G. S., Meesala, M., Maturi, M. H., Meduri, K., & Gonaygunta, H. (2025). Generative AI-Enhanced Cybersecurity Framework for Enterprise Data Privacy Management. *Computers, 14*(2), 55. DOI: 10.3390/computers14020055

Naghshbandi, S. N., Varga, L., Purvis, A., Mcwilliam, R., Minisci, E., Vasile, M., Troffaes, M., Sedighi, T., Guo, W., Manley, E., & Jones, D. H. (2020). A review of methods to study resilience of complex engineering and engineered systems. *IEEE Access : Practical Innovations, Open Solutions, 8*, 87775–87799. DOI: 10.1109/ACCESS.2020.2992239

National Institute of Standards and Technology. (2022). *Computer security incident handling guide (SP 800-61 Rev. 2).* https://csrc.nist.gov/publications/detail/sp/800-61/rev-2/final

National Institute of Standards and Technology. (2023). *Artificial intelligence risk managementframework(AIRMF 1.0)*. https://www.nist.gov/aiml/ai-risk-management-framework

NATO Cooperative Cyber Defence Centre of Excellence. (2022). *Exercise Locked Shields 2022 concludes: Largest international live-fire cyber defence exercise*. NATO CCDCOE. Retrieved from https://shape.nato.int/news-archive/2022/exercise-locked-shields-2022-concludes

Naveed, H., Khan, A. U., Qiu, S., Saqib, M., Anwar, S., Usman, M., Akhtar, N., Barnes, N., & Mian, A. (2025). A comprehensive overview of large language models. *ACM Transactions on Intelligent Systems and Technology*, *16*(5), 1–72. DOI: 10.1145/3744746

Naz, S., & Xu, T.-B. (2024). A Comprehensive Review of Piezoelectric Ultrasonic Motors: Classifications, Characterization, Fabrication, Applications, and Future Challenges. *Micromachines*, *15*(9), 1170. Advance online publication. DOI: 10.3390/mi15091170 PMID: 39337830

Netskope announces general availability of zero trust secure access for hybrid it environments (2020). https://aithority.com/security/netskope-announces-general-availabilityof-zero-trust-secure-access-for-hybrid-it environments/

Ng, M. Y., Helzer, J., Pfeffer, M. A., Seto, T., & Hernandez-Boussard, T. (2025). Development of secure infrastructure for advancing generative artificial intelligence research in healthcare at an academic medical center. *Journal of the American Medical Informatics Association : JAMIA*, *32*(3), 586–588. DOI: 10.1093/jamia/ocaf005 PMID: 39836496

Niaz, A. A., Ashraf, R., Mahmood, T., Faisal, C. M. N., & Abid, M. M. (2025). An efficient smart phone application for wheat crop diseases detection using advanced machine learning. *PLoS One*, *20*(1), e0312768. DOI: 10.1371/journal.pone.0312768 PMID: 39775380

NIST – National Institute of Standards and Technology. (2012). *Guide for Conducting Risk Assessments* (NIST SP 800-30 Rev. 1). National Institute of Standards and Technology.

NIST – National Institute of Standards and Technology. (2018/2023). *Framework for Improving Critical Infrastructure Cybersecurity* (Cybersecurity Framework, v1.1 and subsequent updates / draft 2.0 discussions).

NIST. (2022). *Artificial intelligence risk management framework (AI RMF 1.0)*. National Institute of Standards and Technology, U.S. Department of Commerce., DOI: 10.6028/NIST.AI.100-1

Nokhwal, S., Nokhwal, S., Pahune, S., & Chaudhary, A. (2024). Quantum generative adversarial networks: Bridging classical and quantum realms. *Proceedings of the 2024 8th International Conference on Intelligent Systems, Metaheuristics & Swarm Intelligence*, 105–109. DOI: 10.1145/3665065.3665082

Noviandy, T. R., Idroes, G. M., Maulana, A., Hardi, I., Ringga, E. S., & Idroes, R. (2023). Credit Card Fraud Detection for Contemporary Financial Management Using XGBoost-Driven Machine Learning and Data Augmentation Techniques. *Indatu Journal of Management and Accounting*, *1*(1), 29–35. DOI: 10.60084/ijma.v1i1.78

Novozhilova, E., Mays, K., Paik, S., & Katz, J. E. (2024). More Capable, Less Benevolent: Trust Perceptions of AI Systems across Societal Contexts. *Machine Learning and Knowledge Extraction*, *6*(1), 342–366. DOI: 10.3390/make6010017

Open, A. I. (2023). GPT-4 technical report. https://arxiv.org/abs/2303.08774

OpenXcell. (2023). *Generative AI in cybersecurity: Benefits & use cases.* OpenXcell Blog.

Orpak, K. (2025). Generative AI and cybersecurity: Exploring opportunities and threats at their intersection. *Maandblad voor Accountancy en Bedrijfseconomie*, *99*(4), 221–230. DOI: 10.5117/mab.99.149299

OWASP. (2025). *OWASP Top 10: 2025—The ten most critical web application security risks*. Retrieved from https://owasp.org/Top10/2025

Palo Alto Networks. (2023). *What is generative AI in cybersecurity?* Cyberpedia.

Pan, Z., Yu, W., Yi, X., Khan, A., Yuan, F., & Zheng, Y. (2019). Recent progress on generative adversarial networks (GANs): A survey. *IEEE Access : Practical Innovations, Open Solutions*, *7*, 36322–36333. DOI: 10.1109/ACCESS.2019.2905015

Papernot, N., McDaniel, P., Goodfellow, I., Jha, S., Celik, Z. B., & Swami, A. (2017). Practical black-box attacks against machine learning. In *Proceedings of the 2017 ACM on Asia conference on computer and communications security* (pp. 506-519).

Park, J. S., O'Brien, J., Cai, C. J., Morris, M. R., Liang, P., & Bernstein, M. S. (2023). Generative agents: Interactive simulacra of human behavior. *Proceedings of the 36th Annual Acm Symposium on User Interface Software and Technology*, 1–22. DOI: 10.1145/3586183.3606763

Park, J., Seo, Y., & Cho, J. (2023). Unsupervised outlier detection for time-series data of indoor air quality using LSTM autoencoder with ensemble method. *Journal of Big Data*, *10*(1), 66. DOI: 10.1186/s40537-023-00746-z PMID: 36618886

Parsons, E. K., Panaousis, E., Loukas, G., & Sakellari, G. (2023). A survey on cyber risk procedural guidelines and practical evaluation metrics for organizational IT and cybersecurity risk assessment. arXiv. https://doi.org//arXiv.2410.01750DOI: 10.48550

Patil, D. (2024). Artificial Intelligence in Cybersecurity: Enhancing Threat Detection and Prevention Mechanisms through Machine Learning and Data Analytics. Available at *SSRN* 5057410.

Pearce, H., Ahmad, B., Tan, B., Dolan-Gavitt, B., & Karri, R. (2022). Asleep at the Keyboard? Assessing the Security of GitHub Copilot's Code Contributions. *43rd IEEE Symposium on Security and Privacy, SP 2022*. Proceedings - IEEE Symposium on Security and Privacy. DOI: 10.1109/SP46214.2022.9833571

Peoples, K. (2021). *How to write a phenomenological dissertation: A step-by-step guide* (Vol. 56). SAGE.

Pérez-Pérez, I., González-Afonso, M. C., Plasencia-Carballo, Z., & Pérez-Jorge, D. (2026). Transparency Mechanisms for Generative AI Use in Higher Education Assessment: A Systematic Scoping Review (2022–2026). *Computers*, *15*(2), 111. DOI: 10.3390/computers15020111

Phiayura, P., & Teerakanok, S. (2023). A comprehensive framework for migrating to zero trust architecture. *IEEE Access : Practical Innovations, Open Solutions*, *11*, 19487–19511. DOI: 10.1109/ACCESS.2023.3248622

Prabha, D. P., & Priscilla, C. V. (2024). A combined framework based on LSTM autoencoder and XGBoost with adaptive threshold classification for credit card fraud detection. *The Scientific Temper*, *15*(02), 2216–2224. DOI: 10.58414/SCIENTIFICTEMPER.2024.15.2.34

Prates, L., & Pereira, R. (2025). DevSecOps practices and tools. *International Journal of Information Security*, *24*(1), 11. Advance online publication. DOI: 10.1007/s10207-024-00914-z

Pratt, M. K. (2021). Zero-trust model case study: One ciso's experience. https://www.techtarget .com / search security/feature/Even-with-a-roadmap-zero-trust-model-an-ongoing process

Prescriptive Guidance, A. W. S. (2021). Multi-tenant SaaS authorization and API access control. Available: https: //docs.aws.amazon.com/prescriptive-guidance/latest/saas-multitenantapi-access-authorization/welcome.html

Qu, B., Wang, Z., Gu, M., Yagi, D., Zhao, Y., Shan, Y., & Zahradnik, F. (2024). *Multi-task CNN Behavioral Embedding Model For Transaction Fraud Detection.* 286–292. DOI: 10.1109/ICDMW65004.2024.00043

Radaideh, M. I., Pappas, C., Wezensky, M., & Cousineau, S. (2023). Operational data for fault prognosis in particle accelerators with machine learning. *Data in Brief, 51*, 109658. DOI: 10.1016/j.dib.2023.109658 PMID: 37928324

Rahman, M. M., Kshetri, N., Sayeed, S. A., & Rana, M. M. (2024, October 2). *AssessITS: Integrating procedural guidelines and practical evaluation metrics for organizational IT and Cybersecurity risk assessment.* arXiv.org. https://arxiv.org/abs/2410.01750

Rahman, M. W. U., Nevarez, R., Mim, L. T., & Hariri, S. (2025). Multi-Agent Actor-Critic Generative AI for Query Resolution and Analysis. *IEEE Transactions on Artificial Intelligence.*

Ray, P. P. (2023). Web3: A comprehensive review on background, technologies, applications, zero-trust architectures, challenges and future directions. *Internet of Things and Cyber-Physical Systems, 3*, 213–248. DOI: 10.1016/j.iotcps.2023.05.003

Reddy, H. M. (2024). Role of AI in Security Compliance. *International Journal of Scientific Research in Engineering and Management, 08*(11), 1–6. DOI: 10.55041/IJSREM32650

Reddy, P. C. S., Muller, P. S., Koka, S. N., Sharma, V., Sharma, N., & Mukherjee, S. (2023). Detection of encrypted and malicious network traffic using deep learning. In *Proceedings of the 2023 International Conference on Ambient Intelligence, Knowledge Informatics, and Industrial Electronics (AIKIIE)* (pp. 1–6). IEEE. DOI: 10.1109/AIKIIE60097.2023.10390386

Rezvani, S. M. H. S., Silva, M. J. F., & de Almeida, N. M. (2024). Urban resilience index for critical infrastructure: A scenario-based approach to disaster risk reduction in road networks. *Sustainability (Basel), 16*(10), 4143. DOI: 10.3390/su16104143

Riazi, M., Rezvani, R., & Ghanbar, H. (2023). Trustworthiness in L2 writing research: A review and analysis of qualitative articles in the Journal of Second Language Writing. *Research Methods in Applied Linguistics, 2*(3), 100065. Advance online publication. DOI: 10.1016/j.rmal.2023.100065

Rinta-Kahila, T., Penttinen, E., Salovaara, A., Soliman, W., & Ruissalo, J. (2023). The vicious circles of skill erosion: A case study of cognitive automation. *Journal of the Association for Information Systems, 24*(5), 1378–1412. DOI: 10.17705/1jais.00829

Robertson, J., Hollmann, N., Awad, N., & Hutter, F. (2024). Fairpfn: Transformers can do counterfactual fairness. *ArXiv Preprint ArXiv:2407.05732.*

Romanosky, S., & Sayers, E. L. P. (2024). Enterprise risk management: How do firms integrate strategies: A light literature review and case study analysis. *Procedia Computer Science, 251*, 471–478. DOI: 10.1016/j.procs.2024.11.135

Rose, S., Borchert, O., Mitchell, S., & Connelly, S. (2020). *Zero Trust Architecture.* National Institute of Standards and Technology., DOI: 10.6028/NIST.SP.800-207

Rosoff, G., & Chawla, N. (2024). Zero Trust Driving the Upgrade of BUMED's Identity, Credential, and Access Management Strategy. [The Journal of the American Society of Military Comptrollers]. *The Armed Forces Comptroller, 69*, 46–47.

Rout, S., & Jaiswal, K. (2024). Fraud detection using deep learning. *International Journal of Electrical and Data Communication, 5*(1), 07–11. DOI: 10.22271/27083969.2024.v5.i1a.37

Saddi, V. R., Gopal, S. K., Mohammed, A. S., Dhanasekaran, S., & Naruka, M. S. (2024, March). Examine the role of generative AI in enhancing threat intelligence and cyber security measures. In 2024 2nd International Conference on Disruptive Technologies (ICDT) (pp. 537-542). IEEE. DOI: 10.1109/ICDT61202.2024.10489766

Saeed, I. A., Selamat, A., Rohani, M. F., Krejcar, O., & Chaudhry, J. A. (2020). A systematic state-of-the-art analysis of multi-agent intrusion detection. *IEEE Access : Practical Innovations, Open Solutions, 8*, 180184–180209. DOI: 10.1109/ACCESS.2020.3027463

Salvi, A., Spagnoletti, P., & Noori, N. S. (2022). Cyber-resilience of critical cyber infrastructures: Integrating digital twins in the electric power ecosystem. *Computers & Security, 112*, 102507. DOI: 10.1016/j.cose.2021.102507

Samuel Oladiipo, O. (2024). AI for Identity and Access Management (IAM) in the Cloud: Exploring the Potential of Artificial Intelligence to Improve User Authentication, Authorization, and Access Control within Cloud-Based Systems. *Asian Journal of Research in Computer Science, 17*(3), 38–56. DOI: 10.9734/ajrcos/2024/v17i3423

Sanchez-Serrano, P., Rios, R., & Agudo, I. (2025). A decision framework for privacy-preserving synthetic data generation. *Computers & Electrical Engineering, 126*, 110468. DOI: 10.1016/j.compeleceng.2025.110468

Sani, A., Hassan, Z. L., & Balarabe, A. T. (2024). A Logistic Regression-based Model for Identifying Credit Card Fraudulent Transactions. *Asian Journal of Research in Computer Science*, *17*(7), 41–54. DOI: 10.9734/ajrcos/2024/v17i7476

Sanjalawe, Y., ... 'mari, S., & Makhadmeh, S. (2025). Generative AI for Cybersecurity Applications in Threat Simulation and Defense. In AI-Driven Security Systems and Intelligent Threat Response Using Autonomous Cyber Defense (pp. 263-304). IGI Global Scientific Publishing.

Sarkar, S., Choudhary, G., Shandilya, S. K., Hussain, A., & Kim, H. (2022). Security of zero trust networks in cloud computing: A comparative review. *Sustainability (Basel)*, *14*(18), 11213. DOI: 10.3390/su141811213

Sarker, I. H. (2024). Introduction to AI-driven cybersecurity and threat intelligence. In *AI-driven cybersecurity and threat intelligence: Cyber automation, intelligent decision-making and explainability* (pp. 3–19). Springer Nature Switzerland. DOI: 10.1007/978-3-031-54497-2_1

Saurabh, B., Utkrisht, S., Sandeep, S., Kumar, D. P., & Rajkumar, U. (2024, October). Generative AI Enabled Actionable Decision Support in Cyber Security Operations for Enterprise Security. In 2024 ITU Kaleidoscope: Innovation and Digital Transformation for a Sustainable World (ITU K) (pp. 1-8). IEEE.

Sawada, A., Miyagawa, T., Ebihara, A. F., Yachida, S., & Hosoi, T. (2022). *Convolutional Neural Networks for Time-dependent Classification of Variable-length Time Series* (arXiv:2207.03718). arXiv. /arXiv.2207.03718DOI: 10.1109/IJCNN55064.2022.9892605

Saxena, R. K., & Khullar, S. (2026). Introduction to Federated Learning and Threat Landscape. In Jain, V., Khullar, S., Joshi, M., & Jain, D. (Eds.), *Adversarial AI and Data Poisoning in Federated Learning* (pp. 1–24). IGI Global Scientific Publishing., DOI: 10.4018/979-8-3373-6224-3.ch001

Schwab, K. (2015). World economic forum. *Global Competitiveness Report (2014-2015).*

Security, I. B. M. (2023). Cost of a data breach report. IBM Corporation. https://www.ibm.com/reports/data-breach

Sengar, S. S., Hasan, A., Kumar, S., & Carroll, F. (2025). Generative artificial intelligence: A systematic review and applications. *Multimedia Tools and Applications*, *84*(21), 23661–23700. DOI: 10.1007/s11042-024-20016-1

Serena, L., D'Angelo, G., Ferretti, S., & Marzolla, M. (2025). Simulation in Cybersecurity: Understanding Techniques, Applications, and Goals. *arXiv preprint arXiv:2508.06106*.

Shabeena Shah, W., Khadeeja Bilquees, A., & Zubair, M. J. M. (2025). Innovation Unleashed Charting a New Course in Risk Evaluation with Generative AI. *Generative Artificial Intelligence in Finance: Large Language Models, Interfaces, and Industry Use Cases to Transform Accounting and Finance Processes*, 149–157.

Shackleford, D. (2015). *Security orchestration, automation, and response (SOAR)*. SANS Institute.

Shahapurkar, A., & Patil, R. (2023). Concept drift and machine learning model for detecting fraudulent transactions in streaming environment. [IJECE]. *International Journal of Electrical and Computer Engineering*, *13*(5), 5560–5568. DOI: 10.11591/ijece.v13i5.pp5560-5568

Sharma, V., Vashishth, T. K., Tiwari, D., Sethi, P., & Sharma, S. (2025, April). Enhancing cybersecurity: A machine learning approach for phishing website detection. In AIP Conference Proceedings (Vol. 3278, No. 1). AIP Publishing. DOI: 10.1063/5.0261903

Sharma, V., & Kumar, S. (2023). Role of artificial intelligence (AI) to enhance the security and privacy of data in smart cities. In *Proceedings of the 2023 3rd International Conference on Advance Computing and Innovative Technologies in Engineering (ICACITE)* (pp. 596–599). IEEE. DOI: 10.1109/ICACITE57410.2023.10182455

Shieh, S., Lee, S., & Tsai, M. (2022). Strategy and tactics against ransomware. *Computer*, *55*(5), 85–92. DOI: 10.1109/MC.2022.3146733

Shiri, F. M., Perumal, T., Mustapha, N., & Mohamed, R. (2024). A Comprehensive Overview and Comparative Analysis on Deep Learning Models: CNN, RNN, LSTM, GRU. *Journal on Artificial Intelligence*, *6*(1), 301–360. DOI: 10.32604/jai.2024.054314

Shrivastava, S. (2022). Convolutional Neural Network Approach for Mobile Banking Fraudulent Transaction to Detect Financial Frauds. *International Journal of Engineering Technology and Management Sciences*, *6*(1), 30–37. DOI: 10.46647/ijetms.2022.v06i01.005

Singh, L., Randhelia, A., Jain, A., & Choudhary, A. K. (2025). Ethical and Regulatory Compliance Challenges of Generative AI in Human Resources. In Chelliah, P. R., Dutta, P. K., Kumar, A., Gonzalez, E. D. R. S., Mittal, M., & Gupta, S. (Eds.), *Generative Artificial Intelligence in Finance* (1st ed., pp. 199–214). Wiley., DOI: 10.1002/9781394271078.ch11

Sobania, D., Briesch, M., Hanna, C., & Petke, J. (2023). An Analysis of the Automatic Bug Fixing Performance of ChatGPT. *arXiv preprint.* /arXiv.2301.08653DOI: 10.1109/APR59189.2023.00012

Sood, A. K., & Zeadally, S. (2025). Revolutionizing Cyber Defense: Leveraging Generative AI for Adaptive Threat Hunting. *Internet Technology Letters*, *8*(4), e70039. DOI: 10.1002/itl2.70039

Stefaniak, J., & Moore, S. (2024). The Use of Generative AI to Support Inclusivity and Design Deliberation for Online Instruction. *Online Learning : The Official Journal of the Online Learning Consortium*, *28*(3), 181–205. DOI: 10.24059/olj.v28i3.4458

Steinel, R. B., Lim, K., Ku, C. S., & Department of Computer Science, William Paterson University, Wayne, NJ 07470, USA. (2025). Synthetic data generation for Cybersecurity applications: An Exploratory study of GAN models. In *Department of Computer Science, William Paterson University, Wayne, NJ 07470, USA* [Journal-article]. https://www.wpunj.edu/cosh/macs-scholars-program/assets/SyntheticData.pdf

Suhaimi, A., Lim, A. W. H., Chia, X. W., Li, C., & Makino, H. (2022). Representation learning in the artificial and biological neural networks underlying sensorimotor integration. *Science Advances*, *8*(22), eabn0984. Advance online publication. DOI: 10.1126/sciadv.abn0984 PMID: 35658033

Sulaiman, S. S., Nadher, I., & Hameed, S. M. (2024). Credit Card Fraud Detection Using Improved Deep Learning Models. *Computers, Materials & Continua*, *78*(1), 1049–1069. DOI: 10.32604/cmc.2023.046051

Sultana, M., Hossain, A., Laila, F., Taher, K. A., & Islam, M. N. (2020). Towards developing a secure medical image sharing system based on zero trust principles and blockchain technology. *BMC Medical Informatics and Decision Making*, *20*(1), 256. Advance online publication. DOI: 10.1186/s12911-020-01275-y

Sun, J., Liao, Q. V., Muller, M., Agarwal, M., Houde, S., Talamadupula, K., & Weisz, J. D. (2022). Investigating explainability of generative AI for code through scenario-based design. *arXiv preprint.* /arXiv.2202.04903DOI: 10.1145/3490099.3511119

Sutton, R. S., & Barto, A. G. (1998). *No. 1* (Vol. 1). Reinforcement learning: An introduction. MIT press.

Sutton, R. S., & Barto, A. G. (2018). *Reinforcement Learning: An Introduction* (2nd ed.). The MIT Press., https://web.stanford.edu/class/psych209/Readings/SuttonBartoIPRLBook2ndEd.pdf

Symantec. (2023). Internet security threat report. Broadcom Inc. Source: Broadcom https://share.google/w8okW3JUGn309o0ak.

Tang, Y. (2023). Automatic Fraud Detection in e-Commerce Transactions using Deep Reinforcement Learning and Artificial Neural Networks. *International Journal of Advanced Computer Science and Applications*, *14*(7). Advance online publication. DOI: 10.14569/IJACSA.2023.01407113

Templin, T., Perez, M. W., Sylvia, S., Leek, J., & Sinnott-Armstrong, N. (2024). Addressing 6 challenges in generative AI for digital health: A scoping review. *PLOS Digital Health*, *3*(5), e0000503. DOI: 10.1371/journal.pdig.0000503 PMID: 38781686

Teo, Z. L., Quek, C. W. N., Wong, J. L. Y., & Ting, D. S. W. (2024). Cybersecurity in the generative artificial intelligence era. *Asia-Pacific Journal of Ophthalmology*, *13*(4), 100091. DOI: 10.1016/j.apjo.2024.100091 PMID: 39209217

Thoom, S. R.Sreeram Reddy Thoom. (2025). Lessons from AI in finance: Governance and compliance in practice. *International Journal of Science and Research Archive*, *14*(1), 1387–1395. DOI: 10.30574/ijsra.2025.14.1.0235

Tong, L., Wang, X., & Zhao, Q. (2024). *Grid Monitoring with Synchro-Waveform and AI Foundation Model Technologies* (Version 2). arXiv. DOI: 10.48550/ARXIV.2403.06942

Tounsi, W., & Rais, H. (2018). A survey on technical threat intelligence in the age of sophisticated cyber attacks. *Computers & Security*, *72*, 212–233. DOI: 10.1016/j.cose.2017.09.001

Tsai, M., Lee, S., & Shieh, S. W. (2024). Strategy for implementing of zero trust architecture. *IEEE Transactions on Reliability*, *73*(1), 93–100. DOI: 10.1109/TR.2023.3345665

Tu, J., Shieh, S. W., Liu, T., & Chang, L. (2023). *Cybersecurity reference architecture for semiconductor manufacturing environments*. SEMI.

Uddin, M., Irshad, M. S., Kandhro, I. A., Alanazi, F., Ahmed, F., Maaz, M., Hussain, S., & Ullah, S. S. (2025). Generative AI revolution in cybersecurity: A comprehensive review of threat intelligence and operations. *Artificial Intelligence Review*, *58*(8), 236. DOI: 10.1007/s10462-025-11219-5

Varra, L. B., Puttanapura, J., Reddy, C. K. K., Khullar, S., Lazrek, G., & Parantha-man, J. (2026). Exploring the Technical Foundations and Integration Strategies of Generative AI Within Collaborative Robotics Systems. In *Exploring Generative AI for Collaborative Robots in Agriculture 6.0*. IGI Global., DOI: 10.4018/979-8-3373-4207-8.ch004

Vasant, M., Ganesan, S., & Kumar, G. (2025). Enhancing E-commerce Security: A Hybrid Machine Learning Approach to Fraud Detection. *FinTech and Sustainable Innovation*, *14*, 1–9. DOI: 10.47852/bonviewFSI52024882

Vashishth, T. K., Sharma, V., Samania, B., Sharma, R., Singh, S., & Jajoria, P. (2025). Ethical and Legal Implications of AI in Cybersecurity. In Machine Intelligence Applications in Cyber-Risk Management (pp. 387-414). IGI Global Scientific Publishing.

Vashishth, T. K., Sharma, V., Sharma, M. K., Sharma, R., Sharma, K. K., & Sharma, S. (2026). AI-Driven Threat Detection and Incident Response: Advancing Cybersecurity with Machine Learning. In Improving Threat Detection, Network Security, and Incident Response with AI (pp. 51-82). IGI Global Scientific Publishing.

Vemuri, N., Thaneeru, N., & Tatikonda, V. M. (2024). Adaptive generative AI for dynamic cybersecurity threat detection in enterprises. *International Journal of Science and Research Archive*, *11*(1), 2259–2265. DOI: 10.30574/ijsra.2024.11.1.0313

Vikas, D., R. P., Kumar, D., Charan, P., Ingilela, R. S. K., & Rastogi, R. (2023). Intrusion detection in wireless sensor networks using hybrid deep belief networks and Harris Hawks optimizer. In Proceedings of the 2023 4th International Conference on Electronics and Sustainable Communication Systems (ICESC) (pp. 1631–1636). IEEE. DOI: 10.1109/ICESC57686.2023.10193270

Wang, F., & Silva, R. (2023). Autonomous cybersecurity agents. *IEEE Transactions on Dependable and Secure Computing*. Advance online publication. DOI: 10.1109/TDSC.2022.3218912

Wang, H., & Nyamasvisva, T. E. (2025). A zero-trust security model applied in SDN intelligent network. *International Conference on Artificial Intelligence and Machine Learning Research (CAIMLR 2024)*, 22. DOI: 10.1117/12.3058610

Wan, H., Zhang, J., Chen, Y., Xu, W., & Feng, F. (2025). Exploring Gen-AI applications in building research and industry: A review. *Building Simulation, 18*(6), 1251–1273. DOI: 10.1007/s12273-025-1279-x

Ward, R. and Beyer, B. (2014). BeyondCorp: A new approach to enterprise security. vol. 39, no. 6, pp. 6–11.

Waseem, H. M., Islam, S. U., Matragkas, N., Epiphaniou, G., Arvanitis, T. N., & Maple, C. (2025). Review of generative AI for synthetic data generation: A healthcare perspective. *Artificial Intelligence Review, 59*(2), 55. DOI: 10.1007/s10462-025-11440-2

Wassie, F. A., & Lakatos, L. P. (2024). Artificial intelligence and the future of the internal audit function. *Humanities & Social Sciences Communications, 11*(1), 386. DOI: 10.1057/s41599-024-02905-w

Wen, S. (2024). The power of generative AI in cybersecurity: Opportunities and challenges. *Applied and Computational Engineering, 48*(1), 31–39. DOI: 10.54254/2755-2721/48/20241095

Xia, H., Chen, H., Zhang, J. Z., & Kamal, M. M. (2026). Exploring the impact of responsible AI governance on corporate performance: A quasi-natural experiment. *Technological Forecasting and Social Change, 223*, 124425. DOI: 10.1016/j.techfore.2025.124425

Xiong, A., Qiao, C., Tong, Y., Qi, B., & Jiang, C. (2023). *Block-chain Abnormal Transaction Detection Method Based on Auto-encoder and Attention Mechanism. Research Square* Platform LLC.5(4). DOI: 10.21203/rs.3.rs-2969521/v1

Yan, J., Zhang, H., & Li, K. (2025). Synthetic data for enhanced privacy: A VAE–GAN approach. *Information Sciences, 694*, 119052

Yin, H., Zhang, Z., Wang, Z., Ozyurt, Y., Liang, W., Dong, W., Zhao, Y., & Shan, Y. (2022). *Behavioral graph fraud detection in E-commerce* (arXiv:2210.06968). arXiv. /arXiv.2210.06968DOI: 10.1109/ICDMW58026.2022.00105

Yuan, Q., Meng, Q., Tao, J., Li, G., Fei, J., Lu, B., & Wang, Y. (2025). Multi-Agent for Network Security Monitoring and Warning: A Generative AI Solution. *IEEE Network, 39*(5), 114–121. DOI: 10.1109/MNET.2025.3579001

Yu, L., Xu, X., Trajcevski, G., & Zhou, F. (2022). Transformer-enhanced Hawkes process with decoupling training for information cascade prediction. *Knowledge-Based Systems, 255*, 109740. DOI: 10.1016/j.knosys.2022.109740

Yu, P., Xu, H., Hu, X., & Deng, C. (2023). Leveraging Generative AI and Large Language Models: A Comprehensive Roadmap for Healthcare Integration. *Health Care, 11*(20), 2776. Advance online publication. DOI: 10.3390/healthcare11202776 PMID: 37893850

Zaheer, Z., Chang, H., Mukherjee, S., & Van der Merwe, J. (2019). EZTrust. *Proceedings of the 2019 ACM Symposium on SDN Research*, 49-61. DOI: 10.1145/3314148.3314349

Zaidi, T., & Faisal, S. (2018). An overview: Various attacks in VANET. *2018 4th International Conference on Computing Communication and Automation (ICCCA)*, 1–6.

Zaydi, M., Maleh, Y., & Khourdifi, Y. (2025). A new framework for agile cybersecurity risk management: Integrating continuous adaptation and real-time threat intelligence (ACSRM-ICTI). In *Agile Security in the Digital Era* (pp. 19–47). CRC Press.

Zero trust maturity model (2020). Available: https://www.microsoft.com/en-us/security/blog /2020/ 04/02/ announcing microsoft-zero-trust-assessment-tool/

Zhang, B., Liang, P., Zhou, X., Ahmad, A., & Waseem, M. (2023). Practices and challenges of using github copilot: An empirical study. *arXiv preprint*. https://doi .org/arXiv:2303.08733v3 DOI: 10.18293/SEKE2023-077

Zhang, H., & Wang, Q. (2025). How could GenAI work on in-service teachers' knowledge building process? An empirical study based on epistemic network analysis. *International Journal of Educational Technology in Higher Education, 22*(1), 47. DOI: 10.1186/s41239-025-00544-y

Zhou, L., & Chatterjee, S. (2023). Adversarial risks in AI-driven SOC automation. *Journal of Information Security and Applications, 73*, 103124. DOI: 10.1016/j.jisa.2023.103124

Zhuwankinyu, E. K., Moyo, T. M., & Mupa, M. (2024). Leveraging Generative AI for an Ethical and Adaptive Cybersecurity Framework in Enterprise Environments. *Iconic Research and Engineering Journals, 8*(6), 654–675.

Zioviris, G., Kolomvatsos, K., & Stamoulis, G. (2024). An intelligent sequential fraud detection model based on deep learning. *The Journal of Supercomputing, 80*(10), 14824–14847. DOI: 10.1007/s11227-024-06030-y

About the Contributors

Yassine Maleh (Senior Member, IEEE) is an Associate Professor of Cybersecurity and IT Governance at Sultan Moulay Slimane University, where he has been serving since 2019. He is also an Expert Evaluator at Mohammed VI Polytechnic University (UM6P) since 2025. With more than 14 years of professional experience in cybersecurity consulting, training, governance, and strategic transformation, he has contributed to numerous cybersecurity and digital resilience initiatives for Moroccan and international organizations. Dr. Maleh previously served at the National Port Agency (ANP), Casablanca, between 2011 and 2019, where he held the position of IT Service Manager and contributed to the development of information security and IT governance practices within critical infrastructure environments. He is the Founding Chair of the IEEE Consultants Network Morocco and the Founder and President of the African Center for Research in Information Technology and Cybersecurity (ACRITC), established in 2021. He is also a member of the International Association of Engineers and Machine Intelligence Research Labs. Dr. Maleh holds a double PhD in Cybersecurity and IT Management. His research contributions span information security and privacy, Internet of Things (IoT) security, cyber-physical systems, wireless and constrained network security, digital trust, and IT governance. His research interests further include artificial intelligence for cybersecurity, smart systems security, and governance frameworks for emerging technologies. Recognized among Stanford University's list of the "World's Top 2% Scientists," Dr. Maleh has established a strong international scientific presence through an extensive publication record comprising more than 300 scientific publications, including journal articles, conference papers, book chapters, and edited volumes. He has edited over 60 books and authored 10 books in cybersecurity, IT governance, cyber-physical systems, and related domains, including internationally recognized reference works and best-selling professional publications. He currently serves as Editor-in-Chief of the International Journal of Information Security and Privacy and the International Journal of Smart Security Technologies. He also serves as Associate Editor for IEEE Access and several international journals in cybersecurity and digital forensics. In addition, he is the Series Editor of Advances in Cybersecurity Management published by CRC Press Taylor & Francis. Dr. Maleh has been Guest Editor for numerous special issues in leading international journals, including IEEE Transactions on Industrial Informatics, IEEE Engineering Management Review, Sensors, and Big Data. He has also served on the executive and technical program committees of many international conferences and regularly reviews for high-impact journals such as IEEE Network, IEEE Sensors Journal, Ad Hoc Networks, and Cluster Computing. Throughout his academic and professional career, he has chaired and organized numerous international conferences, including BCCA 2019, MLBDACP 2019, ICI2C 2021, ICACNGC 2022, CCSET 2022, IEEE ISC2 2022, and ISGTA 2024. He was also recognized with the Publons Top 1% Reviewer Award in 2018 and 2019 for his outstanding reviewing contributions to the scientific community.

Mohamed Lahby received the Ph.D. degree in computer science from the Faculty of Sciences and Technology of Mohammedia, University Hassan II of Casablanca, Casablanca, Morocco, in 2013.,He is currently an Associate Professor with Higher Normal School, University Hassan II of Casablanca. His research interests include wireless communication and network, mobility management, and QoS/QoE.

Ahmed A. Abd El-Latif (SMIEEE, MACM) received the B.Sc. degree with honour rank in Mathematics and Computer Science in 2005 and M.Sc. degree in Computer Science in 2010, all from Menoufia University, Egypt. He received his Ph. D. degree in Computer Science & Technology at Harbin Institute of Technology (H.I.T), Harbin, P. R. China in 2013. He is an associate professor of Computer Science at Menoufia University, Egypt, and at EIAS Data Science Lab, College of Computer and Information Sciences, Prince Sultan University, Saudi Arabia. In more than 17 years of his professional experience, he published over 280 papers in journals/conferences including 14 books with over 10000 citations. He was also selected in the 2023, 2022, 2021 and 2020 Stanford University's ranking of the world's top 2% scientists. He involved in government and international funded R&D projects related to the widespread use of artificial intelligence for 5G/6G networks. He received many awards, State Encouragement Award in Engineering Sciences 2016, Arab Republic of Egypt; the best Ph.D. student award from Harbin Institute of Technology, China 2013; Young scientific award, Menoufia University, Egypt 2014. He is a fellow at Academy of Scientific Research and Technology, Egypt. His areas of interests are Cybersecurity, 5G/6G Wireless Networks, Post-Quantum Cryptography, Artificial Intelligence of Things, AI-Based Image Processing, Information Hiding,

Dynamical systems (Discrete-time models: Chaotic systems and Quantum Walks). He is the leader of mega grant program "Research of network technologies with ultra-low latency and ultra-high density based on the widespread use of artificial intelligence for 6G networks". Dr. Abd El-Latif is the chair/co-chair of many Scopus/ EI conferences. He is the EIC of International Journal of Information Security and Privacy, and series editor of Advances in Cybersecurity Management (https://www .routledge.com). Also, academic editor/ associate editor for set of indexed journals (Scopus journals' quartile ranking).

***

Shahanawaj Ahamad is working as a Professor in College of Computer Science and Engineering, University of Hail, Saudi Arabia.

Sunil Kumar Alavilli a Lead Engineer at Sephora, holds a Master's Degree in Computer Science from VTU, earned in 2005. With over 15 years of experience, Sunil has developed applications utilizing cutting-edge technologies such as Spring Boot, Databricks, and Machine Learning (ML). He possesses profound knowledge in conducting analysis and identifying critical factors that influence an application's performance and behavior under various conditions.

Otmane Azeroual is a world-renowned senior researcher, lecturer, and thought leader in digital transformation, artificial intelligence, and advanced data-driven research infrastructures. His groundbreaking interdisciplinary work at the nexus of computer science, higher education research, innovation management, and industry has set new standards in how data and AI reshape science and society. His research on the design, deployment, and critical evaluation of Current Research Information Systems (CRIS) — combined with cutting-edge AI-powered analytics — is internationally acclaimed and among the most cited in the field. Dr. Azeroual's pioneering contributions drive the evolution of intelligent data ecosystems that empower Open Science, elevate transparency, and revolutionize strategic decision-making in science policy worldwide. Holding a Ph.D. in Engineering Informatics and a robust foundation in business information systems and software engineering, he has authored numerous high-impact publications in top-tier journals and has been a sought-after keynote and plenary speaker at prestigious global conferences. His expertise is recognized by editorial boards and scientific committees internationally, where he shapes the future agenda of research data science. Bridging academia and private industry, Dr. Azeroual uniquely fuses rigorous theoretical insight with practical innovation. His leadership in both sectors fuels transformative digital strategies and sustainable technological solutions. As an inspiring educator, he equips emerging researchers and professionals with cutting-edge knowledge in AI, data science, research analytics, and project management — preparing them to excel in complex, dynamic environments. Passionate about harnessing AI for evidence-based governance, Dr. Azeroual actively collaborates across disciplines to build resilient, transparent, and data-driven research infrastructures that set global benchmarks. His visionary work not only advances scientific understanding but also catalyzes paradigm shifts that benefit institutions, governments, and society at large.

Chirra Baburao is an esteemed academic and researcher with expertise in public policy, entrepreneurship, start-ups, and the impact of AI on various sectors. Holding Master's degrees in Commerce, Management, and Psychology, he has over a decade of industry experience in IT, operating as a Technopreneur through his MSME-registered firm, Bobbycomputers&Communications. Currently, working with Sir C.R. Reddy Educational Institutions, Eluru, Andhra Pradesh, India, as Research Convener (Research & Development).He is also a PhD(submitted) at GITAM School of Business, Visakhapatnam, and a former Research Associate (ICSSR) at Gujarat National Law University (GNLU), Baburao excels in qualitative, quantitative, and mixed research methods. He has completed 15 Swayam courses, participated in over 40 webinars, and presented 10 papers at national and international conferences. His research focuses on MSMEs' role in public policy, technological disruptions, and environmental issues. His recent work explores AI's impact on consumer behavior, smart cities, and healthcare, published in reputable journals and conferences, making him a prominent figure in his field.

Subramanyam Boyapati has a Bachelor's degree in Electronics and communications engineering from Anna University in 2008. Currently working as a Senior Engineer in American Express from June' 2015.

Aditi Chauhan is working in School of Humanities and Mass Communication, IIMT University, Meerut, U.P, India

Puneet Chauhan is an Academian with a strong academic foundation and a passion for teaching, he plays a vital role in shaping the technical skills of his students. His primary area of interest lies in Software Engineering, where he focuses on modern development methodologies, software design principles, and emerging technologies.

Nikhil Kumar Goyal is currently working as Assistant professor at poornima university jaipur

Venkataramesh Induru is currently working as Operation Lead - IT Operations Associate Manager for multiple Identity and Access Management projects. 16+ years of experience in multiple IDAM Products (i.e. ForgeRock IAM, Oracle IDAM suite, Oracle Waveset (former SUN IDM) and Tivoli IDM) with Design, Development, Operations, Environment Support and Security Operation skills

Mohammad Ishrat serves as an Associate Professor at the School of Computing Science and Engineering, VIT Bhopal University, Sehore, Madhya Pradesh, India. His research expertise spans Artificial Intelligence & Machine Learning (AIML), Data Science, and Future Networks. With numerous publications in SCI and Scopus-indexed journals, he has also authored several book chapters.

Pooja Jaiswal received the B.Sc. degree in Science from J.K. Institute of Applied Physics & Technology, University of Allahabad (U.P.) in 2007. She received the B.Tech & M.Tech degree in Electronics and communication from J.K. Institute of Applied Physics & Technology, University of Allahabad (U.P.) in 2010 & 2012. Her research interest includes Quantum computing and Image Processing with Deep learning and their applications. Presently she is pursuing PhD from J.K. Institute of Applied Physics & Technology, University of Allahabad, India.

Shyam Sundar has excellent knowledge of Machine learning and its applications.

M. Robinson Joel received the Doctorate Ph.D degree in Computer and Information Technology from the Manonmaniam Sundaranar University, Tirunelveli in March 2019. He completed his M.Tech in Manonmaniam Sundaranar University, Tirunelveli 2002. He is currently working as an Associate Professor in the Department of Computer Science and Engineering, KCG College of Technology, Chennai. He has 16 years of teaching experience.

Bhavya Kadiyala has Master's degree in Bioinformatics from Indiana University-Purdue University Indianapolis (2019). She has worked as a Data Architect at Center for Biomedical Informatics (CMBI) at University of Tennessee Health Science Center post her graduation, where she worked on her first research paper with her Director Dr. Davis.

Wasim Khan received the B.Tech., M.Tech., and Ph.D. degrees.With over 17 years in academia, he is currently a Seasoned Expert in computer science engineering. He has made significant academic contributions, evidenced by numerous patents and a vast array of publications, including conference papers and book chapters. He is currently an Assistant Professor(Senior Scale) with the

Symbiosis Institute of Technology, Symbiosis International (Deemed) University, Pune. His research interests include machine learning, deep learning, social network analysis, anomaly detection, and network intrusion detection.

Shikha Khullar is an accomplished academic and researcher with a Ph.D. in Data Mining and Artificial Intelligence. She currently serves as an Associate Professor at Poornima University, where she is recognized for her dedication to academic excellence and her dynamic involvement in radical research. With a deep-rooted passion for innovation and discovery, Dr. Khullar actively engages in interdisciplinary research that bridges technology and real-world applications, particularly in areas such as intelligent systems, smart data analytics, and sustainable digital solutions. Her work is characterized by a forward-thinking approach, where she not only explores theoretical models but also contributes to practical implementations that address pressing societal and industrial challenges. At Poornima University, she has been instrumental in mentoring young minds, guiding Ph.D. scholars, and contributing to curriculum development in emerging areas such as Artificial Intelligence, Blockchain, and Smart Agriculture Technologies.

Yashwant Kumar Kolli is an experienced Technical Project Manager with a demonstrated history of working in the information technology and services industry. Skilled in CMS, TMS, Content Targeting using Adobe Experience Platform & performance optimization. Strong program and project management professional with a Master of Technology (M.Tech.) focused in Computer Science and Engineering from Nagarjuna University.

Manish Kumar is presently working as Associate Professor in Department of Biochemistry, Faculty of Science, P. K. University, village-Thanra, Karera, Shivpuri (M.P.)- 473660, India. He did his B.Sc. (H) Biochemistry, M.Sc. Biochemistry from Bundelkhand University, Jhansi (U.P.) and M.Phil. Biochemistry from Singhania University, Jhunjhunu (Rajasthan). He did his doctoral degree Ph.D. Biochemistry from Sam Higginbottom University of Agriculture, Technology and Sciences, Prayagraj (U.P.). He received best thesis research award for Ph.D. Biochemistry from UPKAR's foundation, Lucknow as well as young scientist award in biochemistry field. He has Co-supervised 14 PG students and supervising 6 Ph.D. students. He has been published many research papers and review papers in national and international journals with good Impact Factor and NAAS rating. He has teaching experience more than 8 years and research experience more than 14 years.

Vijay Singh Rana Kumar is an accomplished academic researcher with experience in the field of Computer Science and Engineering. He holds an MCA, M.Tech(Computer Engineering) and is currently serving as an Assistant Professor at

J.V. Jain College Saharanpur. India. Vijay Singh Rana Specializes in Artificial Intelligence (AI), Machine Learning(ML)

Karthik Kushala holds a Bachelor's degree in Computer Science and Engineering from Jawaharlal Nehru Technological University, Hyderabad (Class of 2009). I have been working as a Senior Software Developer at Celer Systems Inc. since April 2017, specializing as a Full Stack .NET Developer.

Hanh Le is a passionate researcher and accomplished Full Stack Software Developer with deep expertise in software development, data analytics, data science, and cloud computing. She holds a Ph.D. in Information Technology and a Master's in Computer Science, bringing both academic rigor and a solution-driven mindset to her work. With extensive experience in front-end and back-end development, she specializes in scalable, database-driven applications that support evidence-based decision-making. Dr. Le has led transformative tech initiatives across healthcare, law enforcement, and retail, translating complex needs into high-performing systems. She values interdisciplinary collaboration, believing that impactful innovation often arises at the intersection of fields. Her blend of technical skill, research excellence, and collaborative spirit continues to drive progress in academia and industry alike.

Mohamed Sithik M is obtained his Ph.D. in Information and Communication Engineering from Anna University in Chennai in 2022. He is an Assistant Professor (Senior Grade) in the Department of CSE (CS) at Vel Tech Rangarajan Dr. Sagunthala R&D Institute of Science and Technology, Avadi, Chennai -600 062.He has over 16 years of teaching and research experience and published more than 10 technical papers in journals and conferences. Cryptography and Network Security, IoT, AI and Machine Learning, Deep Learning, Cloud computing, are some of his research interests.

M. Thanjaivadivel is a highly accomplished and skilled researcher in the field of Computer Science and Engineering. He completed his Bachelor's in Computer Science and Engineering from DMI College of Engineering affiliated with Anna University, followed by a Master's in Information Technology from VIT University, and a PhD in CSE from Vel Tech University. Dr. Thanjaivadivel has published numerous research papers in reputed international journals, conferences, and workshops.

Rajakumar Muthusamy Palani is currently working Department of Artificial Intelligence and Data Science, St. Joseph's College of Engineering, Old Mamallapuram Road, Chennai- 600 119, Tamil Nadu, India. His research interests include soft computing, machine learning techniques.

Shatrughan Mishra is working in the field of electronics & communication engineering as Assistant Professor for more than 10 year. A research enthusiast in the area of Solar cells, fundamentals of Digital Electronics & Microprocessor.

Shivani Mishra is a Research Scholar in English Literature and a faculty member in the Department of Applied Sciences and Humanities, with over fifteen years of teaching experience. Her research interests include contemporary Indian fiction, cultural materialism, neoliberalism, and the intersection of literature and social change. She has published several papers in reputed journals, with a focus on the works of Aravind Adiga, exploring themes of class, materialism, and capitalism. Passionate about interdisciplinary studies, she integrates literary criticism with cultural and social theories to offer fresh academic perspectives.

Venktesh Mishra has completed his B.Tech degree in Electronics & Instrumentation Engineering from U.P. Technical University Lucknow, India in 2006 and M. Tech degree in Electrical Engineering from MNNIT Prayagraj, India in 2013. He has completed his Ph.D. from University of Allahabad; Allahabad, India in the area of application of Power Electronics converter in renewable energy sources. He has published several papers in international journals and conferences. His area of interest includes Power electronics and Wind Energy Conversion Systems and Quantum computing. Venktesh Mishra, working as Associate Professor since last 16 years in field of Department of Electronics and Communication Engineering, United College of Engineering and Research Naini, Prayagraj, U.P., India, 211010.

Rajani Priya Nippatla has Bachelor's degree in Bio-Medical Engineering from Osmania University (2000). She is currently a Senior Technical Lead, working for employer Kellton Technologies Inc with the State of California Client FI$Cal (Financial Information System for California). She has over 17 years of experience in Information Technology / Computer Science, with emphasis on Finance Domain, Cloud Services, Data Warehousing and Modelling, Data Security, Business Intelligence and Enterprise performance Management.

Nandita Pradhan is the head of the ECE and CRT department. She did B.E. in Electronics and Telecommunication Engineering in 1985, M.E. in Communication Systems from the Govt. Engineering College, Jabalpur in 1991 and Ph.D. in Electronics and Communication Engineering from AKTU, Lucknow. She began her professional journey as a Lecturer in the Department of ECE at Government Engineering College, Jabalpur in 1985 and served in that position until 1997. Currently she worked as a Head of the Department of ECE in United Group of Institutions, Prayagraj, India.

Vijai Anand Ramar is lead of Automation Team with 20+ Years in Healthcare As the Lead of the Automation Team, I bring over 20 years of experience in the healthcare domain, specializing in large-scale automation, AI-driven solutions, and process optimization. My expertise includes Python Automation Development, Artificial Intelligence, Generative AI for Synthetic Data Creation, and AI-Driven Member Engagement & Retention, all aimed at enhancing efficiency and accuracy in healthcare operations.

Priya S received the Bachelor's Degree in Information technology from Ganadipathy Tulsis Engineering College, Vellore in 2006, the Master's Degree in Computer Science and Engineering from SRM University, Chennai in 2012, and the Philosophy of Doctorate degree in Computer science and Engineering from SRM Institute of Science and Technology, Chennai in 2024, respectively. She is currently working as an Assistant Professor (SG) at the Department of Computer Science and Engineering, School of Computing, Vel Tech Rangarajan Dr. Sagunthala R&D Institute of Science and Technology, Avadi, Chennai. She has over 16 years of teaching experience .She research areas include Machine Learning, Cloud Computing, Deep Learning, Software Engineering and Web Development. She has quality of publications to his credit, including Journal Articles, Conference Publications, Patents, Books and Book Chapters.

S. Ramamoorthi is obtained his Ph.D. in Information and Communication Engineering from Anna University in Chennai in 2024. He is an Assistant Professor (Senior Grade) in the Department of CSE (CS) at Vel Tech Rangarajan Dr. Sagunthala R&D Institute of Science and Technology, Avadi, Chennai -600 062.He has over 16 years of teaching and research experience and published more than 10 technical papers in journals and conferences. Cryptography and Network Security, IoT, AI and Machine Learning, Deep Learning, Cloud computing, are some of his research interests.

S. Thirumal, M.E., Ph.D., is currently serving as an Associate Professor in the Department of Computer Science and Engineering at Vels Institute of Science, Technology and Advanced Studies (VISTAS), Chennai. With over 13 years of experience in teaching and research, he has established a strong academic and professional presence in the field of Computer Science. He earned his Doctorate in Computer Science from the Hindustan Institute of Technology and Science in 2023. His areas of expertise include Machine Learning, Artificial Intelligence, Software Engineering, and Data Analytics. He has authored and co-authored numerous SCOPUS-indexed journal and conference publications. A prolific innovator, he holds multiple published and granted patents in IoT, AI, and smart healthcare technologies.

S. P. Santhoshkumar received the Bachelor's Degree in Electronics and Communication Engineering from Anna University, Chennai in 2006, the Master's Degree in Software Engineering from Anna University of Technology, Coimbatore in 2011, and the Philosophy of Doctorate degree in Information and Communication Engineering from Anna University, Chennai in 2024, respectively. He is currently working as an Assistant Professor (SG) at the Department of Computer Science and Engineering, School of Computing, Vel Tech Rangarajan Dr. Sagunthala R&D Institute of Science and Technology, Avadi, Chennai. His research areas include Machine Learning, Cloud Computing, Deep Learning, Software Engineering and Web Development. He has quality of publications to his credit, including Journal Articles, Conference Publications, Patents, Books and Book Chapters. Also, he received best faculty awards in national level.

Rakesh Kumar Saxena, M.Tech (Dayalbagh Educational Institute, Agra, 1999) and Ph.D. (RGPV Bhopal, 2016), is currently working as Professor in Computer Science Department at Poornima University, Jaipur, Raj. India. He is Fellow member of The Institution of Engineers India, and member of IACSIT, ISTE Delhi. He was awarded as Chartered Engineer by IE (I) in 2017. His research focuses on soft computing, AI, ML, DL and has led projects funded by AICTE, MSME, and the World Bank. He has published 43 research papers and Book Chapters in IEEE Xplore, AIP, and other Scopus/SCI-indexed journals and Books published by Wiley, IGI Global Scientific Publishing.

Vikas Sharma is an active academician and researcher in the field of computer science with 8 years of experience. He earned M. Tech degree specialized in Computer Science. He is involved in academic development and scholarly activities. He is member of International Association of Engineers, The Society of Digital Information and Wireless Communications, Global Professors Welfare Association, International Association of Academic plus Corporate (IAAC), Computer Science Teachers Association and Internet Society. His research interest includes Cloud Computing, Artificial Intelligence, Machine Learning; published more than 55 research articles with 4 books and 90 book chapters in edited books. He is contributing as member of editorial and reviewers' boards in conferences and various computer journals and edited books published by Elsevier, CRC Press, Taylor and Francis, Springer, IGI global, Wiley Publication, IET Publication, De Gruyter, River Publication etc.

Ajay Sharma with more than 20 years of teaching and research experience is a core researcher in the field of Bio Medical Instrumentation, Advanced Embedded Systems & Vital signal processing. Has a number of national and International publications related to this field. By profile he is an Associate Professor in the department of Electronics and Communication, apart from this he is heading over the "Foreign relations Cell" of United University, Prayagraj, India. In addition to this he is the "Cultural Chief" of United group of Institutions. A very dynamic, hardworking and goal centric academician with his unflinching attitude he took his organization to the newer heights. He is also the member of reviewer panel of various "Scopus" & "SCI" indexed international journals.

Sweta Singh holds a B.Tech. in Electronics and Communication Engineering (U.P.T.U Lucknow), M.Tech. in VLSI Design (Banasthali Vidyapeeth, Rajasthan), and a D.Phil. in Electronics and Communication Engineering (University of Allahabad, Prayagraj). She has over 12 years of teaching and research experience, having served at reputed institutions including MNNIT Prayagraj, BBS CET Prayagraj, K.N.I.T. Sultanpur, Government Girls' Polytechnic, Faizabad and Dr. R.M.L. Avadh University Faizabad. Her research interests include microstrip patch antennas, MIMO systems, reconfigurable antennas, VLSI architecture, and 5G/ satellite communication. Dr. Singh has published several papers in reputed journals and international conferences (IEEE, Springer, PIERC), and contributed to multiple book chapters in the field of wireless communication. She actively participates in FDPs, workshops, and training programs, and is dedicated to academic excellence, innovation, and student mentorship. Currently she is working as an Assistant Professor in the Department of Computer Science Engineering & Technology at United University, Rawatpur, Prayagraj.

Satya Prakash Singh is working in the field of electronics as Assistant Professor for more than 17 years. A research enthusiast in the area of the fundamentals of Electronics, communication, and Antenna Design and simulation for modern communication technology.

Vaishali Sonwane is Associate Professor in Poornima University India.

Sachin Tomar is working as an assistant proefessor in SRM University and with a strong academic foundation and a passion for teaching, he plays a vital role in shaping the technical skills of his students. His primary area of interest lies in Software Engineering, where he focuses on modern development methodologies, software design principles, and emerging technologies.

Tushar received B.Tech degree in Electronics and communication from U.P.T.U, Lucknow (U.P.) in 2007. I received the M.B.A. degree in R.T.M. from Jiwaji University, and Gwalior (M.P.) in 2009. I am "Gold medalist" in M.E. in Communication, Control and Networking from M.P.C.T. Gwalior, M.P. My research interest includes Antenna and Microwave communication and their applications. Presently I am pursuing PhD and acting as an Assistant professor in United college of Engineering & Research, Prayagraj, India.

Chaitanya Vasamsetty has Master's in Information from University of North Texas (2017) and Bachelors in Mechanical Engineering from GITAM university (2013). He has work experience of 10 Years in IT. He worked for 2 years at Tata Consultancy Services India, 2 years of experience as Graduate Assistant at University of North Texas, 7 years of experience at Elevance Health.

Tarun Kumar Vashishth is an active academician and researcher in the field of Computer Science with 22 years of experience. He earned Ph.D. Mathematics degree specialized in Operations Research; served several academic positions such as Dy. Director, HoD, NAAC Coordinator, Academic Coordinator, Member Secretary of Department Research Committee, Assistant Center Superintendent and Head Examiner in University Examinations. He is involved in academic development and scholarly activities. He is member of International Association of Engineers, The Society of Digital Information and Wireless Communications, Global Professors Welfare Association, International Association of Academic plus Corporate (IAAC), Computer Science Teachers Association and Internet Society . His research interest includes Cloud Computing, Artificial Intelligence, Machine Learning and Operations Research; published more than 50 research articles & conference papers with 2 book and 80 book chapters. He is contributing as member of editorial and reviewer's boards in conferences and various computer journals and edited books published by Elsevier, CRC Press, Taylor and Francis, Springer, IGI global, Wiley Publication, IET Publication, De Gruyter, River Publication etc.

Ajit Kumar Yadav, born on 1 July 1984, is an accomplished academician and researcher in the field of Electrical Engineering. He completed his M.Tech in Electrical Engineering from the prestigious Motilal Nehru National Institute of Technology (MNNIT), Prayagraj, and obtained his B.Tech in Electrical Engineering from the Institute of Engineering & Technology (IET), MJP Rohilkhand University, Bareilly. Currently, he serves as an Assistant Professor in the Department of Electrical Engineering at United College of Engineering and Research, Prayagraj. With over 14 years of teaching experience and 2 years of industry experience, Mr. Yadav has developed strong expertise in electrical engineering education, research, and practical applications. His academic journey reflects a commitment to knowledge dissemination, mentoring students, and contributing to advancements in engineering education and technology.

Index

A

B

C

D

E

F

G

H

I

K

L

M

N

P

R

S

www.ingramcontent.com/pod-product-compliance
Lightning Source LLC
LaVergne TN
LVHW080905300926
849162LV00003B/557